Fat

Fat

Fighting the
Obesity Epidemic

Robert Pool

OXFORD
UNIVERSITY PRESS

2001

OXFORD
UNIVERSITY PRESS

Oxford New York
Athens Auckland Bangkok Bogotá Buenos Aires Calcutta
Cape Town Chennai Dar es Salaam Delhi Florence Hong Kong
Istanbul Karachi Kuala Lumpur Madrid Melbourne Mexico City Mumbai
Nairobi Paris São Paulo Shanghai Singapore Taipei Tokyo Toronto Warsaw

and associated companies in

Berlin Ibadan

Published by Oxford University Press, Inc.
198 Madison Avenue, New York, New York, 10016

Oxford is a registered trademark of Oxford University Press

Library of Congress Cataloging-in-Publication Data
Pool, Robert.
Fat: fighting the obesity epidemic / by Robert Pool.
p. cm.
ISBN 0-19-511853-7 (acid-free paper)
1. Obesity—Molecular aspects. I. Title.

RC628 .P625 2000
616.3'98—dc21
00-036731

9 8 7 6 5 4 3 2 1

Printed in the United States of America
on acid-free paper

To my children,
Alexandra, Remington,
Genevieve, and Noelle

Contents

Acknowledgments

This book would never have been conceived, much less written, without the urging and support of Ralph Gomory and Doron Weber of the Alfred P. Sloan Foundation of New York City. It was at their suggestion that I first looked into the subject of obesity, and, once I had decided that I wanted to do a book about it, the Sloan Foundation provided a generous grant to support the research and writing. I am greatly indebted to both of them.

While researching the book, I spoke with many doctors and scientists who study obesity. I am particularly grateful to three major contributors to the field of obesity research, all of whom spent many hours in personal interviews, telephone conversations, and correspondence helping me understand their work and its implications. They also reviewed the manuscript for this book, spotting errors and offering improvements. They are, in alphabetical order: Douglas Coleman, a longtime genetics researcher at the Jackson Laboratory in Bar Harbor, Maine, now retired; Jeffrey Friedman, a molecular biologist at the Rockefeller University in New York City and the Howard Hughes Medical Institute; and Rudy Leibel, a doctor now at Columbia University in New York City but who was at Rockefeller while doing much of his research into why people find it so hard to lose weight.

A large number of other researchers spoke with me and provided copies of their scientific publications. They include: David Allison, Columbia University; Claude Bouchard, Laval University; Art Campfield, Roche Laboratories; Streamson Chua, Columbia University; Robert Dow, Pfizer; Adam Drewnowski, University of Michigan; Richard Fabsitz, National Institutes of Health; Jules Hirsch, Rockefeller; Sarah Leibowitz, Rockefeller; Leslie Kozac, Jackson Laboratory; JoAnn Manson, Harvard University; Timothy Moran, Johns Hopkins University; Richard Nisbett, University of Michigan; Metin Ozata, Gulhane School of Medicine in Ankara, Turkey; Beverly Paigen, Jackson Laboratory; Ken Paigen, director of the Jackson Laboratory; Xavier Pi-Sunyer, Columbia University; Eric Ravussin, National Institute of Diabetes and Digestive and Kidney Diseases in Phoenix; Bruce Schneider, now at the Food and Drug Administration but at Rockefeller during the relevant period; Leslie Schulz, University of Wisconsin, Madison; A. Donny Strosberg, University of Paris; Albert Stunkard, the University of Pennsylvania; Elizabeth Sugg, Glaxo Wellcome; Richard Troiano, National Cancer Institute; Mary Walker, Synaptic; and Richard

Wurtman, Massachusetts Institute of Technology. The book could not have been written without their help. I have attempted to represent their findings as accurately as possible, while making them accessible and interesting to the reader. If I have failed at any of this, the fault is mine alone.

In addition, I must thank Luther Young, the public relations director at Jackson Laboratory, and Martha Harmon, the lab's archivist, for their help in tracking some of the laboratory's early history pertaining to the breeding of fat mice. Thanks to them, I have been able to trace the crucial developments fifty years ago that led eventually to our current understanding of how the body regulates weight.

I am particularly grateful to two participants in Rudy Leibel's seminal experiment on the effects of weight loss on metabolism. By describing their experiences in vivid detail, P.J. Nelson and Kelli Johnson brought to life what would otherwise have been just one more dry scientific report.

At Oxford University Press, my editor, Kirk Jensen, has been his usual helpful, good-natured, and perspicacious self, offering suggestions and encouragement and getting only the slightest bit testy as the writing of the book dragged on for a year longer than it was supposed to.

Finally, my wife, Amy, has willingly if not always cheerfully put up with the many times that my fixation on the book has left her with a not particularly attentive husband, from the research phase to the writing phase and to the many days she would see me wander off for an hours-long walk to think about exactly how I was going to compress an encyclopedia's worth of ideas and facts into one easily digestible book. She also read the manuscript once it was done and pinpointed a number of shortcomings. Perhaps I could have done it all without her, but I wouldn't want to.

Fat

Introduction: A Most Peculiar Plague

The twenty-two-year-old Turkish man, identified only as Patient 24, was discovered in early 1997 by Metin Ozata. Ozata, a doctor at Turkey's Gulhane School of Medicine in Etlik-Ankara, was assembling subjects for a study of obesity in Turkey, and the twenty-two-year-old male was the fattest he had yet found. In the words of the bland clinical report, Patient 24 was "markedly hyperphagic"—which, translated into layman's terms, means roughly "eats as much as any two normal people." Five-foot-six and 330 pounds with a fifty-five-inch waist and fifty-nine-inch hips, the man could not walk a city block without stopping to rest. Strangely enough, his four brothers and one sister were of normal weight, actually quite thin by American standards. The five had an average body mass index—the standard measure of fatness—of just 23, which works out to 143 pounds on a five-foot-six frame, well below anyone's definition of overweight. Their brother's body mass index was, by contrast, a massive 55.8.

Besides his weight, Patient 24 was unusual in a number of other ways, Ozata found. He had never gone through puberty. He had no beard and very little hair in his pubic region or, except for his head, anywhere else on his body. He had higher-than-normal levels of insulin in his bloodstream and exceptionally low levels of male hormones. His penis and testicles had never gotten larger than a small boy's, while his breasts were more like a woman's than a man's.

To anyone acquainted with the history of obesity research, the set of symptoms displayed by Patient 24 was strikingly familiar. In 1950, researchers at the Jackson Laboratory in Maine had discovered a mutant mouse that grew to three times the weight of normal mice, with immense deposits of fat that left it so round that it had trouble walking. The researchers named the mutation *obese* and bred it into an inbred strain of mice. When the researchers further studied these *obese* mice, they found that they had exceptionally high insulin levels, did not develop sexually, and were infertile.

If Patient 24 had been discovered five years earlier, his resemblance to the *obese* mouse might have been noted, but most likely he would have been written off as nothing more than an interesting case, an obesity of unknown origin accompanied by further hormonal disturbances. In 1994, however, a researcher at the Rockefeller University in New York City had, after years of searching, tracked down the gene affected by the *obese* mutation. The gene, it turned out, instructs the body how to create a hormone called leptin, which is produced in the fat cells and has the job of telling the brain how much fat the body is carrying. The *obese* mice cannot produce leptin, and their brains interpret the lack of leptin as a sign that their bodies are in a state of starvation, even when the mice are so fat they can hardly move.

Working from that information, Ozata and Donny Strosberg, a French scientist with whom Ozata was collaborating, were able to show that Patient 24 was suffering from an almost identical mutation which crippled his body's production of leptin. The 330-pound Turkish man was the human equivalent of an *obese* mouse.

In many ways the discovery is a humbling one. As humans, we pride ourselves on our highly developed brains and the things our brains enable us to do that no animals can. We can reason, we can speak, we can anticipate the consequences of our actions and decide upon the course that will produce the most desirable results and then embark upon it. Yet none of this made a difference to Patient 24.

According to Ozata, the man desperately wishes to lose weight. He has not been able to find a job because of his obesity, and people treat him with less respect and consideration because he is fat. He has tried dieting but has failed because he gets so hungry.

If it were just this one man, perhaps his experience could be written off as a lack of willpower, as the failures of so many of the obese have been. Perhaps, we could tell ourselves, someone else with more strength, with more fortitude, with more character could overcome the mutation. But Patient 24 is not an anomaly. In the past few years, researchers have discovered a number of people with the same or a similar mutation, and the outcome has been depressingly uniform.

In the same 1998 report that described Patient 24, for instance, Ozata and colleagues told of testing a dozen members of Patient 24's extended family for the mutation. Nine of them were unaffected. The other three, including Patient 24, stood out like Sumo wrestlers at a jockey school. The man's thirty-four-year-old aunt had a waist and hips that were almost as large as his, and his six-year-old, 114-pound cousin was already bigger around than most of the normal-weight adults in the family. Since the publication of the original report, Ozata has discovered a distant cousin with the same mutation: a thirty-year-old woman who stands just under five feet tall and weighs nearly 290 pounds. Another seven members of the extended family were obese but died during childhood, so Ozata never had the opportunity to test their DNA. Presumably, though, they all had the same mutation, since Ozata has yet to find a family member without it who was anything but thin to normal.

In England, researchers at the University of Cambridge found two young cousins from a Pakistani family who suffered the same mutation as Patient 24. While all the other family members were of normal weight, the eight-year-old girl weighed 189 pounds, and the two-year-old boy weighed sixty-four. And, in Paris, a group of French researchers uncovered three sisters who had a related mutation, also first discovered in mice at Jackson Laboratory, called *diabetes*. Instead of affecting the production of leptin as *obese* does, the *diabetes* mutation prevents the brain from detecting leptin, but the end result is the same: The brain believes the body to be in a perpetual state of starvation. Thus in both humans and mice the *diabetes* mutation produces an obesity almost identical to that produced by the *obese* mutation. The three girls in France are both grossly overweight and sexually undeveloped. The thirteen-year-old is just under five feet tall and weighs 350 pounds. The nineteen-year-old is five-foot-three and weighs 365 pounds. The third sister, who died at nineteen, was five-foot-three and 293 pounds.

Not surprisingly, each time the mutation has appeared, it has been in highly inbred families. Patient 24's mother and father were first cousins, for instance, and the three Paris sisters were born to parents who were second cousins. This sort of inbreeding, where cousins or other relatives intermarry, is not uncommon in some Third World countries, and it has an effect similar to the inbreeding carried out at Jackson Lab that produced both the *obese* and *diabetes* mutations. Genetic mutations appear regularly in humans and in mice. Many have no effect or are harmless, and many of the potent ones are recessive—that is, the genes inherited from the mother and the father must both be mutants in order to affect the offspring. If the mother and father are genetically unrelated, they are unlikely to carry the same mutation, and so their children are unlikely to inherit two copies of a mutant gene. But if the mother and father are siblings or cousins, the odds against the offspring increase dramatically.

The most striking thing about these scientific reports is the near-absolute power that the genetic mutations seem to hold over their victims. None of the unaffected family members is fat, yet without exception the subjects with the mutation are grossly obese. These are conscious, rational, thinking individuals with as much willpower and desire to be thin as you or I, but they are as helpless to resist the mutation's imperative as are the mice, who presumably never worry about their appearance, about the inconvenience of carrying about an extra body's worth of fat, or about the long-term health consequences of their weight.

For those of us who feel pride in our thinness, especially those who have never been overweight, these unfortunates offer a dose of humility. We have never faced what they face, and no matter how confident we are in our willpower, in our ability to eat only what we decide is good for us, if we are honest with ourselves, we must admit that in the same situation we would likely fare no better.

It is difficult to get precise figures, but overweight Americans spend a staggering amount of money and effort each year on attempts to lose some of their extra flesh. Diet books alone constitute a sizable industry. A key-word search of Amazon.com, the on-line bookstore, finds that customers can choose from more than 1000 books on the subject of weight loss and more than 500 that deal with obesity. According to the Institute of Medicine, in 1995 Americans were spending more than $33 billion a year on weight-loss services and products, including diet foods and drinks. To put this in perspective, more than two thirds of the world's nations have a gross national product—the sum of all economic production in the country—that is less than $33 billion. Each year Americans spend enough money on losing weight to buy every item and service produced in such countries as Chile, Croatia, Syria, or Nigeria.

It hasn't helped. In October 1999, a group of doctors at the Centers for Disease Control (CDC) in Atlanta reported the results of a series of weight surveys that had been taken between 1991 and 1998. In those eight years, the doctors said, the percentage of Americans who were obese increased by half, from 12 percent of the population in 1991 to nearly 18 percent in 1998. In other words, there were some 11 million more obese Americans in 1998 than in 1991. (By "obese," the CDC doctors meant anyone with a body mass index of 30 or greater—or at least 30 percent above one's ideal weight. A person who is five-foot-two would have to weigh at least 163 pounds to qualify; someone who is five-foot-nine would need to be 203.)

And, in reality, the situation is probably much worse than the CDC figures indicate. The surveys were done over the phone, with people asked to supply their height and weight along with other health-related data, and it is well known that overweight people generally underestimate their weight. Furthermore, since the surveys could reach only people who had a phone, they probably missed a disproportionate number of people in lower socioeconomic classes, who are known to be significantly more likely to be obese. A more trustworthy, although not as current, set of numbers was provided by Phase III of the National Health and Nutrition Examination Survey, performed between 1988 and 1994. It found 22.5 percent of American adults to be obese, up from 14.5 percent in the late 1970s.

Working from these numbers and assuming that the trend the CDC surveys found is real, it would not be an unreasonable guess to say that some 30 percent of adults in the United States today are obese. But whatever the precise numbers are, somewhere between one in three and one in four Americans is obese, and the number is growing steadily each year. The situation is not as bad in most other parts of the world, but every Western country is seeing a steady increase in the number of obese.

It is a staggering statistic. The numbers of overweight and obese have grown slowly enough that we have had time to get used to them, to think that it is somehow normal for so many people to be thirty, fifty, 100 or more pounds heavier than they should be. We take it for granted that at any given point in time a third or more of the adult population is trying to lose weight. Historically speaking, however, there is nothing natural about it. We are in the middle of a vast epidemic of obesity.

The cost of this epidemic to individuals and to society is considerable. Fat people are more likely to develop a variety of diseases, such as diabetes and high blood pressure, than people who are not overweight, and they die earlier than their non-obese peers. The Institute of Medicine estimated in 1995 that, in the United States alone, annual health-care expenses for obesity and related conditions come to more than $70 billion—the entire gross national product of Norway or the Czech Republic. And each year, obesity is a factor in the deaths of some 300,000 Americans. On a less lethal level, the obese are subject to a variety of inconveniences and mistreatments, from difficulty in climbing stairs or walking long distances to discrimination and being judged less competent by others.

For more than sixty years, doctors have been trying to figure out how to help. The campaign began in the 1930s, when the medical community first realized that people with fifty or more pounds of surplus flesh were dying younger than their fellows. At the time, doctors assumed that people got fat because they did not understand the relationship between calories and weight or perhaps because they didn't realize the health consequences of obesity. The standard response was to educate patients about nutrition, provide them with some sample meal plans, and expect them to reform their eating habits accordingly. It didn't work. More and more people got fat, although the numbers were still quite low compared with what they are today.

In the 1950s, during the heyday of Freudian psychoanalysis, overeating was often seen as a psychological problem. Psychoanalysts put their fat patients on the couch, probing their dreams for clues about which subconscious drives were causing them to eat too much. The patients may have resolved their repressed conflicts about their mothers or dads, but they remained fat.

In the 1970s, one prominent theory held that the obese were more susceptible to environmental cues, such as the presence of appetizing food, that trigger eating. Psychologists taught the obese to gain control of their eating by making sure they did not come in contact with such cues. This behavioral therapy actually helped some patients lose weight, but most of them eventually regained it.

While doctors and psychologists were trying various techniques to help the obese lose weight, a decades-long procession of scientists and medical researchers—some motivated by a desire to aid the obese, others by simple intellectual curiosity—explored the physical mechanisms that underlie eating and weight. In the 1940s and 1950s, for instance, a series of experiments in rats showed that both hunger and satiety are controlled by a small part of the brain called the hypothalamus. Researchers in the 1950s and 1960s discovered several mutations in mice that caused the animals to become fat and studied the animals in detail. During the 1960s and 1970s, research on the fat cell revealed a variety of differences in the fat cell population between the obese and the lean. In the 1980s and 1990s, studies of underfeeding and overfeeding on human volunteers clarified how the metabolism responds in the face of weight loss or weight gain. And the past ten years saw the identification of the leptin gene, perhaps the single most important discovery to date in the long quest to understand and control weight.

This book tells the story of that quest. It is a century-long medical mystery tale, a slow piecing together of clues to assemble a portrait of the culprit and a description of its modus operandi. At the beginning of the twentieth century, researchers knew little about overweight and obesity beyond the basic fact that weight is a matter of calories in versus calories out. If a person was fat, they could say with certainty that the person must be eating more than his body needed to maintain a normal weight, but they had little clue *why* that might be happening. In the intervening years, doctors and scientists have forged a relatively complete understanding of the factors that determine how much a person weighs. They have traced out the details of appetite, metabolism, and the development of fat cells. They have teased apart the interconnected roles of environment, genetics, and individual behavior and examined how they influence one another. And, in just the past few years, they have taken their analysis down to the molecular level, identifying the hormones and other chemicals that are involved in the body's weight-regulating system.

As a yarn, the story of obesity research has everything one could ask for. It is full of colorful characters, curious experiments, brilliant insights and wrong turns, important discoveries and red herrings, and even the occasional humorous interlude. It sheds light on an issue that, despite the hundreds of books and thousands of magazine articles written about it, is poorly understood by most lay readers. And it brings one face to face with such philosophical issues as free will, personal responsibility, and who or what is to blame when a person eats himself into pants with a fifty-six-inch waist. Strangely enough, it is a tale that has seldom been told, and never, as far as I can tell, all in one place.

As a medical and scientific search, however, the quest to understand and control weight has been only a partial success. On the one hand, we now know in some detail why people get fat. Although researchers cannot, except for special cases such as Patient 24, say exactly why any given person is fat, they have a good theoretical understanding of how genes and environment interact to produce a body that thinks being fifty or a hundred pounds overweight is normal and anything less is a state of starvation. Furthermore, researchers are beginning to identify particular genes that push a person to become fat. And once a person has gained weight, researchers understand why he or she has such a difficult time losing it. Perhaps most impressive is the molecule-by-molecule understanding that researchers are assembling of the body's weight-regulating system and the concomitant ability to develop drugs that act directly on this system.

In September 1999, for instance, the Cambridge doctors who had discovered the Pakistani cousins suffering from the same mutation as Patient 24 reported a heartening success in treating the girl, who had been eight when discovered and was now ten. A year earlier, when the girl was four feet seven inches tall and weighed 208 pounds, the doctors had begun injecting her daily with genetically engineered leptin. The dose was quite modest, calculated to bring her blood levels of leptin up to only 10 percent of what would be normal for a girl of her age and weight, but it nonetheless had a dramatic effect. Her appetite dropped sharply, and where before she had been almost constantly hungry, wolfing down her meals and asking for more, demanding food between meals, and often sneaking something to eat when she was refused, now she ate no more and no faster than her normal-weight siblings, and she stopped between-meal eating altogether. As a result, instead of gaining two to four pounds a month, as she had been doing, now she was losing weight at about the same rate. After a year on leptin she had taken off thirty-six pounds and was seventy pounds lighter than she likely would have been without the treatment.

The Cambridge doctors also tried leptin injections on a three-year-old girl with the same mutation, and the results were equally striking. The girl had been eating 2000 calories a day—enough for many adults—before the treatment. Soon after the injections began, however, she cut her intake by 80 to 90 percent and started taking child-sized meals. As this was written, Ozata had not yet been able to start leptin injections on Patient 24, but there is no reason to doubt that he, too, will benefit from such a course. Thanks to the discovery of the leptin gene, doctors can now help people who, like Patient 24, are missing this major component of their weight-regulating system.

For everyone else, however, the tremendous body of knowledge that researchers have accumulated about eating, metabolism, and obesity has proved to be of mainly academic interest. Despite all the diet books, diet drugs, reduced-calorie and reduced-fat foods, and advice from weight-loss specialists, the obesity epidemic has not slowed. Indeed, it is growing much faster than it was thirty years ago. If the rate of obesity in the general population continues increasing at the same pace it has for the past two decades, half of the adults in United States will be obese by the year 2025. In any practical sense, the quest to understand and control obesity quest cannot be considered a success.

We do, however, have a good idea of why the epidemic has been so difficult to stop. This is something that has puzzled doctors and obesity researchers for decades. Overweight has always seemed as if it should be one of the simplest medical problems to solve: just have people eat fewer calories. But as doctors in the 1930s quickly found out, and as every generation of doctors after them has verified, it's not that easy. Even the most motivated patients have difficulty losing a significant amount of weight and keeping it off. Many people can maintain a loss of ten or twenty pounds by watching what they eat or exercising more; few can sustain a loss of fifty, 100, or more no matter what the technique.

The reason for this difficulty lies with the body's weight-regulating system, which works to keep the body at a certain preferred weight, or set point. If you gain weight much above your set point, the extra fat stores produce more leptin, which acts as a signal to your brain to reduce your appetite and rev up your metabolism until your weight returns to normal. Conversely, if you lose weight much below your set point, your brain responds by increasing appetite and decreasing metabolism. It is this system that keeps most people's weights stable to within a few pounds for years on end, even if they pay no attention to what or how much they are eating. Such systems do a similar job for the obese, only at weights that are far above what is healthy. Even profoundly obese people will generally stay near a preferred weight if they are not dieting or otherwise trying to lose weight. Thus when an obese person loses fifty or 100 pounds, the weight-regulating region of the brain interprets the loss as a sign of a major problem and responds accordingly. The appetite is set on high, the metabolism on low. Doctors who have studied the so-called "reduced obese"—patients who were formerly obese but who have dropped their weight to near-normal levels—find that they share many psychological traits with victims of starvation. They think constantly about food, for instance, and they are deeply hungry in a way that a single big meal cannot assuage. If a fat person is to lose a significant amount of weight and keep it off, he must, in essence, maintain himself on a starvation diet. This is not natural, and few are successful at it for long.

Patient 24 suffers from a variant of this problem. Without leptin, his brain has no way to sense the body's ample fat stores and frantically signals that they must be replenished. If he were to lose much below his 330 pounds, he would quite literally feel as if he were starving.

It is also likely that psychological factors play a role in keeping people fat. The obese, like everyone else, have eating habits that are deeply ingrained. Changing those habits demands a great deal of concentration and commitment, and, after they have been changed, it is always easy to fall back into older ways that seem more natural and demand less conscious effort. Obesity specialists are still debating the relative contributions of the physiological and psychological factors. The balance probably varies from person to person, with a physiological set point playing a larger role in some fat people and psychological factors more important in others. Either way, once a person becomes fat, it is exceptionally difficult to return to a normal weight.

And more and more people are becoming fat for the simple reason that we have created an environment that makes this inevitable. The human body is designed to maintain a healthy weight in conditions that were present through most of human history—that is, with a limited, unpredictable food supply and with relatively high levels of physical activity. When living as hunter-gatherers, eating whatever animals can be killed or scavenged and whatever fruit and veg-etable matter can be taken from plants, humans keep enough fat stores to make it through the occasional lean times but not so much that it slows them down sig-nificantly. Our weight-regulating systems are finely tuned to work well in such an environment. Hunter-gatherers do not have to think about how much to eat in order to maintain a desirable weight. Their bodies tell them.

The rest of us are not always so lucky. Living in a world of high-calorie, high-fat foods, always in plentiful supply, and with labor-saving devices that keep us from having to exert ourselves too much, sometimes our finely tuned internal machines fail us. They tell us to eat more than we need for a healthy, normal weight, and, if we listen to their advice, we get fat. This makes maintaining a healthy weight a very different matter than it was intended to be. Instead of it being a task that is accomplished unconsciously and automatically, it becomes something we have to think about. Even worse, we have to fight against the overeating that our internal voice is telling us is right and natural. The result for many people is that their "natural" weight is far above what the doctors tell them is a healthy weight, and so, to be healthy, they must do something that is quite unnatural—they must stop listening to their bodies and instead make eating a matter of calculation and restraint. The odds against them may not be as high as those facing Patient 24, but they are considerable nonetheless.

This, in brief, is why the obesity epidemic has been so tenacious. The envi-ronment that we have created for ourselves to live in, while a very attractive and comfortable one, is one that our body's weight-regulating systems were never designed for. And an increasing number of people are paying the price.

What can be done? Many obesity specialists have come to the conclusion that the best hope for the obese, and perhaps the only one, is to develop drugs that manipulate the body's weight-regulating system directly. In the past, diet pills have broadly targeted drugs that affected many different systems in the brain and body. To have a significant effect on appetite or metabolism or some other factor influencing weight, they had to be taken in doses high enough to be felt in other areas as well, and so the likelihood of side effects was high. As a general rule of thumb, the more effective the diet pill was in controlling weight, the more likely it was to have undesirable effects elsewhere. But a new generation of weight-loss drugs is under development that depends on the detailed, molecule-level understanding that researchers have assembled of the body's weight-regulating system, and they may be far more effective than the earlier drugs, with far fewer side effects. Some doctors even expect that the drugs will allow them to turn off a person's appetite completely. A person could control exactly when he got hungry and how hungry he got with the right mix of pills.

To some, especially many obesity doctors who have grown frustrated at their inability to help their patients lose weight and keep it off, this may seem an exhilarating vision. To me, it is unappealing, even a little frightening. Already 30 percent of our adult population is obese, making them reasonable candidates for a drug regimen that would safely and reliably help them lose weight down to a healthy range. In fifteen or twenty-five years, when these wonder drugs are finally perfected, the number of obese may well have risen to 40 or 50 percent of the population. If we rely on drugs to keep us thin, half the people in the United States could be popping pills to keep their weight down, and this wouldn't even include the people who want to take off ten or twenty pounds for swimsuit season or high school reunions.

The medical justification for these weight-loss drugs is that obesity is a disease that kills many thousands of people each year. For a doctor treating an obese patient, the calculus is simple: Jane Doe is five-foot-two and 205 pounds. She won't lose more than thirty or forty pounds on a diet, and it always comes back after a few months. If she keeps going this way, she will likely develop diabetes or high blood pressure or heart disease. She will suffer from joint problems when she is older, and she can expect a much shorter life than her thin friends. Should she be given these drugs that will bring her weight down to 130 and keep it there and help her avoid the complications she could otherwise expect? Assuming the drugs are relatively safe, the answer is easy for most doctors: go with the drugs. And, indeed, it is hard to argue with this conclusion on an individual level. But when multiplied by millions of times, it could well lead to a society in which weight-control drugs are nearly as common as coffee in the morning or brushing one's teeth at night.

There is, however, another way to attack the problem of obesity which is not as familiar as the diet-pill option but which begins to make sense once one stops to consider the character of the problem. It starts with the observation that obesity is indeed best thought of as a disease. Granted, it is a most peculiar disease. The pathogen behind it is not a virus or bacteria or even an environmental toxin but rather something that most people think of as quite desirable: the luxurious lifestyle that we in the Western world have developed. Diseases are generally characterized by malfunctions of bodily systems, but the weight-regulating system in the obese is usually functioning exactly as intended, directing the body to stay at a preferred weight; the problem is rather that the preferred weight is too high. And it's difficult to think of something as a disease when it can be cured by something as simple as putting less food in one's mouth. Diseases should be made of sterner stuff. They should demand antibiotics or chemotherapy or, at the very least, chicken soup and bed rest.

Furthermore, to a certain degree the question of whether obesity is a disease is little more than semantics. The meaning of "disease" has changed and expanded over time as maladies that had never been thought of as diseases get that label applied. Schizophrenics and psychotics, for instance, have gone from simply being crazy to being victims of mental disease. Many doctors who treat obese patients have lobbied to have obesity thought of as a disease, in large part to remove the stigma of obesity as a character flaw or personal failing. Pharmaceutical companies too would like obesity to be seen as a disease. It is easier to justify selling drugs to treat a disease than to provide artificial willpower to people who just can't say no to food. So any discussion of whether obesity is a disease tends to get caught up in such side issues.

Nonetheless, it makes sense to think of obesity as a disease and not simply a behavioral problem for the simple reason that the physical functioning of a bodily system—the system that controls eating and fat stores—has been altered in a way that is damaging to the individual. Research performed over the past decade has left no doubt that the obese have set points that are far higher than people of normal size and that their bodies resist weight loss by decreasing the metabolism and so burning fewer calories. Traditionalists might argue that an individual could still keep his weight in check with a conscious effort even if his internal weight-control system is pushing him to be fat, but that's a philosophical debate. If the body's weight-regulating system, which is intended to work automatically and without conscious input from the individual, is not doing its job properly because of the environment in which it is operating, that can reasonably be considered a disease.

When public health officials are faced with a plague that is making its way through the population, they generally respond with a two-pronged approach. First they attempt to treat the affected individuals, protecting them as best as possible from the ravages of the plague, and, second, they look to find the cause of the plague and stop it. In the case of obesity, the response has been almost completely of the first sort. No one has seriously tried to pinpoint the factors that are causing so many people to get fat and change those factors or else protect people from them.

There are at least a couple of reasons for this. One is practical. Whatever the precise reasons for the obesity epidemic—the easy availability of high-calorie, high-fat foods, the lessening of physical activity, the greater appeal of and emphasis placed upon food—they are factors that have come into existence because of their widespread appeal. We like fast food. We like having escalators relieve us of the necessity of climbing stairs, and we like having cars that carry us from one place to another, even short distances that our grandparents would have walked without thinking about it. Even if research were to show that it is our lack of physical activity that is making so many of us fat, it's hard to see how we could go about remaking our world to force us to exert ourselves more.

I suspect, however, that a more important reason is psychological or, perhaps, philosophical. Weight has always been seen as a very individual, a very personal thing. Because eating is under conscious control—you can always decide not to put that fork in your mouth—being overweight seems clearly to be a matter of an individual's decisions, or perhaps of a failure to make decisions. Over time, doctors and the public have changed their attitudes about the nature of those individual decisions—in the 1930s they were thought to be a matter of free will, in the 1950s they were seen as shaped by subconscious urges, and by the 1980s they were assumed to be a product of the body's weight-regulating system—but the focus has always been on the individual. The most important thing to know about obesity was what differentiated an obese person from someone who wasn't obese. What is different about the obese, psychologically, physiologically, or behaviorally, that makes them fat? It was the asking of such questions that led to the explosion of knowledge about eating and weight that has occurred over the past few decades.

But when it comes to treating the disease, the individual approach has been less effective. The best it has to offer is giving drugs to the obese in order to push their decisions toward eating less. To deal effectively with the obesity epidemic— to prevent it, not just ameliorate it—will demand thinking about it in a different way. The question can no longer be, What is it about the obese that makes them fat? but instead must be, What is it about our society, our culture, and our physical environment that makes so many of us fat?

If the history of obesity research teaches us anything, it is that obesity—as least as it is experienced at the turn of the twenty-first century—is not an individual problem. It is a disease caused by a sick environment to which some of us are more susceptible than others. This is not a way of thinking about obesity that comes naturally to those of us who grew up hearing that weight is a matter of willpower, perhaps with a little help from the latest diet fad, and that if you're fat it's nobody's fault but your own. But it is a way of thinking about obesity that must become much more common if we, as a society, are to find a reasonable solution to our common problem. It is toward starting that process of changing minds that this book is dedicated.

ONE

Medicalizing Obesity

The time is 1911. The place, the Laboratory of Physiology at Harvard Medical School. Here, amidst the x-ray devices and other state-of-the-art equipment, Walter Bradford Cannon is preparing for a simple experiment that will shape thinking about hunger for the next sixty years.

Cannon has no way of knowing that, of course. Thirty-nine years old and the George Higginson Professor of Physiology at Harvard, he has spent the past decade and a half tracing out the operation of the digestive system, using the newly invented x-ray machine to watch food and other objects as they pass through the esophagus and into the stomach and the bowels of both experimental animals and human volunteers. That work led Cannon to the question of why people get hungry and, eventually, to the experiment on which he is now concentrating, an experiment that will cap off his studies into the digestive system. In years to come, he will move on to a number of other subjects in physiology. He will show that such stresses as fear or pain or anger or cold cause adrenaline to be released into the bloodstream, triggering the "fight or flight" response. He will develop the theory of homeostasis, explaining how a body maintains a steady level of some physiological variable—temperature, say, or the amount of sugar in the blood. During the First World War, he will explain what causes wound shock and how to treat it. He will become one of the most influential and widely cited physiologists in the first half of the twentieth century and will regularly be mentioned as a candidate for the Nobel Prize in Physiology or Medicine. That he is never chosen will be attributed by some of his colleagues to the breadth of his achievements—the Nobel committee never quite knew which one to focus on. But of all this, his best-known work is destined to be the study before him today.

Assisting Cannon is Arthur Lawrence Washburn, twenty-three, a student who graduated from Harvard University the previous year and entered Harvard's medical school. Washburn is not particularly interested in medical research or, if he is, the experience with Cannon will change his mind, for, as nearly as can be told from a search of the medical literature over the next several decades, Washburn will never contribute to a published research report after this one. He will graduate from the medical school in 1915, serve in the war, then settle in New York City to practice internal medicine for the next fifty years, where he died in 1965 according to an obituary in the *Journal of the American Medical Association.*

Washburn's official portrait from the Harvard yearbook of 1910 shows a clean-cut man, his dark hair slicked down and fastidiously parted on the left, who looks several years younger than the twenty-two he was at the time of the photo. He is wearing a dark suit, white shirt with a high collar, and dark tie. The picture is done in profile from the left side in a style you seldom see these days except for mug shots, and while it gives a clear view of Washburn's finely shaped ear and slightly oversized nose, it leaves one with the sense of not actually knowing what Washburn looked like. Fortunately, we needn't worry about missing him as we wander the hallways of the Laboratory of Physiology. We simply look for a young man from whose mouth snakes a length of rubber tubing.

The idea for this experiment had first come to Cannon in 1905, when he had been listening through a stethoscope to the sounds of his own abdomen and noticed that hunger pangs seemed to coincide with loud gurgling sounds. Those sounds, Cannon assumed, were a good indication that the muscles around his stomach were contracting and relaxing, squeezing the digestive tract and easing off, and this in turn suggested a hypothesis: that gastric contractions were causing his feelings of hunger. At the time, this was something of a radical notion. Hunger was widely believed to be a whole-body phenomenon, arising when the nutrients from a person's most recent meal had been absorbed from the blood and the body's nerve cells, needing further sustenance, sent an SOS to the brain. But Cannon decided that this was unlikely, for several reasons. When he observed his own hunger pangs, for instance, he noticed that they came and went many times over a stretch of twenty minutes or so, and he did not believe the body's nutrient levels would vary quickly enough to account for the sudden comings and goings of the pangs. And researchers knew that eating clay and other items with no nutritional value could temporarily assuage hunger. This made no sense if hunger were driven by the levels of nutrients in the blood but fit perfectly with hunger being driven by what was happening in and around the stomach.

We don't know why Cannon waited five years to test his idea. Perhaps he had other, more pressing investigations into the digestive system. Perhaps he did not at first see a good way to perform such a test. Or perhaps until Washburn came along, no one had been willing to be the subject of such a test. But whatever the reason, it was late 1910 or early 1911 before Cannon and Washburn set out to determine whether stomach contractions were indeed at the root of the sensation of hunger.

"In order to learn whether such proof might be secured," they would write in their 1912 paper detailing the experiment, "one of us (W.) determined to become accustomed to the presence of a rubber tube in the oesophagus." For several weeks Washburn practiced swallowing what the paper described as "a soft-rubber balloon about 8 cm. in diameter" to which was attached a long, thin tube. In reality, what Washburn was swallowing was most likely a condom, for this is what physiologists of that era usually meant when they wrote "soft-rubber balloon," although, for reasons of delicacy, they seldom made that clear. Condoms were cheap, readily available, and of a size that was useful for many purposes, and so they regularly found their way into the laboratory. Eventually the practice would die out, and physiologists would later look back in some embarrassment at the habits of their predecessors. Half a century after Cannon and Washburn's work, in a past-president's lecture to the American Physiological Society, Horace Davenport would remark, "The condom has a place in physiology, but that place is not the stomach." In 1911, however, this is exactly the part of Washburn's anatomy that became most familiar with this particular device.

Each day Washburn swallowed the "soft-rubber balloon" and worked it down into his stomach, where it was inflated through the attached tube and left in place for two or three hours. During this stretch Washburn would go about his usual activities, walking about the medical school, taking part in laboratory sessions, perhaps even attending lectures—with a condom in his belly and a rubber tube snaking up through his esophagus and out his mouth. We do not know from the descriptions of the experiment whether it was just a few inches of tubing that protruded from Washburn's mouth or if it was several feet, but, either way, he eventually got used to it. "After this preliminary experience," Washburn and Cannon would write, "the introduction of the tube, and its presence in the gullet and stomach, were not at all disturbing."

Having reached this point, the two researchers are now ready to observe how Washburn's stomach behaves during those times when he feels hungry. He skips breakfast and lunch, then shows up in the lab around 2 p.m. to be outfitted for monitoring. After he has swallowed the apparatus, the condom is inflated and the end of the tube is attached to a pressure meter. Whenever Washburn's stomach contracts, the resulting squeeze on the condom increases the pressure of the air inside it, which shows up as a blip on the pressure gauge. In this way Cannon can record the strength and duration of each contraction. Washburn, meanwhile, sits with his finger on a key attached to another recording device and presses it down whenever he feels hungry. This gives them two sets of tracings—one capturing stomach contractions, the other recounting Washburn's subjective feelings of hunger—which can later be compared. In order to avoid the possibility that Washburn is unconsciously influenced to feel hungry whenever he sees that a contraction is occurring, the tracing of his stomach contractions are kept hidden from him during the experiment.

As Cannon and Washburn would report in their 1912 article, the resulting data seemed to leave little doubt about the connection between hunger and stomach contractions. A typical session would start out quietly, with Washburn feeling no hunger and the pressure meter recording no contractions. "Sometimes a rather tedious period of waiting had to be endured before contractions occurred," the researchers wrote. Once hunger hit, Washburn would press and release the key a dozen times or so over a twenty-minute period, with the pangs lasting anywhere from thirty to ninety seconds. And, as the researchers discovered when they compared the two sets of records, each pang that Washburn reported was accompanied by a strong squeeze on the balloon in his stomach. When Washburn would let up on his key, the pressure gauge too would ease off.

It was a powerful and convincing study, one that was still being quoted more than half a century later. Although Cannon and Washburn did not get all the details right—the crucial ingredient in hunger is actually a drop in blood glucose levels, which sets off the stomach contractions and also leads to the desire for food—and although it was later discovered that the contractions are closely correlated with hunger in only some people, the experiment was close enough to the truth that for a long time it would define how doctors and scientists thought of hunger.

Cannon and Washburn's experiment came near the end of an era. From the 1820s to the 1920s, doctors and scientists were slowly piecing together a picture of how people digest and put to use the food they eat. At the beginning of that century-long stretch, what happened to food after it left the mouth for deeper regions was mostly a mystery. By the end, the picture was mostly complete.

The start of that era can be labeled quite precisely. It was June 6, 1822. On this day in Michilimackinac, in what is now the state of Michigan, a U.S. Army surgeon named William Beaumont was called to treat a nineteen-year-old French-Canadian trapper who had been wounded in the abdomen with a shotgun blast. Beaumont found the trapper, Alexis St. Martin, with a sizable hole leading into his stomach, one that seemed almost certain to be fatal. Somehow St. Martin survived, but the hole in his abdominal wall never completely closed. Instead he was left with a fistula, or narrow passage, between his stomach and the outer skin. Normally the walls of the fistula were squeezed together, but Beaumont could open the passage by pressing alongside it and, by so doing, peer into St. Martin's stomach.

The opportunity was too good to pass up. At the time, scientists had a rough idea of what went on in the stomach but very few details. So, three years after St. Martin's injury, Beaumont began a series of observations and experiments to investigate digestion. By keeping close track of what happened in St. Martin's stomach throughout the day, Beaumont proved that the stomach does not produce its gastric juices continuously but instead times the secretions to provide digestive juices only when food is anticipated or is actually in the stomach. He retrieved samples of the digestive juices from St. Martin's stomach and sent them to a chemist, who found that their main component was hydrochloric acid. He also detected a second component of the gastric secretions, which another researcher would later identify as pepsin, an enzyme that breaks apart protein molecules. Beaumont's *The Physiology of Digestion*, first published in 1833, became the standard reference on that subject for the rest of the century.

Beaumont also observed the connections between St. Martin's mental states and the state of his stomach, recording stomach movements and the secretion of gastric juices and comparing that with what St. Martin said he was feeling. Beaumont found that after St. Martin had eaten, he would not become hungry again until after his stomach had been empty for some time. Combining this observation with the fact that St. Martin's stomach produced gastric juices only when food was already in his stomach or when he was expecting food, Beaumont speculated that the sense of hunger is caused by the swelling of the gastric glands as they prepare to secrete their juices. Eighty years later Beaumont's proposal would be one of the possible explanations of hunger that Cannon and Washburn dismissed in the process of advancing their own gastric-contractions theory, but at the time it was as good a guess as any.

Forty years after Beaumont was called to St. Martin's side, two researchers at the University of Munich, physiologist Carl von Voit and chemist Max von Pettenkofer, began a series of experiments that would open up the thermodynamics of digestion much as Beaumont had laid bare its physiology. At the time it was already known that humans and other animals get their energy from combustion, a slow-motion version of the same chemical reaction that drives a fire. Hydrocarbons—molecules containing mostly hydrogen and carbon atoms— combine chemically with oxygen molecules to produce carbon dioxide, water, and other hydrocarbon molecules. The body can "burn" three different types of

William Beaumont. Photo courtesy of the National Library of Medicine.

molecules in this way: fats, carbohydrates, and proteins. These combustions release energy, which is captured by the body's cells and used to power all the body's activities, from muscle movements to the building of new tissue.

In 1862 von Voit and von Pettenkofer constructed an airtight chamber with which they could study metabolism in detail. By having a human subject live in their respiration chamber for days at a time, Voit and Pettenkofer were able to measure the amount of oxygen consumed and the amount of carbon dioxide produced and so calculate the amount of energy expended by the subject during that time. Their experiments stretched over eleven years, and by the end they had, among other things, made the first measurements of the daily energy requirements for human beings.

Twenty years later, that work would be extended and refined by a student of Voit's, the American chemist Wilbur Atwater. Collaborating with an engineer named Edward Rosa, Atwater built a much more sensitive respiration chamber which not only measured more precisely the amounts of oxygen breathed in and carbon dioxide breathed out but also provided an accurate reading of the heat produced by a subject inside. By using the chamber to test subjects who were fed various diets, Atwater produced the first tables of the energy values of different foods, which he published in 1896. A gram of carbohydrate, he found, provides the human body with four calories of energy, as does a gram of protein, while a gram of fat provides nine calories of energy. The numbers that Atwater calculated are still accepted as accurate today.

Atwater continued his studies through 1905 and triggered a wealth of other research on the caloric value and nutritional content of food. By the 1920s nutritional scientists had a clear understanding of how the body uses food and what sorts of food make up a healthy diet.

Throughout this century of digestive exploration, the researchers were driven primarily by a sense of intellectual curiosity. Although the nutritional studies toward the end of the era were used to make diet recommendations, most of the research was of no more than academic interest. In particular, as hard as it may be to believe from today's point of view, the men who did this work were not at all concerned with the question of why people get fat.

And so it was that in 1912, after Cannon finished his seminal stomach-contractions experiment, he dropped the entire line of research into the digestive system and went to work on the sympathetic nervous system. Having identified, or so he thought, the source of hunger sensations, it would have been easy enough to compare the contraction-hunger connection between people of varying weights and see if some flaw in this hunger-signaling system might explain overeating. Perhaps, for instance, the obese had stronger, more persistent contractions. All Cannon needed to do was repeat his experiment with a number of volunteers, some fat and some thin. Two generations later another scientist would do just that and set off a decade of research based on the assumption that the obese could not interpret their hunger signals properly.

As for Cannon, he just wasn't interested in obesity studies. At the time, obesity was not something that doctors and medical researchers concerned themselves with, except as a curiosity. Weight was seen not as a medical concern but as a matter of taste or fashion, and the issue of overeating was not even on the table. That, however, was about to change.

Throughout much of the nineteenth century, medical opinion held that it was healthy to carry an extra twenty, thirty, even fifty pounds of fat. Doctors did not countenance extreme obesity of the sort that makes it difficult to walk or carry out other normal activities, but they believed that a decent amount of extra flesh was prudent. It provided a reserve of vitality which would keep a person from becoming run down or excessively tired and would help see a person through an extended illness. Thin simply was not healthy.

From the 1870s to the early twentieth century, for instance, neurasthenia, or nervous exhaustion, was a popular diagnosis. People had only so much nervous energy, the theory went, and anyone who drove himself too hard, particularly in the professions that demanded a great deal of brain work and little physical activity, was in danger of depleting his energy store. Neurasthenia sufferers could be identified by their thinness, physical weakness, nervousness, and associated maladies such as headaches and insomnia. The cure was complete bed rest with no reading or mental stimulation and plenty of food to build up the fat stores.

As a result, the books and magazine articles devoted to weight were quite different from what we are accustomed to today. Instead of offering advice on cutting calories and on which foods fight fat, authors suggested ways to pack on the pounds. In 1901, for example, when the physicians George P. Wood and E. H. Ruddock published *Vitalogy or Encyclopedia of Health and Home*, they included a chapter called "How to Become Fat or Plump." "This is more easily accomplished than is generally supposed," they wrote. "By following the instructions, lean or spare persons will become fleshy or plump." Get plenty of sleep, they advised, drink plenty of water, and eat lots of starchy foods, fats, vegetables, and sweets. And, if you're in a hurry to gain weight, eat as many oysters as you can. "They may be taken in any form, raw or cooked, but they should be eaten without vinegar or pepper."

Attitudes toward extra weight began changing after the turn of the century, and, ironically, it was not doctors but statisticians for insurance companies who drove the change. Insurance companies had a resource that doctors didn't— detailed, long-term health and mortality statistics on thousands of people—and once it became important for insurance companies to examine those statistics, they began to uncover health patterns that doctors could only guess at. In the late nineteenth and early twentieth centuries, American insurance companies began to sell more and more individual life insurance policies, and in order to better understand the risks, the companies began to study the mortality rates of different groups of people. One of the pioneers in this work was Oscar Rogers of the New York Life Insurance Company, and his report, at a 1901 meeting of the Association of Life Insurance Medical Directors, marked a turning point in attitudes toward the overweight.

Rogers reported that among a group of 1500 men who were 30 percent or more overweight, the death rate was 35 percent higher than expected. This was a big enough difference to be important to anyone selling life insurance, so Rogers's work motivated the industry to collect and analyze reams of health and mortality statistics on the fat and the thin. By the 1920s, both actuaries and doctors—who had been following the reports or the insurance company statisticians with great interest—had become convinced that life expectancy for the obese was noticeably shorter than for their thinner peers.

The new view did not, of course, fit well with the old conviction that it was healthy to carry about a certain amount of extra weight, and for a couple of decades doctors debated which belief was correct and if it might be possible somehow to reconcile the old and the new views of fat. In a 1928 issue of *The Literary Digest*, for instance, a German physician, Martin Hahn, is quoted as arguing that the relative merits of fat versus thin depend upon the patient. For the elderly, Hahn conceded, the insurance studies had proved that thin is better since the underweight undoubtedly lived longer. "On the other hand," he said, "young people do better to be somewhat overweight instead of underweight. This gives them a reserve of internal food to draw on for the extreme exertions which are more frequent when one is young; also in case of serious illness."

Hahn's belief that fat might have a good side was becoming increasingly rare, however, and by the 1930s the medical profession had made a total about-face. Excess fat was now to be avoided by everyone all the time. Part of this change in attitude was driven by the insurance industry's continuing studies. In 1930, Louis Dublin of Metropolitan Life published a watershed paper detailing the specific maladies—heart disease, diseases of the arteries, brain hemorrhage, diabetes, kidney disease—that he found to be more common among the obese and to be responsible for their shortened life expectancy. Dublin's paper triggered a wave of research by doctors and medical specialists investigating the connection between corpulence and a wide variety of health problems, and for decades it was pointed to as definitive proof of the many dangers of being overweight.

In retrospect, we now know that the insurance studies of overweight that drove the change in attitude were critically flawed. For one thing, when Rogers first performed his analyses, the data showed that not only the overweight but also the underweight and the over-tall had shorter life expectancies, but for some reason Rogers singled out only the overweight for special attention. More seriously, the analyses were performed not on a sample of all Americans but, quite naturally, only on the subset of Americans who bought life insurance. Thus the subjects were mostly white males who worked in professional jobs. On the whole they were much less likely to be overweight than adults in the general population, so the health of the overweight members of this small group might not be representative of the health of the overweight in general.

But, most important, there was never any proof that being overweight actually caused these health problems. The insurance companies didn't care, of course. To them weight was simply a marker that helped them pick out people who should pay higher premiums. It did not matter to them whether being overweight was the cause of the increased mortality or simply a result of something else—poor nutritional practices, not enough exercise—that was both making people fat and making them more likely to die young.

To the medical profession, on the other hand, this was—or should have been—a crucial distinction. If an extra fifty pounds of flesh makes a person more likely to die from diabetes or heart disease, it is important to help the person lose that weight, and losing the weight should bring the risks down to the level of the general population. If, instead, the risks arise from other factors, then losing the weight may do little or nothing to alleviate the risks. As we shall see later, this is still a matter of some debate within the medical community. A majority of doctors believe that being overweight is itself a risk, but a significant minority questions just how much of a risk it really is. And although careful statistical studies have unambiguously proven what Rogers and Dublin claimed—that the overweight do indeed die younger—it has been frustratingly difficult to demonstrate that losing weight will help them live longer.

As it happened, however, the medical profession in the 1930s accepted without reservation the idea that being fat was hazardous to your health, and doctors began preaching to their patients about the perils of fat. In less than a decade, obesity had gone from something that few doctors worried about to being seen as an important medical issue.

Still, although doctors had accepted obesity as a problem with medical consequences, they did not yet consider it to be a problem of medical origin, and this was an important distinction. Overeating was a behavioral issue, not a physiological one, and thus the corpulent were responsible for their predicament. It was up to them—with the advice and encouragement of their doctors, of course—to get themselves out of it.

When reading magazine articles on dieting and weight loss from the 1930s, one is struck by how little the advice has changed in the intervening sixty years. The language is somewhat outdated, and the sorts of foods proposed in the meal plans are clearly a throwback to an earlier era—meat or fish with breakfast, lunch, and dinner, every day of the week—but otherwise the recommendations would not seem out of place in a modern woman's magazine.

> Do not attempt to make a radical change in your eating habits . . . until you consult your physician.
> Do not attempt to reduce by diet alone. Follow a definite plan of exercises. . . . Lowered food intake will cause a loss of weight, but the exercises will also take off inches and put the muscles in better tone.

Generally speaking, weight loss will be achieved by a decrease of from 800 to 1,200 calories from your previous diet.

You should plan your reducing program over a period of months and not attempt to lose too much in a short time.

By the 1930s, thanks to decades of nutrition and metabolism studies, doctors knew almost as much about safe and healthy weight-loss diets as they do today. Long before being overweight was found to be unhealthy, dieting had been popular among the public as a way of attaining a fashionable thin look, and so doctors and physiologists were accustomed to lecturing the public on the right way to diet. Doctors knew with great accuracy how much food a body needed daily to remain healthy—not just the number of calories, but also grams of protein, grams of carbohydrate, grams of fat, and the necessary trace amounts of various vitamins and minerals—and they were able to tell a patient precisely how many calories to cut from the normal daily intake to lose a pound, a pound and a half, or two pounds a week. Since none of these facts about human physiology has changed, it is no surprise that the diet advice of the 1930s should look so familiar.

What is different about dieting articles from that time is their context and presentation. One does find some of the same optimistic encouragement for the dieter that you still see today—a 1935 issue of *Hygeia* offers cheerily, "Dieting may be difficult for the first ten days or two weeks, but as overeating is a habit, the body becomes accustomed to the new regimen and adjusts itself"—but much of what accompanies the dieting advice of the time sounds preachy and judgmental to the modern ear. Consider this lecture to parents that appeared in September 1937, also in *Hygeia*, which was the general-audience health magazine published by the American Medical Association:

Don't let your child get fat! If you do, it means that both you and your child will go through a period of mental suffering and unhappiness during the all important early teens. . . .

Make them figure conscious. Tell them that we cannot all have beauty of feature but that we can do a great deal toward controlling our figures. Do not wait to have them reach this knowledge through bitter experience. . . .

It cannot be otherwise in this modern world that gives no quarter to the fat person.

Or this from the same AMA magazine in December 1937:

Most fat or plump persons want to be thinner, but at the same time they refuse to recognize the real cause of their trouble, which is, in all but a few cases, simply eating more food than the body needs for its daily activity.

Rather, they regard themselves as victims of an adverse fate over which they have no normal control.

Or contemplate the philosophical musings of a *Hygeia* writer in May 1939 as he tackled the larger meaning of corpulence:

An attribute of man is his power to distinguish right from wrong. The race should be increasingly conscious of its privilege to choose between alternatives in habits for the future betterment of the individual and the race. . . .

To an extent . . . the excessively obese mark themselves as having certain mental traits. They become members of a selective group, characterized in part by a disregard for personal physical appearance. . . .

All weight, normal or excess, is maintained by food that is eaten. There is no other source of flesh for men. Should not one of average intellect be willing and able to dignify the individual and the race by maintaining the conventional semblance of humanity?

Clearly, weight was not simply a medical issue, it was a moral issue as well. The obese were not merely an affront to actuaries, they were an affront to decent, self-respecting people everywhere.

Just why the overweight came in for such opprobrium is a long, complex cultural tale involving societal attitudes about health, appearance, consumption, thriftiness, self-discipline, and personal responsibility, among other things. It is a story told elsewhere in great detail, as in Hillel Schwartz's excellent social history, *Never Satisfied*, and in Roberta Pollack Seid's rave against weight obsession, *Never Too Thin*, and it is beyond the scope of this book to do it justice. Certainly, as these authors argue, the medical community's beliefs about the obese were colored by how the broader society saw them.

But parallel to and reinforcing these social attitudes was a history of medical findings that seemed to imply that the overweight were indeed responsible for their state. This research does not excuse the nasty attitudes many healers had toward their fat patients, but it does help explain why the medical community in the 1930s did not believe there was anything medically wrong with the obese other than their weight.

Doctors had known since at least the late 1800s that obesity could, in some cases, be the result of illness or disease. In 1893, for example, the Boston physician James J. Putnam described a forty-seven-year-old woman whose thyroid gland had stopped producing its normal hormonal secretions. She was listless, her hair had mostly fallen out, and she had become quite fat. An extract from the thyroid glands of a sheep helped bring her back to health, including removing all of the excess fat tissue.

In 1901, the Austrian physician Alfred Froehlich reported the case of a four-teen-year-old boy who had first come to him two years earlier with complaints of headaches and vomiting. Eventually the boy's eyesight started to fail, his headaches became much worse, and he became markedly fat around the mid-section. By analyzing his symptoms in great detail and comparing them with those in a few similar cases, Froehlich concluded that the boy was suffering from a tumor in his pituitary gland.

In such cases, doctors recognized that the cause of the weight problem — glan-dular malfunction, often leading to an artificially lowered metabolism — was clearly beyond the control of the patient, and accordingly granted such patients a special medical category. As the metabolism expert Karl von Noorden wrote in 1907, "It is the general opinion of both physician and layman that there are obese persons whose condition is to some extent independent of overeating or deficient physical exercise, and is rather the result of a 'constitutional tendency.' Such cases cannot be brought under control through intelligent regulation of diet and exer-cise." Von Noorden coined the term "endogenous obesity" for what ailed such people, with the implication that their obesity was innate to their bodies and thus, in effect, inevitable. The rest of the overweight were said to suffer from "exoge-nous obesity," an avoidable condition brought on by things within the patient's ability to control — in essence, eating too much and exercising too little.

The endogenous-exogenous distinction provided a useful way of categorizing different types of weight problems, but it also created an artificial dichotomy that shaped thinking about obesity for decades. Now the overweight must be diag-nosed as either one or the other — responsible or not responsible, shameless or blameless. According to this dichotomy, anyone who was not a victim of a meta-bolic malfunction must be lazy or gluttonous or both.

Throughout the 1910s and 1920s, doctors tended to lean toward the metabolic explanation and characterize most of their fat patients as suffering from the endogenous sort of obesity. Blaming obesity on the glands made sense to the patients, who often insisted that they ate less — or certainly no more — than their friends and colleagues of normal weight. It was also an attractive diagnosis to doc-tors, who would much rather have something concrete to offer their patients as the cause of their problems than simply telling them they ate too much.

Over time, however, research showed that very few of the fat patients whom doctors examined actually had any sort of medical abnormality that could account for their weight. Their glands were fine, their metabolisms were normal, and, furthermore, they were generally not the judicious eaters that they often made themselves out to be. Three researchers at the Western Pennsylvania Hospital in Pittsburgh demonstrated this simply and directly in one 1930 study designed to test the usefulness of a particular diet. Before putting eight of their female subjects on the diet, the doctors asked them to list everything that they ate normally. Then, in a twist that the patients had not expected, the doctors fed the patients for several days exactly what they had acknowledged eating at home, no more and no less. Six of the eight lost weight, as much as five pounds in four days, while the other two stayed even. The average weight loss for the group was two pounds in four days. If only the patients could be kept on a diet of what they admitted to eating, the doctors' work would be mostly done.

This and a raft of similar work pushed medical opinion to the other end of von Noorden's dichotomy. Now it appeared as if most fat patients suffered from corpulence of the exogenous type—which meant that it was completely within their power to fix. A 1937 article in *Hygeia* put it plainly: "If it is not a glandular disturbance that is causing excess weight, then the control of body weight is a matter of will power and knowledge."

In the early days of medical weight consciousness, when doctors were just beginning to preach the gospel of healthy thinness, doctors gave their fat patients the benefit of the doubt and assumed that their sins were unconscious. The obese were not the gluttons that some ignorant members of the public imagined them to be; they had simply fallen into overeating from ignorance or carelessness. It was easy to see how this might happen: A woman who had been walking to and from work each day, a mile each way, might quit her job and stay at home; everything else being equal, she would be burning 200 fewer calories each day, six days a week, which would put 15 pounds on her within a year unless she consciously ate less to compensate. Or a man who married a good cook might eat greater quantities of her food than he had of his own bachelor cooking; if he didn't also exercise more, he would soon become quite fat.

Assuming that obesity was the result of this sort of unconscious overeating, the cure seemed simple enough. Doctors would explain the calorie equation to their patients, provide them with calorie counts for different foods, and instruct them to keep their daily intake below a certain level. They might also encourage them to exercise more. In the more serious situations, where patients were seventy, a hundred, or more pounds overweight, the doctor would prescribe a rigid low-calorie diet with individual food items and serving sizes carefully specified for each meal. In any case, there was just one solution to the problem of overweight: eating fewer calories than the body needed for its daily energy requirements.

Then as now, doctors were certain that such a program would take off the weight—as long as the patient followed it. The metabolic work of Atwater and Rosa had shown that the human body does indeed obey the law of conservation of energy, and a series of careful studies in 1929 and 1930 had removed any lingering doubts about whether the metabolisms of the obese worked the same way as the metabolisms of the lean. For years doctors had reported contradictory results from putting obese patients on diets. Sometimes they lost weight, but sometimes they did not, and some patients even gained weight on low-calorie diets. To discover what was going on, two doctors at the University of Michigan Medical School, L. H. Newburgh and Margaret Woodwell Johnston, monitored a group of obese patients for several weeks as they were kept on a small, carefully determined number of calories each day. At first they found that several patients maintained their weight or even gained, just as other doctors have seen. Eventually, though, all the patients lost weight precisely according to predictions, and, when Newburgh and Johnston took into account how much liquid the patients had drunk and how much urine they had excreted, they found that they could resolve the initial discrepancy quite simply: the patients who did not lose weight in the first week or so of the diet were retaining water. Once their bodies' liquid balance was reestablished, their resistance to weight loss evaporated, and they quickly began shedding the pounds. This, Newburgh and Johnston wrote, accounted for the experience that many doctors had had of putting patients on a diet and getting no results. If a patient would only hang in there, eventually the pounds would melt away.

At this point—the beginning of the 1930s—there no longer seemed to be any mystery as to why people got fat or how they could lose weight, and obesity research lost its appeal to many medical scientists. True, a few cases of corpulence had interesting etiologies—a tumor near the pituitary gland, a thyroid gone haywire—but most were a clear case of staying at the table too long. The cure was equally plain: eat less. Obesity no longer seemed an interesting subject for inquiry, and the field became a research backwater for a decade or more.

Doctors, too, lost interest. Family physicians would hand out calorie charts and diet plans, often along with some condescending comments, to their overweight patients, but few ambitious doctors—or doctors of any kind, for that matter—chose the field as a specialty. As the psychologist Mickey Stunkard would write in 1959, "the treatment of obesity lost its glamour. The physician's job, it seemed, was simply to explain that semistarvation reduces fat stores, to prescribe a diet for this purpose, and to sit by. If the patient lost weight as predicted, this merely confirmed the comfortable feeling that treatment of obesity was really a pretty simple matter. However, if, as so often happened, the patient failed to lose weight, he was dismissed as uncooperative or chastised as gluttonous."

There was just one problem with this straightforward approach to weight loss: it
didn't work. When put on a diet, some patients would take off some weight—ten,
twenty, perhaps even fifty or more pounds—but it wouldn't stay off. Almost
inevitably the pounds would come back, often bringing some friends with them.
When Stunkard spoke at length to a 1958 conference on obesity therapy, a second doctor, Solomon Garb, summarized Stunkard's conclusions in this way:
"Most obese patients will not remain in treatment. Of those who do remain in
treatment, most will not lose significant poundage, and of those who do lose
weight, most will regain it promptly."

In 1959, Stunkard reviewed the records of 100 consecutive patients who came
to the Nutrition Clinic of the New York Hospital to lose weight. He found a
remarkably uniform record of failure. Only twelve of the 100, whose excess
weight ranged from twenty to 120 pounds, were able to lose as much as twenty
pounds, and only one lost forty pounds. Of those, only two had kept the weight
off at the end of two years.

The psychologists Stanley Schachter and Judith Rodin offered this plaintive
assessment of the obesity field in 1974, but it could have been written at any time
in the previous fifteen or even twenty-five years:

> Of all human frailties, obesity is perhaps the most perverse. The penalties
> are so severe, the gratifications so limited, and the remedy so simple that
> obesity should be the most trivial of aberrations to correct—yet, it is among
> the most recalcitrant. Almost any fat person can lose weight; few can keep
> it off.

As the magnitude of this failure became clear, beginning in the 1940s, doctors and medical scientists reacted in different ways. Some continued to blame
the obese, concluding that they must have even less willpower and self-respect
than thought and sometimes condemning them with a surprising ferocity.
Consider the following from the January 1948 issue of *Hygeia*, which seems to
reveal a frustration bordering on anger with the obese:

> Everybody loves a fat man. A round face, a pendulous belly are tokens of
> mirth, symbols of good nature. To Santa Claus, old King Cole and Falstaff
> are applied such blithe adjectives as jolly, rollicking, merry, jovial and
> benign. The thin man, on the other hand, is suspect, and conjures up
> visions of a stingy Scrooge, ghost-ridden Hamlet and a lean and dangerous
> Cassius. Gaunt, dyspeptic, cadaverous, dour and skinny are the stark and
> ugly words that modify the lean.
>
> But it ain't necessarily so! Medical science disputes this time-worn

theory. Science holds that obese individuals are not only poor medical risks but behavior problems as well. Doctors are more apt to point to a gourmandizing Goering as typical of the fat man than to a benevolent St. Nick. And in the thin man they may note aesthetic, spiritual, sensitive and self-sacrificing experiences rather than the sensual pleasures of excessive food and drink.

No longer were the obese jolly and benevolent. Instead they were disturbed and disturbing. At best they were heedless gluttons, at worst their gluttony might be reflective of darker, more unsavory failings.

Not all doctors reacted the same way, of course. Some came to believe that the failure must be theirs, rather than their patients'. The patients wanted to lose weight and tried to lose weight, but they were struggling with something that demanded more than willpower, menu plans, and encouragement to overcome. In short, these doctors began to see obesity not just as a condition with medical repercussions but also as a condition with medical causes, and that conviction was the root of the modern search for the causes of obesity. If obesity was due to something beyond the control of people, then it was the responsibility of doctors and medical researchers to learn what was causing it and how to treat it.

From the beginning, obesity researchers understood that if overeating was something more than a personal choice, then its sources must lie in one of two realms: the physiological or the psychological, the body or the mind. In theory, even though glandular breakdown had been ruled out as a cause for all but a minority of cases of obesity, excess weight might still be caused by a more subtle physiological failing. It might be due to a metabolic deficiency that the tests of the day could not detect. It could be a quirk in the way the body stored fat. It could be an abnormality in the part of the brain that controlled hunger—a particularly compelling hypothesis because researchers at Yale had recently shown that, by damaging one small region of the brain called the hypothalamus, they could create rats that overate and became obese. Or it might be some sort of breakdown in the homeostatic balance that works in both animals and humans to maintain a steady weight—a hypothesis that was advanced for the first time in the early 1950s.

Practically speaking, however, none of these possible physiological explanations for obesity had much value to physicians interested in helping the obese. They were little more than guesswork, and, even if researchers could confirm one of them, it wasn't at all clear how doctors would go about using that knowledge to effect a cure. There simply was not enough known about the physiology of metabolism, of hunger, and of fat cells.

Psychologists and psychiatrists, on the other hand, were ready. They had had several decades of experience investigating the foibles and weaknesses of the human mind and devising ways to treat them. Obesity posed a new challenge to these doctors, but not one that seemed significantly different from the other sorts of anxieties and neuroses that they had tackled. And so it was that from the 1940s into the 1960s, the subconscious became the major battleground in fighting obesity.

"When food is taken in excess of . . . physiological needs," wrote George Reeve in 1942, "it implies needs other than physiological which are in some way met by obesity." Reeve, a psychiatrist from Mt. Sinai Hospital in Cleveland, was one of the first to take seriously the idea that the obese were suffering from something beyond an inability to put their forks down—and, indeed, that such an inability indicated that something else must be going on. In particular, Reeve suspected that overeaters must be overeating because it satisfied psychological needs. If a doctor could identify those needs and provide some way of meeting them besides overeating, perhaps the overeating and the resulting obesity could be cured.

One of the earliest psychological explanations for overeating—and one that is still heard sometimes today—was that it is a coping mechanism. Some people eat when they are sad, others when they are nervous or anxious, still others when they are bored. If an analyst could figure out which environments or situations were most likely to push a patient to eat, it might be possible to avoid overeating by avoiding those situations or perhaps by substituting some other coping activity for eating. The weakness of this approach was that it begged the question of *why* the obese overeat. Almost everyone is sad or anxious or bored at one time or another, but most people don't respond by eating so much that they gain weight. What made the obese different? Psychologists could do no more than answer lamely that if a person had a predisposition to overeating then these various triggers could push them over the edge.

Psychoanalysts, however, thought they could do better. By exploring a patient's childhood and analyzing the patient's dreams, they would find the hidden meanings behind the eating and, by explaining these meanings to the patient, help him or her overcome the urge to overeat.

In 1947 Alfred Schick, a psychiatrist from New York City, offered one of the earliest discussions of the psychoanalytic interpretation of obesity. Although his grasp of physiology was rather limited and out of date—he still accepted that many cases of obesity were caused by glandular problems—his psychoanalysis was cutting-edge. His explanation of why a child's early development could influence his weight as an adult is a masterpiece of the Freudian mumbo jumbo that would dominate psychiatry for the next couple of decades:

In infancy, the ingestion of food is the most important function of self-preservation and the highest available pleasure. Freud points out that originally sexual excitement depended upon this need for nourishment. The sexual activity in that phase is not yet separated from the intake of food. . . . According to Rado [another psychoanalyst], the pleasure derived from eating is not limited to the oral zone but involves the entire digestive tract and the whole organism. Rado holds that in infancy, the entire process of digestion is charged with libido, a condition he calls alimentary orgasm. In the normal adult vestiges of the alimentary orgasm remain.

In this view, an infant's act of obtaining food was intimately connected with many emotionally charged items—self-preservation, sexual gratification, the love of a mother, and being provided for by her—which gave psychoanalysts like Schick plenty to work with when interpreting an adult's eating habits.

In his 1947 paper Schick offered a detailed psychoanalysis of Mary, a twenty-one-year-old daughter of an Orthodox Jewish family. The analysis was designed to illustrate to Schick's fellow practitioners the sorts of things they might look for in their own obese patients, and, indeed, psychoanalytic treatment of obesity did follow very much along the lines that Schick had indicated. It is worth spending some time on Schick's analysis, for it illustrates the state of the art in treating fat patients for the next decade or more.

At seventeen, Schick wrote, Mary had an emotional crisis. Up to that point she had seemingly been well adjusted, but then one Friday afternoon a young man whom she had been dating attempted to kiss her. Distraught, Mary fled home where her family was preparing for their weekly ritual supper, and there she felt an irresistible compulsion to eat as much food as she could stuff into her body. As her parents and two brothers sat at the table she would slip off to the kitchen between courses and gorge herself on "whatever she could find in the refrigerator and cupboards." The next morning she woke up depressed and promised herself she would not repeat the performance, but she soon fell into a pattern of pigging out periodically, especially on sweets and foods that were forbidden at the ritual dinners. It didn't take long for her weight gain to be noticeable enough that her parents took her to several physicians, but none of them succeeded in stemming her weight gain, and within six months "her appearance had become so unsightly and she herself so unhappy that she became a recluse and even gave up her favorite pastime, singing."

The emotional crisis had clearly been triggered, Schick concluded, by the threat that the kissing attempt posed to Mary's suppressed sexuality. "Emotionally immature, Mary could not cope with the sex situation." In his psychoanalytic ses-

sions with Mary, Schick was able to tie her eating to an impressive number of subconscious desires which he uncovered by exploring her childhood and listening
to her recounting of her dreams. Resentful of her mother's strictness, for instance,
Mary wanted to "do away with mother orally," and her "unconscious cannibalis-
tic drive found expression in her pathological eating." On the other hand, Mary
admired her mother and wished to be like her, so she "tried unconsciously to
achieve the union with her mother by eating in the magical belief that she would
thus become the consumed object."

Mary's relationship with her father also played a role in her eating, Schick concluded. Jealous of her mother's relationship with her father, Mary wished to take
her place. Having seen how pleased her father had been with her mother at the
birth of her younger brother, Mary wished to play the same role—to become
pregnant by her father. Because Mary had been told as a child that pregnant
women had babies growing in their stomachs, she came to associate eating and
the stoutness it produced with impregnation and the resulting pregnancy. Thus
in Mary's subconscious mind her eating was "an attempt at union with [her
father] on an oral level. The resulting obesity expressed the biological aim of
every sexual relation: pregnancy."

Adding to the complications was Mary's unconscious desire to be a male,
revealed in a peculiar dream. Five people were sitting around a table, two of
them feeding two others while the fifth one watched. In the dream Mary
declared, "These feeders have an easy job and I want to become a feeder." Later,
with Schick's help, Mary identified the watcher as being her father, the two feeders as her brothers, and the two people being fed as herself and her mother; the
feeding represented both the way a male supports his family and the way he
"feeds" a woman in intercourse. Thus Mary's eating was reflective of a "homo-
sexual attitude," Schick wrote. "Mary, in her unconscious desire to play the part
of the subject and object simultaneously, acted as the feeder and at the same time
fed herself in her eating spells . . . .Her abnormal eating aimed unconsciously at
identification with her father by incorporating his penis. It also indicated a symbolic feeding of the incorporated mother."

Clearly Mary was a very confused young woman. Or, in Schick's more poetic
description, her obesity was "the result of many instinctual cravings co-existing
in the timeless chaos of the unconscious." Fortunately for Mary, Schick was able
to help. "In the course of the analytical therapy, the intervals between her eating
bouts became longer and longer and the fits of eating considerably less severe.
She gradually lost forty pounds, resumed her social contacts fully and returned
to work."

Over the next ten years, an increasing number of psychoanalysts followed in
Schick's footsteps, bringing their particular analytical tools to bear on the prob-

lem of obesity. To judge from the writings of that time, these doctors must have
felt like zoologists who had stumbled onto a new land full of strange and hitherto
undescribed fauna, and soon they had a whole taxonomy of syndromes that they
believed were contributing to obesity.

In 1957, psychiatrist Harold Kaplan and psychologist Helen Singer Kaplan,
both of New York Medical College, surveyed the results of the previous decade
of theorizing and offered a catalog of some of the unconscious meanings for food,
overeating, and obesity that psychoanalysts and others had suggested. Obese
patients, they found, could be classified in two broad categories. Some enjoyed
being fat because it was the only thing they had ever been good at, the only way
they could surpass others. "A big body to them means strength, a type of great-
ness and bigness achieved by becoming more special and stronger than others."
A second group of fat patients saw obesity was a mark of failure and inadequacy,
although it was still useful and comforting in a twisted sort of way. "These feelings [of inadequacy] and the obesity associated with them then can be used to
justify all the failures in interpersonal relationships which the obese patient has."

Kaplan and Kaplan also summarized the various unconscious meanings that
psychoanalysts had attributed to food and eating. Food could symbolize "the
mother, with eating being an attempt to orally incorporate the mother." It could
signify the phallus, so that eating was an "expression of penis envy and a wish to
deprive the male of his penis." The act of overeating could be an "expression of
an unsatisfied sexual craving." It could serve as "a means of expressing hostility."
It was sometimes intended as "self-punishment and self-degradation, oft-times in
response to guilt." Or it could be "a substitute for love, affection, and friendli-
ness" or "a substitute for pregnancy." The researcher's list went on for forty-nine
separate entries, many of them containing several related interpretations.

"Almost all conceivable psychological impulses and conflicts have been
accused of causing overeating," Kaplan and Kaplan noted dryly, "and many symbolic meanings have been assigned to food." Since it seemed that any sort of emotional conflict might result in overeating and, ultimately, obesity, the researchers
argued that obesity is best thought of as a "nonspecific" psychological disorder.
The obese, they said, "may be characterized as emotionally disturbed persons
who, because of the availability of overeating mechanisms in their environments,
have learned to use hyperphagia as a means of coping with their psychological
problems."

After the 1950s the psychoanalytic treatment of obesity gradually fell into dis-
favor, and by the 1970s, although it still had its share of patients, it received little
attention or respect from the rest of the medical community dealing with the
obese. Even a number of psychoanalysts concluded that much of the improvement they saw in their patients—when they saw improvement—was due mainly

to a psychological placebo effect. The patients had faith in their therapists' ability to help them and it was this rather than any real coming to grips with their inner conflicts that produced the cure.

What remained after psychoanalysis had bowed out was the consistent observation that overeating was frequently associated with some psychological turmoil. Study after study had shown that the obese eat too much when they are depressed, when they are happy, when they are lonely, when they are anxious, when they are feeling guilty, or when they are in the grips of any number of other strong emotions. Unfortunately, this was only an observation, not an explanation, for it failed to distinguish the obese from people of normal weight. Many people overeat when they are sad or nervous or whatever, but only some of them overeat so much and so often that they get fat. What makes these different from those who don't?

Doctors today believe the difference to be physiological. Almost everyone eats too much every now and then, but only some people pay for it with a permanent weight gain. These are people whose bodies are primed to gain weight when presented with an abundance of food, and once they have gained weight, their bodies resist taking it off. So, except in a few cases, investigating an obese patient's mental or emotional problems will do little to help them lose weight, although it may help them become better adjusted to their obesity.

Instead, researchers say that if psychological differences between the obese and the lean exist, they are more likely the result than the cause of the excess weight. It is perfectly understandable that a person who is carrying an extra 100 pounds might get depressed or hostile. Job discrimination, social rejection, and physical limitations can do that to you.

Throughout the 1940s, '50s and '60s, a small but growing cadre of doctors and researchers came to specialize in obesity. Many were psychologists and psychiatrists, but their number also included medical doctors and scientists who studied endocrinology and metabolism, the brain, fat cells, or various other elements of the body with a relationship to weight. During the 1960s, the best-known fat doctors were the Dr. Feelgoods who dispensed amphetamines, thyroid hormones, diuretics, laxatives, and other medications that were supposed to help people lose weight, often selling the pills themselves in addition to writing the prescriptions. They were generally not welcomed by other obesity specialists, who tended to view them as profiteers, but nonetheless they added their voices to the chorus insisting that the overweight needed medical help.

Still, that chorus remained a minority in the medical community. As late as 1970, the chief of psychiatric services at the Veterans Administration Research Hospital in Chicago could write, "Most physicians regard obesity as a sin and treat fat patients with disdain befitting a moral leper." That view is fading today, but many doctors continue to suspect that the overweight are in some way responsible for their problem.

Nonetheless, although their numbers were small, by the 1960s the coterie of obesity doctors and researchers had, in all the ways that mattered, redefined obesity. Within that group there was almost total agreement that overweight was a condition that demanded medical intervention—that it was, in essence, a disease. They did not agree on what the nature of that disease was likely to be, but they did agree it was not something a patient could wish away. And since it was these specialists who defined knowledge about obesity for the rest of the medical community, obesity's status was set. Granted, it might take years or even decades for other physicians to come around or else to retire and leave the field to younger doctors who were open to this new view of obesity, but the deal was done.

The sociologist Jeffery Sobal refers to this as the "medicalization of obesity"— the process by which obesity ceased being seen as a moral problem for which an individual bears ultimate responsibility and instead came to be considered a malady or sickness. As Sobal sees it, this medicalization was at least as much a sociological phenomenon as a scientific one. The medical and scientific arguments for why obesity should be considered a disease did play a role, particularly in swaying individuals, but other factors, such as the formation of a well-defined community of obesity specialists and even the use of "obesity" to describe the field, were equally important, if not more so.

The name of the malady is not a trivial matter, Sobal notes. Previous labels such as corpulence, plumpness, or fatness carried moral overtones—they implied a condition for which the fat person was responsible. It was important to replace those terms with a new one that had none of the connotations and could instead imply a medical problem. "Obesity" was it, and getting people to refer to obesity instead of corpulence was a vital step in the medicalization of the field.

With obesity medicalized and its status as a disease established, doctors and researchers were still faced with the issue of exactly what sort of a disease it was. And that, as we shall see, would prove to be not an easy question to answer.

TWO

The Answer
That Wasn't

The decision to eat—when, what, how much—calls into play a host of factors, some of which we can sense and others that act clandestinely, beyond our conscious reach.

The most obvious of these factors, and the one that people tend to associate most strongly with eating, is hunger. Hunger, properly understood, is a physical sensation that humans share with every other sort of animal, a craving that comes from deep within the primitive parts of the brain and signals the body's need for food. It was hunger that Cannon and Washburn believed was being generated by rhythmic contractions of the empty stomach and which we now know to be triggered by changing levels of glucose in the blood.

But hunger is merely one factor among many in determining when and how much to eat. Even rodents base their gustatory decisions on considerations other than hunger. Rats can easily be trained to eat only when a light is on, for instance, or to eat all their food quickly in one big feeding instead of the usual pattern of spacing it out throughout the day. Humans, with their hugely inflated cerebral cortices, have far more complicated deliberations.

In modern, clock-driven societies like our own, the biggest single factor influencing when people eat may well be time of day. As the clock ticks toward meal time, we start to anticipate the food, perhaps unconsciously, perhaps with a very conscious contemplation of the menu, and by the time the hour has come, we are primed for consumption. It is not really so different from the rats taught to gobble a day's food in a single fifteen-minute period. Besides the clock, our eating decisions take into account such things as the presence or availability of food, the sight and smell of it, whether other people are eating, our diet goals, our emotional state, and whatever else may be competing for our time and attention, as well as all the subconscious factors that the Freudians uncovered. Somewhere in the brain, probably in the cerebral cortex, these various factors are digested, weighed, balanced, and compared to come up with a single decision: eat, or not eat.

Once a person has started eating, the decision to stop takes into account a different set of factors, and again the physical sensations are just part of the story. Both the distension of the stomach and the food-triggered release of hormones from the gastrointestinal tract send satiety signals to the brain, but these are only suggestions, not orders. A man served his favorite dessert may eat on well past satiation. A woman on a diet or in a hurry to get back to work may stop before her body says it's full.

The question facing anyone who wants to understand obesity is which of these many, often interrelated factors is responsible for people eating too much. In theory, of course, the problem could be exercising too little rather than eating too much, but this has always seemed unlikely. It is so much easier to consume than to expend—a 300-calorie candy bar is gone in three minutes, a 300-calorie jog lasts for thirty—that an imbalance between the two has always been assumed to be due mainly to overconsumption. And so for sixty years the major emphasis in obesity research has been on understanding eating and explaining why some people eat more than they need.

By the 1960s it was clear that psychoanalytic theories were not helping much. More promising was the research into the internal systems regulating hunger and satiety, research that had been progressing steadily since the 1940s. Working mostly on rats, physiologists had traced the sensations of hunger and satiety to the part of the brain called the hypothalamus and had shown that overeating or fasting could be triggered by destroying one part of the hypothalamus or another. Although the implications for overeating in humans were not at all clear, the work highlighted the importance of internal physiological signals and pushed obesity researchers to think more along these lines.

Against this background took place one of the most memorable episodes of obesity research. It involved several giants of psychology and a theory that wove together environmental, physiological, and psychological factors in a way that was intellectually irresistible. Unfortunately, it became clear after nearly a decade of work that the theory was all wrong. Nonetheless, the tale has quite a lot to say about what obesity is and is not.

It was 1934 when Hilde Bruch, a German-born pediatrician, immigrated to the United States. Because she was surprised to see so many fat children in America compared with what she had known in Europe, Bruch decided to specialize in childhood obesity. At first she focused on metabolism, but when she realized how few patients actually had glandular disorders, she switched gears and took further medical training to become a psychiatrist. By the late 1950s, the innovative Bruch had become one of the most influential thinkers in the still-young field of obesity research, and her 1957 book, *The Importance of Overweight*, was the best-known popular treatment of obesity. And so it was that in 1961, when Bruch offered a new hypothesis for why people overeat, people took it seriously.

Bruch's idea was simple and revolutionary. Most previous theorizing about weight had assumed that the obese were simply ignoring the signals they received from their bodies and eating for reasons other than hunger. But from her work with obese psychiatric patients Bruch believed that many of them did not recognize sensations of hunger. They were never really hungry, and they were never really sated, so they couldn't use these cues to know when to eat or when to stop. Instead, they regulated their eating in ways quite different from normal people, often in response to emotions they were feeling or what they sensed other people expected of them. Without internal signals and with too many occasions to eat and too much food around them, they overate and became fat.

But why did they not sense hunger in the same way that most people do? Here Bruch made the sort of intellectual leap that she was already well known for among her peers. Reasoning from research done on the development of behavior in rats, Bruch hypothesized that such bodily drives as hunger are not completely innate but are partly dependent on learning in childhood, so that improper or dysfunctional parenting could keep a child from making the proper associations. If, for instance, a mother responded to every cry of her baby with a bottle, no matter whether the baby was hungry, tired, lonely, or had a dirty diaper, then that child might grow up unable to tell the difference between hunger and other sorts of emotional distress. Such "conceptual confusion" was the defining characteristic of obese patients whom she had seen, Bruch wrote: "These people are unable to recognize when they are hungry or satiated, nor do they differentiate need for food from other sensations and feelings of discomfort. They need signals from the outside to know when to eat and when to stop; their own inner awareness has not been programmed correctly."

Bruch's hypothesis was provocative and seemed to explain many of the observations psychiatrists had made about the obese over the years. Furthermore, although it was quite speculative, Bruch could offer as confirming evidence a series of experiments performed two years earlier by Mickey Stunkard, chairman of the psychiatry department at the University of Pennsylvania School of

Medicine and perhaps the most highly respected researcher in the obesity field.

Stunkard had become involved in obesity research in the early 1950s when he uncovered an unusual eating pattern in an obese girl he was treating: she was not hungry in the morning, ate modest lunches and dinners, but then stuffed herself through much of the night. Investigating further, Stunkard discovered this same pattern in a number of obese patients. He dubbed it the "night-eating syndrome," and his 1955 paper describing it broke new ground in obesity research. Unlike the papers of psychoanalysts, which tended to offer two or three case studies and then generalize from them, Stunkard's work covered twenty-five obese patients and thirty-eight normal-weight controls. Of the twenty-five obese subjects, who had been referred to a special clinic at New York Hospital because they had not responded well to previous treatment, sixteen had full-blown night-eating syndrome and another four showed some of its signs. By contrast, none of the thirty-eight controls had it. Instantly, the night-eating syndrome became one of the best-documented psychological traits associated with obesity.

After that Stunkard quickly made a name for himself with several papers that took psychological research to a new level of rigor. In 1957 he described the depression and emotional upset that hit a collection of obese patients once they had been on a diet for a few weeks or months and had lost weight. Although other psychiatrists had argued that diets might not work—and might even damage a patient—if their psychological problems weren't solved first, Stunkard's careful study proved it in a way no others had. Two years later he published a detailed inquiry into binge-eating. That same year he reported, in a paper described in the last chapter, what a dismal failure medical weight-loss programs were.

It was about this time that Stunkard was studying stomach contractions in some of his obese patients using a variation of the gastric-balloon technique that Cannon and Washburn had applied nearly six decades earlier. In two of the obese women he was testing, Stunkard discovered that there seemed to be no connection between contractions and hunger. The women consistently denied feeling hungry even when his instruments showed their contractions to be at a maximum. This was puzzling. Like everyone else, Stunkard had accepted without question the contraction-hunger connection that Cannon and Washburn had found. But the experience with the two women made him decide to go back and ask the questions that Cannon and Washburn had ignored: Was it possible that the obese did not sense stomach contractions in the same way that others do? And could this help explain their overeating?

Recruiting seventeen obese and eighteen normal-weight women who were patients at the University of Pennsylvania Hospital's medical clinic, Stunkard repeated the Cannon-Washburn experiment thirty-five times, inserting a stomach tube into a subject and monitoring her gastric contractions while asking every fifteen minutes if she was hungry. After consolidating the results for the fat patients and for the thin patients, he discovered something that Cannon and Washburn had missed. Among the non-obese subjects, the behavior was similar to what Cannon and Washburn had seen: the women tended to report hunger during contractions and no hunger when their stomachs were quiescent. Stunkard did not find the exact congruence that the earlier two had — sometimes a woman might report hunger when no contractions were present, and sometimes she would not be hungry when her stomach was contracting — but statistically there was a clear connection between contractions and hunger.

Among the obese women, however, this pattern disappeared. They were no more likely to be hungry when their stomachs were contracting than when their stomachs were quiet. And, strangely enough, the obese women reported being hungry much less often than the other women. Although they had fasted overnight for tests that began at nine o'clock the next morning, six of the overweight women claimed never to feel hungry throughout the entire four-hour experiment.

Perhaps, Stunkard speculated, the overweight women had learned to deny their hunger in response to a disapproving society. Pressured to lose weight, they learned to block out feelings of hunger altogether in an effort to lose weight. Thus they lost the ability to discriminate between hunger and nonhunger. Once this happened, he reasoned, the obese would be left without their best defense against overeating — their own internal hunger signals — and would have to fall back on guesses about how much they had eaten and how much was enough.

But, as Bruch pointed out, there was another way to interpret what Stunkard had seen. Perhaps the disconnection between hunger and stomach contractions was not a result of obesity, but a cause. Perhaps these obese women who could not hear their body's hunger signals had been deaf to them since childhood. Seen in this light, Stunkard's experiment seemed to provide a striking experimental corroboration for what Bruch had seen clinically in her psychiatric practice.

Until this point, Bruch's hypothesis was still nothing more than conjecture — a provocative and sweeping conjecture, granted, but one that needed experimental verification to be accepted as a plausible explanation of why people gain weight. And Bruch was not equipped to provide that verification. She was a healer and a thinker, not an experimentalist. Had it been left to her, her ideas would never have gone much beyond intriguing musings. As it happened, however, Bruch's theory would catch the attention of someone who knew just what to do with it, and he would take it from there.

Stanley Schachter spent his long career wandering into this area of social psychology and that, offering a few critical insights, performing a few telling exper-

iments, then wandering off again, leaving the scientists who remained to contemplate a field forever transformed by his input. He was brilliant, innovative,
and bold. When Schachter died in June 1997, he left behind a prodigious body
of research in several different areas along with some forty students who had
earned their Ph.D.s under him, including several who would themselves rise to
the top of their fields. But perhaps his most enduring legacy among psychologists
was his approach to research. Schachter was an exceptionally clever experimenter who took pride in devising ways to test a hypothesis in ever more strin-
gent detail. But, more than that, he and his students quite clearly had fun. The
hallmark of a Schachterian experiment was an appreciation for the foibles of
human nature plus an ability to incorporate those foibles into the design of the
experiment. And when he began to study eating and weight, Schachter would
have more foibles to work with than he could shake a fork at.

Schachter had stumbled into the obesity field by chance, following the implications of a line of experiments that had nothing at all to do with weight. In the
late 1950s, first at the University of Minnesota and then at Columbia University,
he had pioneered a new way of thinking about human emotions. Up to that time
most scientists had assumed—generally without thinking too deeply about it—
that emotional states mirror underlying physiological states: anger corresponds
to one distribution of chemicals in the body and brain, fear to another, joy to a
third, and so on. It was a supposition that seemed so obvious, so natural, that few
thought to question it. Schachter did. Suppose, he said, that a subject were sur-
reptitiously injected with adrenaline or some other chemical that excited his sympathetic nervous system. The subject would notice his body tingling or trem-
bling, his heart beating faster and perhaps a bit irregularly, his breath coming
more quickly—all the usual symptoms of the fight-or-flight response. Not knowing that all these physical sensations were the artificial result of the drug, how
would the subject interpret them?

Schachter suggested that the subject would look to his environment for cues
to what might have triggered his new physiological state. "Should he be at the
time watching a horror film, he would probably decide that he was badly frightened. Should he be with a beautiful woman, he might decide that he was wildly
in love or sexually excited. Should he be in an argument, he might explode in
fury and hatred. Or, should the situation be completely inappropriate, he could
decide that he was excited or upset by something that had recently happened."
In short, Schachter argued, a single physiological state could be interpreted as
any of several different emotions depending on the situation. It was too simplistic to think that emotion could be reduced to the chemicals coursing through
the body and brain.

To test his hypothesis, Schachter devised a crafty experiment. He recruited

185 subjects for a "study of the effects of vitamin supplements on vision." They were told that each would receive an injection of "Suproxin," a vitamin compound. In reality, the Suproxin was either a dose of adrenaline or a placebo, so that, within a few minutes of injection, some of the subjects would feel fight-or-flight symptoms while the others would be unaffected. The adrenaline group was further divided into two subgroups. The first was told to expect side effects: "Probably your hands will start to shake, your heart will start to pound, and your face will get warm and flushed." The second was told the "vitamin" injection would have no side effects. When the adrenaline hit their systems, they would not attribute it to the shot but would instead, Schachter predicted, interpret the symptoms according to external cues. And to provide these cues Schachter set up two scenarios, one designed to elicit euphoria, the other to spark anger.

In the first, a subject was put into the test room with "a stooge who had been introduced as a fellow subject and who, following a completely standardized routine, acted in a euphoric-manic fashion, doing such things as flying paper airplanes, hula-hooping, and the like, all the while keeping up a standard patter and occasionally attempting to induce the subject to join in." In the second scenario, intended to provoke anger, Schachter asked a subject to fill out a questionnaire that was insultingly and outrageously personal. It asked such questions as, "With how many men (other than your father) has your mother had extramarital relations? 4 and under ____; 5-9 ____; 10 and over ____." To raise the tension several notches, Schachter put each of these subjects in a room with a stooge, again supposedly a fellow subject, who filled out the questionnaire with visibly growing fury, finally ripping the thing up, throwing it to the floor with a growl of "I'm not wasting any more time; I'm getting my books and leaving," and storming from the room. All the while, Schachter or one of his students was observing through a one-way mirror to see how the subject responded. Afterward each of the subjects was asked to answer a series of questions designed to measure euphoria and anger.

Those subjects who had been given adrenaline and told to expect no side effects behaved just as Schachter had predicted, interpreting the quickening pulse and the flushed face to mean they were feeling the same things as the "subjects" with whom they were paired. Those in the room with a euphoric partner, he wrote, "tend to catch the stooge's mood with alacrity; they join the stooge's whirl of activity and invent new manic activities of their own." On the other hand, the subjects who had been given the placebo or who had gotten the adrenaline but been told what to expect "tend simply to sit and stare at the stooge in mild disbelief." The situation was similar in the second setting.

Later, Schachter used similar combinations of adrenaline and a suggestive environment to manipulate amusement—as indicated by laughter while watching a slapstick movie—and fear or anxiety in other unwitting subjects. By the end of this series of experiments, he had shown that emotions were not the simple product of underlying physiology that they had seemed; they depended in large part upon how a person interpreted those inner sensations. And so in the mid-1960s, when Schachter came across the work of Hilde Bruch and Mickey Stunkard, he was well prepared to build on it.

If, as Bruch had suggested, the obese never learned as infants to associate the physiological signals of hunger with the psychological state of hunger, two different outcomes seemed possible. They might interpret any sort of arousal—fear, anxiety, anger—as hunger, in which case they would eat at times when their bodies did not need the food. Or, alternatively, they might never sense hunger at all and decide when and what to eat according to other cues.

Richard Nisbett, a graduate student of Schachter's at Columbia in the early 1960s, remembers that when his mentor first began working on obesity, he focused on the first alternative—that overweight people interpret almost any sort of internal arousal as hunger. It was obviously an attractive hypothesis for Schachter, who had already used adrenaline arousal and the proper setting to generate euphoria and other emotions. Now, if Bruch was right, he should be able to use adrenaline to bring on hunger in much the same way—but only in the obese, not in those of normal weight. Preliminary experiments found nothing of the sort, however, and Schachter quickly decided that the obese were not more likely to confuse an adrenaline rush with hunger.

This left the second alternative—that overweight people don't feel hunger at all, at least not in response to the inner sensations that signal hunger to most other people. This fit well with Stunkard's work showing that the obese were no hungrier during stomach contractions than between them, but it raised the questions: What does cause hunger in the obese? How do they decide when and how much to eat? After thinking about it for a while, Nisbett says, Schachter came up with a new direction. "One day he told me he had this idea: the obese are controlled by external circumstances."

In other words, overweight people, having no recognizable hunger signals from within, would take their cues for when and how much to eat from the world around them. When they spoke of "hunger," it was not the same sensation that caused those of normal weight to think about their next meal, but it was instead a psychological state triggered by something outside their bodies. Schachter was not the first psychologist to suspect this was the case, but he would be the first to put the hypothesis to systematic testing.

Not knowing which external cues might be important to the obese, Schachter marshalled his army of students to examine different possibilities, such as taste, time of day, and whether or not food was present and visible. At the same time they would check to make sure that internal cues such as amount of food in the stomach or anxiety did not play a role in how much the obese ate.

Nisbett was put to work on the effects of taste. Most people will eat more of good-tasting and less of poor-tasting food, but Schachter reasoned that the pattern should be greatly exaggerated in the obese if indeed they are more sensitive to external factors. Recruiting several dozen Columbia undergraduates, Nisbett gave each a quart of "vanilla bitters" ice cream and asked them to rate the taste, eating as much of it as they liked. A variety of Schachterian twists and subterfuges were added so that the subject would not guess that the amount of ice cream he ate was the variable Nisbett was most interested in.

Half of the subjects got a premium vanilla ice cream. The other half got a bargain version adulterated by Nisbett with the bitter chemical quinine. As expected, all three groups that Nisbett had divided the subjects into—underweight, normal, and overweight—ate more of the unadulterated ice cream, but the overweight subjects were clearly more influenced by taste than the others. For instance, compared with the underweight subjects, the obese ate nearly twice as much of the good stuff and barely half as much of the bad as did the lightweight subjects. In this one case at least, the obese were more sensitive to an external cue—taste—than were the non-obese.

In another experiment, Schachter and a student, Larry Gross, showed that overweight subjects were more influenced by time—in particular, by how close it was to dinner time—than those of normal weight. But perhaps the most devilish of all Schachter's work on obesity was an experiment he did with students Ronald Goldman and Andrew Gordon to measure the effects of fear on eating. The subjects, all of them male students at Columbia, were told they were participating in an experiment designed to test how tactile stimulation affects taste. Half were "pre-loaded" by being offered a plate of roast beef sandwiches and told to eat their fill, and the other half were kept hungry. Then, after filling out a questionnaire, each subject was seated at a table with five bowls of crackers, supposedly low-calorie crackers aimed at the commercial market, and asked to rate the taste of the crackers on a number of scales.

But before the subject began to eat the crackers, the experimenter explained how the rest of the test would go. After the subject finished rating the crackers, he would be hooked up to an electrical stimulation machine, have an electric current run through his skin, and then asked once again to rate the crackers to see if the stimulation had affected his taste sense. Half of the subjects—the "low fear" group—were told that the electrical stimulation would be the lowest level possible and that at most they would feel "a slight tingle in your skin." As for the others, Schachter tried to scare them as much as possible without having them walk out of the experiment:

In high-fear conditions the experimenter pointed to an 8-foot-high, jet-black console loaded with electrical junk and said, "That machine is the one we will be using. I am afraid that these shocks will be painful. For them to have any effect on your taste sensations, they must be of a rather high voltage. There will, of course, be no permanent damage." The subject was then connected to the console by attaching a very large electrode to each ankle. While doing this, the experimenter looked up at the subject and asked, "You don't have a heart condition, do you?"

Before eating, the subjects filled out a questionnaire designed to measure their fear of the expected electrical stimulation. They were left alone for fifteen minutes to rate the crackers while the experimenter watched through a one-way mirror and counted the number eaten. Then the experimenter returned, explained the deception, and asked the subject not to reveal the ending to other students.

Once again the results supported Schachter's hypothesis. Eating the roast beef sandwiches ahead of time decreased the number of crackers the normal-weight subjects "tested" but had no effect on the obese. Similarly, the non-obese subjects ate less when anxious about the approaching shocks, but not the obese. In short, normal-weight subjects were influenced by internal factors—the amount of food in their stomachs or electric shocks on their minds—but the obese subjects were mostly oblivious.

Schachter's series of experiments, published as four back-to-back articles in a single 1968 issue of the *Journal of Personality and Social Psychology*, rocked the obesity research world. Almost overnight the internal-external hypothesis became the leading contender to explain why the overweight eat too much: Normal-weight people, sensitive to the internal signals of hunger and satiety, ate just what their bodies needed; the overweight were guided instead by external messages, and a world full of tasty, fattening food led them to eat more than was good for them.

It was a plausible theory, and it tied together a number of widely held stereotypes about the obese: that they were unusually attentive to the appearance and taste of food, that they were more emotional, that they were less able to resist temptation. But it left one big question unanswered: If it was true that the obese were less attuned to their internal signals and more in tune with external ones, was this a cause or a consequence of obesity? Stunkard had assumed, after seeing a lack of internal sensitivity among the obese in his gastric-contraction experiment, that it was a consequence of society's disapproval, which pushed obese women to deny their hunger. Bruch, on the other hand, had hypothesized that the lack of sensitivity to internal signals was learned in childhood and was a cause of overeating.

The most direct way to decide the issue would have been to perform prospective studies in which young people of normal weight were tested for internal versus external responsiveness and watched to see who got fat. This would take far too long and cost too much to be practical, however. So Schachter would resort to indirect evidence based on an apparent parallel between obese humans and obese rats. It would be one of the strangest stories in the history of the field.

Psychologists trace the first hint that a particular segment of the brain might control weight and appetite to a medical case described in 1840. A fifty-seven-year-old woman, the wife of a gardener, had become exceptionally fat in the last year of her life. For many years before that she had been suffering from various neurological symptoms—vertigo, headaches, and mental deterioration—and when she died the autopsy revealed a tumor of the pituitary gland that had grown so large it was distorting the entire lower part of her brain. Over the next sixty years, the medical literature produced several other clues like this one, cases of obesity associated with a tumor in the same area near the pituitary gland, but they were scattered and apparently unrelated, and no one put the pieces together. Not until 1901 did anyone formally suggest that obesity might be caused by damage to this part of the brain.

That suggestion came from Alfred Froehlich, the Austrian physician who reported the peculiar case of an obese fourteen-year-old boy with a variety of neurological symptoms, including headaches and vomiting, progressive blindness in his left eye, and sensitivity to tapping on the left side of his skull. On the basis of his observations, Froehlich concluded that the boy suffered from a pituitary tumor. And in reviewing the medical literature, Froehlich ran across several earlier cases in which children with pituitary tumors had two of the same symptoms—obesity and underdeveloped genitals—that his own patient exhibited. So Froehlich proposed that the two symptoms, when seen together, were evidence of a tumor in the pituitary gland. The condition he described came to be called Froehlich's syndrome.

Froehlich's report came to be widely known and helped set off the early twentieth-century vogue for blaming obesity on glandular disorders. By the 1920s, doctors were indiscriminately diagnosing practically every overweight patient as suffering from some hormonal insufficiency, although Froehlich himself never took part in it. He believed that his syndrome, as properly defined, was restricted to only a handful of children, and in later years he would complain that what had been intended as a specific medical diagnosis had come to be a blanket excuse for weight gain. Every obese child, he said, was presented to him as if he or she were a Froehlich case.

Froehlich was right to be skeptical about the widespread diagnoses of glandular problems, but he proved to be wrong about something else. The fatness of his patient—and of others with the same syndrome—actually had nothing to do with the pituitary. Later, doctors found that tumors near the pituitary but not touching it could produce obesity of the same type as Froehlich's patient, while other studies showed that tumors completely restricted to the pituitary gland left a patient's weight unaffected. The implication was that some organ near the pituitary, not the pituitary itself, was implicated in obesity, but for nearly four decades after Froehlich's original observation, no one could say just which brain structure it was.

The breakthrough making it possible came in 1939, with the development of stereotaxic surgery, a technique for locating—and destroying—small, carefully circumscribed pieces of the brains of rats and other lab animals. A researcher would anesthetize the rat, immobilize its head, and then, after referring to a three-dimensional map of the rat's brain, insert a needle into the brain so that its point ended up in the middle of whatever section the researcher wished to study. A short jolt of electrical current would kill the brain cells around the needle's tip, and, once the rat awoke and recovered from the surgery, the researcher could observe the effects this damage caused in the rat's behavior. By varying the amount of the current and the time over which it was applied, the researcher could wipe out anything from a few neurons to a major piece of the brain.

Within a year, two Northwestern University researchers, A. W. Hetherington and Stephen Ranson, applied the technique to solve the mystery of Froehlich's syndrome. They proved that obesity is produced by damage to the hypothalamus, a cherry-sized (in humans) organ deep within the brain and near the pituitary gland. The hypothalamus controls the sympathetic nervous system, which in turn controls such nonconscious activities as heartbeat and the secretion of hormones. It is the hypothalamus that triggers the body's fight-or-flight response in reaction to a threat. The gland also oversees body temperature, mood and emotions, sleep, sexual behavior, and appetite. Hetherington and Ranson showed that a rat whose hypothalamus is burned out while young inevitably becomes quite fat as an adult. If the operation is done on an adult rat, it gains weight as well but becomes plump rather than obese.

The Hetherington-Ranson finding is one of only a handful of studies in the history of weight research that can accurately be called revolutionary. For the first time scientists had located unequivocally a crucial element of the body's weight-control system. And not just in rats—the evidence from tumors and the similarity between rat and human left no doubt in anyone's mind that the hypothalamus plays a key role in regulating eating in people as well.

Hetherington and Ranson's work set off a wave of research into the behavior of rats made fat by hypothalamic lesions. The next major study came in 1943, when John Brobeck, Jay Tepperman, and C. N. H. Long of Yale proved that the hypothalamic rats become fat because they overeat. The lesioned rats, they found, were a bit more lethargic than intact rats, so they probably expended less energy, and some strange things seemed to be going on with their metabolisms, but the major difference between them and normal rats was that they ate several times as much food.

The voracious appetites of these lesioned rats, which many researchers would confirm over the years, would become a part of the field's lore, repeated from teacher to student and colleague to colleague and sometimes slightly embellished in the process. As the tale is usually told, the aftermath of the surgery proceeds something like this: As soon as the rats awaken, even before they have shaken off the effects of the anesthetic, they stagger to the trough of rat chow and plunge in, gobbling down pellets as if their lives depend on it and stopping only when their stomachs can hold no more. After enough time has passed that some of the food has made its way into the intestines and created a bit of room in the stomach, the rats begin again.

The original account by Brobeck, Tepperman, and Long is only slightly less dramatic. There is no mention of the rats staggering to the trough, but the animals "voraciously gnawed and ate chow pellets" as soon after the surgery as they were able. Several of the rats inhaled food particles to the point that they had trouble breathing, and one died. When the researchers autopsied that animal, they found that the entire portion of its digestive system from the mouth to the stomach was distended with food. After that, the researchers kept the rats away from the food until the anesthetic had worn off completely, and they had no further fatalities.

The rats, which weighed between 150 and 250 grams before surgery, would gain as much as twenty to twenty-three grams in the first eighteen hours afterward—the equivalent of an man of average weight gaining fifteen or twenty pounds in less than a day. Most of that gain was food sitting in the stomach and intestines, waiting to be digested. For the next several months, the rats gained weight rapidly, eventually plateauing at a weight that was, on average, 70 percent higher than the rats without lesions.

Although no one could ask the rats how they felt, their actions seemed to leave little doubt: Damage to the hypothalamus—and in particular to a small section of it called the ventromedial nucleus—had created a tremendous hunger in the animals, one that was not satisfied until the rats were incredibly fat.

Since that time, doctors have periodically come across people with damage to the same part of the hypothalamus, and the results are consistently the same: the patients get quite fat. One of the most dramatic cases came in September 1964, when a twenty-two-year-old woman, a bookkeeper, was admitted to the New York Hospital in New York City because her family and friends had noticed severe changes in her behavior.

According to the report of the doctors who examined her, "She became withdrawn but was given to frequent outbursts of unprovoked laughing, crying, and, at times, rage." She was also constantly hungry, obese, and diabetic. The doctors, diagnosing a tumor in the hypothalamus, treated her with a variety of drugs to control her diabetes, her hormonal imbalances, and her mood swings. Despite the drugs, the woman continued to hit, scratch, bite, and throw things at her attendants. "Although these [outbursts of violence] initially appeared to be unprovoked," the doctors reported, "we subsequently noted that the withholding of food, which she consumed in quantities of 8,000 to 10,000 calories per day, invariably evoked aggressive behavior. Near the end of her hospitalization, continuous feeding was found to be the only method which succeeded in maintaining the patient in a reasonably tractable state." In two months of hospitalization, the woman gained fifty-three pounds, nearly a pound per day. At the end of that time she died suddenly, apparently of a heart attack.

Upon autopsy, the doctors found that a tumor had destroyed both the right and left ventromedial nucleus of the hypothalamus while touching almost nothing else—almost exactly the same damage done by Hetherington and Ranson to rats. It was this destruction that had left the woman voracious and frenzied until she was fed.

It was Schachter's student Nisbett who first noticed the similarities between obese rats and obese people. In mapping out the first experiment that Schachter had suggested to him, the test of whether fat humans were more responsive to the taste of food, Nisbett had recalled reading about the lesioned rats. In particular, he remembered one 1950 experiment in which the rat psychologists, in order to see how the rats would respond to less appealing food, had added quinine to the rats' chow. So when Nisbett designed his own test, he decided that he, too, would use quinine. "It was basically being cute," he says. When he performed the experiment, however, he found an eerie parallel between the species.

In the quinine experiment, three researchers at Yale, Neal Miller, Clark Bailey, and James Stevenson, had set out to determine whether lesioned rats really are hungrier than normal rats, according to the standard psychological measures of hunger. Up to this point researchers had assumed that, because the lesioned rats ate more, their hunger must be at a constantly elevated level, but it was possible that something other than hunger was at play.

To test this, the three researchers added quinine to rat food and offered it to both lesioned and intact rats. The results were surprising: Provided with a good-tasting, high-fat diet, the fat, lesioned rats ate 50 percent more than the rats of normal weight, but, when offered the quinine-adulterated version, the fat animals lost their appetite and ate almost nothing. The normal rats cut their consumption only by half—not nearly as much as the fat rats—and ate several times as much of the adulterated food as did the lesioned animals. The researchers concluded that the obese rats' hunger was of a limited type: they ate more good-tasting food, particularly food that was high in fat, but they ate much less when the taste was unpleasant. They were hungrier than normal rats, but also finickier.

That was exactly what Nisbett would find in his taste experiments on human subjects nearly a quarter of a century later: the obese ate proportionately more of the good-tasting ice cream and proportionately less of the bitter stuff. Which got Nisbett thinking: Was the similarity between rats and humans just coincidence, or was something else going on?

After his taste test, Nisbett next examined the effects of a different sort of external eating cue: how much food is present. He offered his subjects, all of them male students at Columbia, roast beef sandwiches after they had spent half an hour hooked up to electrodes. Then he left the subject alone with the food. In some cases, three sandwiches had been left out on the table; in other cases, it was just one. Either way, the subject was told he could get more from the refrigerator.

Nisbett found that underweight and normal-weight students ate the same number of sandwiches no matter how many had been left on the table: about one and a half for the underweight, and almost two for the normal weight. The overweight were different. They ate an average of one and a half sandwiches when one sandwich was left out but an average of two and a third when three were in sight. The results could be interpreted as the obese being more sensitive to external cues. Futhermore, Nisbett realized, their behavior was strikingly similar to that observed in lesioned rats.

In a series of experiments performed in the late 1940s, Miller, Bailey, and Stevenson had found that rats with damage to the hypothalamus would not work as hard for their food. In a bar-pressing test, where the rats had been trained to push on a small bar in order to get a pellet of food, normal rats pressed twice as often—and so got twice as much food—as the lesioned rats. Normal rats ran faster down an alley at the end of which they could get food, and, when fitted with a tiny harness that held them back, the normal rats pulled harder against the harness, trying to reach the end of the alley.

When Nisbett, who had by now received his Ph.D. and left Schachter's group for a job at the University of Michigan, published his results, he pointed out the similarities between his work and the experiments on lesioned rats. Like the obese students, fat rats ate more food than normal rats only when it was freely available. If they had to work to get it, they ate less. In closing his article, Nisbett suggested, "The analogy between the hypothalamic obese rat and obese humans should be further explored." Over the next several years Nisbett would do just that, with a series of experiments following up on the ones he performed at Columbia. But it would be Schachter and a group of his remaining students who would truly take the suggestion to heart.

Schachter described the program triggered by Nisbett's observations in *Obese Humans and Rats*, a remarkable and somewhat bizarre book he wrote in 1972 with his student Judith Rodin. Intrigued by the parallels that Nisbett had noted, Schachter decided to test for parallels between fat rats and fat humans on every imaginable measure of behavior. Tracking down every observation he could find about rats with lesions in the ventromedial hypothalamus, Schachter then looked for experiments on obese and normal-weight humans that seemed to test the same sort of behavior; if he found no similar study on humans, he designed his own, trying to make it as close as possible to the original study on rats. At times this would lead to experiments as devious and convoluted as anything that Schachter and his students had ever done or would ever do.

In shock-avoidance experiments, for instance, psychologists had found that lesioned rats would work harder to avoid a painful shock than would normal rats. Since it wasn't feasible to put human subjects in a maze and give them shocks until they found the way out, Rodin devised what was intended to be a rough equivalent. Volunteer subjects, all female New York University undergraduates, were hooked up to what appeared to be a large shock-dispensing apparatus. Each subject had electrodes attached to her wrists and then was handed two envelopes, one labeled "Shock" and the other "Money." Inside each were four puzzle pieces that were to be assembled into an eight-by-ten rectangle. Piecing together the money puzzle would win the subject a cash prize, while solving the shock puzzle would allow the subject to avoid a shock from the machine. The subject was told that she could work on either puzzle or both, but that she would have only three minutes to solve them.

What the subject didn't know was that neither puzzle was solvable, although both were designed so that this would not be obvious with only three minutes of trying. Instead, Rodin was interested in how the subjects would allocate their three minutes. "We assume," she wrote, "that the proportion of time that they spend working on the shock-avoidance puzzle is a loose analog to the effort the experimental animal exercises to avoid shock." Of course, no one got shocked at the end of the three minutes.

When Rodin had finished, she found that her subjects had performed as predicted: The overweight girls spent an average of only eighteen seconds out of three minutes on the money puzzle, while the normal ones devoted three times as much to it. The parallel with rats stood up, Rodin wrote. "When threatened with an electric shock, both kinds of [obese] subjects work more efficiently, harder, or longer than do normal controls to avoid painful stimulation."

Schachter and Rodin's book reviews fifteen such comparisons between obese humans and rats and concludes that in thirteen of them the two species behaved quite similarly—too much to be explained by coincidence. Instead, it seemed reasonable to suppose that the humans might be overeating for a similar reason that the lesioned rats were. There must be "something awry with the hypothalamus of the obese human," they wrote. Nothing as obvious as a hole burned in it, of course, but perhaps something akin to what Bruch had suggested—that the neurons in the hypothalamus of an obese person had never made the proper connections. Whatever it was that might be wrong in the hypothalamus of obese humans, Schachter and Rodin assumed it had a similar effect to the lesions in the rats, and they went on to build a theory that would explain the observations made on both rats and humans.

Schachter's original hypothesis clearly had problems. If, for instance, the obese were as sensitive to external food cues as he suggested, they should be eating all the time. Every time they saw a billboard or television advertisement, every time they passed a restaurant or refrigerator, they should grab a bite. Yet in surveys the overweight report eating fewer meals—they're much more likely to skip breakfast or lunch—than people of normal weight. How is it that the obese can so easily make it through a morning without falling victim to at least one of those external cues?

The explanation, Schachter and Rodin suggested, is that the obese are not sensitive to all external cues, but only to the salient ones—those that are particularly noticeable or near-at-hand. A roast beef sandwich on a table in front of you is more tangible than one in a refrigerator.

Schachter put his students to work testing this new hypothesis. In one memorable experiment, Lee Ross set out to measure the temptation offered by cashew nuts under various conditions. After the usual sort of misdirection, Ross sat each subject at a table with five objects in easy reach: a toy car, a set of chessmen, candlesticks, marbles, and a can of large, salted cashews that the experimenter opened in front of the subject. The subject was then told to relax, listen to the instructions that would be played on a tape recorder, and act naturally. He could play with the marbles, eat the nuts, whatever. Half the subjects were left in the room with only one dim red bulb providing illumination, so that they could make out the can and the other objects but could see no details, while the other half got normal lighting. Furthermore, some of the subjects listened to a tape designed to draw their attention to the nuts—"think of the light salty taste, the rich toasted quality, and the taste of really fine cashews"—while others got tapes talking about marbles or tapes that didn't focus on anything in particular.

When Ross compared how many nuts the different groups ate, he found that the obese subjects were indeed more influenced by the salient cues. Those who both had good light to see the nuts and listened to a tape talking about nuts ate more than three times as many cashews as those who sat in a dim room and listened to a tape about marbles. By contrast, the normal-weight subjects ate the same amount of nuts no matter what the lighting or the subject of the tape. The obese, it seemed, were indeed more sensitive to food cues, as long as they were compelling enough.

From there, Schachter and Rodin took a bold conceptual leap, the sort of leap that, if it is right, separates the scientific greats from the rest of the research world. They suggested that this extra sensitivity to eating cues was just one facet of a larger pattern: that the obese are, for some reason hidden within the hypothalamus, more sensitive to external stimuli of all sorts than are those without overeating problems. They were more likely to remember a word or an image they saw only briefly, more likely to be moved to tears by the picture of a mother holding a dying child, more likely to be frightened by things that go bump in the night. Obesity was merely the most visible symptom of a broader syndrome, one that might well have benefits as well as disadvantages.

For nearly a decade, Schachter, Rodin, and others explored the implications of this "externality hypothesis," and for many psychologists it became the accepted explanation for obesity. Indeed, the internal-external distinction was put to work by psychologists in a number of areas besides obesity. As Rodin noted in 1981, almost every introductory psychology textbook published in the previous eight years had included a discussion of internality and externality. Purely in terms of adoption and acceptance, it was a wildly successful theory.

For the obese the externality hypothesis was a mixed bag. It sure beat being told they were gluttons with no self-respect or willpower, and it was an improvement over being labeled a candidate for the psychoanalyst's couch, but the new picture of obesity had its own negatives. Perhaps the obese weren't as unpleasant to be around as some of the lesioned rats—who were "finicky, irascible, emotional, and generally bitchy" in Schachter and Rodin's words—but they did not have the sort of solidity and internal balance that you would like in a bank president, say, or a next-door neighbor. Compared with people of normal weight, they were hypersensitive and liable to be pushed around by whatever emotional currents were swirling around them. But they couldn't help it, any more than the rats could. It was just their nature.

No one took the externality hypothesis and the parallels between lesioned rats and obese humans more seriously than Flemming Quaade, a surgeon from Denmark. In the early 1970s, Quaade slid a needle into the hypothalamus of sev-

eral severely obese patients, attempting to stimulate hunger by sending an electric current into that part of the brain. Twenty years earlier, researchers at Yale
had located a part of the hypothalamus that seemed to have the opposite job from
the ventromedial nucleus: it increased hunger rather than restrained it. When
this section was tickled with an electric current, a lab animal, even one that had
just eaten, would go after its food; if the section was burned away, the animal
would lose its hunger and stop eating altogether. Quaade thought he saw a way
to help his fat patients stop eating so much. So in three of them who had reported
feeling hungry when nudged by his probe, Quaade upped the current enough to
destroy the surrounding neurons and, he hoped, weaken or cripple the hunger
center there. It worked, he reported, but only temporarily. After the surgery, the
patients ate less and lost as much as twenty pounds, but the weight came back
within a few weeks. It was impossible to say whether the transient weight loss was
due to damage to a hunger center or simply to the trauma of having a part of one's
brain burned away.

The medical world—or at least that part of the medical world that noticed
what a relatively unknown doctor in Copenhagen had done to his patients—was
appalled that someone would treat obesity by putting permanent, if small, holes
in the brain. Quaade was unrepentant, arguing that his therapy was less drastic
than the then-common intestinal-bypass surgery, but he stopped nonetheless.
Holes in the brain that helped someone lose weight were one thing; holes in the
brain that left one as heavy as before were another altogether.

Quaade's clinical experiments, which he conducted between 1971 and 1973,
came during the heyday of the externality hypothesis. But even as they were going
on, the tapestry that Schachter had so cunningly woven was beginning to unravel,
and a decade later, it would be little more than a collection of brightly colored
threads that had once seemed to make a whole.

The unraveling began in 1971 when Stunkard revisited his 1959 gastric contractions experiment, which had captured Hilde Bruch's attention and helped
launch the internal-external hypothesis. With a more sensitive measure of
hunger, he tested twenty-four subjects—sixteen obese and eight normal-weight—
and found that, contrary to his earlier study, the obese were just as likely as the
normal subjects to associate stomach contractions with hunger. Furthermore, he
found this time that only a minority of either the fat or the thin patients actually
did make this association. Recanting his earlier position, Stunkard concluded
that gastric contractions were not an important part of the hunger sensation in
most people and that there was no difference in how the obese and the non-obese
responded to these internal signals. With this report, one of the two main strands
of the internal-external hypothesis was pulled away: there was no reason to
believe that the obese were less sensitive to internal sensations than anyone else.

By the mid-1970s the other main strand was loosened as well. A number of experiments designed to observe the heightened externality of the obese were coming up blank. One of the most compelling was a 1977 report by Rodin. She tested four separate groups of subjects, including teenage girls at a weight-reduction camp and overweight women at a diet clinic, and found that the fattest of the subjects were no more and no less externally responsive than the lightest.

At about the same time, Nisbett weighed in with an analysis that challenged Schachter's core distinction between external and internal personality types. In general, Nisbett found, people cannot be classified as either external or internal. Instead, each person is a hodge-podge, responding well to some external stimuli and ignoring others, attuned to some internal signals and oblivious to others. A person who seems to be an external sort by one test might well seem an internal type according to a second.

In late 1977, when Rodin spoke at an international conference on obesity, she entitled her talk, "Has the distinction between internal versus external control of feeding outlived its usefulness?" Yes, she concluded, it has. In the short run, she said, people may gain weight because they are tempted by food cues, but over time this susceptibility to external signals seemed to have no relation to how heavy a person became. Some people who are highly susceptible to food cues stay thin, while others who are barely susceptible at all become quite obese. Whether or not a person becomes obese, Rodin concluded, "is determined by mechanisms for weight regulation that have little or nothing to do with external responsiveness."

To her credit, Rodin faced the disintegration of the theory she had helped create with equanimity and integrity. For several more years she wrote and spoke about the subject, describing the problems with the internal-external hypothesis and wrestling with what had gone wrong. In retrospect, she said, it was clear that almost from the beginning a number of studies had found overweight people no more responsive to external cues than their lighter-weight peers, but in the excitement of the chase these had often been ignored. Many studies had found support for the internal-external hypothesis, Rodin reiterated, but, ten years on, it seemed likely that many of these results were simply due to chance. Because there is such a wide variation among people as to their internal and external sensitivities, and because the early studies tended to look at relatively small groups of subjects, it was inevitable that in some experiments the selection of subjects would be such that the heavier ones were, on average, more sensitive to external stimuli. The positive results from these studies were taken as proof of the externality hypothesis, while studies with negative results were often explained away by one post hoc rationalization or another.

That does not quite answer the question of just why the studies coming out of

Schachter's lab were so uniform in their support of the internal-external hypothesis. If random chance were the only factor at work, then Schachter and his students should have had as many experiments finding the obese to be internally motivated as they had experiments finding them externally motivated, and the majority of experiments should have seen no connection at all between weight and internality-externality. Perhaps it was coincidence. Or perhaps Schachter's faith in his hypothesis was so great and his students' deference to him so utter that Schachter was never apprised of the errant trials; instead, the students would take more data or reanalyze what they had until the results came out the way they were supposed to.

We will likely never know. By the time Rodin was disavowing the internal-external hypothesis, Schachter had moved on. In 1978, he was studying cigarette smoking, where he once again invigorated a field with new and clever experimentation. One of his best-known studies concluded that smokers seemed to be addicted to the nicotine in their cigarettes, for when they switched to brands with lower nicotine levels, they smoked more cigarettes to compensate. In contrast to Rodin, Schachter seems never to have revisited the obesity area after the publication of their book.

With the disappearance of the internal-external hypothesis, only one, still puzzling, observation remained to be explained: the similarity in behavior between fat humans and fat rats. If it was not due to the obese of both species being more sensitive to external stimuli, what was it?

It was Nisbett who had the critical insight. Many of the obese subjects in the experiments were likely to be on diets of one sort or another, he reasoned. Either they were consciously counting calories or else they simply ate less than they wanted. Reasoning from work done in the 1960s that implied the number of fat cells a person has is fixed sometime in childhood or adolescence, Nisbett argued that an adult has a preferred weight, or set point, determined by the number of fat cells, and that the body has some mechanism, probably headquartered in the hypothalamus, that acts to maintain that weight. A person could eat as much as his body requested and stay at that preferred weight or else consciously eat less in order to keep his weight at a lower level, in which case he would be hungry much of the time.

Many of the obese subjects in the experiments were restricting their eating to this degree, Nisbett argued, and this explained why they often seemed to behave like hypothalamic rats. The rats with the hypothalamic lesions were clearly hungry—nothing else could explain why they ate so voraciously in the weeks following their surgery—and it was reasonable to believe that constant hunger created behavioral changes in an animal, whether a human or a rat.

Later, Peter Herman, a student of Schachter's who ended up at the University of Toronto, revised Nisbett's ideas to come up with what is the current under-standing of what Schachter and his students were really seeing. The important factor is not whether a subject is constantly hungry, Herman suggested, but whether a subject is consciously restraining himself and eating less than he would if following the dictates of his body. Then Herman performed a series of experi-ments demonstrating that people with high levels of restraint, whether overweight or not, indeed do react quite differently to external stimuli than people who are not so restrained.

In one typical study, Herman collected equal numbers of restrained eaters and unrestrained eaters who had been matched for weight, so that there were fat restrained eaters and thin restrained eaters, fat unrestrained eaters and thin unre-strained eaters. On the usual Schachterian pretext of giving a taste test, he fed the subjects two, one, or no small milkshakes and then asked them to "test" a pre-mium ice cream, eating as much as desired to get an accurate rating. He found, as expected, that the unrestrained eaters who had first filled up on milkshakes ate less ice cream than those who not gotten a milkshake.

But, surprisingly, exactly the opposite happened with the restrained eaters. Those who had drunk two milkshakes ate *more* ice cream than those who had drunk one, who in turn ate more than those who had had no milkshakes. Herman was astonished, but quickly decided what must be going on. When the restrained eaters were forced to bust their diet by having the milkshakes, their restraint evaporated. Since they had already gone over their daily caloric limit, they simply ate as much as they wished. And two milkshakes did a more complete job of knocking out the restraint than one.

Herman labeled this effect "disinhibition," and he went on to demonstrate that it happens in a variety of settings. Drinking alcohol before a taste test was an effi-cient means of disinhibition, for instance. Many of the effects that Schachter and his students found could be interpreted as a disinhibition effect rather than a result of increased sensitivity to external factors, Herman said. The fact that obese students ate more when anxious, for example, would make sense if the anxiety were removing the usual eating restraint they imposed upon themselves; the unrestrained eaters, on the other hand, ate less because anxiety acts to depress the appetite.

What remained after the demolition of the internal-external hypothesis was the observation that it is extremely difficult to find consistent behavioral differ-ences between the obese and the normal that can explain why some people get fat and others do not. Behavior may well play a role, but it is not so straightfor-ward and powerful a role as people like Bruch and Schachter hoped. And so attention in the field would turn increasingly toward the physiology of weight.

THREE

There's No Place Like Homeostasis

The thing P. J. Nelson remembers most from her year and a half in the Clinical Research Center on the third floor of Rockefeller University Hospital is the liquid formula. For months on end it was her breakfast, her lunch, her dinner, and her between-meal snacks. It was her turkey dinner at Thanksgiving and her hot dogs on the Fourth of July. It lingered on her taste buds each night as she went to sleep and greeted her in the morning. "It was god-awful," she says. "The worst formula in the world."

She didn't really mind the taste so much, she recalls—"It had kind of a mealy taste, not so bad, just chalky"—and once she learned to dissolve the orange-flavored potassium tablets in water and mix that in with the formula, the taste was vaguely pleasant. Even the texture was bearable. The formula would slide over the tongue like thirty-weight motor oil, but she got used to it. No, what made the formula so awful was the quantity.

When she was 320 pounds and holding, P.J. had to drink 4500 calories of the stuff each day. The attendants would deliver it in the morning in large cups—"They were kind of like a Big Gulp at the 7-Eleven," she remembers—and her assignment was to finish three and a half of them by bedtime. "You were drinking that formula the whole freakin' day. You were just forcing it down. And it was awfully hard to stretch that potassium."

Later, when she was losing weight, life was more pleasant. Each day she had just 800 calories—three small glasses of the stuff—to drink. A few swallows and they were gone. None of the constant sipping, sipping, sipping, and after a while her body seemed to forget how little was going into her stomach, and she wasn't even hungry anymore. "It sort of wears off," she says. "Eventually the hunger does stop."

For eighteen months, this was P.J.'s job: she drank exactly how much of the formula she was given, and no more. She could drink as much water as she wanted, and diet beverages, but nothing with any calories in it. Otherwise, she was free to roam the hospital and do pretty much as she chose.

When she had first arrived, weighing 290 pounds, her doctors told her to eat enough food—anything she wanted, as long as it was fattening and in great quantity—to get up to 320. From that point on, she would have nothing but formula until she was done with the experiment. For a month she drank enough formula to maintain 320 pounds, then the doctors started taking her down. Two months at 800 calories a day, and she was back at 290, at which point the doctors stabilized her weight, and out came the Big Gulp cups again. It was easier this time, though, since she needed only about 3000 calories a day to maintain that weight, and she didn't have to gulp nearly so constantly. After several weeks at 290 pounds, it was back to 800 calories a day and watching the numbers at the morning weigh-in going steadily down. When another thirty pounds was gone, the doctors stabilized her again. Each time P.J. reached a new plateau, the doctors spent a couple of weeks varying her intake, giving her more calories one day, less another, in order to figure out just how much her body demanded to stay put at this new weight. At the end of that time the doctors were able to keep her steady to within an average of a fraction of an ounce per day.

After eighteen months of this, P.J. was thinner than she had been at any time since her sophomore year in high school. She left the hospital at around 190 pounds, a weight she was sure she could have never achieved on her own.

"When I was thirteen, I was two hundred and fifty pounds," P.J. says. Two years later, as a sophomore in high school, she went on her first major diet when she wanted the lead role in the musical Annie Get Your Gun. It took her three months, she recalls, but she did it. "I did do Annie Oakley. I did get down to one hundred and seventy-five pounds. That was when I was fifteen." From then on her weight had been a roller coaster, usually heading slowly up, but sometimes, because of a diet or illness, taking a short, steep plunge before turning upward again. After high school she went into the theater, where she made a career out of performing as the funny fat girl, the big woman with the big voice in such musicals as Hello Dolly, Funny Girl, and Gypsy. But as she got older, the constant travel wasn't so much fun anymore. "Not only did I turn thirty on the road," she says dryly, "but it was in Toledo." And the nearly 300 pounds that was now her normal weight began to bother her more, not just because of the potential health problems but because of her appearance as well. "My other half really hates me fat," she says. So she agreed to take part in a study that her doctor had told her about, a trial at Rockefeller University Hospital that was looking at the effects of weight loss on metabolism, a trial that would take a year or more of her life but which would leave her thin—at least for a while.

No one promised that she would keep it off, she remembers. In fact, they were careful to let her know that her chances were not very good. Before starting the study, P.J. spoke with Jules Hirsch, one of the three doctors in charge. "I got the whole nine yards about how only five percent of people who lose weight keep the weight off," she remembers. "He said, 'Maybe you'll be in that five percent.' I was sure I could."

There is an intricate psychological dance that goes on here, notes Rudy Leibel, another of the three doctors and the one who conceived and designed the study in which P.J. took part. The obese patients who take part in the study generally have been unable to lose weight on their own, and the Rockefeller doctors, to entice them into the study, make one iron-clad guarantee: You *will* lose weight. If a subject followed the rules of the study—lived in the hospital, ate nothing but the liquid formula, drank nothing but water—he or she could not fail, since it is physiologically impossible not to lose weight on 800 calories a day. Even the occasional pizza sneaked into the hospital rooms by some desperately hungry subjects would only slow the weight loss slightly. On the other hand, the doctors were always careful to point out that maintaining the lower weight after leaving the hospital would be up to the patients, and experience says that they will probably regain what they lost. Leibel says: "We always tell them, 'The likelihood you'll be able to keep it off is very low, but you will not fail to lose the weight." The patients who enroll—there have been several dozen over the past decade— are trading on hope. Each knows the odds, but each figures, First things first— lose the weight, then worry about keeping it off.

At the end of her time in the study, P.J. moved back into her apartment, started looking for work to pay the credit card charges that had been piling up, and began assembling a new wardrobe. "It was fun getting into reasonably sized clothes instead of tents," she remembers. And, pointedly, she gave away all her "fat clothes." After investing a year and a half of her life in losing this much weight, she was sure that she would never need them again.

Under a microscope, fat cells look much like a collection of soap bubbles, transparent and roughly spherical, but with their sides pressed inward by the cells around them. A typical fat cell is roughly a tenth of a millimeter across—somewhat thicker than a strand of hair—but that is only an average. Some are twice that size and others less than half as large. Filling the interior of each cell is its reason for existence: a tiny, clear droplet of triglyceride, the body's long-term energy-storage chemical. Each molecule of triglyceride is a short chain of three fatty acid molecules, and it is these fatty acid molecules that the body burns in chemical reactions to release energy. The fatty acids are a particularly efficient way of storing energy: a gram of typical fat will generate about nine calories of energy when oxidized, compared with only four for proteins or carbohydrates.

Each fat droplet weighs only about one billionth of a pound, but an average adult has thirty billion fat cells, which works out to thirty pounds of fat in storage, or enough energy to run the body for forty or fifty days. Some people have much less fat, of course — researchers have observed adults with as little as two pounds of fat — and some have much more. The extremely obese may carry 300 or 400 pounds, enough to supply their energy requirements for a year to a year and a half. Medical journals tell of one 450-pound man who fasted under medical supervision for a year and two weeks, taking nothing but zero-calorie liquids, and lost nearly 280 pounds without any ill effects.

Throughout the 1950s, the fat cell had been mostly ignored by obesity researchers. They knew that the obese had greater fat deposits than the lean and that those fat deposits consisted of clumps of individual fat cells, but fat tissue had generally been assumed to be the passive receptor of the excess calories that people took in — an expandable gas tank, so to speak. The idea that the fat cells themselves might offer clues into obesity did not become popular until the 1960s, when a young M.D. would almost single-handedly make adipose tissue a fashionable area of research.

Jules Hirsch came to the Rockefeller Institute for Medical Research in 1954 after two years of military service in the Coast Guard and the U.S. Public Health Service. He was just twenty-seven, but he had graduated from medical school at twenty-one and had put in two years as an intern and two more as a resident before going to the Coast Guard. Soon after he came to Rockefeller, Hirsch began studying lipids, or fats, in the blood. These lipids were known to be a major contributor to atherosclerosis, and Hirsch examined how the amounts and types of fat that a person ate influenced the amounts and types of fat in the bloodstream. From fats in the diet and bloodstream it was a natural step to look at fat deposits in the body. "The biggest lipid compartment in the body is adipose tissue," he explains, looking back on those days four decades ago. If he wanted to understand fats in the blood, he would have to understand fats in the fat cells, so in 1960 he devised a tool for examining the fat cells of patients. It was a simple tool, the sort of thing that seems obvious as soon as it is described, but it opened a new window into the body for obesity researchers.

To collect fat cells for study, Hirsch would insert a large needle through the skin and into a fat deposit, preferably a large, squishy one. "[T]he buttock is usu-

Jules Hirsch. Photo courtesy of Jules Hirsch. Reprinted with permission.

ally the most convenient site," he commented dryly in his 1960 paper describing the new technique. After anesthetizing the target area, he stuck the needle an inch or so under the skin, injected some saline, and pulled back on the plunger to create suction at the tip of the needle. He then pushed the needle back and forth inside the fat deposit, breaking up the fat cells somewhat, and pulled the needle back out. "In this manner," he wrote, "a portion of the injected saline is recovered along with numerous minute shiny fat droplets which cling to the inner surface of the syringe."

With the easy access to the adipose tissue that the technique offered, Hirsch began to study how the makeup of the body's fat cells changed with diet. Although the fatty acid composition in the cells changed quite slowly, Hirsch found that he could control that composition by controlling the diet. "Over several years we could, for instance, make a person a corn oil individual," he says. If the person were fed a diet in which all the fats were in the form of corn oil, eventually his fat cells themselves would become almost pure corn oil. Or if a person were fed an extremely low-fat diet, his own fat deposits would become a "hard lard tissue" much like that of hogs.

From there Hirsch began to study the metabolism of adipose tissue, looking for differences between obese and lean patients. He suspected that their metabolisms differed at the level of the individual fat cells, but to test his idea, he needed some way to calculate the number of fat cells in a sample of adipose tissue. Once he knew the number of cells, it would be a simple matter of division to calculate the metabolism per cell and compare it among subjects. And so Hirsch set off in a new direction that would, quite by accident, transform the study of fat.

In the mid-1960s there was no good way to determine the size or number of fat cells in a tissue sample. The bits of adipose tissue, snipped out during surgery or sucked up into a needle during an aspiration, were white, blobby things that offered up their vital statistics only grudgingly. It was possible to take a thin slice of the tissue, mount it on a slide, and view it through a microscope, but counting and sizing the cells in this way was tedious, eye-straining work. Or one could use chemical means to measure the amount of DNA in a sample and, since each cell in the body contains a fixed, well-known amount of DNA, one could then estimate how many cells the sample contained. But adipose tissue contains a great many types of cells other than fat cells—blood vessels, connective tissue, various immune-system cells—and so the numbers derived this way were always suspect.

To get around these difficulties, in 1966 Hirsch developed a simple, accurate way to count and size fat cells. He would take a bit of adipose tissue whose weight had been determined, then dissolve it and separate out the fat cells from the other types of cells to create a collection of individual, triglyceride-filled spheres floating in a saline solution like a school of miniature jellyfish in a thimble of sea water. He next passed this solution through an electronic counter that automatically tracked the number of particles larger than a minimum size. By repeating the measurement at varying minimum sizes, Hirsch could determine how many fat cells were in the sample and what their sizes were.

Although he had developed the cell-counting method to help out with his metabolism studies, Hirsch first took the opportunity to ask some basic questions about the size and number of fat cells. Did the obese have more fat cells than the lean, for instance, or were their fat cells simply larger? At the time, no one knew.

In his first investigation with the new technique, Hirsch counted and sized the fat cells from some of the fattest patients at the Rockefeller obesity clinic. What he discovered was that their obesity was due mainly to having far more fat cells than the average person. Their fat cells were larger than normal, true, but they got only so big—about four times the normal size in lean subjects—before reaching a maximum beyond which they apparently could not grow. As researchers would later show, once a person is at least sixty pounds overweight, his fat cells have usually reached this maximum size. Beyond sixty pounds overweight, being fatter demands having more, not just bigger, fat cells.

Hirsch then asked the natural questions of why the obese should have more fat cells than the lean and whether the presence of those additional fat cells was a cause or an effect of their obesity. Hypothesizing that influences early in life might help determine the number of fat cells, he tried a simple but clever experiment with rats. Collecting a number of male rats born at the same time, he mixed up the litters, putting them with various mothers and creating some litters with just four babies and others with twenty-two. Since all the infants were competing for the mother's ten teats, the rats in the smaller litters would be much better fed in their first twenty-one days of life, up to the time they were weaned. After weaning, the rats were all fed standard rat chow, as much as they wanted, whenever they wanted it, and Hirsch then measured how much fat they had developed at various ages up to maturity at four and a half months.

As expected, the rats from the small litters — who got all of mom's milk that they wanted — were larger at weaning than the rats from big litters. Furthermore, the rats from the small litters increased their size advantage over the next several months, growing to be half again as large as the other rats by the age of twenty weeks. When Hirsch examined the rats, he found that, as expected, much of their difference in size was due to fat tissue. In the particular area he measured, the rats from the small litters had more than three times as much fat as their thinner relatives. But it was the details about the fat that would get everyone's attention.

When Hirsch counted and sized the rats' fat cells, he discovered that early in life the major difference between the groups of rats lay in the number of fat cells: at ten weeks the rats from small litters had nearly twice as many fat cells as those from large litters. In older rats, however, there was also a difference in size: the small-litter rats had fat cells twice as large as those from large litters.

From this evidence, Hirsch proposed that fat cells develop in much the same way that neurons and many other types of cells were believed to do. The number of fat cells, he suggested, is fixed early in life when the precursors to fat cells are growing and dividing. At some point before adulthood, the process halts, and the number of fat cells then is the number that the organism — rat or human or other animal — will have for the rest of its life. In Hirsch's experiment, the rats from large litters had stopped producing new fat cells by fifteen weeks, while those from small litters continued making them until at least twenty weeks, giving them double the number of fat cells that their thinner cousins had.

By contrast, Hirsch said, the size of the cells can change throughout life. Individual fat cells begin expanding early in life and keep growing for as long as the rat or person is gaining weight. Once an animal matures and the number of fat cells is fixed, all the growth of the adipose tissue comes via this enlargement of the fat cells.

The work, and Hirsch's interpretation of it, set off a decade of research on fat cells, much of it performed by Hirsch and his students, that built up a detailed picture of the role that the fat cell plays in obesity. Doctors now know, for instance, that obese humans generally have both too many fat cells and exaggeratedly large fat cells, but that the two types of excess arise in different situations and have different implications. People who have been fat since childhood generally have an inflated number of fat cells. People who become fat as adults may have no more fat cells than their lean peers, but their fat cells are larger. In general, people with an excess of fat cells find it harder to lose weight and keep it off than the obese who simply have enlarged fat cells. In one 1977 study of obese women who lost weight, those who had enlarged fat cells were able to maintain their weight loss for an average of nearly a year. Those who had an excess number of fat cells kept the weight off for only fifteen weeks. And those whose fat cells were both too numerous and too big lasted only twelve weeks. Another study done in the same lab in Göteborg, Sweden, found that dieting obese women could usually lose weight up to the point that their fat cells were the same size as those in normal-size women, at which point they hit a wall. Losing weight suddenly became much more difficult, and the women tended to become frustrated, go off their diets, and start to regain the weight they had lost.

As Hirsch and others followed up on that original 1968 experiment, they found that some of the details were wrong in the predictions that Hirsch had made for how the fat cell works, but the general picture has held up surprisingly well. The details of when fat cells form, for instance, are more complicated than Hirsch had assumed. In 1979, Hirsch's student Jerome Knittle published a study tracking the size and number of fat cells in fat and thin humans beginning at four months of age. The obese, he found, form fat cells continuously through age twenty-four. By contrast, the non-obese form new fat cells only up to age two and then again from age ten to eighteen. Knittle also found that the difference in fat cell size between the obese and non-obese appeared earlier than Hirsch had predicted from his rat experiments, actually preceding the appearance of a difference in fat cell number. Such discrepancies were relatively unimportant, however. What mattered more was that obese children, as Hirsch had predicted, were growing new fat cells at a time when the normal children were not and so ended up in adult life with more fat cells than their thinner peers.

The idea that the number of fat cells is fixed by adulthood has also had to be modified in light of further experimental evidence. In 1978, yet another of Hirsch's students, Irving Faust, showed that adults rats could be induced to grow new fat cells if they were offered a tasty, high-fat diet. The new fat cells appeared only, Faust concluded, if the existing ones expanded beyond a certain threshold. It seemed that if the rat's fat cells got close enough to their maximum size, it was a signal to the body that more fat storage would soon be needed, and more fat cells were produced. Although the evidence is less conclusive in humans, it appears that people, too, will develop new fat cells as adults if their existing ones get large enough.

It is even possible that fat cells, once formed, can be gotten rid of, albeit with a lot of effort. In 1988, Swedish doctors examined a group of extremely obese patients who had lost large amounts of weight after surgery to reduce their stomach size. In the patients who had kept the weight off for a year, the doctors found that not only had the size of the patients' fat cells dropped sharply but apparently a sixth or more of the cells had disappeared altogether.

Today, the picture of the fat cell's life cycle is very similar to what Hirsch proposed in 1968, and, for the obese, it is a depressing situation. They are stuck with an excess number of fat cells which are next to impossible to dispose of, and it is almost as difficult to shrink their size and keep it shrunk. In 1983, Hirsch and several students put rats on a low-calorie diet for so long that their fat cells lost almost all their fat and could not even be identified as fat cells under a microscope. Nonetheless, once the rats were allowed to eat what they wanted, the fat cells quickly filled back up with triglycerides to their original size.

Rudy Leibel doesn't remember the date exactly, or even the year—he thinks it was sometime in 1977—but twenty years later the words are still with him. "Late one evening," he recalls, "an obese mother brought in an obese child to see me. He was seven or eight." At the time Leibel was a pediatric endocrinologist at Cambridge Hospital outside Boston, specializing in weight problems. It was a frustrating job, for the more he learned and the more he worked with overweight children, the more he came to realize that there was really very little he could do for them. He could recommend good nutritional practices, he could talk to the parents about the importance of minimizing fat and calories in the diet, and he could encourage exercise, but it often seemed as if he was working against some overpowering force. Many of the children's bodies seemed programmed to become fat no matter what they did, or their parents did, or he did. So he was trying to explain all this to the boy's mother that night, trying to tell her that there was only so much he, or anyone, could do.

Abruptly she rose and pulled her son up with her. "Randall, let's get out of here," she said. "This doctor doesn't know shit."

For months afterward, Leibel would replay the scene in his mind, and eventually it came to take on a larger significance, symbolizing his failure as an obesity specialist and the failure of the entire obesity community. "I remember thinking, 'Man, she's right.'" But he had no idea what to do about it.

It was at about this same time that Leibel heard a talk by Ethan Sims, a researcher at the University of Vermont medical school who ten years earlier had performed a series of seminal experiments on the body's response to weight gain. Sims had recruited inmates at the Vermont State Prison to stuff themselves on four meals a day until they had gained an average of 25 percent of their body weight: forty pounds for someone who weighed 160 at the beginning of the experiment, fifty for someone who weighed 200. It wasn't easy. A typical subject needed five months of overeating, sometimes at a rate nearly twice his usual caloric intake, to gain the weight, and of the nine who took part in the experiment, only six could make it to the target of at least a 25 percent weight gain. One could gain only 18 percent, and two others had to stop at a 21 percent gain.

Sims's goal had been to see whether this sort of artificial obesity would produce the same types of physical, hormonal, and metabolic changes that doctors were used to seeing in their obese patients: an increase in the number of fat cells, for instance, and a rise in the amount of insulin that the body secretes in response to a meal. Many of these changes were indeed mirrored in the prisoners who gained weight, but Sims found several intriguing differences. Once they had become fat, for instance, the prisoners had a far tougher time staying fat than did the obese patients doctors were used to seeing. To maintain their extra weight, they had to eat about 50 percent more calories than they had been eating before the start of the experiment—more than consumed by many obese patients who were much heavier than the fattened-up prisoners. And when the prisoners went to lose the weight they had put on, they found it much easier than did most overweight people. Within three months of exercise and eating whatever they felt like eating—no longer forcing themselves to eat far more than their appetite requested—they were back at their starting weight. Only two of the prisoners, both of whom had gained weight very easily, found it difficult to take the pounds off. Sims also reported observations that anticipated Hirsch's work on the fat cell: the weight gain for the prisoners seemed to have come about almost completely by an expansion of the fat cells, which doubled in size during the experiment, and not an increase in their number.

As Leibel listened to the details of Sims's work, he thought he heard a clue about why it is so difficult for the obese to lose weight. "I remember thinking, 'This is trying to tell us something.'" It seemed that there were physiological differences between the fat and the thin that went far beyond what they chose to eat, and, as he mulled over what might have been going on, Leibel began to wonder if he might be of more help to the obese as a researcher than as a clinician. He could spend the next twenty or thirty years of his life explaining to his patients that he didn't know shit, or he could try to do something about that abysmal ignorance.

In the spring of 1978, Leibel had come from Boston to Manhattan for a meeting of the Pediatric Research Society conference and was staying at the Hilton at Columbus Circle, across Central Park from Rockefeller University. At Rockefeller, Leibel knew, was one of the best-known obesity research labs in the world, run by Jules Hirsch. Leibel was familiar with Hirsch's work but had never met him. "I just walked across the park, walked into the lab, and started talking to people," he remembers. Hirsch was out that day, but Leibel would end up having dinner with some of the other members of the lab, and by the end of the evening he was hooked.

"Four months later I moved my whole family here." He had been an assistant professor of pediatrics at Harvard's medical school and vice chairman of pediatrics at Cambridge Hospital, but he took a fellowship at Rockefeller at half the pay. He, his wife, and their eight- and two-year-old daughters had been living in a large Victorian house in Brookline. They moved into an 850-square-foot apartment in Rockefeller's faculty house. "This was all to help Randall," Leibel says now, nearly two decades after the move.

In person, Leibel is energetic and engaging, clearly in love with what he does, and, unlike most scientists, a good storyteller. Scientists tend to be obsessive about details, down to the most minute, and such details are death to a good story. Leibel instead is a big-picture guy, interested in the big truths and always on the lookout for an anecdote or an example that will illustrate a point he is trying to make. Like any good researcher, he is driven by an intellectual curiosity, by the desire to understand how things work, but he is a doctor first, looking for ways to help his patients, and his conversations always return to them. Randall is grown now and almost certainly an obese adult—statistically speaking, obese eight-year-olds, especially those with obese parents, have little hope of becoming anything else—but there will always be other Randalls, and this is what drives Leibel.

When Leibel walked into the Hirsch laboratory in the spring of 1978, it was an intense, exciting time. Hirsch and his colleagues were mapping out the effects of eating on adipose tissue and of adipose tissue on eating. It seemed completely believable that the lab might uncover a crucial piece of the obesity puzzle, one that pointed, if not to a cure, at least to an effective way of preventing or treating overweight. Leibel, with the words of Randall's mother still hanging in his ears, was smitten.

But it was more than the promise of the research that appealed to Leibel. Hirsch's observations about the nature of obesity resonated with what Leibel had seen in his own patients. The older doctor, after two decades of working with the obese in the Rockefeller clinic, had come to the conclusion that their condition had very little to do with eating. "The abnormality is not a food intake disorder," he says now, repeating a message he has offered many times since the 1970s. "It is a fat storage disorder." When severely obese patients were brought down in weight with very-low-calorie diets, Hirsch found, they often exhibited the same sorts of stresses and psychological upsets that doctors had observed in normal people in times of starvation: an almost obsessive preoccupation with food, increased anxiety and irritability, difficulties in observing their own body size and shape objectively. As Richard Nisbett, Stanley Schachter's student, had concluded from a different line of evidence, the bodies of the obese interpreted anything close to a normal weight as tantamount to starvation.

The problem, as Hirsch argued at an obesity conference in 1977, was best thought of as a homeostatic disturbance: an incorrectly set balance among the various systems that interact to determine body weight. The notion of homeostasis is an old one, and has been applied to a wide variety of bodily functions, from body temperature to the level of glucose in the blood and the balance of ions inside and outside a cell. A system in homeostasis is at a rough equilibrium and tends to return to this equilibrium whenever it is pushed away. A person whose internal body temperature drops too much below 98.6 degrees will start shivering; if the temperature gets too high, he will sweat. Something similar—although much more complex—was going on with body fat, Hirsch believed. "When people lost fat, they weren't cured of their obesity," he says. They were simply fat people whose bodies were being kept artificially at a weight far below where the bodies wanted to be.

Recently, Hirsch told the story of a patient whom he had been following for nearly thirty years. He had met J.W. in October 1969, when J.W. was forty-one years old and a successful editor and chemist. In college in the late 1940s, J.W. had been six-foot-five and 220 pounds. After graduation he had grown to nearly 300; then, before his marriage in 1960, he had lost weight, with great difficulty, back down to about his college weight; after that he had steadily gained weight at a rate of nearly a pound a week for the next eight years. By 1968 he had reached 515 pounds, and he checked himself into a hospital for a forced diet. When he came to see Hirsch the next year, he had already regained much of the weight he had lost. "I hospitalized him for weight reduction," Hirsch said, "and since then I have hospitalized him at the Rockefeller University Hospital twenty-five times. Many of these hospitalizations have been for prolonged periods of weight reduction." Hirsch would feed him 600 to 800 calories a day of the liquid formula, the same stuff that P.J. Nelson and the other experimental subjects would get, and J.W. would invariably lose weight. While in the hospital, J.W. would receive psychiatric counseling, exercise training, and behavior modification therapy, and after leaving the hospital he would be seen by Hirsch and his colleagues regularly. None of it helped. "[T]he patient's weight seemed inexorably to float back to the five-hundred-pound level."

When speaking of J.W. to an audience, Hirsch likes to show a graph that plots J.W.'s weight over the years. It resembles nothing so much as a jagged saw with about a dozen teeth. The line tracing J.W.'s weight plunges up, then down, up, then down, over and over again. From 1969 to 1993, the graph records seven different times that J.W. lost at least 100 pounds, sometimes more than 200, and a few other times that he lost somewhat less. After each loss he rebounded to around 500 pounds. At the time that Hirsch told the story, in mid-1998, J.W. had reduced to 212 in order to undergo surgery to replace a diseased heart valve but had begun to move up again. Past history would imply that he will eventually hit 500 pounds once more.

Clearly, Hirsch concludes, the various bodily systems—appetite control, metabolism, and others—that determine J.W.'s weight are in homeostasis only when his weight is around 515 pounds. When J.W. loses weight in a hospital stay, it pushes those systems out of balance and they respond by trying to return the weight to its proper setting. Unfortunately for J.W., what his body believes to be a proper setting is far too high to be healthy.

The idea that the body naturally maintains a certain weight is not new. For more than a century, researchers have realized that the body has some mechanism for keeping its weight at a fixed point, or set point. Both animals and people maintain relatively stable weights over long periods of time, even in the face of food supplies that vary in type and amount of food.

The body's weight-control system is exceptionally sensitive. As Leibel notes, the average American man or woman will gain about twenty pounds between the ages of twenty-five and fifty-five, or about two-thirds of a pound per year. This implies an average excess of calories in versus calories out of about 2400 calories per year, or about seven calories per day. By comparison, a single soda cracker is about twelve calories. Since the average non-obese adult takes in some 900,000 calories per year, or about 2500 calories per day, this is a remarkable feat. The body does not control each day's eating to within seven calories out of 2,500, of course. You might eat a thousand calories more than normal on Thanksgiving and a thousand calories less on a busy, stressful day when you forget about food. But over weeks and months the numbers average out, and you end up eating exactly what you need to keep a steady weight.

For most of the century, this internal weight-control system was assumed to have little or nothing to do with overweight and obesity. The homeostatic balance, normally so precise, was simply thought to have failed in the obese. Perhaps fat people had feebler systems that could be overwhelmed by the hedonistic appeal of high-calorie, high-fat foods. Perhaps some particularly powerful emotion drove them to overeat despite the best efforts of their weight-control systems. One way or the other, it seemed reasonable that once an obese patient's weight returned to normal, the weight-control system should help keep it there.

Hirsch didn't think so. If obesity were an aberration, a simple excursion from the set point, then a fat patient who lost weight should find his body getting more comfortable as it moved back toward the set point and find it was easy to keep the weight off. But the reverse was true. The closer a fat person got to his "ideal" weight, the less comfortable he got and the greater the pressures for eating became. Hirsch concluded that the obese must be suffering from a homeostatic balance that had settled far higher than normal. The obese were not fat because they ate too much; they ate too much because they were fat—because their bodies wanted to be at a weight far higher than the insurance tables indicated was healthy. Losing weight moved them away from what their bodies considered to be the proper weight and triggered the body's defenses against starvation.

Upon arriving in Hirsch's lab, Leibel threw himself into the quest to understand how the body monitored and controlled its weight. One of his first investigations was a search for signals that fat deposits might use to communicate with the brain. More than twenty years earlier the psychologist Jean Mayer of Harvard, noting that people tend to maintain a stable amount of body fat, proposed that the body must contain a "lipostat"—some system that monitored fat deposits and, much as a thermostat does with temperature, acted to keep the amount of fat in the body constant. If fat stores got too low, the lipostat would somehow increase the appetite and push the person to take in more calories; if fat stores got too high, the appetite would be temporarily suppressed. If Mayer was right, fat cells must release some chemical messenger that would let the brain or other parts of the body know how much fat had accumulated, but no one had been able to discover such a messenger.

Leibel thought the messenger might be glycerol. It was a likely suspect. Glycerol is the part of the triglyceride molecule that remains when the three fatty acids are removed, and the level of glycerol in the blood was known to be related to the size of a person's fat cells. It made sense that large amounts of glycerol in the blood might be interpreted by the body as a sign that the levels of fat are too high and that food intake should be cut back. So Leibel injected glycerol into rats and measured its effect on appetite and weight. The rats did cut their eating for a few days and lost weight, but the effect disappeared within a week. And when Leibel tried giving glycerol to human patients who were on diets in the Rockefeller clinic, he found that it had no effect on their hunger or on their weight loss. It seemed to be a dead end, and he dropped it.

Rudy Leibel. Photo courtesy of Rudolph Leibel. Reprinted with permission.

At some point in the early 1980s, Leibel realized that the records of Rockefeller might offer some clues to the set point. For more than a decade, Rockefeller doctors had been taking in obese patients and keeping them on very-low-calorie diets until they had lost dozens, sometimes hundreds, of pounds. As part of the reducing program, the patients would allow the doctors to make detailed measurements of them before and after the weight loss, and sometimes during as well. If the obese were suffering from a set point that was too high, and if the body responded to weight loss by trying to return to that set point, Leibel reasoned, then the reduced-obese patients should be different in important ways from either normal-weight patients or fat patients who hadn't lost weight.

Indeed, researchers had long suspected that weight loss affected the metabolism, but the evidence had been spotty and inconsistent, so Leibel devised a way to test that idea with the Rockefeller archives. Combing through records covering 1965 to 1979, he identified twenty-six patients who met his criteria: They had been admitted to the program at or near their maximum weight; they had stayed at least six months; and they had maintained a stable weight for at least three weeks before their weight loss began and for at least three weeks at the end of the weight loss. Leibel also identified a set of twenty-six normal-weight patients of approximately the same age and weight as the obese subjects who had been at Rockefeller for studies of cholesterol balance in the blood.

Because all of the patients had been fed the usual Rockefeller liquid formula, the records of their daily formula intake told Leibel exactly how many calories each patient got each day, which in turn provided an indirect measure of the patients' energy expenditure during the periods of weight stability. As long as a person is neither gaining nor losing weight, every calorie ingested is balanced by a calorie burned by the body to provide energy for its daily activities. Changes in the amount of water in the body can confuse the calculations, but as long as researchers are careful to keep track of fluid in versus fluid out, the numbers are quite reliable. So from the records of the Rockefeller clinic Leibel was able to come up with three sets of figures: the daily energy expenditures of the twenty-six obese patients before their weight loss; the energy expenditures after the weight loss; and, for the purpose of comparison, the energy expenditures of the twenty-six normal-weight patients. The results were published in 1984.

Leibel found that the non-obese group, which consisted of twelve men and fourteen women who weighed an average of 138 pounds, needed an average of 2,280 calories per day to maintain weight. By contrast, the obese group, an identical number of men and women who weighed an average of 335 pounds, needed 3,651 calories a day. This wasn't surprising—the obese subjects weighed nearly two and a half times as much as the control group, so it seemed reasonable that they might need an extra 1,400 calories a day to maintain that weight. What was surprising, though, was the comparison after the weight loss. After the twenty-six obese patients had lost an average of 115 pounds apiece, they weighed an average of 220, and at this reduced weight their bodies demanded just 2,171 calories a day. In other words, these reduced-obese patients, who still weighed an average of eighty pounds apiece more than the lean subjects, had to eat 100 calories a day less to maintain their weight.

Fat people have often claimed that they can gain weight even while eating less than their skinny friends, and here was proof, at least for the extremely fat: Once they had lost 100 pounds, they would start to regain that weight unless they kept their calorie intake below what thin people normally ate each day.

To pinpoint exactly what had happened to the metabolisms of the obese patients when they lost weight, Leibel performed some additional calculations that took into account the varying body sizes of the subjects. When comparing the energy requirements of different people, researchers have found that the important variable is a person's fat-free mass—the weight of the body minus all the fat. A 160-pound person with forty pounds of fat has the same fat-free mass as a 200-pound person with eighty pounds of fat—120 pounds of muscle, bone, organs, and other nonfat tissue—and because they have the same fat-free mass, they will require roughly the same number of calories each day to maintain their weight, even though one is forty pounds heavier than the other. Of course, other factors than fat-free mass can influence metabolism. One person might be much more active than the other, for example, and so have a higher daily energy expenditure. But among people with about the same activity level, fat-free mass offers a good measure of what the daily energy budget should be. Fat itself adds little to the body's energy requirements.

Leibel, unfortunately, did not know the fat-free mass of his subjects, since it had been recorded in the clinical records for only some of them, so he fell back on surface area measurements, or the number of square inches of skin. Studies by other researchers had shown that surface area is a good proxy for metabolic rate: people whose bodies have the same surface area will burn roughly the same number of calories each day. This allowed Leibel to come up with one figure— the number of calories burned per day divided by the surface area in square meters—that should be roughly the same in all the patients. And when Leibel compared the lean subjects and the obese subjects before they had lost weight, he found that it was: while maintaining their weights, the lean patients consumed an average of 1,341 calories per square meter per day, and the obese patients took in 1,432. But the reduced obese were another story altogether. Once they had lost weight, the obese patients needed only 1,021 calories per day per square meter to maintain—a drop of 28 percent from what their bodies had required before the weight loss.

In short, after the fat patients reduced, their basal metabolic rates plunged, to the point that if they were to avoid gaining weight they needed to eat fewer calories per day than lean subjects who weighed eighty pounds less. This was exactly what one would expect if Hirsch was right about homeostasis. When the obese lost fat, their bodies were pushing them back in the opposite direction by slowing their metabolic rates. The lowered metabolism made it harder to keep losing weight or even to maintain the weight loss since, just to stay in place, the patients had to eat far less than a normal person with the same fat-free mass did. By contrast, the obese who were at their "natural" weight—300-plus pounds—and who were not on a diet had metabolisms that worked at the same rate as those of everyone else.

In a follow-up study, Leibel set out to see how long the metabolism would stay artificially low in people who had lost weight. Recruiting four women who had dropped forty to eighty pounds and kept it off for four to six years, he brought them to the clinic, fed them on the liquid formula, and measured how many calories a day were needed to keep them at a stable weight. When he did the same calculations as before, he found that the women were maintaining on an average of 1,031 calories per day per square meter—almost exactly the same energy requirement that he had found in the earlier set of patients immediately after their weight loss. Even after half a dozen years, it seemed, the body remembered the weight it had been and was still pushing to get back there.

As striking as Leibel's study had been, it was ultimately unsatisfying. Scientists are never comfortable going back and reanalyzing someone else's data, and with good reason. The original data, accumulated for a different purpose, often fail to include many of the details that the later researcher wants—in Leibel's case, fat-free mass and detailed measurements of the patients' metabolic rates, to name just two. More important, the design of an experiment—exactly what is done and how—determines what can be learned. The older work had been designed with very different questions in mind than Leibel wanted to ask.

So Leibel decided to repeat the studies, this time with his own patients and his own experimental protocols. "We would do it right," he says. He would recruit both obese and lean patients and submit each to exactly the same manipulations of their weight. They would all drink exactly the same formula. They would all be put through the same battery of tests and measurements designed specifically to monitor how metabolism varied with changing body weight and fat-free mass. In an additional twist, some of the subjects would be overfed until they gained 10 percent of their body weight; if homeostasis was at work, the body should resist gaining weight with the same tenacity it showed against losing weight. The subjects in the weight loss group—including all the obese patients—would diet on 800 calories of the formula a day until they lost 10 percent of their weight and then be stabilized for testing. (Some, like P.J. Nelson, would gain 10 percent first, then start losing.) The normal-weight subjects would be released after one cycle of weight gain or loss, but the obese patients could keep going, losing weight in 10 percent increments, until they decided to stop.

In 1985 Leibel began recruiting patients and bringing them into Rockefeller for this new set of weight manipulations. Some, like P.J., came through doctor referrals. "My doctor had been unsuccessful in convincing me to lose weight, and he was worried about my health," she remembers. After hearing about Leibel's program, he recommended that she give it a try. Most of the subjects were recruited, though. "Doctors tend to send very sick patients," Leibel explains, and because ill patients might have metabolic abnormalities unrelated to their obesity, any obese patient who was not otherwise healthy got turned away. Instead, Leibel fell back on newspaper and radio advertisements for most of his volunteers. With each obese subject, he made the same bargain. "We offer the opportunity to go down to what we mutually agree is a safe and healthy body weight."

Most subjects ultimately drop between 30 and 50 percent of their starting weight, some even more. To lose that much of themselves, some patients have spent as much as two years at Rockefeller.

Finding normal-weight volunteers to serve as controls for the experiment was trickier. Who would choose to spend several months as a guinea pig in a weight-modification experiment, with minimal compensation other than room and board? The answer, Leibel realized, was: college students. To recruit his control subjects he sent out notices to colleges and universities, to the attention of the people whose job it was to help place students in work/study programs or summer jobs. The pitch: Come to Rockefeller University for a semester or a summer, live and eat for free in the hospital, and get a job or an internship on campus. The food may not be so good, but a stint at Rockefeller will look great on your resume, and, hey, you can't beat New York for museums and shows.

Kelli Johnson was one student who found that pitch appealing. In the spring of 1991, toward the end of her freshman year at Kalamazoo College in Michigan, she was looking for summer work that would give her some experience in her planned career field, science, and she found several possibilities in a book in her school's job office. "The one at Rockefeller was the most involved and paid the best," she says. For $40 a day she would work in the Hirsch lab at Rockefeller, learning basic lab skills, helping take care of the mice, and doing whatever small jobs needed doing. "I was sort of a gofer." But it was good experience, she says, and she got credit toward graduation at Kalamazoo for the work.

She entered the experiment at 125 pounds, which was the heaviest she had ever weighed in her life. When Leibel stabilized her weight at the beginning of the experiment, she needed to drink about 2000 calories of the formula a day, and, perhaps because she never had to down several Big Gulps worth of it a day, the formula never bothered Kelli as it had P.J. "It took some getting used to, but it was tolerable." What she couldn't get used to was the hunger. Unlike P.J., who lost her appetite after a few days in the 800-calorie weight-loss portion of the experiment, Kelli never adapted. "I was terribly hungry," she remembers. "It was just three small glasses a day. I saved it up for night since I could sleep better on a full stomach."

During that sleep she would make up for everything she was missing while awake. "I would dream about pizza and be mad in the morning that I hadn't dreamed about ice cream." She became obsessed with food. She bought cookbooks just to read the recipes. She hoarded food in her room—she didn't eat any of it, she just wanted to know it was there. "One time I called my dad and started to cry because I was so hungry."

The one thing that made it bearable was seeing the weight loss each morning at the weigh-in. Having gained weight her freshman year at college, she enjoyed seeing it slip away. Within a month she was down to 112 pounds, 10 percent lighter than when she had arrived, and she made the same promise to herself that P.J. had. "I was so happy. I swore I would never go back."

The responsibilities for the patients were few. Get up every day at 5:30 or 6 a.m. to have your vital signs checked. Drink the assigned amount of formula, drink as much water as desired, and take vitamin tablets. And don't eat or drink anything else.

Naturally there were a few slip-ups. "Most occurred when patients were in the weight-loss phase," Leibel says. "They are allowed out of the hospital then, and sometimes the temptation gets too great." Because the patient's weight was tracked so closely, it was usually obvious when someone had gone off diet, and Leibel encouraged them to confess so that he could asterisk their records for the next couple of days. But ultimately, although he never told the subjects, Leibel didn't care about the occasional furtive pizza or hamburger. The focus of the study was on what happened at the plateaus, when the subject's weight was held constant, and if somebody ate a little extra during weight loss, it did little more than put off the next plateau by a day or two.

The worst part about those long weight-loss periods was finding something to do with the time. Although most of the normal-weight controls had jobs around the hospital, many of the obese were full-time patients, and for them the experiment was often a test of their ability to keep from being bored. "You have to be able to keep yourself entertained," P.J. says. "There were a gazillion projects I was working on." She kept up with her music, she worked with a friend on a book, and for a while after she went in she continued a part-time job with her actors' credit union. The hospital provided a VCR for occasional movies and allowed the subjects to take part in its recreational therapy classes in arts and crafts. "I made wallets, did a few belts, and tried the pottery thing but I couldn't get that wheel to work for nothing," P.J. says. "And lots of ceramics. Every person I knew got ceramics for Christmas."

At the plateaus, the subjects were kept much busier and discipline was tight. No one was allowed out of the hospital, and Leibel closely monitored everything that went into — and came out of — his subjects. And they went through a battery of tests designed to pin down exactly how their bodies were behaving at that particular weight.

The first thing Leibel needed to know was exactly how many calories each subject was taking in to maintain his or her weight, and the use of the liquid formula made that relatively straightforward. The formula was mixed according to a simple, unchanging recipe: a powdered carbohydrate and a powdered protein blended into a corn-oil base, in a ratio such that the carbohydrate accounted for

45 percent of the calories, the protein 15 percent, and the fat 40 percent. In past Rockefeller studies the proportions had been varied so that researchers could study the effects of different percentages of carbohydrate, protein, and fat, but this time Leibel fed every subject the same diet. To make sure that he knew exactly how many calories each patient was ingesting, he periodically tested the formula for calories per gram with a bomb calorimeter—a device in which the formula is burned and the heat from that burning is measured. From there, calculating the total caloric intake was as simple as weighing the formula that each patient drank and multiplying by the factor of 1.36 calories per gram. The formula was supplemented by vitamins and minerals as well as salt.

Because the body does not use all of the calories it takes in, Leibel had to account for this too. Standard digestibility data, determined years ago by the Department of Agriculture, told him that the patients would absorb about 92 percent of the calories in the formula and the rest would be excreted. To make sure that his subjects' digestion of the formula did not change as they gained or lost weight, Leibel collected stool and urine samples at each plateau and tested them for calorie and protein content. Once the excretion was taken into account, Leibel calculated that his subjects were getting 1.25 calories for every gram of formula they ingested. To get her 4500 calories per day at her highest weight, P.J. needed to drink 3600 grams of the stuff, or nearly eight pounds, every day. Kelli, on the other hand, never needed to consume more than about four and a third pounds. But however much a patient drank, Leibel could say to within a few calories a day how much each patient needed to maintain weight at a plateau.

This in turn told Leibel how much energy each patient expended daily, but it did not tell him how that energy was being used. Scientists who study metabolism break energy expenditure into three categories. The largest is the resting, or basal, metabolic rate, which is the energy expended to run the body's essential functions, from pumping blood to keeping the body's individual cells operating. In sedentary adults the resting metabolic rate usually accounts for between 60 and 70 percent of the total energy expenditure. A second category is the thermic effect of food, or the calories expended by the body in response to a meal— mainly the energy needed to digest the food and process it into molecules that the body can use. This is normally about 10 percent of the daily energy expenditure. The rest of the body's daily energy budget is the energy expended in physical activity. It is normally 20 to 30 percent of the total, but it can be much higher in athletes, laborers, and other physically active people.

One of Leibel's goals was to determine which of these three categories could account for the drop in energy expenditure that he had found in the earlier study. Was the resting metabolic rate dropping? Was the body getting more efficient in processing food? Were the subjects becoming less active as they lost weight? Any or all were reasonable possibilities.

So each of the subjects was run through a collection of tests designed to pinpoint how his or her body was using the calories ingested each day. To measure the resting metabolic rate, Leibel had a subject lie in bed with his or her head encased in a clear hood. By keeping track of the amount of oxygen and carbon dioxide going into and coming out of the hood, Leibel could measure how much oxygen a subject was using and from that calculate the rate of energy expenditure. The measurement was carried out at 8 o'clock in the morning, before the patient had been given anything to eat. Leibel repeated the procedure an hour later after having the patient drink a carefully measured amount of formula. By seeing how much more energy the body used while the formula was being digested than when the stomach was empty, Leibel could determine the thermic effect of food.

Finally, Leibel determined how much of each subject's body weight was fat and how much was lean tissue. He used several methods, checking them against one another, but the most common was simple underwater weighing, which offers a measure of how much a person weighs compared with the weight of an equal volume of water. Because fat is not as dense as bone or muscle, people with higher percentages of body fat weigh less relative to their volume than do people with less body fat and more muscle and bone. To be weighed under water, P.J. remembers, the patients would step into a small pool of water, kneel on a scale, and expel all the air from their lungs. "That was not always so easy. Sometimes you floated away if you didn't breathe out enough."

When he had accumulated data from some forty patients over a decade of testing, Leibel analyzed the results and published them in the *New England Journal of Medicine* in March 1995. The work remains the definitive study of how people's metabolisms change in response to changes in weight.

When you gain weight, Leibel found, your body responds by burning more calories. After a 10 percent weight gain, his subjects' metabolisms had jumped an average of 16 percent more than expected, among both the obese and the nonobese subjects. Leibel knew that his patients' metabolisms should increase somewhat, since about a fourth of their weight gain was lean tissue, not fat, and the extra fat-free mass would demand extra calories to support it. But the 16-percent increase in energy expenditure was over and above the expected gain due to the extra lean tissue.

Most of the increase, Leibel found, came in the nonresting energy expenditure, whose rate—measured in calories per pound of fat-free mass—jumped by about 60 percent. Because Leibel had no way of measuring the nonresting energy expenditure directly, that number was determined to be the total energy expenditure — calculated as the total calories ingested while at a stable weight — minus resting energy expenditure and the thermic effect of food. Theoretically, non-resting energy expenditure should be mainly the energy needed to sit, walk, and do other physical activities. Strangely enough, however, when Leibel observed his patients' movements over the course of a day, he saw no difference between pre- and post-weight gain, so the jump in energy expenditure could not be explained by the simplest hypothesis: that the patients were more fidgety and moved around more when they were heavier.

The opposite happened when his patients lost weight: their metabolisms slowed down. After a 10 percent weight loss, they used 15 percent less energy than expected. Again, most of the change in energy expenditure came in the nonrest-ing category, and, again, observation revealed no difference in how much the sub-jects moved around. Surprisingly, however, the drop in energy expenditure was a result almost completely of the first 10 percent weight loss. Losing another 10 percent of body weight did not cause any further drop in energy expenditure, aside from the expected drop due to the loss of lean tissue.

The results imply, Leibel says, that the body tries very hard to keep its weight at a preferred level. Gain weight above that point, and your metabolism jumps, burning more calories in an attempt to shed the extra pounds. Lose weight below that set point, and your metabolism will slow down and conserve calories, trying to build your weight back up to its previous level. Leibel's experiment did not pin-point exactly where this resistance to weight change kicks in — whether a gain of just a few pounds is enough to trigger it, or whether it demands a shift in body weight of 5 percent or more — but the way that people's bodies stay within a few pounds of a set point year after year would seem to imply that the weight-control mechanism is quite sensitive to changes in weight. Certainly, by the time you've lost 10 percent of your weight, your body is pushing back as hard as it can, since additional losses do not cause the metabolic rate to drop any further.

From Leibel's perspective, the most important message of his study is what it says about the obese. Although they weigh far too much for their own good, their weight is, in one sense at least, every bit as normal for them as the weight of lean people is for them. Everyone — obese, lean, and in between — has a "natural weight" that the body tries to maintain. Get too heavy, and the body will act to push the weight back down; too light, and the body pushes the weight back up. Leibel found no difference in the force of the push between the obese and the lean. A natural three-hundred-pounder would have just as must trouble staying at 270 pounds, or 10 percent below the usual body weight, as a natural one-hun-dred-pounder would have staying at ninety pounds.

Furthermore, Leibel says, the metabolisms of the obese are almost identical to those of the lean when measured at the set point: the two groups expend almost the same energy per pound of fat-free mass. The only difference he finds is that the resting energy expenditure of the obese tends to be somewhat higher when compared on the basis of fat-free mass. The reason, he suspects, is simply that an obese person's heart and lungs work extra hard because of the additional flesh weighing them down.

Although Leibel's experiment looked at the set point only from the perspective of metabolism, he and other obesity specialists believe that hunger must also be affected by excursions from the set point: get too heavy, and you feel less hungry than usual; too light, and you feel hungrier. It is certainly true for rats, who eat more when their weights have dropped below their set point and then slow down their eating when their weight comes back up. Testing this in humans is much harder since so many factors other than hunger can affect how much a person eats. In Leibel's experiment, for instance, people were restricted to drinking the formula, which seems to do funny things to the appetite. But the fact that the human body can maintain a constant weight over months and years implies that hunger must be closely regulated along with metabolism.

Together, Leibel believes, the changes in metabolism and hunger that accompany a departure from the set point make it difficult to keep the body at a weight that is not natural, and the farther one gets from the set point, the harder it is to stay there. Keeping a few pounds off is relatively simple; keeping fifty or a hundred off demands a discipline that few can muster.

Almost any doctor who works with the obese will tell you that successful long-term losers are a monomaniacal lot, completely obsessed with their weight. Bruce Schneider, a clinical researcher now at the Food and Drug Administration, was working in Hirsch's lab in the early 1980s when Leibel advertised for people who had maintained a weight loss of 100 pounds for at least a year and a half. "He got six people," Schneider recalls, "and all of them were wacked." One woman had to—*had* to—jog six miles a day. If she didn't, she became extremely upset. Another constantly fantasized about food. "You were basically dealing with chronic starvation," Schneider says.

The obese who return to a normal or close-to-normal weight may look healthier, may even be healthier by the usual standards of how long they will live and how likely they are to suffer from diabetes, atherosclerosis, and heart disease, but their bodies don't see it this way. As far as their bodies can tell, they are starving, and that doesn't feel healthy at all.

It was late 1994 when Kelli Johnson returned to the Hirsch-Leibel lab for another go-round. After leaving the lab in the summer of 1991 at 112 pounds, 10 percent lighter than when she had entered, and swearing that she would keep the weight off, Kelli had gradually regained about half of it, to 117. Now, needing a senior thesis to graduate from Kalamazoo College, she thought of Leibel. He was continuing to gather data on people gaining or losing 10 percent of their body weight, and he was offering the same incentive to normal-weight volunteers. Kelli could get free room and board at the hospital, and Leibel arranged for her to work with Rockefeller researcher Michelle Bloom on a search for differences in gene expression between obese and normal mice, but one thing was different: Since Kelli had already participated in the weight-loss portion of the experiment, this time she would have to gain 10 percent of her body weight.

It was during Kelli's second stay that Hirsch's paper would appear in the journal and reporters from around the country would descend on his lab to hear about the results. Being articulate, attractive, and familiar with the theory behind the experiment, Kelli was a natural subject for interviews, and Leibel recommended her to reporters who wished to talk to someone who had taken part in the study. Later, she would remember her fifteen minutes of near-fame with a detached amusement: "It was nice for my mom to be able to turn on NBC and see the lab and catch a glimpse of me."

Gaining twelve pounds and keeping them was not so nice, however. After spending a month on the formula stabilized at 117 pounds and going through the same battery of tests as before, Kelli was switched to solid foods for her weight-gaining period. Breakfast, cooked in the hospital kitchen, consisted of pancakes, sausage, cereal, juice, and milk. Lunch included two entrees plus side dishes, and dinner was "this gross amount of food." She drank cans of Ensure between meals, had whatever snacks she could force down, and kept a six-pack of sugared colas in her room's refrigerator. Sometimes she went out to dinner with friends, trying to enjoy the New York City cuisine. "It was fun for about the first day, but after that it was work."

She remembers going to her job once, doubled over because she had eaten so much. Michael Rosenbaum, Leibel and Hirsch's collaborator on the study, happened by and asked if she was okay. "I ate too much," she managed to force out. "That's what I want to hear," Rosenbaum replied, and walked on.

It took her another month to get to 130 pounds, at which point she entered the last, least enjoyable phase of the experiment. Uncomfortable because of the extra weight, she had to drink about 2700 calories of the formula each day to maintain those pounds. "I didn't like the formula, and I didn't like the weight." For a month she was put through the usual series of tests, and then she was released. She went back to Kalamazoo to write her senior thesis and graduate. "When I finished the study," Kelli remembers, "the weight just poured off. In a matter of weeks it was gone."

That quick weight loss is normal among the lean controls who have gained 10 percent of their body weight, Leibel says, which is why he has no qualms about releasing them at the higher weight. "They are always back to normal within six months, sometimes less." Their bodies are programmed to be at the lower weight.

After graduation, Kelli began working out at the gym regularly and eventually settled near the weight at which she had left Rockefeller the first time. "I walked down the aisle at one thirteen," she says, "and I stayed there until I started reproducing."

Leibel guesses that Kelli's normal set point may be around 118 pounds, the weight she was maintaining as a senior in college. When she entered his study at 125 pounds, she was heavier than she had ever been, and he suspects that she was probably several pounds above her set point because of a transient weight gain during her freshman year. After graduation, she kept herself a few pounds below her set point by steady exercise. Neither of these situations is surprising. The set point seems to have a certain give to it, so that a person can stay a bit above or a bit below it with relatively little effort, but the tendency will always be to drift back to that one weight.

Indeed, Leibel's series of experiments offers a compelling, if unintended, demonstration of the power of the set point. For not only has every person who ever gained 10 percent of body weight for Leibel quickly returned to normal after the trial, but none of the obese subjects who, like P.J. Nelson, swore that their time at Rockefeller would not be in vain, has managed to keep the weight off. Not even P.J., who had been so sure she would be the exception that she got rid of all her fat clothes.

When P.J. left the hospital she knew exactly how much she needed to eat each day to maintain her new weight—2200 calories—and she had already made the transition from the formula back to solid food while still in the hospital. Furthermore, she had had a year and a half of dietary discipline, eating only what she was supposed to and, one might hope, losing some of the taste for good food that might be her downfall. But 2200 calories a day was little more than half of what she had been eating daily when she had been 290 pounds, and, more important, her body did not believe that 2200 calories was nearly enough for a day's nutrition.

"It's an enormous discipline to keep the weight off," she says now. "I have discipline in learning my lines, in preparing for a show, but not in dieting. If there's a goal, like playing Annie Oakley, it's a lot easier because your mind is set on that goal." But back in the real world, without someone else telling her how much and what to eat, P.J. began to listen to her body.

"Once I was out of there," she remembers, "I was eating and gaining weight and feeling guilty." She remembers checking back in with Jules Hirsch after the experiment and seeing his disappointment in her weight gain, which made her feel even more guilty. "For a couple of weeks I was busy sticking my finger down my throat," she says. Eventually, though, she decided she didn't want to go down that path. "I thought, 'People die from this.' And I couldn't go out with people and excuse myself to go to the ladies room and stick my finger down my throat and hope nobody comes in."

She left Rockefeller in November 1987. By August 1988, when she was performing as Mama Rose in *Gypsy*, she had gained fifty pounds and weighed 240. From there she gradually inched up to where she had been when she entered the study, and by October 1991 she weighed between 280 and 290 pounds. It was then that she fell seven feet to the floor from a loft bed and broke her left leg, which was followed by several months "sitting in a wheelchair, being back home with mother, eating everything she put in front of me because she's trying to make me healthy." After that she was far heavier than she had ever been. "By the time I started walking I was clearly over three fifty because my doctor's scale only went up to three fifty."

Gradually she lost weight again, and at one point, after a nine-month bout with "horrible diarrhea," she dropped down to 250. Once the diarrhea stopped, however, she immediately put the weight back on. "I got up to two eighty, two ninety. I was sort of maintaining there. It seemed to be all right to be at that weight. It's what I had always been."

That was in 1997. Later that year, after her father was diagnosed with congestive heart failure and her mother with Alzheimer's, her doctor put her on medication to deal with the family stress, and the pills, besides creating what P.J. terms "lovely bald spots," also pushed her back up to 320 pounds. But once she gets off the medication she expects to drop back down again. "Two hundred seventy is my natural plateau," she says. "It would take far more work for me to stay at two fifty. And to stay at one eighty I would have to be as rich as Oprah and have someone manage it for me."

The existence of the set point and the tenacity with which the body defends it answer, to at least a small degree, one of the major questions that have driven weight research for much of the past century: Why it is so difficult to lose weight? It is difficult because the body has a mind of its own, and it fights any large excursion from the weight it wants to be.

This fact dispels the simplistic idea that all fat people are gluttons or sloths. A four-hundred-pounder who is maintaining his weight at his set point is no more a glutton than a hundred-fifty-pounder at his set point. Each is following the dictates of his own body, eating what seems natural and right. And while the four-hundred-pounder will probably be less active than the one-hundred-fifty-pounder, that lack of physical activity is not what's keeping him heavy.

Likewise, it is clear that the various psychological disorders hypothesized for the obese over the years are at best secondary factors. You may cure an obese patient of depression or an oral fixation, but if his set point is still artificially high he is going to find it tough to lose weight.

Leibel and Hirsch use such observations to argue that the existence of the set point absolves the obese of any blame for their condition. Obesity is a disease, they say, and the obese are its victims. A growing number of obesity researchers agree with them. That attitude has made only small inroads into the population at large, but, not surprisingly, it has resonated with the fatter members of the population and has helped many of them accept their weight as the natural consequences of a malfunction in the bodies and brains over which they have no control.

Certainly P.J. Nelson has come to see her own fatness in a different light, and she has much more modest goals for herself than when she first visited Jules Hirsch and spoke about what to expect from her weight-loss experience. "I feel pretty horrible at this weight," she says of her current 320 pounds. "I would be an ass if I thought I could get down to two hundred again, but I could be really happy to get down to two seventy. Of course, now that my left leg is shorter [after breaking it], I probably am not going to be able to handle my two seventy as well as I did before. But I just want to be *comfortable*."

On her desk, P.J. keeps a picture of an attractive woman. The woman is not thin, really, but no one would call her fat. It is P.J. herself at one hundred eighty-something pounds, shortly after she left the Rockefeller study. She is wearing an eye-catching off-white dress with a red blazer. Her light brown hair is perfect— "It was a good hair day," she comments—and atop it is a jaunty tam-o'-shanter. "It's a really swell picture," P.J. says with the dispassion she might use in discussing a photo of a fellow performer or a distant cousin, "but I look at it and think, 'Who in the world is that person?'" Once, for a few months, she saw that face looking out of the mirror at her, but that was more than a decade ago, and the chances are near zero that she'll ever see that face again. P.J. knows it, but she just can't feel too bad about it. "I don't have a clue who that person is."

FOUR

The Legacy of the Great Fire

It has been more than fifty years, but people in Maine still talk about the '47 Fire. Over eight days a string of wildfires burned more than 300 square miles of the most beautiful parts of the state. The blazes, feeding on trees and brush that had been parched for months and pushed this way and that by capricious winds, left graveyards of black stubs where pine and spruce forests once had stood, carpets of ash in the place of woodland pastures, and piles of rubble punctuated only by the ubiquitous Maine chimneys where the map showed that nine towns should be. The damages, measured in today's dollars, amounted to more than $2.4 billion.

As destructive as the fire was, however, it was not an unmitigated disaster, for, in a twist that would seem contrived in a novel or movie, the fire set in motion a series of events leading to the most important discovery to date in the history of weight research. That discovery—the identification of the hormone leptin— could eventually prove to be worth more than all the real estate scorched by that memorable blaze. We will get to leptin in good time, but first we shall follow the series of episodes that laid the groundwork for its discovery. For some reason, perhaps related to the retiring nature of its main character, the story has never been as well known as it should be.

On a map, Mount Desert Island resembles a horseshoe-shaped earring dangling off the jagged ear that is the coast of central Maine. Densely forested, dotted with lakes and sounds, and ringed with steep cliffs and rocky outcrops that stretch far into the sea, the island has long attracted out-of-staters looking for cooler weather and a bit of nature. They arrive after Memorial Day, when the temperature has risen enough to make the Atlantic breezes seem pleasant instead of chilling, and they depart toward the end of October, when the recently brilliant leaves go dull and fall off the trees.

From the late 1800s through the 1920s, when the Rockefellers, the Mellons, and other giants of industry were advertising their wealth with houses to rival those of European royalty, Mount Desert Island—and particularly the town of Bar Harbor on its eastern shore—was a favorite location for their summer homes. B. F. Goodrich, the rubber company magnate, had a home at Bar Harbor, as did members of the Pulitzer, Rockefeller, Vanderbilt, and Drexel families. Edsel Ford, the son of Henry, lived a few miles away in Seal Harbor. The Chicago banker A. T. Stotesbury spent more than $1 million in the 1920s to build Wingwood House, a fifty-room Georgian Colonial mansion, in Bar Harbor. Summer was a gay time, with dozens of yachts in the harbor, scores of expensive automobiles motoring through town, and Great Gatsby parties at the "cottages," as the summer homes were usually called, and at the island's huge Victorian hotels.

The '47 Fire erased this bit of Bar Harbor. In the four days from October 21 to October 24, sixty-seven summer homes burned, many of them to the ground. Gone were houses owned by the author Mary Roberts Rinehart, the conductor Walter Damrosch, and the late financier Henry Morgenthau Sr. Most of the island cottages would never be rebuilt. The old, opulent Bar Harbor had actually been fading for nearly two decades, the fortunes of its wealthy summer residents having been nibbled away by the income tax, the stock market crash of 1929, and the Great Depression, and many of the summer homes had been deserted for years, their owners planning to tear them down. The fire saved them the trouble and provided them with insurance proceeds to boot. Other absentee owners, unlucky enough to have their aging mansions spared by the fire, would pay to demolish their houses in the coming years. Thus passed Stotesbury's Wingwood House, as well as Kenarden Lodge, built by the railroad magnate John Steward Kennedy in the 1890s, and several others.

By the 1960s, Bar Harbor was a town catering to visitors of more modest means. No yachts, no chauffeurs, no caviar on the lawn. Today, the hotels in Bar Harbor are clean and comfortable but far from opulent, and the shops in the small downtown cater to Baby Boomer tourist tastes: artwork, gifts, and T-shirts, most of them with a Bar Harbor or nautical theme. The era of the cottages, although still described with a wistful pride to visitors of the town, is gone.

A mile or so outside Bar Harbor, on an ocean bluff among the sites of several former cottages, is the Jackson Laboratory, an independent research lab best known for the hundreds of different strains of mice it raises and sells to scientists worldwide. Like many of the cottages, there was little of Jackson Lab left after the fire moved through. Unlike the cottages, however, it was rebuilt, and thereby hangs our tale.

The Jackson Lab had opened eighteen years before the fire, in 1929, when Clarence Cook Little, a biologist and past president of the University of Maine and the University of Michigan, inaugurated a laboratory aimed at studying cancer using techniques from the emerging field of genetics. Little believed that hereditary factors played a role in the development of cancer, and he further believed that the best way to study the role of these hereditary factors was to use a laboratory animal, such as the mouse. By breeding strains of mice that were susceptible to various types of cancer, Little planned to create a tool for medical researchers to understand how and why people get leukemia, lymphomas, breast cancer, skin cancer, and other types of cancer.

The funding to start the laboratory came from three wealthy benefactors. Edsel Ford, whom Little had met years earlier while running a summer research program at Bar Harbor, would pay half of the cost to erect a building and operate the laboratory for five years. The other half would be split by Roscoe B. Jackson, head of the Hudson Motorcar Company and another summer resident of Bar Harbor, and his brother-in-law, Richard Webber, who owned a chain of department stores in Michigan. After Jackson died suddenly on a trip to Europe, his widow agreed to maintain the funding, and Little named the new institution after him: the Roscoe B. Jackson Memorial Laboratory.

By 1947 the lab was thriving not just as a cancer research facility but as a supplier of inbred and partly inbred mouse strains to laboratories in the United States and other countries. Like humans, wild mice have a great deal of genetic variation, and this variation is a headache for any researcher trying to figure out the etiology of a disease like cancer. If mouse A develops breast cancer and mouse B doesn't, is it because A was exposed to higher levels of some putative carcinogen than B or because A is naturally more prone to developing breast cancer than B? Without mice that are genetically very similar, it can be impossible to separate out genetic causes from environmental ones. The solution is inbreeding: mate brother with sister, pick a male and female from the resulting litter and mate them, and so on for a number of generations. After about twenty repetitions, the mice are born with identical genetic makeups except for the unavoidable difference that a female has two X chromosomes and a male an X and a Y. Mouse breeders at Jackson Laboratory had created dozens of inbred strains that differed from one another in various ways, particularly in their susceptibility to develop cancer and in the types of cancer that appeared.

Such pure inbred strains are laborious to develop and maintain. The breeders must maintain careful records in order to keep track of genetic relationships and be able to trace out mutations that arise. But more important—and more difficult—is keeping the line pure. Mice are ingenious sorts, well adapted to living alongside humans without being detected and to sneaking into and out of manmade structures, even those meant to be mouse-proof. A female mouse in estrus entices every male mouse within smelling distance, which makes keeping mice out of cages where they don't belong a much more important task than keeping them in cages where they do. If, despite precautions, a rodent Romeo makes it into Juliet's cage without detection, it is still no problem if Romeo has some physical characteristics distinct from Juliet's—say a brown coat instead of a white one. Then the offspring from their union will clearly have been sired by someone other than one of Juliet's brothers, and the mistake goes no further. But if the differences between Romeo and Juliet are more subtle, the intrusion can go unnoticed, and what was once a pure line can become as messy and unsettled as the relationship between the Montagues and Capulets.

Most of the 90,000-plus mice at the Jackson Laboratory in the third week of October 1947 lived on the top floor of the main building. The original section of the structure, a 54-by-99-foot, three-story box built in 1929, was wood-frame with a brick exterior. A second unit, added in 1938, was 54 feet by 52 feet with a steel-and-concrete frame and a wooden roof with slate shingles. Work had begun on a third section, the same size as the first. The concrete for the floor above the basement had been poured, and the frames for pouring the walls and upper floors were in place. In the various structures, the mice were kept in wooden boxes covered with creosote, a flammable liquid used as a wood preservative. The boxes were piled on wooden racks which had, for more than a decade, been treated regularly with the even more flammable kerosene. This is not normal mouse-handling practice, but at Jackson Lab the wooden racks had somehow become infested with bedbugs, and the mouse keepers used kerosene to keep the bugs in check.

In the afternoon of October 23, a Thursday, the wind on Mount Desert Island shifted from southwesterly to coming from the northwest. Suddenly the wildfires that had been mostly contained by the island's fire crews took off in a new direction, into parts of the tinder-dry forest that had so far been untouched. With winds as high as fifty miles per hour at its back and a supply of new fuel in front of it, the fire shot southeastward toward the coast. In its path lay Bar Harbor, the cottages on the coast, and Jackson Laboratory. Most of the lab's personnel had already evacuated. With the word of the approaching fire, the last few departed, and by 4:30 the place was deserted, except for the mice. Shortly before 5 p.m., the fire reached the lab.

When Jackson Laboratory workers returned the next day, they found little left. The original wooden building, which had held 30,000 mice, had burned to the ground. All that remained was its boiler room, which had been built with concrete walls and ceiling. The second unit fared somewhat better. Its steel-and-concrete walls, built to be fireproof, remained intact, but its interior was gutted. Most of its 60,000 mice had died in the fire. The few survivors were so grievously injured that they all were euthanized.

According to local newspaper accounts, Little, the director, surveyed the ruins of eighteen years of work and vowed to go on. "Rebuild? Of course we'll rebuild," he said. A few mice had survived in other parts of the laboratory that had been out of the fire's path, and with these the lab workers began to reestablish some of their strains. To help this effort and to replace the varieties for which the lab had no survivors, scientists and medical researchers from around the United States, Canada, and Great Britain sent mice from their own labs. The mice were descendants of mice originally obtained from the Jackson Laboratory, or, in a few cases, mice that had been born at the lab and shipped out before the fire. Within two years, the lab had received so many donations of mice that it was able to reestablish all but one of the strains it had maintained before the fire. During the same two years, funded by grants and donations, the lab renovated the gutted Unit 2,

Jackson Laboratory after the Fire of '47. Photo courtesy of the Jackson Laboratory. Reprinted with permission.

finished Unit 3, built a partial replacement for Unit 1, and constructed a fourth unit, all of which gave the laboratory a great deal more space than it had had before the fire. By 1950, the Jackson Laboratory had rebuilt and more.

During the reconstruction, many of the lab's researchers moved temporarily to other institutions to carry on their work. One of them was Nathan Kaliss, who was studying the immune system's effects on tumor growth. After the fire, Kaliss took up residence at the American Sloan-Kettering Institute in New York City. When he returned in 1948, he brought a breeding pair of mice that had been provided by a Sloan-Kettering colleague, J. J. Biesele, back with him. The male in the pair had been shipped to Biesele from Jackson Laboratory on October 22, the day before the wildfire swept through the grounds. The female was from a colony that Biesele had bred in a pen, rather than in a single cage as was standard at Jackson Laboratory. She was the daughter of the Jackson Lab male and a dam from Biesele's colony that Biesele believed to be of the same strain.

In normal circumstances, mouse genealogy is a subject of interest only to mouse breeders, but here we must wade briefly into the nitty-gritty of strains and substrains and who was descended from whom. It will be the only way to keep track of the players as we go along.

The strain in Biesele's colony, one of the oldest and most popular of the Jackson Lab's inbred mouse lines, was known as C57 Black, or C57BL in the abbreviated argot of the lab. It could be traced back to a line established by Clarence Cook Little himself nearly a decade before he founded Jackson Laboratory. Little had bought three mice, one male and two female, from Abbie Lathrop, a Granby, Massachusetts, fancier who bred and sold mice to other collectors. When Little mated the male with the female that had been number 57 in Lathrop's records, the large litter included both black and brown mice, so Little separated them by color and began inbreeding. He labeled the resulting two lines C57 Black and C57 Brown. (The second female, number 58, was the matriarch of yet a third line, C58.) Thirty years and more than 100 generations of inbreeding later, the C57BL strain was still sturdy and prolific—two characteristics that are rare among highly inbred mice—and so it was a favorite for a variety of uses. Over time it had been divided into a number of substrains as mutations appeared or as breeders introduced a few new genes for one purpose or another. The particular line that Kaliss believed he was carrying back from Sloan-Kettering was denoted C57BL/6J, usually referred to as Black-6 by the mouse geneticists who worked with it.

The first hint that something might be amiss came after Kaliss had inbred the mice from the Sloan-Kettering pair for several generations. When he put tumors derived from Black-6 mice into his own mice, they rejected them—a clear sign that his mice were genetically distinct from the normal Black-6 line. At first Kaliss dismissed the discrepancy as probably a single mutation in one of the genes that instruct the immune system which tissues to accept and which to reject. Clearly his colony of mice constituted a new substrain—which was given the label C57BL/Ks and called Black Kaliss—but it seemed to be just one more simple variant of the standard Black-6 mouse. As the years passed, however, a number of other differences between Black Kaliss and Black-6 appeared, until by the 1970s Kaliss and others began to wonder if his strain was pure C57 Black after all. But it would not be until the 1990s that mouse geneticists had tools powerful enough to answer that question with any confidence.

In 1995, a team led by the Jackson Lab's Beverly Paigen examined the chromosomes of Black Kaliss in great detail, comparing them with the chromosomes of Black-6 and other mouse strains. An interloper did indeed sneak into Biesele's colony at Sloan-Kettering, Paigen concluded, and the female mouse that Kaliss brought back with him to Jackson Lab was one of its descendants. Judging from the genetic evidence, three of the grandparents of that female mouse were C57 Black but the fourth was DBA, the oldest of all the inbred mouse lines. Little had created DBA in the years before World War I and named it for its coloring, which was a light fawn with none of the barred agouti pattern typical of wild mice: thus Dilute Brown non-Agouti, or DBA. According to Paigen's genetic analysis, the genome of the Black Kaliss mouse is mostly Black-6, but about one in every eight of its genes is descended from DBA.

And somewhere in that one-eighth lies a set of genes that, beginning in the late 1960s, would put researchers on the long path toward uncovering the secrets of the set point.

The first truly obese mice known to researchers appeared at Jackson Laboratory two years after the great fire. It was not the first fat mouse, because mouse researchers had already developed lines that were undoubtedly overweight. The yellow agouti mouse, for instance, generally weighs about twice as much as a normal mouse, and the difference is mostly fat tissue. It is the Orson Welles of mice, larger than life but not grotesquely so. The rats with lesions in their hypothalamus, on which so much work was done in the 1940s, were similarly stout. But this new animal took corpulence to previously undreamed-of heights. It was a Sumo wrestler among mice, a sideshow freak, three or four times as heavy as an average mouse while being no longer.

The picture published with the first scientific description of the mouse shows it from above, standing, or perhaps sprawling is a better word, next to a mouse of normal size. With its ears and snout providing only small deviations from a shape that is otherwise almost perfectly round, the mouse looks more like a furry balloon with a tail than a living creature. The two women who discovered the mouse, researcher Margaret Dickie and a research associate, Priscilla Lane, named it *obese*, abbreviated as *ob*.

A number of researchers studied the mouse over the next few years, but the results were contradictory and disappointing. The *obese* mutation had appeared in a non-inbred line of mice that Jackson Laboratory maintained for investigating the chromosomal location of various mutations. Researchers at the lab crossed it into the Black-6 line to create a pure inbred strain of obese Black-6 mice that would become the standard for work at Jackson Laboratory, but scientists in other places crossed them with different strains, often not bothering to produce a pure inbred line for their work. As a result, researchers working with one strain of the fat mice often did not replicate the results of researchers working with another, and interest in the *obese* mouse waned.

Sixteen years after the discovery of *obese*, another fat mutant appeared in the cages of Jackson Laboratory. This mouse was just as fat as the *obese* mouse, but it was another characteristic that first called it to the mouse breeders' attention.

"The mouse was picked up because the cages were wet," remembers Douglas Coleman, a longtime Jackson Lab researcher and one of the first to study the new mutation. The mutant had appeared in one of Kaliss's colonies of Black Kaliss mice. A mouse handler had noticed that a few of the animals were drinking prodigious amounts of water and excreting equally prodigious amounts of urine — some 20 milliliters daily, Coleman recalls, compared with about 1 milliliter a day

The *obese* mouse. Photo courtesy of Jeffrey Friedman.

for normal mice. "And," Coleman says, "not only were they wet, but they were ripe." The urine of the mutant mice had a particularly pungent smell.

It is no surprise that it was a mouse caretaker who spotted the new mutant, Coleman notes. Throughout the lab's history, these handlers have usually been the ones to notice mutations that the lab's researchers then breed and study. Because the caretakers deal with the mice daily, they are in the best position to notice anything different in their behavior or appearance, and, indeed, lab tradition has it that one of the main reasons Little decided to locate in Maine was the character of the Maine people who would work there—careful, capable, and observant. These remain the qualities that are looked for in the mouse handlers. (A second reason for the choice was Bar Harbor's mild summer weather. In the days before inexpensive air conditioning, this made it possible to raise thousands of mice at a reasonable cost.) Despite the caretakers' importance, however, they seldom receive credit for their finds other than internal acknowledgment at the laboratory, and the name of the discoverer of this particular mouse does not seem to have been recorded.

Today, researchers at the Jackson Lab have a well-developed system for seeing that mutants such as the fat, smelly one that appeared in Kaliss's colony are not overlooked. They hold weekly meetings at which they display mice that have a different phenotype—that is, act or look different—from the others of the colony into which they are born. With as many mice as Jackson Lab breeds, there are always a few of these "phenodeviants," and most of them are of little or no interest to the laboratory staff, either because they duplicate past mutations or because the mutation itself is mundane. But occasionally a new mouse type appears that does catch someone's eye, and that scientist will breed the mutants or the parents of the mutants to establish a mouse line with the new characteristic.

Thirty years ago procedures weren't so formalized at the lab. There was no weekly meeting and often no attempt made to see if other researchers might be interested in a mutation. "Everyone had phenodeviants," Coleman says. "Often you just got rid of them." In the case of the fat, pee-happy mice found in Kaliss's colony, this could have easily happened. Kaliss himself wasn't interested in the mice—he had other research directions—and these animals were stinking up his cages. But Kaliss suspected that they might be suffering from a rodent version of diabetes, which in humans is characterized by an increased thirst and sugar in the urine, and he knew that Katharine Hummel, another researcher at Jackson Lab, was interested in the disease. So Kaliss asked her if she wanted to take them off his hands. Hummel agreed, and Kaliss handed over all the affected mice, the fat ones as well as the breeding pairs that had produced them.

Hummel in turn called in Coleman and asked if he would help her with the biochemical analysis of the new fat mouse. She wanted him to determine

The *diabetes* mouse. Photo courtesy of the Jackson Laboratory.
Reprinted with permission.

whether the mice were indeed suffering from diabetes. With no inkling that he was stepping into something that would consume a large percentage of his time over the next twenty-five years, Coleman said yes.

From the start, Coleman and Hummel had an advantage over the researchers who had studied the *obese* mouse fifteen years earlier: the new mutation had appeared in the highly inbred Black Kaliss strain, which made it much more convenient to analyze. So within a few months they knew the basic details of the new mutation. The mice got fat, although not as fat as the *obese* mice, growing to about twice normal weight. And they were diabetic: their levels of blood sugar were three times the normal level, the sugar in their urine was much higher than normal, and the islets of Langerhans—the part of the pancreas that produces insulin and that is damaged in human diabetics—were abnormal. Hummel named the new mutation *diabetes*, abbreviated *db*.

Because the *db* mice resembled the older *ob* line in a number of ways—in addition to being fat, for instance, they were also sterile—Hummel, Coleman, and Margaret Dickie tested whether the *diabetes* mutation affected the same gene that was involved in the *obese* line. Although they had no clue what the genes were—this was twenty years before researchers would clone the first few genes from the mouse—they had a straightforward method to determine whether genes hit by the two mutations were in fact the same gene. Both mutations were autosomal recessives—that is, a mouse had to inherit a defective gene from both of its parents for the mutation to manifest itself. A mouse that carried only one defective gene was, to all appearances, perfectly normal. If both the mother and father had one defective gene and one normal gene, then approximately one-fourth of the mice in a litter would inherit two defective genes and become fat. (Mice with two defective genes were sterile and did not reproduce.) So the researchers crossbred mice with a single *ob* gene against mice with a single *db* gene. If *ob* and *db* had been different defects in the same gene, then one-fourth of the mice born from those unions should be fat. As it turned out, none of the mice got fat, and the researchers could conclude that *obese* and *diabetes* were defects in two distinct genes. The *db* mouse truly was a new mutant.

Up to this point, the situation with the fat mice had seemed straightforward: *obese* and *diabetes* seemed to be two unrelated mutations that, although they each produced fat mice, appeared to have little else in common. Then Priscilla Lane, the co-discoverer of the *obese* mouse, walked into Coleman's office with a conundrum. As Coleman remembers it, "Skippy Lane brought in another mouse and said, 'Tell me whether this is *ob* or *db*.'" She had found in the lab's colonies yet a third mutation that produced fat mice, but she was confused about its identify. To judge from the physical characteristics of the mice, the new mutation seemed to affect the same gene that the *obese* mutation did. The mice gained weight the same way that the *ob* mice did, and they did not develop diabetes as *db* mice did. On the other hand, breeding experiments implied that the mutation in the new mice affected the same gene that the *diabetes* mutation did. When mice with this new mutation were crossbred with mice carrying the *ob* gene and mice with the *db* gene, it was only the progeny from the *db* unions that got fat. Clearly the new mutants were suffering from a defect in the same gene hit in the *db* mice. But if the new mutation was a variant of *db*, why did it not produce diabetes? And why did it appear so much like *ob*?

It was an intriguing puzzle, and Coleman set out to solve it. In gathering information about the mice, he learned that Lane had discovered the new mutation in a strain of brown mouse. According to standard mutation-naming procedure, because the mutation struck the same gene as the *diabetes* mutation, the new one was labeled *diabetes-2J*, or *db-2J*. Once it was identified as a possibly interesting mutation, the brown *db-2J* mice were crossbred with Black-6 mice to create a line of Black-6 mice with the *db-2J* mutation. It was this strain that presented Coleman with his conundrum: Why did Black-6 mice with two copies of *db-2J* not develop diabetes?

Coleman suspected that the explanation might lie with the genetic differences between the strains of mice. The original *diabetes* mutation had appeared on the Black Kaliss strain and had been maintained on it ever since. Although Black-6 mice were genetically very similar to Black Kaliss, perhaps they were different enough that the same mutation would produce dissimilar outcomes. Other researchers were dubious, Coleman remembers. "Everybody said it's not the inbred background. They didn't think it could be that big an effect." Nonetheless, Coleman bred the *diabetes-2J* mutation into a line of Black Kaliss mice and compared them with the Black-6 mice that had been given the same mutation.

What he found astonished him. In the Black Kaliss mice, the *db-2J* mutation had exactly the same effect as *db*: early in life the mice overate, became fat, and had high levels of insulin in the bloodstream; by the time they were four or five months old—the mouse equivalent of the late teens—they had developed diabetes; afterward, as the disease took its toll, they lost weight and died, sometimes in what for humans would be their twenties or thirties. By contrast, the Black-6 mice with the *db-2J* mutation ate a lot, gained weight, and had high levels of insulin in the first few months of life, but as they aged they continued to get fatter and fatter, and they never developed full-blown diabetes. These mice lived well into rodent middle age before they were, in the sanitary circumlocution of the laboratory, "sacrificed and autopsied."

In short, the *db-2J* mutation behaved like *diabetes* when it developed in the Black Kaliss mice and like *obese* when it was put into a Black-6 line. The root of Skippy Lane's confusion lay in the fact that the Black Kaliss mice were much more susceptible to diabetes than were the Black-6. As Coleman eventually figured out, both strains overeat and become fat, pushing their pancreas to produce more and more insulin, the hormone that controls the level of sugar in the bloodstream. In the Black-6 mice, the islets of Langerhans can meet the demand by becoming larger and increasing in number. Thus, although the Black-6 mice become hugely fat, they are otherwise relatively healthy. In the Black Kaliss animals, however, the islets collapse under the strain. The pancreas secretes less and less insulin, the levels of blood sugar skyrocket, and the animals die from complications of diabetes.

Surprisingly, Coleman found, the *ob* gene also behaved in exactly the same way. When the *ob* mutation was inserted into the Black Kaliss line, the mice not only got fat but also developed diabetes. In Black-6 mice, by contrast, *ob* did not lead to diabetes. The explanation for the difference was the same as for the difference in *db*: the pancreas in the *obese* Black Kaliss mouse was unable to keep up with the demand for extra insulin caused by the overeating and obesity, and it sputtered out, while the pancreas in the *obese* Black-6 mouse could stand up to the strain.

Later, Coleman would try to track down which genes in particular explain why Black-6 mice are so resistant to diabetes and Black Kaliss mice so susceptible, figuring that the information might point to a way to keep obese humans from developing diabetes. He found hints that part of chromosome 12 in the mouse might be involved in helping the islets of the Black-6 mice meet the increased demand for insulin, but he got no further. Other researchers have tried and failed as well. Beverly Paigen, the Jackson Lab geneticist who traced the origins of the Black Kaliss strain, found three different places in the mouse genome that appear to play a role, but again the connection is weak. She suspects that the difference in how the pancreas responds may arise from the interaction of several genes or groups of genes.

But whether or not Black Kaliss ever helps cure diabetes, this mouse strain that appeared so mysteriously at Jackson Lab in the wake of the '47 Fire has already made its mark—by setting in motion a long chain of events that would eventually culminate in the discovery of leptin. "It was lucky the *diabetes* mutation occurred on that strain," Coleman explains. "Otherwise we would have just thought it was similar to the *obese* mouse and put it away." If the *db* mutation had appeared in Black-6, for instance, the affected animals would have not drunk so much and peed so prodigiously, and, without those signs that the mice were diabetic, Katharine Hummel would never have been interested. If Hummel hadn't been interested, she would have never asked Coleman to look at the mice, and, as we see below, if Coleman had never gotten involved with the *ob* and *db* mice, a major chunk of what scientists now know about the regulation of weight would be missing. All this because a horny mouse of the wrong lineage sneaked into a breeding colony that wasn't within 300 miles of the Jackson Laboratory.

Doug Coleman could be a poster child for why movies about real scientists don't work. Anyone who writes about science or who talks to scientists about their public image eventually hears this complaint: "Why can't Hollywood portray scientists as they really are instead of as caricatures and villains? It's no wonder the public mistrusts science." And it's true, of course. Scientists in the movies aren't generally the sort you'd want living next door to you, or even on the same planet. If they are not menaces like Victor Frankenstein or Dr. Strangelove, they are buffoons like Rick Moranis in *Honey, I Shrunk the Kids*.

To get an image of Doug Coleman, take every characteristic of these movie scientists and, except for the intelligence and the curiosity, throw them out. In appearance he calls to mind Richard Dysart, the actor who starred in the television show *L.A. Law* as the law firm's steady and earnest senior partner, Leland McKenzie. He is quiet but intense, measured in his speech but animated when he hits upon a subject that interests him. These days, years after leaving Jackson Laboratory and retiring from science, that subject is more likely to be nature conservancy than fat mice. Coleman is a member of a local conservation group and spends much of his time as a volunteer helping people with legal papers involving conservancy issues. He has worked to restore fifty acres of Maine forest that he and his wife own to its pristine, natural condition, efforts that won him the Maine Forest Stewardship Award in 1998. For our interview he is dressed in not

Douglas Coleman. Photo courtesy of the Jackson Laboratory.
Reprinted with permission.

the white coat of the movie scientist but a plaid flannel shirt and casual pants—
normal attire for the researchers at Jackson Lab.

During his thirty-three years at the lab, the dramas that filled Coleman's life
were of the sort that is hard to build a blockbuster movie around: weeks and
months of tedium dotted with small victories and defeats and, every now and
then, a breakthrough, with most of the action taking place in Coleman's head as
he slowly pieced together an understanding of this or that aspect of mouse physiology and genetics. From 1958, when he first went to work at the lab, to 1991,
when he retired, Coleman got to work each day at 7 a.m., which usually made
him the first to arrive. He loved it, he says. He couldn't wait to get in to see what
the day had in store. But it never consumed him. Unlike many researchers, who
can be found in their labs at all hours, Coleman would work an eight- or nine-
hour day, then leave. And when he reached sixty and retired, it was a clean break.
No ongoing projects that brought him into the lab two or three days a week, no
part-time consulting, and, he avows, no regrets. "Research is a hard business," he
says, trying to explain how he could walk away from something that had been
such a large part of his life for so long. "You have days of despair and days of
euphoria." To do science the way Coleman did—"I'm pretty much a loner; every

experiment done was pretty much done by myself" — is tiring, both physically and psychologically. Coleman left the laboratory when he could still have been productive, even if he had scaled his work week down to a couple of days, but one gets the sense that he knew part time wouldn't work. He couldn't flip the switch halfway off.

Like any good scientist, Coleman spent his career following his nose, taking on research when the questions intrigued him and passing on those items that held no appeal. A bit ruefully he relates how George Snell, who for years had an office next to Coleman's at Jackson Lab, would drag him into seminars and discussions of his work, trying to get Coleman to become involved. Coleman, who had his own interests, resisted and so missed out on the discovery of how the major histocompatibility complex regulates a body's immune response, a breakthrough that won Snell the Nobel Prize in 1980. Perhaps, Coleman muses, if he had given in to Snell's entreaties he might have shared that prize. But, on the whole, he has no regrets. "I never complained about my career," he said in one interview in late 1997. "I was satisfied in my own mind." Six months after that interview, Coleman was elected to the prestigious and exclusive National Academy of Sciences, the biggest honor that a U.S. scientist can receive, short of the Nobel Prize. The recognition was late in coming, but that was probably because Coleman's research was so far ahead of its time. It would not be until the mid-1990s, twenty years after he had finished his most important work on fat mice, that other researchers would build on it and come to understand its importance.

As he tells it, Coleman never set out to study obesity. When he was nearing the completion of a Ph.D. in biochemistry at the University of Wisconsin, Madison, he heard from a former Wisconsin graduate student who had gone to work at the Jackson Laboratory that the lab was looking for another biochemist. Was he interested? Coleman, who had taken several courses in oncology, knew of the laboratory's reputation in cancer research. So he took a job there, expecting to stay no longer than a couple of years, learning some new research techniques and then moving on. After his arrival, he won a grant from the National Institutes of Health (NIH) to study muscular dystrophy, but he soon found himself wandering into different areas. "That was the beauty of this institution," he remembers. "They let you do that." Fortunately for Coleman, the NIH was understanding too. At some point he realized that he had been spending far more time on diabetes than on muscular dystrophy, but when he confessed this to his funding officer at the NIH, he was told not to worry about it and just to keep sending in progress reports on whatever he was doing.

Within a few years of arriving, Coleman was becoming known around the country as a comer. "I was beginning to get a reputation in biochemical genetics," he recalls, and he could have easily taken a job somewhere else. But by this time he was sold on Jackson Lab. He liked the atmosphere there, the friendly collaborativeness among the researchers on staff. It fit his own style of mostly going it alone but working with others when their skills and expertise could complement his.

And so it was that when Katharine Hummel wanted someone to analyze the biochemistry of the new line of diabetic mice, she turned to Coleman. "I was just in the right place at the right time," he says. "I was young, I was inquisitive." And he was energetic. He set out to learn everything he could about the diabetic mice, and quickly uncovered a number of surprising traits. The *db* mouse could fast almost indefinitely, for instance. Normal mice died after a few days without food, but the *diabetes* mutation seemed to do something to the mouse that allowed it to metabolize fat and survive. And the *db* mouse was astonishingly resistant to insulin. They could be given 40 units of insulin—"enough to kill a horse," Coleman says—and scamper away unfazed.

Coleman, whose work had always been well regarded by scientists working in his immediate area but not widely recognized beyond its borders, suddenly found himself invited to describe the new mouse at one conference after another. It was an exciting time. Not only did he get to visit many of the appealing cities where scientists like to hold their international conferences—places such as Paris and Copenhagen—but he was able to meet many of the scientists whose work he had read and admired.

Meanwhile, he was continuing to investigate the *diabetic* mouse. (And also carrying on with other lines of research, Coleman notes. Even at the times he focused most intensely on *db* and *ob* mice, he says, he never spent more than half his time on them. He made it a rule always to have at least two major lines of research going at once; that way if one of them wasn't going well, perhaps the other would be.) In particular, Coleman had noticed that *db* mice had unusually high levels of insulin in their blood from the time they were a couple of weeks old until they were in the final stages of dying from diabetes. Perhaps, Coleman hypothesized, some insulin-releasing factor was circulating in the blood of the *db* mice, signaling the pancreas to pump out large amounts of insulin. To test this, he turned to parabiosis, a little-used technique that takes a pair of mice and joins their circulatory systems, turning them into the rodent version of Siamese twins.

An animal caretaker was the only member of the Jackson Lab staff who was familiar with parabiosis—roughly speaking, Greek for "living life side by side"—so Coleman asked her for instructions. Soon he was creating his own side-by-side mice.

"It's gross," he says. "I would not do this today." The operation is simple, but it is not for the queasy. You begin by cutting the skin along the left side of a mouse from under the forearm all the way to the end of the body—a 1½-to 2-inch incision on a 3-inch mouse—and then spreading open the skin, pulling it back from the cut. Next you cut the peritoneum, the membrane that lines the abdominal cavity and holds the guts in, creating a hole about the size of a dime. Repeat all this on the right side of a second mouse so that you have two mice with slit-open sides and holes in the peritoneums. Place the mice side by side, head to head and tail to tail, and sew together their peritoneums around the edges of the dime-sized holes. Squirt some powdered antibiotic over the whole area in the hope of preventing infection. Then bring the skin of the mice together along the slits, belly skin to belly skin, shoulder skin to shoulder skin, back skin to back skin, and connect the different areas of skin with surgical clips so that what once was two separate mouse coats now becomes one continuous coat that covers two mice. Finally, run a suture from the large muscle over the left shoulder blade of the first mouse to the same muscle over the right shoulder blade of the second, and pull the suture tight so that the mice cannot pull apart.

"It didn't seem to hurt the mice," Coleman says. "A fat mouse would get up [after the anesthesia wore off] and go right to the food hopper." Nor did the mice seem to have difficulty adjusting to life in tandem. A pair of joined mice would quickly learn to move together instead of pulling in different directions, and even the males seemed to accept their twins as partners rather than as interlopers. "Males are normally not real friendly," Coleman says. "They like to fight. You didn't see any of this in the parabiosed mice."

After a few days, the skin of the two mice grows together, as do the peritoneums. More important, the small blood vessels known as capillaries grow across the incision in the peritoneums and skin, uniting the circulatory systems of the two previously separate mice. Inbred mice can live joined this way, Coleman notes, because all the mice in a litter are essentially identical twins, so their immune systems will not reject the skin and blood vessels of the other mouse. Once the healing is complete, a small amount of the blood circulating in each animal will make its way into the other animal. In an average pair, Coleman says, about 1 percent of the blood is exchanged each minute.

It was this exchange that Coleman was counting on to reveal something about the cause of the high insulin levels in diabetic mice. By joining the blood supply of a *db* mouse with that of a normal mouse, he hoped to see changes in one mouse or the other. If indeed an insulin-releasing factor was circulating in the *db* mouse, triggering the delivery of extra insulin, then a normal mouse parabiosed with a diabetic mouse should see its own insulin levels rise. On the other hand, if some factor in the blood of normal mice was inhibiting insulin release, then the insulin levels in a diabetic mouse should be decreased when the animal's blood supply was connected with that of a normal mouse. Coleman was hoping for the latter, as it might point toward a way of keeping insulin levels down in humans who developed the adult-onset variety of diabetes. What he really expected, though, was that the parabiosis experiment would simply come up empty-handed. "Most of the time nothing happens. Either there is no factor or not enough factor gets across [from one mouse to the other]."

As it turned out, the correct answer was "None of the above." After several weeks and a number of pairs of conjoined mice, Coleman was distressed to discover that one mouse after another was dying. Of course, once one mouse of a pair had died, the second, whose circulatory system was now attached to a corpse, was quick to follow. Coleman assumed he was doing something wrong. "The first few that died, I thought, 'I'm just a damn poor surgeon'—which I am."

He threw out the first three or four pairs that died without further investigation, but as the deaths mounted, he began watching the mice to see what was killing them. His first guess was that, since the deaths were occurring in pairs with one *db* mouse and one normal mouse, the bodies of the mice were rejecting each another. Although both the *db* mice and the normal mice were from the Black Kaliss line, perhaps the two strains were not genetically similar enough to avoid rejection. But he saw no sign of such an immune response in the mice.

Then Coleman noticed that the normal mouse of each dead pair was always very thin, with no fat on it. Nor, he says, did these thin mice have anything in their stomach or intestines. Intrigued, Coleman began observing the mice closely from the time of the surgery, and he discovered that he could see the normal mouse getting visibly thinner within a few days of the operation. Although he could not weigh the animals separately, he could measure the blood sugar of the individual mice in a joined pair, and he found that the glucose levels in the normal mouse fell to a level found only when a mouse is getting nothing to eat. Furthermore, Coleman and the animal caretakers never saw the normal animal in a pair consume anything. "You can't watch a mouse for 24 hours, so you could never prove it didn't eat," Coleman says, but the evidence was overwhelming: the normal mice were starving themselves to death.

Coleman was perplexed. "I started groping through the literature," looking for anything that might offer a clue. Eventually he found that clue in a paper published nearly ten years earlier, in 1959, by G. R. Hervey at the University of Cambridge. Hervey had parabiosed normal rats and rats with lesions in the hypothalamus. As usual, the lesioned animals overate and became fat, but their Siamese twins—the normal rats joined to them—ate much less than usual and became quite thin. Just as Coleman saw in his own rodents, Hervey reported that often the normal animal in the pair would die, apparently from self-imposed starvation.

Hervey hypothesized that the bodies of rats must send some signal through the bloodstream to the brain saying how fat they are, and that if the rat gets too heavy the brain will cut back on appetite until the body returns to an appropriate weight. The lesioned rats were deaf to this signal, Hervey thought, because the part of the hypothalamus that responds to the signal had been destroyed. But the brains of the normal rats in the joined pairs were receiving this signal from the bodies of the connected fat rats, and so they would not eat. In effect, the normal rats believed they were too fat and were trying to lose weight. But no matter how little a normal rat ate, and no matter how emaciated it got, its fat partner was still pumping signals through their conjoined bloodstream saying, "Don't eat." And so the normal rat would starve.

Something similar must be happening in his mice, Coleman decided. The fat *db* mice must be producing large amounts of a "satiety factor" which their brains ignored, probably because the *diabetes* mutation caused some sort of damage to the hypothalamus. A normal mouse attached to a *db* mouse would heed this satiety factor and not eat.

It was a defining moment for Coleman. The original goal of his parabiosis experiments—to find some factor in normal mice that suppressed insulin production—had fallen through. A diabetic mouse that was surgically connected to a normal mouse did take a little longer to develop the disease, but this delay appeared to have nothing to do with any alleviating factor the *db* mouse received from the bloodstream of the normal mouse; instead it was likely due to the shock of the surgery. But in the process of testing this hypothesis about diabetes, Coleman had stumbled upon an entirely new line of research. He had never before been interested in obesity or appetite, but this lead was too good to pass up. For the next decade, much of his time and energy would be devoted to proving that he had indeed seen an anti-appetite factor in the blood of the *db* mouse.

Coleman's parabiosis experiment was published in 1969, but it would not be until 1973 that he got the one more clue he needed to deduce what was really going on in fat mice. In 1971, Coleman had figured out that the diabetes that developed in the *db* mouse was dependent on the type of mouse the mutation appeared in—a full-blown, fatal disease in the Black Kaliss strain, and a mild case or no case at all in Black-6 mice—and in 1973 he had shown that the *obese* mutation causes exactly the same symptoms as *diabetes*, down to the variation of severity between the different strains. Now Coleman understood that the only reason *ob* and *db* had initially seemed so different was that one had been bred into Black-6 and the other into Black Kaliss.

Given this, Coleman decided to repeat the parabiosis experiment with *obese* mice in addition to the diabetic and normal mice. Because he had already bred both the *ob* and *db* mutations into Black-6 lines of mice, he could surgically join them without having their bodies reject each other, and this he proceeded to do. Coleman paired *obese* mice with normal mice, *obese* mice with diabetic mice, *obese* mice with *obese* mice, and, as a control, normal mice with normal mice. Then he let them grow, watching how much they ate, how much weight they gained, what their blood sugar concentrations were, and what their insulin levels were.

The results were published in what is arguably one of the two most important papers in the history of obesity research, the other being the announcement twenty-one years later of the discovery of leptin, which built on Coleman's report and answered the key question raised in it. In his paper, published in 1973, Coleman reported what happened when the various types of mice were joined in parabiosis. If *obese* mice were paired with *db* mice, they suffered the same fate that the normal mice joined to *db* mice had four years earlier: they starved themselves to death. By contrast, when *obese* mice were surgically connected with normal mice, both mice survived, although in these partnerships the *obese* mouse did not get as fat as would normally be expected. Paired *obese* mice gained as much weight as would be expected if they had been kept separate. And two normal mice in union each gained somewhat less weight than normal.

Although at first sight it is not clear what to make of these varying outcomes of the parabiosis, Coleman argued that they pointed almost inescapably to one conclusion. Normal mice, he said, must produce a satiety factor that signals the brain how fat the mouse is and slows down eating when the body gets too heavy. The brain of *db* mouse, as he had previously suggested, does not respond to this factor, so the mouse eats and eats and eats, getting fatter and, in certain strains, developing diabetes. Because the *db* mouse is so fat, its body produces large amounts of the satiety signal in an urgent but unsuccessful effort to tell the brain to go easy on the mouse chow. On the other hand, Coleman said, the *obese* mouse clearly responds to the satiety signal. The wasting deaths of the *ob* mice joined to the *db* mice showed that their brains were receiving the signal that the bodies of the *db* mice were sending, and when an *ob* mouse was joined to a normal mouse it cut down on its eating in response to the more modest amount of satiety signal that the normal mouse produced. Why, then, did an *obese* mouse get obese in the first place? The *ob* mutation, Coleman hypothesized, must prevent the satiety signal from being produced in the first place. Thus no matter how fat the mouse got, its body had no way of telling its brain to stop eating.

This hypothesis, Coleman saw, would also explain why the syndromes caused by the *ob* and *db* mutations were so similar. They were both interfering with the same feedback system designed to cut back on appetite when the body got too fat. An *ob* mouse could not produce the satiety factor, and a *db* mouse could not respond to it, but the end result was the same: the animal kept eating long past the time that normal animals would stop.

Today, the most modern interpretation of Coleman's experiments is slightly different from his reading a quarter of a century ago, but the bottom line is impressively close. Researchers now know that leptin, the hormone that *ob* mice cannot produce, is not a "satiety factor" in the most literal sense of a substance that creates a sensation of fullness or satiety and shuts down eating. Instead leptin is a more general "fat signal" that tells the brain how much fat the body has accumulated. If the body gets too fat, the increased level of leptin circulating in the blood triggers a general lessening of the appetite and signals the body to burn off some of its fat stores. Conversely—and this is an aspect that Coleman had no way of foreseeing—if the body gets too thin, the lowered leptin levels produce an increase in appetite and cause the body to hold onto what fat stores it has.

For nearly twenty years before Coleman's experiment, weight researchers had discussed the possibility that the body had a "lipostat"—a system that maintains a steady amount of fat stores—but no one had any way of testing that hypothesis or tracking down such a system. Now Coleman—who, not being a weight researcher himself, was unfamiliar with the idea of a lipostat—had offered the first compelling evidence that the body does indeed depend on a blood-borne chemical, probably produced in the fat cells and detected in the hypothalamus, to monitor and regulate the amount of fat in the body.

Furthermore, Coleman had provided a way to track down that chemical, if one could assemble the necessary molecular genetic tools: find the chemical whose production the *ob* mutation disrupts. Although it was not clear at the time, even to Coleman himself, this would be the lasting contribution of his work. Today, researchers recognize leptin as being the key element in the system by which the body maintains a stable weight over long stretches of time—the system that Jules Hirsch and Rudy Leibel hypothesized must exist from their weight-gain and weight-loss experiments, and the system that makes it nearly impossible to lose weight and keep it off for any length of time. And Coleman had pinpointed the *ob* mouse as holding the key to leptin.

Some scientific breakthroughs are immediately recognized and hailed by the scientific community and the world at large. The discovery of high-temperature superconductors is one example. The birth of the sheep Dolly, the first mammal to be cloned from a mature, adult cell, is another. Other breakthroughs must wait years or decades to receive their due. Coleman's was of this sort.

It probably didn't help that Coleman was not an obesity researcher. Science is an insular pursuit, and researchers tend to pay most attention to the work being done by other specialists in their particular field. At the time of Coleman's parabiosis experiments, many weight specialists were looking to the mind rather than the body for answers, and because his studies were reported in such journals as *Biochemical Genetics*, the *American Journal of Physiology*, and *Diabetologia*, his findings went unnoticed by the majority of the doctors and researchers worrying about weight. The reigning fad in that field was the externality hypothesis, with its focus on how overweight people responded to external stimuli, and the fact that normal mice starved themselves to death when joined parabiotically to diabetic mice did not seem nearly as germane to the obesity establishment as whether fat people would eat fewer sandwiches than normal-weight people if they had to get up and open a refrigerator to retrieve the sandwiches.

Even among the physiologically minded researchers who were looking at the possibility that obesity is caused by malfunctions in the body's weight-regulation system, Coleman's interpretation of his experiments did not gain much of a following. Several hypotheses were vying with the lipostatic theory to explain how the body maintained a stable weight over long periods of time. One, for instance, held that mice—and probably humans too—regulated appetite according to the amount of glucose in their blood, and particularly the difference between the levels of glucose in the arteries and in the veins. Another suggested that the starting and stopping of eating was part of the body's regulation of its internal temperature. Coleman's experiments supported the idea of a lipostat, but he was walking into an argument that had been going back and forth for years before he had stitched together his first pair of mice, and his data and his opinions were given little heed by the mostly older, more well-known researchers who dominated the obesity field at the time. "I was always the young pup," he recalls.

In response, Coleman set off on a series of experiments that took him much deeper into the details of how mice regulate their body weight, examining such questions as whether obese and diabetic mice maintain a lower body temperature and thus can divert more of their food than normal mice into fat stores. Eventually, he says, he convinced himself that his original hypothesis must be correct: that the fat cells produce some sort of satiety factor that travels through the bloodstream to the brain.

Convincing the rest of the weight establishment would have to wait, though, until the elusive satiety factor could be pinned down. For years Coleman himself looked for it, but he had taken off in a completely wrong direction, hypothesizing that fatty acids—since they are produced by fat cells and circulate in the blood—might be carrying the fat reports to the brain. And so the discovery of leptin would not come until 1994, when the world of obesity research would be shaken up by a young, mostly unknown medical researcher who had been a sophomore in high school when Douglas Coleman first puzzled over why the mice in his parabiosis experiment were starving to death.

FIVE

That Eureka
Moment

Scientific discoveries, like people, have lineages, and the more genealogically minded researchers can trace the ancestors of their own work back through multiple generations. Rudy Leibel and Jules Hirsch, for instance, often describe their work on the metabolisms of the obese as the descendant of eighteenth-century studies by Antoine Lavoisier, who proved oxygen's role in combustion. Lavoisier begat von Voit and von Pettenkofer, the nineteenth-century researchers who studied the thermodynamics of food, who begat Atwater and Rosa, the developers of an extremely precise respiration chamber, who begat others, and so on, leading eventually to Leibel and Hirsch's own work.

The 1994 discovery of leptin has quite a different family tree. One prominent line included the discovery of the *obese* mouse and Doug Coleman's studies of that mouse. A second had its roots in early work on satiety factors.

It was 1937 when a researcher named N. F. MacLagan discovered, quite by accident, one of the first chemicals known to regulate appetite. MacLagan was following up on previous work that had found digestive secretions in the stomach to be regulated by a blood-borne substance released by the intestines. The earlier researchers had shown that by grinding up the intestines of a dog, chemically extracting a portion of the brew, and injecting the extract into rabbits, they could decrease the rabbits' gastric secretions. The chemical purification methods of the time were too crude to isolate the active ingredient completely, so the researchers could not say exactly what it was, but they named it enterogastrone, from the Greek words for intestine and stomach.

What MacLagan found was that when he injected such an enterogastrone brew into rabbits, they ate less. It was not a huge effect, but it was reliable: some substance made by the intestines was acting as an appetite suppressant. MacLagan reported his finding in the scientific literature, but he had other interests, and no one followed up on the appetite-suppressing effects of enterogastrone until the 1960s. At that time, two nutritionists at the Harvard School of Public Health, Zvi Glick and Jean Mayer, repeated MacLagan's work in mice and rats with similar result, but still no one knew what the active ingredient was.

Finally, in 1973, three medical researchers at the New York Hospital-Cornell Medical Center in White Plains, New York, proved that the ingredient of interest was the hormone cholecystokinin. CCK had first been described forty-five years earlier as a substance released by the intestines that causes gallbladder contractions—thus its name, from the Greek words for "gallbladder" and "stimulating." CCK's main job is to help prepare the body for digestion. When released by the intestines in response to the presence of food, it triggers the gallbladder and pancreas to release enzymes that help break food into its component parts. It also prompts the stomach to slow its contractions; without CCK's intervention, the stomach would dump its contents into the small intestines so quickly that they could not be properly digested. All this was known prior to 1973. What the three New York researchers—James Gibbs, Robert Young, and Gerard Smith—showed was that CCK also creates a sense of satiety when it is released from the intestines, and, furthermore, that the effects of CCK on appetite were dramatically larger than any that had been seen for another chemical.

Injecting CCK into hungry rats would cut their feeding by as much as half, the researchers reported. The effect lasted for only half an hour, however, and after that, the CCK-treated rats actually ate more than the untreated rats. As Gibbs, Young, and Smith correctly deduced, CCK is broken apart in the bloodstream rather quickly, and the hunger-suppressing effects last only as long as it does. After the first half-hour, the CCK-treated rats were hungrier than the others because they had eaten less.

The three scientists supposed, as had earlier researchers who had studied the effects of enterogastrone, that CCK exerted its effect on hunger by halting stomach contractions. Since the classic work of Cannon and Washburn, it had been generally assumed that stomach contractions were responsible for the feeling of hunger. It made sense that something that stopped the contractions should thus dampen hunger.

A few months later, Gibbs, Young, and Smith expanded on the work in what would become one of the classic papers on the regulation of eating. They had surgically implanted into half a dozen rats a "chronic gastric fistula," a tube sewn into the stomach and left hanging beneath the rat so that, when the tube was opened, anything liquid in the rat's stomach would drain out. By feeding the rats a liquid diet, the researchers could, simply by keeping the tube open, guarantee that almost none of what the rat was eating made it into the small intestine.

The researchers first kept the fistulas closed and put the rats on a fast-and-feed cycle, giving them no food for seventeen hours and then making liquid food available. Despite the tubes hanging from their stomachs, the rats behaved just like any other rats offered food after a fast. They ate rapidly at first and gradually slowed down until, after ten minutes or so, they stopped eating entirely, groomed themselves for a bit, and went to sleep. Fifteen or twenty minutes later they would wake, eat a bit more, and for the next couple of hours they would nibble—if nibble is the right word for a liquid diet—at their food, taking a bit here and a bit there, never with anything like the intensity of the first few minutes after breaking their fast.

Having established the rats' normal pattern, the researchers then opened the fistulas and repeated the test. Again the rats attacked the food with the usual zest of animals who haven't been fed for seventeen hours, but this time, with their food draining out through the fistulas as fast as they could imbibe it, they did not slow down after five minutes. At ten and fifteen and twenty minutes, they were still stuffing themselves. After twenty-five they did relax a bit, but throughout the test period they ate and ate and ate. They never stopped to groom themselves for any length of time. They never fell asleep. The implication was clear: the act of eating itself was not enough to satiate the animals. The food had to make its way through the stomach and into the intestines before the rats would be satisfied.

To show that the intestines were signaling this satiety by releasing CCK, Gibbs, Young, and Smith injected the hormone into the abdomens of rats that were "sham feeding"—eating the liquid food and simultaneously having it drained out of their stomachs. Once the CCK hit their systems, the rats slowed their eating and, with high enough doses, they stopped altogether, groomed, and took a nap. They were getting no more food into their intestines than before, but now they thought they were. The CCK was telling the rats, "You're full and happy; relax and go to sleep."

Given CCK's powerful effects on eating, it was probably inevitable that someone would try to link it to the *ob* and *db* mice, and, as it turned out, that someone would be Rosalyn Yalow, winner of the 1977 Nobel Prize for physiology and medicine for her development of radioimmunoassays in the 1950s. It would not be her finest hour.

Yalow, who had no previous experience studying the regulation of feeding, was attracted to the subject by a 1976 experiment performed by G. J. Dockray, a physiologist at the University of Liverpool. Using the radioimmunoassay technique that Yalow had pioneered a quarter of a century earlier, Dockray had shown that one molecular version of CCK was found in the brain as well as in the intestines. From this, it seemed reasonable that the two parts of the body might be communicating via CCKs. Perhaps when food entered the intestines, the resulting CCKs traveled not just to the gallbladder, pancreas, and stomach, but to the brain as well. If so, then perhaps CCK shut down hunger not indirectly, by stopping the contractions of the stomach, but directly, by carrying a "You're full" signal to the brain.

The hypothesis was particularly attractive, Yalow saw, because it could explain what was wrong with *ob* and *db* mice. If CCK were the satiety factor that Douglas Coleman had hypothesized a few years earlier, then a mouse that did not produce CCK or whose brain could not detect it would not know when to stop eating. So, with her student Eugene Straus, Yalow set out to check the hypothesis on *ob* mice.

After buying a breeding pair of mice from Jackson Lab, each with one copy of the *ob* gene, Yalow and Straus raised several litters that contained both *obese* mice, with two copies of the mutant gene, and lean siblings, which had one or no copies. For comparison, they also studied several litters of another strain of mice known as LAF-1. If Yalow's supposition was correct, the fat mice should have less CCK in their brains than the others.

To find out, the two researchers relied on a radioimmunoassay of a type that is still standard in the business. The mice are killed, and their brains removed and quick-frozen on dry ice. The frozen brains are then dropped into hydrochloric acid, and this mixture is poured into a tissue grinder, which reduces it to a form that can be tested for CCK. First a preparation of radioactive molecules that have been designed to latch onto CCK molecules and no others is added to the mixture; the brain tissue is then rinsed, which washes away all the radioactive molecules that have not attached themselves to CCK molecules in the brain; and, finally, the researcher measures the radioactivity of the brain tissue. The amount of radioactivity is a measure of how much CCK was in the brain.

When Yalow and Straus were done, the results agreed nicely with what they expected: the *ob* mice had only about a third as much CCK in their brains as their lean littermates, and only about a fourth as much as the normal mice from the other strain. In their article describing the results, published in January 1979 in the prestigious journal *Science*, Yalow and Straus wrote that the study "unequivocally" showed that *ob* mice had less CCK in their brains than other mice and that it "suggested" that the lower levels of CCK in their brain might be the cause of the mice's obesity.

Coleman's satiety factor, it seemed, had been found. There was just one problem: the experiment was wrong. While her Nobel Prize was still warm from the King of Sweden's hands, Yalow was proving that even the best scientists can make mistakes.

It was Bruce Schneider, a young M.D. who had recently left Yalow's lab after spending a couple of years there on a postdoctoral fellowship, who first realized that she had goofed. By coincidence, he himself had been focusing on CCK since moving from Yalow's group to Jules Hirsch's lab at Rockefeller University. Schneider had wondered if *obese* mice might produce a slightly different form of CCK, one that was less effective in producing satiety, and, to test that possibility, he had spent a year and a half looking in great detail at cholecystokinin in mice, both *obese* and normal. By the end of that time he had convinced himself that whatever differences might exist between fat and normal mice, they had nothing to do with CCK. The hormone had exactly the same chemical form in fat and normal mice. Its levels in the brain were exactly the same in fat and normal mice. Indeed, he found, CCK levels in the brain hardly varied at all, no matter what was going on in the rest of the body. They did not change, either up or down, after meals. They did not change after mice had been starved for seventy-two hours. They did not change when mice got very fat. If CCK in the brain played any role in regulating satiety, he concluded, it was a subtle one. A negative result like this, Schneider knew, would not get his work published in *Science*, but that's the way it goes. Much more of a scientist's time than most people would guess is spent simply eliminating possibilities.

Schneider had done this work without knowing that Yalow had plunged into the same area. He first realized that she had toward the end of 1978, when Hirsch returned to his lab after attending a conference in San Francisco where Yalow had presented her CCK data. "She announced that she had discovered the cause of genetic obesity," Schneider remembers Hirsch telling him.

It put Schneider in a difficult position. From his own studies he was sure Yalow was wrong, but he was a young researcher, just a few years removed from his M.D., and she was a highly regarded senior scientist, and one who, as the head of the lab where he had spent his postdoctoral fellowship, was a mentor of sorts to him. "It's terrifying to be getting a different result from a Nobel laureate," Schneider says now, looking back. Science, despite its egalitarian reputation, has a pecking order, poorly defined sometimes and not always adhered to, but quite real nonetheless. Full professors outweigh assistant professors, who outweigh postdocs, who outweigh graduate students. Faculty members at the more prestigious universities outweigh those at second-tier schools, who outweigh those at the rest. And Nobel laureates are at the top of the heap, while recent trainees are way down the ladder. Most of the time the pecking order is not an issue, but when it comes to deciding among conflicting claims, the scientist farther up the ladder tends to be given the benefit of the doubt.

Nonetheless, once Yalow's paper had appeared in *Science*, Schneider decided that he could not let it go unchallenged. He wrote up his own results and published them in the *Journal of Clinical Investigation*. Then he waited.

And waited. At first, he recalls, few people believed his results. Yalow certainly didn't. But other researchers, attracted by the controversy and by the possibility that CCK might play a major role in the control of appetite, repeated the experiment, and by 1982, Schneider remembers, several had confirmed his results. Schneider himself went back and redid the experiments with a different, more powerful technique and got the same answer. CCK levels in *ob* mice were no different from those in normal mice. No one replicated Yalow's results, not even Yalow, who never published on the subject again. The final proof, if further proof was needed, came in 1989. With the advent of more powerful techniques for mapping genes, Schneider and several colleagues were able to prove conclusively that the CCK gene was not involved in the *ob* mutation. Researchers already knew that the *ob* gene, whatever it was, lay on mouse chromosome 6, while *db* lay on chromosome 4; Schneider's group localized the CCK gene to mouse chromosome 9. The mutation that created the *obese* mouse had nothing to do with CCK.

Today, researchers are still not sure exactly how CCK causes satiety. It apparently triggers the vagal nerve, which runs from the gut to the brain, to signal the brain that food is in the intestines. It also seems to act on the stomach to slow the rate at which food is squirted from the stomach into the small intestine, which distends the stomach and adds to a feeling of fullness. And it has a separate, perhaps independent, role in the brain's appetite center, where its injection decreases feeding in lab animals. But it does not travel from someplace in the body through the bloodstream to the brain, as Coleman's satiety factor did.

The dispute between Yalow and Schneider was, from a scientific point of view, nothing more than a sideshow, a spat that was quickly forgotten by all but the principals. On a historical level, however, it played a small but pivotal role in the history of weight research. For, in the middle of all the fuss, a young M.D. arrived at Rockefeller who became intrigued by the question of how weight is regulated and who decided, after playing a minor role in the CCK squabble himself, that his future lay not in ministering to patients but in grappling with the fundamental questions that only basic science can answer.

Jeffrey Friedman is the boy at the head of the class, the guy you'd like to dislike because he's so much smarter than everybody else but you can't because you see how hard he works and you know that in his own mind he doesn't measure himself against you or anyone else but himself. He is brilliant, and he clearly knows it, but he doesn't come off as cocky or arrogant because he is not too impressed with how smart he is. Instead, he appears driven by the fear that somehow, some day, he might fail at something because he didn't try hard enough.

It wasn't always that way. Friedman remembers loafing through high school, doing just enough to stay near the top of his class. He graduated when he was sixteen, having skipped the fifth grade, and entered a joint program between Rensselaer Polytechnic Institute and the Albany Medical College that offered him the chance to earn a bachelor of science degree and an M.D. simultaneously. During his six years there, he found himself doing less and less as he realized that he could get good grades without going to class; his friends called him "the Sponge" because of the way he soaked up information just before the test and still did well. At twenty-two, with his B.S., magna cum laude, and his medical degree, he headed for the Albany Medical Center Hospital for his residency.

Three years later, in spring 1979, he was finishing up a stint as the chief resident in the hospital's Department of Medicine and wondering where he should go from there. He had a prestigious medical fellowship lined up, but, because he had been slow with his application, it wouldn't start for another year. So, with the help of a mentor at Albany, he arranged for a year's research fellowship at Rockefeller, working with Mary Jeanne Kreek.

Kreek, an expert on addiction, gave Friedman the job of learning how to make a radioimmunoassay for beta endorphins, the brain's pleasure molecules, and for help Friedman turned to Bruce Schneider, who had been using the radioimmunoassay technique on CCKs. Whenever Friedman wasn't working on the assay for endorphins—a project that was ultimately unsuccessful—he would help Schneider out with some of the CCK experiments he was performing to test his claims against Yalow's. Friedman often found himself engrossed in discussions with Schneider about what CCK might or might not be doing in the body and how one might go about finding out for sure. "The world of science was opening up to me," he says.

At the same time, the world of science was opening up, period. The revolution in molecular biology was under way, and it was becoming clear to anyone who paid attention how much power was being unleashed by gene cloning and the other tools of molecular biology. Friedman faced a choice. In fall 1981 he was scheduled to start a fellowship in gastroenterology at Brigham Hospital in Boston, which would have served as a nice springboard into a career in academic medicine. But he felt he had found his calling in the research world he had seen at Rockefeller. It engaged him intellectually, but, more important, for the first time he was in a situation where he couldn't coast and still get top marks. "There is no ceiling on the amount of effort to do well in research," he says. Equally important, he sensed that great things were about to happen in the field of molecular biology, and he wanted to be part of it.

Friedman wrote letters to several of the pioneers in the cloning field, asking about a job, but found that no one was interested in hiring an M.D. with a year of research experience. So, realizing that it was the only way he would be taken seriously in molecular biology, Friedman decided to go back to school and signed up for the Ph.D. program at Rockefeller.

He spent four years there working with James Darnell, who, as Friedman remembers, "was among the handful of leading molecular biologists doing cloning," and by 1985 had finished his Ph.D. dissertation on gene expression in the liver—determining which genes are turned on in liver tissue, and which are turned off. By this time he had received an offer to stay at Rockefeller for another year as a postdoctoral fellow. And he had developed a deep-seated interest in the mechanisms by which the body controls eating.

From the time he had arrived at Rockefeller, Friedman says, he had been intrigued by how the body's chemicals shape emotions. There is nothing more cold or impersonal than chemical reactions, and there is nothing more intensely human than emotional states, yet the one clearly influences—some would say completely determines—the other. Kreek's studies of endorphins had offered a glimpse into this enigma, as had Schneider's work on CCK, and the latter work in particular had captured Friedman's interest: What chemical reactions might underlie our sensations of hunger or satiety? This, he thought, was a question he would like to answer.

Throughout his doctoral work, Friedman had continued to talk with Schneider about CCK, and in 1983 he used the expertise he had picked up in Darnell's lab to clone the gene responsible for producing CCK in brain tissue. He showed that it was the same gene that produced CCK in the gut, and he compared the activity of the gene in the two types of tissue. That same year, Friedman demonstrated that the CCK gene did not lie on mouse chromosome 6 and thus could not be the gene responsible for the *obese* mutation, although the result was not published for several years.

Initially, after getting his Ph.D., Friedman focused on CCK, planning to learn everything he could about how and when the body produced it and what controlled its quantity. "I wanted to see if molecular biology could tell us how good a candidate CCK was as a weight-reduction factor," he says. But somewhere along the way another idea had begun to take root, and it slowly began to supplant CCK in Friedman's mind.

For some time he had been watching the cloning work of the molecular biologists with interest. By the early 1980s, researchers had cloned a number of genes from the fruit fly, isolating them from the rest of its DNA and making them available for study. Cloning genes from mammals was much harder because they have so much more DNA for the genes to hide in, but by the mid-1980s molecular biologists were beginning to assemble the tools to do that as well. In particular, Friedman remembers hearing lectures by two prominent cloners, Lee Silver and Lou Kunkel, that convinced him that it should be possible to clone a mammalian gene. This was a suitable challenge, he thought—difficult and demanding the most advanced techniques available, but ultimately feasible.

Furthermore, Friedman knew just which gene he would like to clone. Yalow's failed attempt to prove that *obese* mice suffered from a dearth of CCK had left him wondering, "If it's not CCK, what is it?" He and Schneider had talked about it at some length, and there seemed only one way to get an answer. As Schneider remembers it, Friedman vowed, "I'm going to go and clone the gene."

DNA is often described as a blueprint, and this is a reasonable metaphor since the information necessary to build an organism is contained within its DNA. But perhaps a better way to think of DNA is as a multivolume cookbook. The human genome consists of twenty-three pairs of chromosomes—the volumes—and each of them contains a large number of recipes. Altogether there are somewhere between 50,000 and 100,000 of these recipes, each of which is a gene—a relatively short stretch of DNA that encodes the instructions for making a particular protein. (Proteins in turn are the basic building blocks with which a human or any other organism is constructed.) In most cases the DNA contains two copies of a recipe, one on each chromosome of a pair, and the two copies may provide slightly different instructions. Besides genes, the chromosomes contain stretches of DNA responsible for turning the genes on and off and also a great deal of DNA that seems to have no purpose whatsoever.

Finding and reading a recipe in this cookbook is not easy. Each volume consists of millions of letters in one long string. The alphabet that the cookbook is written in has only four letters—A, C, G, T—so that a short excerpt from the cookbook might look something like this: . . .AATGCCGATA. . . . Each of these letters represents one of four molecules called bases—adenine, cytosine, guanine, and thymine—that are strung together to form a strand of DNA. The sequence of these bases holds all the information necessary to make a protein, so reading a gene recipe amounts to determining the series of bases that constitute the gene.

Today, decoding a gene is a relatively straightforward job—not easy, but usually able to be done with well-established methods. It is the sort of thing that a molecular biologist will hand over to his graduate students as a way of proving they have learned enough to earn a Ph.D. Fifteen years ago, however, when Friedman set out to determine what gene was behind the *obese* mutation, it was not simple at all. Indeed, it was not even clear that it was possible.

The major problem—indeed, the only problem of real difficulty—lay with finding the genes. Somewhere within the three billion letters of the mouse genome cookbook lay a single recipe, a few thousand letters long, that was the gene Friedman sought. Initially, all that was known about this particular gene was that a mutation in it was responsible for the *obese* mice. By the early 1980s, researchers had mapped the *obese* gene to mouse chromosome 6, which limited the search to a single cookbook of a hundred million letters or so, but when Friedman set out to find the gene, that was the extent of what was known about it.

To understand what was involved in the search, it is necessary to understand a bit more about DNA. It is a long, winding molecule which, if you zoom in on a short stretch of it, resembles a spiral staircase without the railing. Untwist the spiral and you find a simple ladder whose outer pieces are the so-called phosphate backbones, twin chains of phosphate molecules that run along the outsides of the strand of DNA. Bridging these two strands and forming the steps on the ladder are the base pairs. Each base pair is a chemically joined couplet of bases, and the chemical attraction between the bases is such that an adenine is always coupled with a thymine and a cytosine with a guanine. Because of this pairing, the sequence of base pairs along a strand of DNA is normally written by listing the bases along one strand; the complementary members of the base pairs are implicit.

As one moves along a strand, each triplet of bases specifies one particular amino acid—CGA specifies arginine, for instance—so that a series of, say, 300 bases will correspond to a chain of 100 amino acids. These amino acids are strung together to create a protein, and each cell contains machinery that can start from a gene and assemble the proper sequence of amino acids. Once it is put together, the strand of amino acids folds in on itself in complicated ways to produce the protein.

Once a gene has been isolated, decoding the recipe is straightforward. The gene is cloned—copied by the millions—and, once enough copies of the gene are available, well-understood techniques of molecular biology are applied to determine the sequence of bases that lie within the gene. But figuring out which small stretch of DNA within the entire genome holds a particular gene is far harder than finding a needle in a haystack. At least a needle looks different than a piece of hay; nothing obvious separates one particular gene from the countless other stretches of DNA that make up the collection of chromosomes in a mouse or a man.

The one exception is the case in which the protein itself has already been identified. Then one can work backwards to find the gene by determining the chain of amino acids that make up the protein, figuring out which sequence of base pairs will specify that chain, and looking for that particular sequence in the chromosomes. In reality, it's somewhat more complicated than this because several different triplets of base pairs can code for the same amino acid, but knowing the sequence of amino acids still provides enough information to locate the gene. Once the gene is found, it can be cloned and sequenced.

But when the protein has not been found, this option is not available, and in the case of the *ob* gene, no one knew what the corresponding protein was. It wasn't CCK, and no one had any other likely candidates. Friedman would have to comb through the haystack.

The only thing that makes such searches possible is the particular way in which the genes from mother and father are passed on to an offspring. Each parent has two copies of each gene (except, in the case of the father, for genes on the X and Y chromosomes, which are not paired). An offspring gets one copy of each gene from the mother and one from the father. When Gregor Mendel, the father of genetics, performed his famous studies on peas in the late 1800s, he decided that the traits determined by genes were passed on independently. The color of peas on a plant, for example, said nothing about whether the peas would be rough-skinned or smooth. In the early twentieth century, however, Thomas Hunt Morgan found that this was not quite right. Certain traits, such as white eyes and miniature wings in the fruit flies that Morgan studied or baldness and hemophilia in humans, tend to be inherited together. The reason, as would later be discovered, is that the genes for these traits lie close to one another on the same chromosome and such neighboring genes are likely to stay together during meiosis, the process that reduces forty-six chromosomes to twenty-three in preparation for forming an egg or a sperm cell.

Morgan, as would many geneticists who followed, observed which traits were likely to be inherited together and how great that likelihood was, and used that information to form a rough genetic map. Two traits that were inherited together had to lie on the same chromosome—if they were not physically connected in this way, they would have no chance of staying together through meiosis—and, furthermore, the more likely they were to be passed on together, the closer they must lie on the chromosome. Morgan's genetic map was the beginning of a broad program that has now resulted in a nearly complete map and sequencing of the human genome: a listing of almost every gene, where it lies on what chromosome, and what its sequence of base pairs is. A map of the mouse genome will not be far behind.

Twenty years ago, though, the genetic maps of mouse and human consisted mainly of blank spaces with the locations of a few genes noted here and there. The organism for which the most complete map had been assembled was the fruit fly, with its brief life cycle, small amount of DNA, and plethora of mutations.

The short time between fruit fly generations made breeding easy, their numerous mutations gave fly geneticists plenty of easily recognized traits that they could use in breeding experiments to see which traits were inherited with which, and the size of the genome—only about a twentieth that of the mouse or the human—made it much easier to construct a closely detailed map. So by the early 1980s, molecular biologists had begun to clone genes from the fly, taking advantage of the detailed genetic maps to zero in on the genes' location.

This work on the fruit fly demonstrated just how useful the new cloning techniques could be, particularly in uncovering details about an organism's development and function, and other scientists began to wish for that power in their own work. Friedman was one of them.

Sitting in his office in September 1997, three years after he discovered the leptin gene, Friedman recalls the tentative beginnings of that project a dozen years earlier. He had initially been attracted to the idea of cloning the *obese* gene in mice by hearing about cloning efforts under way in humans. It was clear, he says, that the technology was far enough along that this was a doable, if very difficult, proposition. "I assumed that if you could clone a gene out of a human, you could clone a gene out of a mouse more easily, if anything." He would soon realize how wrong he was.

Efforts to construct genetic maps for the mouse and human had been hampered by their relatively large genomes, by the lack of mutations and other traits that could be followed from generation to generation, and by the long time between generations compared with the fruit fly and other model organisms studied by geneticists. What made genetic maps feasible in mammals, Friedman notes, was the discovery of various ways to create an almost endless supply of "traits" that could be followed very easily from generation to generation and used in the maps.

The first such technique depended on the ability of certain naturally occurring enzymes that cut sections of DNA at precisely defined points. For example, the enzyme *Eco* RI, isolated from the common bacterium *Escherichia coli*, looks for the sequence GAATTC and snips the DNA between the G and the A. As it turns out, that sequence will pop up hundreds of thousands of times in the mouse or the human genome. Many of those locations will be the same from animal to animal or from person to person, but some of them will vary. One person may have GAATTC at a particular point on chromosome 13, while another has GGATTC at that spot; *Eco* RI will cut the first person's DNA at that point but not the second. And, with a little cleverness, the presence or absence of GAATTC at a particular site represents a trait that is just as identifiable as white eyes in a fruit fly or *ob*-type obesity in the mouse.

The cleverness works this way: A molecular biologist takes a collection of DNA and treats it with the restriction enzyme, which breaks the DNA into segments of varying lengths. Exactly what the lengths are will depend on where the sequence GAATTC appears on the chromosomes. Then, using a well-developed technique called gel electrophoresis, the researcher determines the various lengths of the fragments (or at least of the shorter ones) that have been created by the enzyme's cutting action. This set of numbers—the lengths of the fragments—is a genetic characteristic that varies from individual to individual.

Most important, it is sometimes possible to determine the presence or absence of a sequence such as GAATTC in different animals. Suppose, for example, that one mouse has fragments created by *Eco* RI that measure 250 and 350 base pairs long, while in a second mouse the shortest fragment is 600 base pairs long. It is clear what must have happened: the first mouse has an extra GAATTC near the middle of the 600-base-pair sequence, so that the sequence was cut there in the first mouse but not the second. The extra GAATTC site is a specific characteristic that sets the first mouse apart from the second and which can be used in genetic mapping just as well as any physically observable trait. Indeed, it is actually more useful than many physically observable traits, because such traits are often difficult to identify with certainty—Is this mouse fat enough to be *obese* or not?—whereas the presence or absence of a particular sequence is clear-cut.

The usefulness of these restriction sites goes beyond providing easily identifiable traits for the mapping of genetic characteristics. Because the actual DNA sequence there is known, even if it is only six base pairs long, it is something that a molecular biologist can use as a starting point to work along the strand of DNA. Such sites are called markers because they physically mark a particular spot on a chromosome.

In the mid-1980s, researchers were accumulating such markers in both the human and the mouse genomes. But, as Friedman found out, very few had been found on the mouse. To zero in on the *obese* gene, he would have to use every marker that anyone discovered and create a number of them himself. That in turn would demand a major research project involving the breeding of thousands of mice, so Friedman was pleased when, in the spring of 1986, he discovered a partner who would share some of the effort: Rudy Leibel.

For eight years Leibel had been working with Jules Hirsch, trying various approaches to uncover the physical mechanisms controlling weight. He had already shown, based on retrospective studies of Rockefeller patients, that the reduced-obese had slower metabolisms than people who had never been fat, and he had tested glycerol, a part of the body's fat molecules, to see if it might be the chemical messenger that tells the brain how much fat is being stored in the body. It wasn't, but Leibel was still interested in finding that messenger, and cloning the *obese* gene seemed a promising angle to do it. He and Friedman agreed to collaborate on the search, with Friedman directing the molecular aspects of the project and Leibel being in charge of breeding and tracking the multitudes of mice they would need.

By the fall of 1986, Friedman and Leibel had some preliminary funding for the cloning project and were ready to begin breeding the mice. The strategy was to take two strains of mice, the *obese* Black-6 mice and normal mice from a line unrelated to Black-6, and interbreed them. *Obese* mice have two copies of the mutant *obese* gene, and normal mice none, so that all the children of such pairings would have one mutant gene and one normal. Because mice with one copy of *ob* look and behave like normal mice, there was no way to tell which was which, so these first-generation mice would be mated with pure *obese* mice, creating a second generation half of whom had two copies of the *obese* gene and were fat, and half of whom had one copy and looked normal. Friedman would then look for genetic markers that were usually inherited along with the *obese* gene. These, he could assume, must lie very close to *ob* on chromosome 6. The goal was to find markers so close to the gene that only one or two mice in a thousand would inherit the *obese* gene without also inheriting the marker. Some basic genetic calculations indicated that Friedman and Leibel would need to breed and test about two thousand mice to find markers this close, but, once they had done that, it would be possible for Friedman to pinpoint the location of the *obese* gene to within half a million base-pairs or so, and that would be a small enough section of chromosome that he could then use other methods to capture the gene.

All of this depended upon finding the right markers. If there were no markers close to the gene, it would be impossible to pin down, so Friedman threw himself into the search. He spoke regularly with other scientists studying the mouse genome, attended conferences, and watched everything that was published in the field. He volunteered to serve as coordinator of international efforts to map mouse chromosome 4, on which the *db* gene was known to lie. For a while he also served as co-chair of the committee handling chromosome 6, where the *obese* gene sat, and even when he was not officially involved in keeping track of the chromosome 6 results, he kept in regular contact with the scientist who was. He wanted to make sure he was among the first to hear of any new markers that might be of use.

At the same time, Friedman and Leibel were running a parallel effort to look for the *diabetes* gene, whose mutation had almost exactly the same effect in mice as the *obese* mutation. Friedman also was continuing to work on CCK. That research, he knew, would provide him with concrete results to report—nothing spectacular, but he could count on solid progress and a steady stream of publications, something that is important for a scientist looking to prove himself. By contrast, finding the *ob* or *db* gene would be a major victory, but, if he failed, he could be left with little or nothing for his efforts.

Indeed, for its first five years, his gene search would produce no publications for Friedman. Nonetheless, by 1988 he had decided to go for broke and put all his resources into finding one of the obesity genes. "CCK was a safer bet," he says, "but I didn't want to do anything that would compromise my chances of finding *ob* or *db*."

Looking back on that decision with pride and a bit of awe, Friedman tries to explain why he did it. Part of it was the atmosphere at Rockefeller. It is a place where being good is not enough. Researchers are expected to be seminal. They are supposed to set agendas that researchers at other places will follow. CCK didn't offer much of a chance for this sort of research, but the gene search did. "I knew this was my chance to make my mark," Friedman says.

And, he says, he was curious about what it would feel like to make such a discovery, to feel the flash of eureka that accompanies it. "In talking to senior sci-

Jeffrey Friedman. Photo courtesy of Jeffrey Friedman. Reprinted with permission.

entists, I always wanted to know what that moment was like," he recalls. "I wanted that moment."

By 1991, the team trying to clone *ob* and *db*, which now included a graduate student, some postdoctoral fellows, and several technicians, had found two markers quite close to *obese*. For one of them, labeled *Pax4*, only two mice out of nearly a thousand tested had inherited *ob* without inheriting the marker. For the other, D6Rck13, none of the first thousand or so mice tested had inherited *ob* without also getting the marker. D6Rck13, which would prove to be the key marker in the search, was isolated by microdissection, a technique for creating markers in which a chromosome is cut up into a number of pieces. Nathan Bahary, a graduate student in the group, had been sent to London in 1987 to learn the technique from Steve Brown, one of the few people in the world who knew how to perform the delicate chromosome slicing. "It took a long time to make it work and a long time to find the markers," Friedman remembers. "Years."

Those years were taking a toll on Friedman. "When the project started in 1986," he says, "it was purely joyous. I knew it could be done, and I knew it would be important. It seemed like this great adventure." But by now it was becoming clear just what a gamble he had taken. Other researchers at Rockefeller were beginning to wonder when his research was going to show results, and he was beginning to worry that if he didn't have something soon the funding for his project—provided by the National Institutes of Health and Howard Hughes Medical Institute, with whom he was an investigator—would dry up. "It was clear my career was going to sink or rise based on whether the project was a success," he recalls.

He drove himself harder, and at the same time became increasingly worried that someone else would beat him to the gene. In science there is little glory reserved for second place, no matter how close the finish. "By around 1992 or 1993, whenever I got a phone call from someone I wasn't expecting, I would think they were calling to say someone else had gotten it." He had heard of two or three other groups looking for *obese*, and once another researcher, working from information that Friedman had collected, described a gene at a mouse genetics conference that he thought might be the one. And there was always the chance that someone might simply stumble across it. Researchers were regularly cloning genes whose identities and functions were unknown. If such a "candidate gene" fell in the right part of chromosome 6, it would be relatively simple to determine whether it was *obese*. "Over the years," Friedman says, "several positional cloning efforts [i.e., the approach he was taking] have evaporated at the hands of the candidate gene approach—to the great chagrin of those who spent enormous effort on positional cloning. Because of this, I was always quite vigilant about keeping track of the map position of new genes."

The years had also taken a toll on Friedman's collaboration with Leibel. The two complemented each other nicely, Bahary recalls, since they had different strengths and different weaknesses, but, as the search got closer to its goal, tensions grew between them over just whose project it was, and each grew suspicious that the other was attempting to claim too much credit. In 1992, they agreed to end their collaboration. Friedman would continue the search for the *ob* and *db* genes on his own, while Leibel would continue his own studies of the severe diabetes that *ob* and *db* mice develop. When requested, Leibel would provide Friedman with data about the mice whose breeding he had overseen during their partnership, but he would have nothing else to do with the cloning effort.

As Friedman bred and tested more mice, he found one, mouse 167, that was recombinant for the D6Rck13 marker—that is, it had inherited *ob* without inheriting that marker—but it did have the *Pax4* marker. This was important, for it implied that the two markers were on different sides of the *ob* gene. They bracketed it, pinpointing its location on the chromosome to somewhere between them. The markers were approximately 2.2 million base pairs apart, still too large a region in which to easily locate *ob*, but by 1993, Friedman was able to apply a newly developed tool—yeast artificial chromosomes—to narrow that region down to just 650,000 base pairs. This was a small enough region to start fishing for the gene directly.

At this point, Friedman turned to two other newly developed methods to look for the gene, cDNA selection and exon trapping. The latter technique identifies exons, the segments of genes that hold the specific instructions for building a protein. Large stretches of a gene, called introns, are discarded during the cellular process that uses the information in the gene to produce a protein, and early in 1994 researchers had described a way to grab onto whatever exons lay in a stretch of DNA. Friedman had quickly assigned a member of his team, Ricardo Proenca, to learn the exon-trapping technique, and Proenca generated 200 candidates which Friedman and his team winnowed down to four genes that lay inside the area where he expected *obese* to lie.

If a gene is active in a certain type of tissue—fat tissue, say, or liver tissue—a researcher can detect its presence by looking for the corresponding RNA. The RNA, a molecule closely related to DNA, acts as a middleman in the protein-making process: the sequence of base pairs in the gene's DNA is copied into a sequence of base pairs expressed in RNA (minus the introns), and the RNA then serves as a template for making a protein. Thus, if a cell is actively producing a protein, that activity will be revealed by the presence of RNA with the proper sequence of base pairs.

When Margherita Maffei, another member of Friedman's team, tested the various exons for RNA expression in normal mice, she found that one of them, labeled 2G7, had exactly the pattern they were looking for. RNA corresponding to 2G7 was present in fat tissue but in none of the other tissues they had examined: brain, small intestine, stomach, pancreas, lung, heart, liver, spleen, and testis. "When I saw something that was in fat and nowhere else," Friedman says, "I got pretty excited." But the true test of whether 2G7 was part of the *obese* gene would be how it acted in *obese* mice.

In recounting those final days, Friedman remembers what he was doing and how he was feeling on an hour-by-hour, sometimes almost a minute-by-minute, basis. It is clear that he has told this story a number of times before for other people and, probably, that he has gone back over it by himself a few times as well, savoring the memory.

By the beginning of 1994 a new variant of the *obese* mutation, *ob-2J*, had been found, and Friedman's team was working with both *ob* and *ob-2J* mice. Thus his team set out to test whether the RNA from 2G7 was present in the two different strains of *obese* mice. On May 6, Friedman remembers, he gave a lecture and showed their data up to that point. The next day was a Saturday. Yiying Zhang, another of Friedman's team, ran a test called RT-PCR (for reverse transcriptase-polymerase chain reaction), looking for RNA corresponding to 2G7 in the fat tissue. The *ob-2J* mice had none of the RNA, although the *ob* mice did. Zhang ran into his office to tell him the news.

"All this time," Friedman says, "I had never lapsed into thinking about getting it." He had, of course, thought about what it would mean for him and his career, but he had never allowed himself to fall into full-fledged daydreaming. "I was holding myself back a little." But now his reserve was beginning to crack. Zhang's RT-PCR indicated that the *ob-2J* mice had some mutation that prevented them from translating the 2G7 intron into RNA, which was strong evidence that 2G7 was part of the *obese* gene. But because the *ob* mice were producing RNA from the exon, it was not conclusive proof. That proof should be found, Friedman knew, in another type of test for the presence of RNA, a Northern blot analysis that Maffei had set up. But Maffei was gone for the day, her analysis only half-done. "I went through her desk, I went through her refrigerator, and I found the blot," Friedman remembers. Then he finished the setup for the analysis and left it to cook overnight.

He went home, but he couldn't sleep. By dawn he was on his way back to the lab, and at 6:30 a.m. he was holding the finished Northern blot. "I don't want to be melodramatic about this," he says, "but my whole life was this project." He did have a girlfriend, Lily Safani, whom he had met in the summer of '91 when a friend had convinced him to take a summer share of a house on Long Island. "I developed this [Northern blot] film, and I called Lily up and said, 'We've got it.'"

What Friedman saw was a particular pattern in the Northern blot, which,

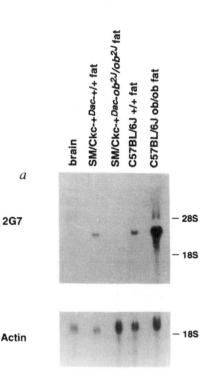

The Northern blot that triggered Jeff Friedman's "eureka moment." Photo courtesy of *Nature* magazine. Reprinted with permission.

unlike the RT-PCR technique, gave a good relative measure of how much RNA was being produced in each tissue sample. Again the *ob-2J* mouse showed no sign of RNA from the *obese* gene. The *ob* mouse, on the other hand, had RNA levels twenty times higher than those in normal mice. Friedman immediately recognized what must be going on. The *ob-2J* mutation was such that no RNA was ever produced from the gene, while *ob* mice were producing RNA from the gene, but, for some reason, the protein made from that RNA was not effective. The fat cells in these mice, in an effort to make the protein, kept increasing the amount of RNA until it was twenty times its normal level. "I knew when I saw this that Coleman was right and this [*ob* protein] would be a hormone," he says.

That afternoon he had tickets to a playoff game between the New York Knicks and the Chicago Bulls. He went, and he still remembers an amazing dunk made by John Starks of the Knicks. Later he and Lily went to Pete's Tavern. "We sat outside and I told Lily and my friend Wayne, 'This is going to be big.' Wayne bought champagne. They sort of believed me and sort of didn't."

Friedman would spend the next six months in the lab, nailing down all his evidence and learning as much as he could about the *obese* gene. Once he had identified it, he was able to map out the precise sequence of base pairs that composed it. He found that the gene carried the instructions for making a protein of 167 amino acids, which he at first referred to simply as the *ob* protein. He discovered that the *obese* mutation was caused by the change of a single base, from cytosine to thymine, which in turn created a "stop" message in the middle of the gene that shut production of the *ob* protein down after only 105 amino acids and made it nonfunctional. As for the *obese-2J* mutation, Friedman surmised that it was caused when a virus inserted some DNA between the two exons that make up the *ob* gene and so prevented the second of the two exons from being translated into RNA. In December, he published his findings in *Nature*, the most prestigious journal for genetic discoveries.

Eight months later in *Science*, Friedman, in collaboration with Stephen Burley, another Howard Hughes Medical Institute investigator at Rockefeller, reported how the *ob* protein affected mice of various sorts. *Obese* mice, which could not produce any of the protein themselves, lost weight dramatically when injected with protein. The *diabetes* mouse, on the other hand, was not affected at all; as Douglas Coleman had predicted more than twenty years earlier, it did not respond to the presence of the *ob* protein. Normal mice given injections of the *ob* protein lost weight to the point that they had almost no body fat. In light of these effects, Friedman proposed that the protein be called leptin, from leptos, Greek for "thin."

In the summer of 1995, Friedman was promoted from associate professor to full professor at Rockefeller and granted tenure, an implicit recognition that he had demonstrated the change-the-world ability that the university seeks. And a year later, having finished the job he had set for himself more than eight years earlier, Friedman got married. "I was not consciously waiting for *ob* to be resolved before getting married," he says now, "but I think that subconsciously I was waiting. It was difficult for me to consider getting married until the *ob* project had come to completion, either by my group or someone else." He has slowed down a bit since then, especially with the birth of Alexandra and Nathalie in the summer of 1998, but his lab remains on the forefront of research into leptin, and Friedman himself is still the main expert on the gene he isolated and the protein that it encodes.

By any measure, Friedman was correct when he told Lily and his friend Wayne that the discovery was going to be big. But even he didn't realize how big.

Five months after his publication of the discovery of the *ob* gene, the drug company Amgen announced it was buying rights to that discovery for a sum that astonished veterans of the pharmaceutical industry. Amgen agreed to an up-front payment of $20 million, reportedly the largest ever made for rights to a university-held patent. One third went to Friedman and six other members of his and

Burley's laboratories, and the other two-thirds were divided between Rockefeller and the Howard Hughes Medical Institute, which was Friedman's employer although his lab and office were at Rockefeller. The deal also specified that Amgen would make future payments if the development of leptin into a drug passed certain milestones—payments that could eventually add up to several times the initial $20 million—as well as royalties on the sale of any drugs developed from the patent. Amgen's hope, of course, was that leptin would prove either to be a useful fat-fighting drug itself or that it would lead to the discovery of other drugs.

The discovery of leptin has also proved to be a major scientific event. Since 1994, researchers in hundreds of labs around the world have jumped into the study of leptin. An October 5, 1999, search of Medline, a database listing all the papers published in major medical and biological journals, found more than 1500 publications with "leptin" in the title.

A surprising number of those actually have little or nothing to do with obesity, at least not directly. It turns out that, because the amount of fat stored has implications for a number of the body's systems, leptin plays many roles besides regulating weight. The timing of puberty is one example. Researchers have long known that prepubescent girls with more body fat begin menstruating earlier than their thinner peers, so it was a natural question to ask whether leptin might play a role. It does. When four researchers at the University of California, San Francisco, treated a group of young female mice with leptin, they found that the leptin-treated mice grew more slowly than the others and had less body fat, but they became sexually mature earlier. Normal female mice are five to six weeks old before they become pregnant for the first time; the leptin-treated mice were a week ahead. Apparently, when a young female's brain is deciding whether to begin the changes of puberty, one of the main signals it pays attention to is the level of leptin in the bloodstream. This makes sense because if a female were to become pregnant before her body had enough fat reserves, it could be dangerous for both her and her baby.

Leptin has also been found to affect both the immune system and the growth of blood vessels. Because malnourishment and starvation hurt the body's ability to defend itself against infection, researchers at Hammersmith Hospital in London tested leptin in mice that had been starved to the point that their immune systems were barely functioning. Leptin returned the immune systems to normal even while the mice were still starving. A group of scientists at three institutions in the United States, reasoning that fat cells must grow new blood vessels in response to changes in the amount of fat stored, tested the effect of leptin on the corneas of rats. Leptin, they found, causes the corneas to grow a network of tiny blood vessels. Presumably, it has the same effect in fat cells, but since it is much harder to detect tiny blood vessels in opaque fat cells than in the transparent cornea, the researchers did not test this.

By far the most important aspect of leptin, however, is the one that Friedman had in mind when he first started looking for it: its role in the body's weight-regulating system as the main signal that lets the brain know how much fat the body has stored. Much of the research on leptin over the past five years has been devoted to understanding exactly what leptin's role is in the body's weight-regulating system and how it works.

After Friedman's cloning of the *ob* gene, his team and others quickly showed that the level of leptin in the blood is closely related to the amount of fat in the body. Fat mice and fat people have higher levels of leptin; thin ones have lower levels. This dashed some of the early hopes generated by the leptin discovery, hopes that the obese might be victims of bodies that, for some reason, did not produce enough leptin. If this were the case, it should be possible to treat obesity by providing leptin, just as insulin-dependent diabetes is treated by providing insulin. As it turned out, however, the obese have leptin blood levels many times higher—sometimes as much as twenty or fifty times higher—than people of normal weight.

The same investigations into leptin levels uncovered two other basic facts. First, levels in the blood vary widely, particularly among the obese. With just a few exceptions, people with low body fat have leptin levels that are close to zero, some of them so close as to be undetectable. If leptin levels are plotted versus body fat, the resulting graph shows an almost exponential growth, from near zero to very high levels. This is nothing more than an average, however, and there are many exceptions. Some obese people have leptin levels that are quite normal, while some mildly overweight people have higher leptin levels than people who are much fatter. The second fact that has come out about leptin levels is that when the obese lose weight, the amount of leptin in their blood drops, sometimes quite dramatically, although again there is wide variation.

Studies of lab animals have shown that leptin levels do, as expected, affect how much an animal eats. If too little leptin is circulating, a mouse or other animal will overeat and put on fat; too much, and it will lose its appetite and lose weight.

The implication of the findings is that the obese, or most of them anyway, have a resistance to leptin. If a person of normal weight had as much leptin circulating in his bloodstream as the average obese person, his appetite would be so depressed that he would eat little and lose weight rapidly. The obese do not do this, which implies that although their brains respond to leptin, the response is muted compared with the brains of thinner people.

Because the obese do respond to leptin, there is hope that leptin treatment could help at least some obese people lose weight. In May 1996, Amgen began

Phase I clinical trials of leptin, and, although this phase of the Food and Drug Administration's drug-approval process is designed merely to test the safety of a drug and see how well it is tolerated by people, researchers performing the trials reported that leptin does indeed seem to help some people lose weight. The subjects who both dieted and received the highest dose of leptin lost an average of nearly sixteen pounds over six months, from an average starting weight of nearly 200 pounds. Subjects who dieted and received a placebo lost only about four pounds. The leptin's effectiveness varied widely, however. Of the eight patients who received the highest dose of leptin, one lost no weight and one actually gained. The implication seems to be that people get fat for different reasons and that the effectiveness of a given treatment will depend on what has gone wrong in a given person's body.

The major downside to leptin treatments for obesity is that it must be injected. If it were swallowed, it would be broken down into its component amino acids in the stomach and would be quite useless. Furthermore, studies of lab animals have shown that leptin is most potent at reducing weight when it is given continuously, instead of as single injections, so a leptin treatment regimen would probably demand several injections a day, or perhaps the surgical insertion of a leptin pump. At some point, a drug company may find a drug that mimics the effect of leptin and can be swallowed, but this is likely many years in the future.

For now, then, leptin as an obesity treatment is no more than a sideshow. The real significance of Friedman's discovery is how it has opened up the entire weight-regulation system to analysis by the tools of molecular biology and biochemistry. With leptin in hand, researchers have started to trace out that system, which until 1995 had been mostly a black box.

Here is what we now know about the body's weight-regulating system. Weight—or, more accurately, fat storage—is regulated in two ways, through appetite and through metabolism, through how much energy you take in and how much energy you expend. There are clearly some relations between the two types of regulation, but they seem mainly independent of each other, with the major connection between them being that they both are tied tightly to the amount of fat in the body.

Eating is itself controlled by two regulatory subsystems, one short-term and the other long. The short-term system oversees when you eat and how much you eat on a day-to-day basis. The purpose of the system is to tie your meal size and frequency to the immediate metabolic needs of your body. Think of it in terms of a financial budget: you may have money saved in the bank that can be drawn on if it is needed, but it's better to pay for your day-to-day living expenses out of day-to-day earnings.

The short-term system weighs a number of factors before sending a hunger signal: changes in the concentration of blood sugar, body temperature, blood levels of various amino acids, and levels of various hormones. After one has eaten, the satiety signals generated by the presence of food in the stomach and intestines play their own role in this short-term system. CCK, the hormone that Rosalyn Yalow suspected as the culprit in *obese* mice, is mainly a satiety factor and acts mainly in the short-term regulation of eating.

The long-term system has quite a different job, which is to keep the body's reserve of energy stores stable. It does not concern itself with such transitory issues as how much glucose is in the blood but rather with how much fat the body is carrying, a number that changes much more slowly. Depending on the amount of fat stores, the long-term system will push the short-term system this way or that. If the fat stores drop too low, it will act to increase hunger; if they get too high, it will make hunger less than it would normally be and perhaps bring on satiety earlier. Leptin functions mainly in this long-term system. High levels of leptin do not act as a satiety factor, shutting off eating in lab animals. Instead, the leptin level is more subtle in its effects, modifying an animal's total daily intake by modulating meal size, altering the interval between meals, and perhaps causing a meal to be skipped altogether.

In other words, the long-term system acts mainly by modifying the short-term system. If you gain weight above your set point, the long-term system makes you less hungry than you might otherwise be, or perhaps causes satiety to occur more quickly than it might otherwise have. If you drop below your set point, the long-term regulator will cause your feelings of hunger to be exaggerated and your feelings of satiety to be attenuated.

In humans, of course, there is another level of decision-making altogether. Somewhere in the cortex the hunger signals generated by the short-term system and modified by the long-term system are combined with all the other factors that influence eating in humans—habits and patterns, time of day, who's around, what else is going on, how good the food looks, how strong the resolve is feeling at the moment—and a decision is made: whether to eat, when to eat, what to eat, how much to eat.

So much is going on in the making of any individual eating decision that it is impossible to separate out the factors. One could never say—truthfully—that "My leptin levels made me eat that cheesecake." But it is possible to look at the cumulative effect of dozens or hundreds or thousands of individual eating decisions and ask why you ended up at 180 pounds instead of 150. And from that point of view, "My leptin made me do it" is a much more defensible proposition.

Many of these general details about the body's weight-regulating system were known even before Friedman discovered leptin, even though no one knew exactly how the brain kept track of fat stores. Friedman's real contribution was to open up the long-term regulatory system to study, and in the past five years researchers have pieced together a much better idea of how it works.

The most intriguing detail to come to light in that time is that the brain seems to have two different neural pathways that respond to changes in leptin, one that kicks in when leptin levels drop and another that reacts when they rise. Both pathways begin in the hypothalamus, the part of the brain that scientists in the 1940s and 1950s burned holes in to create obese rats. If leptin levels drop too low—or, as in the case of the *obese* mouse, are completely gone—neurons in the hypothalamus detect that and send signals out to other regions in the brain that eventually cause various physiological responses to starvation, such as greatly increased appetite, a drop in metabolic rate and body temperature, decreased activity in the immune system, and lowered reproductive function. No one has yet traced out the neural pathways over which these signals travel, but some of their components have been identified. For instance, it is clear that neuropeptide Y, or NPY, is deeply involved in the response to low leptin levels.

For years NPY has been known as an incredibly potent appetite stimulant—inject it into the brain of a rat, and the animal will eat greedily, even if it has recently finished a meal. But in 1996, when researchers at the University of Washington in Seattle genetically engineered mice that did not produce NPY, the animals ate normally and grew to be of normal weight. They were not, as one might predict, any smaller or lighter than mice whose brains had the usual amount of the appetite-stimulating chemical. The dilemma was resolved later that year when the same research team bred their NPY-deficient mice with *obese* mice to get mice that had neither NPY nor leptin. These mice were midway in weight between normal mice and *obese* mice—fat, but not roly-poly. They were also midway in fertility. Whereas few *obese* males and no *obese* females are fertile, a significant minority of both sexes was fertile in the NPY- and leptin-deficient mice. The implication is that NPY must play a role in both the overeating and the infertility that come from a lack of leptin.

The pathway that carries a signal from the hypothalamus in response to high leptin levels is equally obscure, but, again, at least one likely component is known. The melanocortin-4 receptor sits in the hypothalamus and, when stimulated, cuts eating sharply in mice. Conversely, when the receptor is blocked, mice overeat and get fat. And when mice are genetically engineered to lack the melanocortin-4 receptor, they get fat and have very high leptin levels. Apparently, as they gain weight their bodies produce more leptin, but their brains cannot respond fully to the leptin because the melanocortin-4 receptors are gone. The implication is that the melanocortin-4 receptor is one part of the system by which the brain responds to high leptin levels.

Besides leptin, NPY, and melanocortin-4, researchers have identified a number of other chemicals that act in the brain to affect appetite. In 1998, for instance, scientists at the University of Texas Southwestern Medical Center in Dallas stumbled across two neuropeptides—small proteins that carry signals between neurons—that, when injected in the hypothalamus, cause rats to increase their eating as much as sixfold. They named the related chemicals orexin A and orexin B, from the Greek work for appetite. Corticotropin-releasing hormone, or CRH, and the closely related urocortin both have the opposite effect, cutting food intake and leading to weight loss when injected. They seem to play a role in the effect of stress on appetite, but CRH, at least, is also regulated by leptin. When leptin is injected into the hypothalamus, it causes an increased production of CRH, which in turn lessens the appetite. Other chemicals involved in the brain's weight-regulating system—what Friedman has called "the alphabet of weight control"—include melanocyte-stimulating hormone (MSH), agouti-related hormone (AGRH), glucagon-like peptide-1 (GLP-1), bombesin, galanin, and serotonin.

Most of these have effects on appetite, but some also alter metabolism. For example, when NPY is applied to the paraventricular nucleus (a part of the hypothalamus), it slows down a rat's metabolism by attenuating the signals sent by the sympathetic nervous system to brown fat, a type of fat that the rat burns when it needs to increase its body temperature.

Although the way in which these different pieces of the fat-regulating system fit together remains a mystery, we now know that the body has a complex system with leptin at its heart that regulates appetite and metabolism in order to keep the body at a stable, preferred weight. But how does the body settle on this preferred weight, and why is it so high for so many of us? That demands a different sort of answer.

SIX

The Parable of
the Pimas

A century and a half ago, when tens of thousands of Forty-Niners were making their way to the gold fields of California, the more adventurous of them chose the southern route, traipsing through the lower reaches of what is now New Mexico and Arizona and following the meandering east-west path of the Gila River. That route avoided the high mountains of the trails to the north, which could be particularly dangerous in the winter, but it took the traveler through the center of Apache country, which stretched for a hundred miles or so west from the modern Arizona-New Mexico border. The Apaches, who raided neighboring Indian tribes regularly, were nearly as warlike in reality as they were portrayed to be in the old Westerns, and they had little tolerance for the bands of wagon-train adventurers who never asked permission to pass. Many of the fortune-seekers and would-be settlers who crossed into Apache lands would never see the Golden State.

And so it was, the chronicles of that time report, that travelers were relieved and grateful to make it to a verdant stretch of land near where the Gila meets the Salt River, south of what is now Phoenix. There dwelt the Pimas, a group of friendly Indians who had farmed the lands along the Gila for centuries, since long before the first Spanish padres had wandered up from Mexico, looking for savage souls to save. Unlike the Apaches, the Pimas tolerated visitors and even welcomed them. According to one well-known story, when Kit Carson, the famous Army scout, visited the Pimas in 1846, he was told, "Bread is to eat, not to sell. Take what you want." To the California-bound who had survived the Apaches, the Pimas offered supplies for the next part of their journey.

It was not their bread that was most valued by the travelers, however. It was their protection. The stretch along the Gila River on which the Pimas lived was the most fertile agricultural land in the region, and, except for times of drought and the occasional flood, the Pimas were able to grow and gather from the desert more food than they needed. The neighboring tribes — not just the Apaches but Yumas, Yavapai, and Mohave as well — were less well endowed, and they raided the Pimas regularly. As Frank Russell, an anthropologist who studied the Pimas extensively at the turn of the century, reported, "Every three or four days small parties of five or ten would come to steal livestock or kill any individual that might have gone some little distance from the villages. Larger war parties came once or twice a month."

In response the Pimas had developed a militaristic culture in which martial prowess was prized and in which an important part of a boy's education was learning to use the war club and shield. "In those days," an old Pima would write a century later, "a Pima warrior coming toward you holding one of those shields in front of him, jigging, side-stepping, watching every move you made from over the edge of a shield, was considered very dangerous. If you shot an arrow at him, he merely side-stepped, holding the shield at an angle in the path of the arrow. When it hit the shield, it only glanced off to one side. And before you were ready for a second shot, the warrior was upon you, knocking the weapon out of your hand and putting his war club into effective use. A Pima warrior with those weapons was a man to look out for."

The Pimas kept pickets posted around their villages to spot approaching raiders, and a Pima warrior always kept his weapons at hand. It was expected that every so often he would have to drop what he was doing and run to meet a group of raiders. Occasionally, a Pima chief would decide to avenge some outrage and mount an attack upon the Apaches, and then a thousand or more warriors might gather and march upon the enemy's home ground. In the pitched battle that followed, as many as several hundred Indians might be killed.

Given their hospitality to strangers and their willingness — at times it seemed almost an eagerness — to engage their enemies, the Pimas often found themselves in the role of defending those who were weaker or who needed protection. Several decades before the gold seekers passed through on their way to California, the Pimas had welcomed into their lands the Maricopas, a band that had broken off from the Yumas to the west. The remaining Yumas, a much larger group, followed the Maricopas to Pima territory, attacked them regularly for years, and would have annihilated them had it not been for the shields and war clubs of the Pimas. One of the great battles in the Pimas' history came in 1857,

A group of Pima Indian scouts in the late 1800s. Photo courtesy of the National Anthropological Archives. Reprinted with permission.

when an army of Yumas, Mohaves, and other allies marched up the Gila River to assail the Maricopas. The Pimas collected every available warrior to oppose them, and the resulting fray lasted through the day. When it was over, the Yumas had been routed and left more than 400 dead on the battleground—victims of arrows, short lances, war clubs, and knives. (At the time, none of the tribes yet had firearms.) Four years later, a U.S. Cavalry officer who camped on the site of the battle would report that "the ground was strewed with the skulls and bones of the slaughtered warriors." The defeat was so devastating that the Yumas never again bothered the Maricopas or the Pimas.

When Americans began passing through—and eventually settling near—the Pimas' territory, they also were shielded from the Apaches and other aggressive tribes. "Since the year 1849 [they] have acted in the capacity of and with even more efficiency than a frontier military," wrote one observer in 1858. "They have protected American emigrants from molestation by Apaches, and when the latter have stolen stock from the emigrants, the Pimas and Maricopas have punished them and recovered their animals." Meanwhile, many Pima men agreed to serve as guides for the Army in its running battle with other tribes. In 1879, the *Eleventh Annual Report of the Board of Indian Commissioners* would conclude that American settlers "could not have inhabited that region had it not been for the fidelity with which the Pimas and Maricopas constantly defended them against the Apaches."

Many of the modern descendants of those Pima warriors still live along the Gila River, on a 372,000-acre reservation south of Phoenix that was established in 1859. The land has changed noticeably in the 150 years since the Forty-Niners came through. The Gila, whose plentiful waters once made Pima lands so fecund, is now little more than a trickle. It has been diverted by upstream farmers and by the city of Phoenix, which sits just above the northern boundary of the reservation. The strips alongside the river, once covered with fields of wheat, beans, squash, and corn, are now dusty and barren. Away from the river, things have changed less. Mesquite trees, saguaro cacti, and yuccas still dot the desert. The sky is still spectacular, deep blue in day, ebon at night, and, except for the occasional thunderstorm in July and August, almost completely cloudless. And in the distance the mountains squat, low and craggy, still ready for the next band of Apaches to retreat with their plunder.

Like the river and the lands alongside it, the Pimas have been changed by the coming of the white man. Their centuries-old culture is now to be found mainly in books. Everyone speaks English, and only a few remain fluent in Piman. Many in the tribe are Christians, and the rich collection of tales by which the Pimas traditionally explained the creation of the earth and their place on it has been largely forgotten. The old Pima family dwellings, round huts made from sticks and covered with several inches of dirt, are gone. In their place are small, poorly made houses of the sort that you would find in any other impoverished section of the American Southwest. But nothing has changed so strikingly as the Pimas themselves.

When the white settlers first arrived, they found Indians straight out of a Frederic Remington sculpture. The bodies of the Pimas were thin and sinewy, their legs chiseled by regular running, their arms strong from the bow, the war club, and the plow. Today, the Pimas are fat. Not just chubby or overweight, like the average American couch potato, but obese. Fleshy arms. Bellies that hang over belts and push against dresses. Faces so full and round that the strong jaw lines and high cheekbones one sees in photographs from the 1800s have all but disappeared, leaving the adults with gentle, almost childlike visages. The average Pima man in his early thirties is five-foot-seven and weighs 220 pounds. The average woman is five-two-and-a-half and 200. The heaviest weigh as much as 500 pounds. The Pimas are the second-fattest group of people in the world, saved from being the fattest only by the inhabitants of Nauru, an eight-square-mile island in the western Pacific Ocean whose extensive guano-derived phosphate deposits have made the people of that island some of the wealthiest and most leisurely in the world.

Besides being exceptionally fat, the Pimas suffer from a plague of Type II diabetes, the version of that disease that targets primarily overweight adults, and its ravages can be seen everywhere. Because diabetes sabotages the body's ability to regulate the sugar in its bloodstream, blood sugar levels fluctuate widely, leading to such side effects as high blood pressure, kidney failure, blindness, and a gradual shutting down of the blood supply in the extremities, a condition that suffocates the limbs and often forces their amputation. The Pimas have the highest known rate of diabetes in the world. Half of all adults over thirty-five are diabetic—eight times the rate in the general population—and by the time a Pima reaches fifty the chances are about two in three that he or she will be diabetic. Because diabetes strikes the Pimas much younger than the general population, the extra years of battering by fluctuating blood sugar levels results in much more serious complications. On the reservation one finds tribe members in their thirties or forties who are dependent on dialysis, have lost a limb, or have been blinded by the disease. Some don't live to see fifty.

What has happened to the Pimas? The answer can be summed up in two words: Western civilization.

It was 1694 when the first Spanish padres arrived in Pima lands, and from then on the Pimas would be a continuing target of various efforts to civilize them—that is, to make them, in big ways and small, more like their earnest civilizers. Throughout the eighteenth and nineteenth centuries, Christian missionaries were regular visitors to the Pimas and recipients of their hospitality, but it was not until the surrounding area had been settled by American farmers that the civilizing began in earnest.

The Americans, having won the territory containing the Pimas' lands in the Mexican War, insisted that the territory's inhabitants behave in a proper manner. The Pimas, never quite understanding what all the fuss was about, were generally willing to go along. When the town of Phoenix passed an ordinance requiring Indian men, who normally wore nothing more than a breechclout, to wear trousers while inside the city limits, the Pimas responded by stashing some overalls in a mesquite thicket just outside the city limits. Whenever a Pima man went into Phoenix he would retrieve a pair from the thicket and put it on; upon leaving, he would disrobe and leave the overalls for the next Indian. Later, when the Indian Department demanded that Pima men build adobe houses and cut off their long hair before they could receive free wagons from the government, the Pimas gradually acquiesced. And when the government opened schools on the reservation—a day school in 1871, and a boarding school in 1881—Pima parents sent their children, reasoning that it was important for them to learn about the outside world. But the one factor that put the Pimas on the road to obesity was the establishment of the Gila River reservation.

By the late 1850s a growing number of settlers were putting down stakes along the river, and the U.S. government sought to minimize the tension between them and the friendly Indians by delineating which land belonged to the Pimas—and which did not. At first the Pimas, who numbered about 4000 at the time, resisted the idea, arguing that the entire Gila River valley was theirs. But after assurances that the reservation would include all their villages and agricultural lands and that these domains would thus be protected from any encroachment by the settlers, the tribe agreed.

The reservation would not, however, include surrounding lands that the Pimas used for hunting and gathering and which were particularly vital to the tribe in those years—about one in every five—that drought shrunk the Gila to a trickle. Taking those lands away from the Pimas would limit the tribe's access to many of its traditional nonfarm foods. Even worse for the Pimas, the agreement did not secure them water rights to the Gila. Accustomed to thinking of the river as something that nobody owned or could own, the Pimas probably never imagined they needed to worry about getting a fair share of the Gila's water.

By the mid 1860s a number of settlers had set up farms a few miles upstream of the Pima reservation and began taking water from the river to irrigate their fields. A few years after that, several mines and smelters were built farther up the river to take advantage of mineral lodes that had been discovered there, and these diverted even more water from the Gila. Finally, beginning in 1874, a group of Mormon farmers set up shop yet farther upstream, near the New Mexico border. These demands on the Gila's water, combined with a severe drought that lasted through much of the 1870s, reduced the Gila to a dry bed where it ran through the Pima reservation.

It was during this drought that many of the tribe left the land of their ancestors and moved north to the Salt River. It still had plenty of water, and the Mormon settlers who lived along it had invited the Pimas to share. It was not a disinterested offer—the Mormons were looking for protection from the Apaches—but it was nonetheless one that the Pimas found attractive. In 1879, the Salt River Indian Reservation was established, just east of Phoenix and abutting what is now Scottsdale. Ironically, the long drought ended that same year, and a large percentage of the refugees returned to the Gila valley. Today, Pimas can be found on both reservations, but the majority live on their original lands along the Gila.

It is both fascinating and depressing to read through the tribal chronicles of the second half of the nineteenth century and see the rapid changes in the Pima culture that followed the influx of white settlers and the building of their cities near the Indian villages. Although the tribe had no written history, it did keep "calendar sticks," three- to four-foot long wooden staffs with a long series of notches and carvings that the stick's keeper used to help him remember various events and the years in which they occurred. Some events recorded on the sticks were important, others seemingly trivial, but all that made it onto the sticks had been deemed worthy, for one reason or another, of being remembered. Thanks to the anthropologist Russell, who interviewed two keepers of calendar sticks and recorded their narratives, we have a record of Pima chronicles from 1833 to the turn of the century.

In the early years, the narratives consist almost exclusively of fights with the surrounding tribes. From 1835–36, for instance: "One summer afternoon, when only women and old men were at home, the Apaches came and killed two Pimas, a man who was irrigating his field, and a boy who was hunting doves." Or from 1851–52: "Two Apaches were discovered near the Maricopa village by Whyenânâvim, a Maricopa warrior, who killed one of them before they could escape. The Pimas went on a campaign against the Apaches on Salt River, near where the present reservation is located, and one of their number was killed."

The earliest mention of a plague was in 1844–45, when cholera swept through the tribe. "Those stricken with it usually died within twenty-four hours, but if they recovered they were well again in three days. From four to ten died each day." Later, epidemics caused by contact with the outside became almost common- place: in 1860–61, "a plague which killed its victims in a single day"; in 1866–67, "a sickness characterized by shooting pains that resembled needle and knife pricks" and, later the same year, "a devastating fever"; in 1867–68, malaria; in 1871–72, measles, which was deadly to many of the Pimas; in 1875–76, a repeat of the sickness that caused shooting pains; in 1876–77, smallpox; in 1882–83, another bout with measles; in 1884–85, an epidemic that the calendar stick keeper did not specify; in 1896–97, smallpox; and in 1898–99, measles again. Until the 1890s it was normal for the tribe to blame a plague on malevolent med- icine men. If an epidemic stayed too long or killed too many, the tribe decided which medicine men must be causing it and put them to death. Sometimes that didn't work and a second purge was necessary, but eventually the epidemic would stop.

Beginning in the late 1870s, several years into the drought that had left the Pimas hungry and anxious, the chronicles begin to mention tribe members being killed in drunken fights. The Pimas had always brewed and drunk alcoholic bev- erages during the saguaro harvest, but otherwise intoxication was frowned upon, and killing another Pima—except a medicine man who was using his magic to harm others—was disgraceful. By the late 1880s, however, the combination of *tizwin*, the Indians' home brew, and homicide was so common that it could be noteworthy when nobody died: "Tizwin was made at Gila Crossing," Russell recorded for the year 1888–89, "but no one was killed in the resulting debauch." The drunks and the trouble makers were never more than a small minority of the tribe, Russell says, and the other Pimas scorned them, but their presence indicates the strains in Pima society as more and more of its traditional foundations crumbled away.

By the beginning of the twentieth century the Pimas were already a much different tribe. Peace with the Apaches had been established years earlier, and they had become a less warlike, more sedentary people. They still farmed along the banks of the Gila and Salt rivers, but the unpredictability of the water supply had made them partly dependent on trading posts and government programs for their sustenance, and this introduced new, white man's foods into their diet. They relied less and less on provisions gathered from the desert, and the hunting and trapping of large animals was gradually dying out as the animals themselves were becoming more rare, although rabbits, hares, and quail remained staples.

It was at this time that the first mention of the Pimas being overweight appears. In 1905, Russell wrote that the Pimas were "noticeably heavier than individuals belonging to the tribes on the Colorado plateau to the north and northeast, and many old persons exhibit a degree of obesity that is in striking contrast to the 'tall and sinewy' Indian conventionalized in popular thought."

There are few records concerning the Pimas over the next several decades. A poor and mostly forgotten people, they did continue to receive government support, but they were not drafted during World War I and were not granted U.S. citizenship until 1924. Still, researchers who study the Pimas have pieced together the essentials of their story during that period.

Over time, the Pimas' diet gradually shifted away from wheat, beans, squash, and produce gathered from the desert and began to resemble that of the rest of the country. Beginning in the 1930s, federal and state programs provided high-fat foods such as bacon and cheese. After World War II, the U.S. Department of Agriculture expanded the types of foods supplied to include milk, canned meats, fruits, vegetables, and dry cereals. Gradually traditional dishes such as cholla bud stew, made from the dried buds of the cholla cactus, and posole, whose main ingredients are crushed wheat kernels and tepary beans, were joined by—or sometimes supplanted by—such modern delicacies as cheddar cheese melted over a flour tortilla, corned beef with gravy, and ground beef cooked with macaroni, onion, and canned tomatoes. Researchers at the National Institute of Diabetes and Digestive and Kidney Diseases (NIDDK) in Phoenix have estimated that the traditional Pima diet took about 70 percent of its calories in the form of carbohydrates, 15 percent in protein, and 15 percent in fat. By the 1950s the proportions had changed to 61 percent carbohydrate, 15 percent protein, and 24 percent fat. In 1971 it was 44 percent carbohydrate, 12 percent protein, and 44 percent fat—a tripling of the fat content.

Meanwhile, the Pimas were also cutting down on physical exertion.

"Fat Louisa," an early victim of the Pimas' genetic propensity to obesity. Photo courtesy of the National Anthropological Archives. Reprinted with permission.

Historically, they had always been an active people. Farming with primitive tools is hard work, as is hunting and gathering, and the constant fighting with other tribes—particularly the need to get to a battle quickly and, if necessary, to retreat quickly—demanded being able to run long distances without tiring. It was not until late in the nineteenth century that the Pimas or other Indians in the area had more than a few horses, so pursuing, attacking, and fleeing were done almost exclusively on foot. From the time they were young, Pimas practiced running, and one of their favorite games was a race in which each participant kicked a small ball on the ground in front of him as he ran. The shorter races were about a mile; longer ones could stretch for twenty-five miles or more. After the turn of the century, the running games became less and less common and finally disappeared. The Pimas did, and still do, continue to farm, but the percentage of the tribe involved in agriculture declined, and, as with farming in the rest of the country, the introduction of mechanized farm machinery made the labor less and less strenuous for those still tending the fields. Today the Pimas engage in no more physical activity than other Americans.

The twenty years following World War II seem to have been a critical time for the Pimas. By all accounts, before the war it was still relatively rare for a Pima to be obese, although no one seems to have made specific measurements of the Pimas' weight during that time. Similarly, diabetes was uncommon before the war, and here the evidence is more definite. In 1905 Russell's extensive report on the Pimas made no mention of diabetes, although he listed twenty-eight other diseases that affected the tribe's members, from acne and eczema to cataracts and consumption. In 1940, an epidemiologist tracking the occurrence of diabetes in Arizona saw no greater prevalence among Pimas than in the general population. But by 1963 the rates of both diabetes and obesity among the Pimas were so high that when the National Institute of Arthritis, Diabetes, and Digestive and Kidney Diseases—NIDDK's predecessor—stumbled across them while surveying the Pimas for rheumatoid arthritis, the institute quickly made the tribe the focus of an entirely new program. Within two years the institute had in place a project to track, study, and treat the diabetes and obesity among the Pimas. Since then, surveys of the Pimas have traced a steady increase in both obesity and diabetes above already high rates of the early 1960s.

The researchers who study the Pimas believe it was the Second World War itself that triggered the massive changes among the Pimas. When the United States mobilized to fight the war, it brought the Pimas into close contact with the surrounding American society, so that when the rest of the country entered the affluent postwar years, the Pimas would jump in too. In the decades leading up to the war, the Pimas had been a poor people, struggling to survive, and thus had been mostly bypassed by the changes taking place in the rest of the country. But the war opened up a new, modern world to them. Pima men and men from other Indian tribes were drafted into the armed services, where they fought side-by-side with white soldiers (even as black soldiers were being kept in their own units). Many of the Indians who weren't drafted still left the reservations to go to work in factories. And the federal government leased a site on the Gila River reservation to house and feed 15,000 Japanese-Americans who had been forced to leave their homes on the Pacific Coast in the wake of fears that some might aid a Japanese invasion. The Japanese community, run by a staff of 150 white Americans, was Arizona's fourth-largest city during the war.

The paychecks from the armed services and the factories and the rent checks from the federal government fueled a short-lived economic boom on the reservations and provided a taste of prosperity that few Indians had sampled before the war. When the war was done, the checks stopped, but the taste would remain. Henceforth Pima society would embrace increasingly large chunks of American popular culture: clothes, music, cars, movies—and food. But their taste for the Western life would prove more expensive than anyone imagined.

For any individual Pima, it is perfectly legitimate to speak of that Pima's weight in terms of his or her set point—how the brain has decided for one reason or another that the correct weight is some fifty or a hundred pounds above what is healthy and how it resists attempts to lose weight below that point. But when faced with the magnitude of what has happened to the Pima tribe, a whole people struck by an epidemic of obesity, this focus on the individual seems somehow beside the point. What one really wants to explain is the plague itself, not the details of how it affects any one person. And for this there is perhaps no better approach than to look halfway around the world to another desert and another set of desert dwellers who also suffer from the Pimas' plague.

The sand rat is found throughout much of the North African and Arabian deserts, from Algeria and Sudan eastward through Egypt and into Israel, Jordan, Saudi Arabia, and Syria. By appearance it is a rather nondescript rodent, but its lifestyle is notable. Making its burrow at the base of a saltbush plant, the sand rat gets all of its nourishment as well as all of its water from the leaves of the saltbush. This arrangement allows the sand rat to stay close to his burrow and avoid wasting energy foraging for food, but the saltbush leaves make a severe diet. Not only are they quite salty, up to twice as salty as sea water, but they are low in calories and in nutritional value, which compels the sand rat to spend most of its time feeding—removing a leaf, scraping off the salty outer layer with its teeth, chewing and swallowing the inner portion, then repeating the performance over and over, eating half or more of its weight in saltbush leaves each day. The advantage of this choice of food is that the saltbush leaves offer a dependable, year-round supply of food, and one that no other desert rodents will touch.

When sand rats are captured and raised in a laboratory instead of the desert, an appalling transformation takes place. Raised on regular rat chow, the bland fare developed to provide lab rodents with all their nutritional needs, sand rats born in the lab will overeat to the point that they weigh twice what their desert cousins do. They become so fat that their bellies drag on the ground, their insulin levels rise to dangerous heights, and they develop diabetes. Many die young, and, among those who live long enough, their eyes become clouded by cataracts to the point that they cannot see.

The parallels between the sand rat and the Pima are obvious—two desert creatures brought into a luxurious life find themselves fat and diabetic—and, indeed, scientists believe that precisely the same forces are at work in the two situations. But by focusing on the sand rat instead of the Pima, we can see just how far we can go in explaining these developments without bringing such messy complications as consciousness and free will into play.

Although scientists are still piecing together the specific physiologic details of why the sand rat becomes fat and diabetic, the broad outlines of it are clear.

Having evolved to exist on a diet of saltbush leaves, which are low in caloric content, the sand rat is extremely thrifty in its use of energy. Its basal metabolic rate is low compared with other rodents, even other desert rodents, so it expends less energy in maintaining basic bodily functions, and it is superefficient in storing any excess energy as fat, which enables it to maintain energy reserves even with a diet that offers little energy to spare. These adaptations allow the sand rat to thrive on a diet that would starve another animal, but the same adaptations make rat chow a deadly feast. Eating rat chow provides many more calories in a much smaller volume of food than the sand rat is designed to handle, and the sand rat eats more than it needs and transforms the excess into fat. The extra calories also prompt the insulin-producing cells in the sand rat's pancreas to pump out large amounts of insulin. Eventually, as blood sugar levels rise higher and higher and the pancreas tries frantically to produce enough insulin to process it, the insulin-producing cells fail under the strain, and diabetes sets in. Many chow-fed sand rats die of the disease by eight to ten weeks of age, barely into rat adulthood. Death by affluence.

The researchers who study the Pimas believe they suffer from a very similar "thrifty gene" malady. For hundreds or thousands of years before the white man arrived, the Pimas had lived in the desert, dependent upon native plants and animals and whatever they were able to raise by farming along the Gila River. When the rains failed, as they did twice a decade on average, the crops dried up and even the desert was less bountiful. If a drought lasted more than a year or two, starvation loomed. So, as with the sand rat, the Pimas most likely to survive were those with efficient metabolisms and whose bodies stashed away a little something extra in times of plenty. The ancestral Pimas who would been best suited for our modern world—who would have stayed lean and healthy in the face of corn-fed beef, dairy products, and sugared sodas—died off in the periodic famines because their bodies had not kept enough reserves.

For centuries or perhaps millennia, then, having a body that was more efficient at using energy and storing fat was an advantage for those among the Pima tribe. This caloric efficiency helped keep Pimas alive in times of famine, and it never really hurt them because their low-fat, low-calorie diets and their active lives kept them relatively lean even when food was plentiful. But in the second half of the twentieth century, when the Pimas' eating and exercise habits came to resemble those of the rest of the United States, the efficiency backfired. Now, day after day, year after year, the Pimas' bodies are socking away a few extra calories for a famine that never comes. They, like the sand rat brought into the laboratory, are victims of a mismatch between the environment for which their bodies are designed and the environment in which they live.

No one knows which particular genes are at fault in either the Pimas' or the sand rat's increased propensity to get fat (although a number of researchers are performing genetic tests on the Pimas in hopes of finding them), but there is no doubt that genes are to blame. And, more generally, several decades of research have shown that genes play a major role in determining how likely any of us are to become fat. For years geneticists have been studying groups of related people—parents and children, siblings, and twins—and measuring how similar they are in terms of fatness or thinness. The most common measure of fatness in these studies is body mass index(BMI)—weight in kilograms divided by the square of the height in meters. In general a BMI of 25 or below is considered normal to thin; 25 to 30 is overweight; and over 30 is obese. A person who is five-foot-nine and 155 pounds has a BMI of 23; five-foot-two and 174 pounds works out to a BMI of 32.

When genetics researchers compare the BMI of siblings, they find them to be much more alike than the BMIs of people who are not related to each other. To make sure that this similarity is not due simply to siblings having been raised in the same household and taught to eat the same way, researchers also compare adopted siblings, who grow up in the same home but are not related. Adopted siblings, it turns out, are not much more alike than people who have never met, and, once the adopted siblings leave home and live apart, even that small similarity disappears. As difficult to believe as it may be to those who blame their eating habits on mom or dad, one's family environment has almost nothing to do with how much he or she will weigh as an adult. If it did, adopted siblings would be more similar.

By contrast, identical twins who were separated at birth or shortly afterward and who were raised apart have BMIs that are very close. Since the twins are being raised by different sets of parents in different homes, often in different cities, the closeness of their weights must be due almost completely to the fact that they share the same set of genes.

The standard way that scientists express the importance of genes in determining a trait such as BMI is in terms of the trait's "heritability"—in essence, a measure of how much of a trait's total variation among a group of people is caused by the genes. In the case of BMI, studies of identical twins reared apart imply a heritability of about 70 percent. That is, on average, about 70 percent of the difference in BMI from one person to the next is caused by genetic differences. This is exceptionally high, and it implies that genetics play a major role in determining a person's weight. By comparison, the heritability for IQ is about 50, as are the heritabilities for a number of personality traits, such as thrill-seeking behavior or anxiety.

It's easy to get carried away with that 70 percent figure—which is, admittedly, quite impressive—and conclude that genes are almost everything in determining what a person weighs, but it's not quite that simple. Several caveats are in order. First, the 70 percent figure is still being debated. Genetic studies other than the separated-twin work sometimes find much lower heritabilities—as low as 30 or 40 percent. Still, researchers in the field tend to find the separated-twin studies to be the most persuasive because they are the most direct and demand the fewest assumptions, so the heritability seems likely to be closer to 70 percent than 40. And even if the lower figure is correct, even 30 or 40 percent heritability implies that genes play a major role in determining what someone weighs.

A second qualification is that all of the calculations about heritability are statistical ones, done by looking at dozens or hundreds of subjects, and they say nothing about individuals. You cannot tell yourself that your genes deserve 70 percent of the credit, or the blame, for your weight, and, indeed, that statement does not even make sense. As you are growing up, genes and environment interact in a complex way to create the person you become, and it is impossible to separate out the influence of one from the other. Only by looking at groups of people is it possible to, in effect, average out the effects of the environment and isolate a figure for the genetic component.

A third and most important thing to remember is that the heritability figures are calculated for groups of people growing up in roughly the same environment. Although the twins in these studies have been separated and reared separately, they are still raised in the same country, often the same city, as their siblings, so they are exposed to similar foods, similar eating customs, similar messages from the popular culture. Perhaps the best-known study of identical twins reared apart, which was published in 1990, analyzed twins born and raised in Sweden. Because Sweden is a relatively homogeneous society, most of the twins were exposed to very similar environmental influences growing up, and so one would not expect the environment to play a large role in causing differences in weight. If it were possible to do a separated-twins study in which, say, one of each pair of twins was raised among the Pimas and the other among the !Kung San, a hunter-gatherer tribe in the Kalahari Desert, then the environment would be seen to play a much larger role. The subjects raised among the !Kung San would all be thin because of the tribe's diet and active lifestyle, while those who grew up among the Pimas would have a range of weights, from thin to fat, depending on their own genetic heritage. When the twins raised apart were compared with the twins raised together, the calculated heritability would be much smaller than 70 percent, perhaps as little as 10 or 20 percent. So the statement that BMI is 70 percent heritable means that, in a given cultural environment such as Sweden or the United States, genes explain on average 70 percent of the variation in BMI from one person to the next; it does not mean that genes explain 70 percent of the variation in BMI across all countries and all cultures.

In other words, the 70 percent figure can be deceptive because it downplays the importance of the environment. And if there is one lesson to emerge from the experience of the Pimas, it is that the environment is by far the most important factor in determining whether someone will become fat.

Somewhere between 700 and 1000 years ago, the ancestors of today's Pimas split into two groups. Some ended up in Arizona; their descendants would shelter the Maricopas, play kickball, and eventually settle down on the Gila and Salt River reservations and grow fat. Another group retreated to a remote mountainous region of northern Mexico, where they seldom had contact with the outside world and where they are still leading lives much like those of their distant ancestors. Genetically, the two groups of Pimas are indistinguishable—they have not been separated long enough for appreciable differences to have appeared. So in 1991, when researchers from NIDDK in Phoenix had a chance to collaborate with a Mexican scientist to study the Mexican Pimas, they grabbed the opportunity.

The Mexican Pimas live in the village of Maycoba, 500 miles south of the Gila River reservation. Hidden in the Sierra Madre mountains, a mile above sea level, Maycoba can be reached only by four-wheel-drive vehicles. When the NIDDK team first visited the village, it took them ten hours to drive there from Hermosillo, the capital of the state of Sonora and the nearest large city. Later, when the Mexican government opened a winding but paved road that cut through the Sierra Madres relatively close to Maycoba, the trip would be reduced to just five or six hours. The Pimas in Maycoba have no electricity, no running water. They grow corn, beans, and potatoes in the traditional way, using hoes to cultivate small plots of land. They raise vegetables in small gardens, and they breed livestock.

Despite their remoteness, the Maycoba Pimas are not completely untouched by the outside world. Many of them leave the village to work on ranches, in mines, or in road construction. And they supplement their home-grown foods with products purchased from the outside: eggs, powdered milk, shortening, coffee, even sodas. It would seem as if these Pimas live in a world much like the one that Frank Russell described for the Arizona Pimas at the beginning of the twentieth century: still mostly a traditional culture but one that is being steadily encroached upon by the outside.

When the researchers from Phoenix compared the physical characteristics of the Mexican Pimas and the Arizona Pimas, they found the Mexican tribe to be very much like what their Arizona cousins must have been like a century earlier. The Mexicans are a couple of inches shorter than the Arizona Pimas of today, and far thinner: the men tested in Maycoba weighed an average of 153 pounds versus 199 for a group of similar-aged men at Gila River, and the women 132 pounds versus 188. A few of the Mexican Pimas were obese, but the very fattest would be classified as only average-obese among the Arizona Pimas of the 1990s. And diabetes is still relatively rare among the Mexican Pimas, although more common than among the general population: out of sixteen men and nineteen women tested on the original visit, only one man and two women were diabetic.

It would be a mistake to hear these comparisons and conclude that the Pimas of Mexico lead some sort of idyllic, back-to-nature existence. "These people have a very tough life," says Leslie Schulz, one of the NIDDK team that traveled to Maycoba. They live in unsanitary conditions and, partly because of that, are often ill. "And," she says, "I don't remember a single [Mexican] Pima who can read or write, or even sign their name." But their near-traditional lifestyle does shield them from the obesity and the diabetes that a more affluent way of living has visited upon the Arizona tribe. Unfortunately, it seems inevitable that as civilization, with its fatty foods and labor-saving devices, trickles into Maycoba, the Pimas there will grow fatter and fatter and will suffer more and more from diabetes, cardiovascular disease, and other illnesses of affluence. But for now, at least, they remain protected by their poverty, living a life close enough to the one their bodies are adapted to.

The comparison of the Arizona Pimas and their Mexican cousins spotlights the almost irresistible power of the environment to shape weight, not just among the Pimas and perhaps a few other groups with thrifty genes, but for everyone in the developed world. To one degree or another, we all face the same mismatch between the environment for which we were evolved and the environment we have created for ourselves to live in. To one degree or another, we all are suffering from the Pimas' plague.

Modern humans evolved as hunter-gatherers, dependent for their nourishment on the supply of game and on whatever fruits, nuts, berries, roots, leaves, and other vegetable matter was available. Because little in that diet was high-fat or high-calorie, and because its supply was variable, our distant ancestors faced the same pressures—albeit to a smaller degree—that the more recent ancestors of the Pimas did: Their bodies must have been able to operate efficiently and to maintain a certain energy reserve even when subsisting on the normally low-fat, low-calorie diet of a hunter-gatherer, and when a large animal was killed and eaten, their bodies must have been ready to store that fat for leaner times.

For hundreds of thousands of years, as long as humans lived as hunter-gatherers, they had no trouble with diabetes or obesity. The evidence for this is circumstantial, but convincing. Among the few tribes today who still follow the hunting-gathering way of life, for example, researchers have found no cases of obesity. And in prehistory, the one exception to this rule seems to be the people who produced the well-known Paleolithic "Venus" figurines, small statues of usually very obese women, presumably representative of fertility. But, according to the anthropologist Peter J. Brown, these people—who may well have been the first humans to get fat—were probably not the nomadic hunter-gatherers they are often assumed to be, but instead had established permanent settlements from which they hunted large animals such as reindeer and the woolly mammoth and at which they stored food for times of scarcity. In the main, obesity seems not to have appeared until after the development of agriculture and never to have affected more than a small percentage of any population until recently, when industrialized economies have created a luxurious living environment unlike anything ever seen before.

It is a sad irony. It has often been said that humans are very adaptable creatures, and that is true. We can live in the Tibetan highlands, in the rain forests of Brazil, in Europe during the Ice Age, or in the Sahara Desert today. And because of this adaptability, we have always assumed that we could create almost any sort of environment for ourselves and thrive. We have also assumed that whatever environment we created for ourselves would likely be an improvement over what we had. Today, however, we have run smack into the limits of our adaptability. We have created for ourselves an environment—a food-rich, activity-poor environment—that makes a great number of us sick, and so far there has proved to be little we can do about it.

The idea that the modern world's labor-saving devices and overabundance of food have something to do with obesity is not new, of course. It has long been recognized that decreasing activity levels and the increasing availability of food make it easier for people to get fat. But there is more, far more, to the role of the environment than simply making it easier for people to get fat, and understanding the current epidemic of obesity demands seeing that role in a different way than it is usually seen.

Most often we think of the environment as little more than a backdrop against which we live our lives. It may constrain our choices, giving us the opportunity to do certain things—eat cheeseburgers, sit in front of a television—and not others—skirmish with the Apaches, suffer through periodic famines—but it does not really affect who we are. If we were born 200 years ago or 2,000 we would be the same people, just wearing different clothes and doing different jobs.

But that is not true. Our genes, except for very simple cases such as hair color or the shape of our noses, represent no more than possibilities or probabilities. The ultimate outcome—which scientists call the phenotype, to distinguish it from the genotype, or the genetic instructions—depends on our interaction with the environment as we are developing. Take two genetically identical rats and, immediately after weaning, start feeding one on a tasty, high-fat diet and put the other on rat chow. When they reach adulthood, the first will be heavier, so put him on a diet until he weighs no more than the other. Now take these identical twin rats who weigh exactly the same and let both have as much as they want of a high-fat diet that encourages overeating. The first one, the one that ate the fatty foods as a juvenile, will grow to be much fatter than the second, which will get chubby on the high-fat diet but never truly obese. Their different environments have transformed the first rat into an animal that is "naturally fat" while leaving the second relatively resistant to weight gain.

The environment is not a passive setting for, but rather an active player in, an organism's development, and if we are to understand what has happened to the Pimas—or what is happening to much of the rest of the country's population—we have to take into account the way that the environment shapes and molds a person into something different from what he would have been in another setting. From this perspective, the Pimas are fat not because they eat fatty foods and don't get enough exercise—although that is certainly the immediate cause—but because the environment that molds them has changed from traditional Indian to modern Western, and when that modern Western environment gets hold of people with thrifty genes, the result is no less in doubt than what happens with the sand rat.

This is an important distinction. If one thinks of the Pimas' obesity in terms of their eating and exercise habits, the focus is placed on individuals and the choices they make, and there is certainly a place for this approach. When a doctor is counseling a patient, for instance, the focus should be on that patient's choices, for that is all—short of drugs or surgery—that the doctor has to work with. But it makes little sense to explain the differences between the modern Pimas and those of 200 years ago in terms of choices. Two hundred years ago the Pimas were not being born to diabetic mothers whose high blood sugar levels were fattening them up even before birth. Two hundred years ago Pima children were not raised with television and fast foods. Two hundred years ago an adult Pima couldn't have eaten a diet that was 40 percent fat even if he or she had wanted to, and physical activity was a way of life, not a doctor's prescription.

The same thing is true for all of us, although, because of genetic differences, it is not quite so strikingly obvious in the general population as among the Pimas. As our environment has changed, we have become a different people, but this is something that most people—even many obesity researchers—have not yet come to grips with. To read most of what is written today about obesity, one would think that we are still the same generally thin people we were 200 years ago, except that the temptations of the world have put a few extra pounds on some of us. In short, the old image of a thin population is seen as still being the norm, and our current overweight condition is an artificial one — we have been displaced from the norm by too many doughnuts and too few push-ups, but we could get back there easily enough if we only knew the right techniques. Those same old skinny people are just hidden under several inches of adipose tissue.

But there is a new norm now, a few dozen pounds heavier than it used to be. Look around: the overweight and obese people you see are not anomalies. They are the natural result of the world in which they grew up and in which they live. They are the people of the early twenty-first century, and there will only be more of them as time goes on. By remaking our environment, we have remade ourselves. We are the sand rats in the laboratory cages. We are the Indians trapped in the white man's lifestyle. Any rational plan to solve our problems with weight must start from this basic understanding.

SEVEN

Setting the
Set Point

Early in 1999, weight research made the news when three doctors
from the Mayo Clinic offered the latest in a long line of possible explanations for
obesity. After recruiting sixteen volunteers, twelve men and four women, the
researchers had determined how many calories a day each needed to maintain
his or her weight and for eight weeks fed each of them 1,000 calories a day more
than that. By the end of the experiment they had overeaten a total of 56,000 calories — enough to tack on sixteen pounds of fat, if every calorie could have been
stored away as adipose tissue. Not surprisingly, every one of the volunteers gained
weight, but some gained much more than others. One was nine pounds heavier
at the end of the six weeks than at the beginning, while another put on only thirteen ounces. The rest were spread out between those two extremes, gaining an
average of six pounds apiece.

This itself was not news, of course. Many times before scientists had fattened
up volunteers and noticed that some had an easier time gaining weight than others. But this time the three scientists, James Levine, Norman Eberhardt, and
Michael Jensen, had added an extra twist: they were able to say with some certainty what happened to all the calories that had not ended up as fat.

To do this they measured how much energy each subject was expending daily,
both before and after the period of overeating, with a technique called doubly
labeled water. Then, like Leibel and Hirsch several years earlier, they measured
their subjects' basal metabolic rates and also the thermic effect of food — how

many calories their bodies burned to digest their meals. By subtracting the basal metabolic rate and the thermic effect of food from the total daily energy expenditure, they could calculate how many calories each subject was burning in physical activity.

The twist that set this experiment apart from earlier ones was the researchers' further subdivision of the physical activity into exercise activity—running, walking, biking, climbing stairs, and so on—and nonexercise activity, which included everything else. Assuming that some of their subjects might increase their activity level, either consciously or unconsciously, once they started gaining weight, the researchers told the subjects that they could do no exercising—no jogging, no biking or swimming, no rowing or stair-climbing—and they enlisted family members and coworkers to spy on the subjects to make sure they were keeping their word. The researchers also put pedometers on the subjects for a couple of days to get a measure of how much they were walking around. In this way they could be sure that the subjects' physical activity—at least that part of the activity that set off the pedometer—remained approximately constant throughout the experiment. They had no way of measuring the nonexercise activity directly, but by keeping the exercise activity constant, the researchers could assume that any increase or decrease in the total calories burned in physical activity was due to what they termed NEAT: nonexercise activity thermogenesis.

At the end of the eight-week experiment, the researchers weighed and measured their subjects and looked at where the extra calories went. Just under 40 percent, on average, had ended up as fat and another few percent as lean body mass, mostly the muscle and support tissue needed to take care of the extra fat. The remainder—about 570 of the extra 1,000 calories a day—had been burned off, and, by comparing the metabolic measurements from the beginning and end of the experiment, the researchers could determine how the body had used this energy.

Some of it had gone to increased basal metabolic rates. By the end of the experiment, the subjects were spending about 5 percent more calories each day—or about 80 calories per day—for their bodies' basic housekeeping chores. The subjects were also burning an average of an extra 140 calories to process their daily meals, which wasn't surprising, since they were processing 1,000 calories a day more than they had been. But the largest jump in energy use—about 330 calories per day, on average—was spent on nonexercise physical activity. In other words, the researchers calculated that their subjects had burned off about a third of the extra calories they had eaten simply by increasing the sort of physical movement—fidgeting, standing up, sitting down, and so on—that was too subtle to be picked up by a pedometer.

This all was interesting but not surprising, given what other researchers, such as Leibel and Hirsch, had reported. What set this study apart—and what got the attention of headline writers across the country—was the tremendous differences in energy expenditure that the three researchers observed among their subjects. Some of them had little increase in NEAT as they gained weight—one even saw a drop—while others had large jumps. One subject was burning nearly 700 calories a day more in nonexercise physical activity at the end of the experiment than at the beginning, about the same amount that would be burned in running seven miles a day. That's a lot of fidgeting. Not surprisingly, this subject gained only two pounds. The subject who gained only thirteen ounces over the course of the experiment was burning an extra 600 calories a day in NEAT and also had significant jumps in his basal metabolic rate and the thermic effect of food.

Overall, Levine, Eberhardt, and Jensen concluded, it was the difference in the NEAT between the subjects that explained most of the difference in weight gain. Those whose bodies responded to the overeating with extra fidgeting or other nonexercise activity gained the least amount of weight; those whose NEAT remained stable gained the most.

Interestingly, the four subjects with the lowest change in NEAT during the experiment were the only four females who had taken part. If that represents a true difference between men and women and not just a fluke, it could mean that women's bodies put up less natural resistance to gaining weight than men's when they eat too much.

The area that Levine, Eberhardt, and Jensen were exploring is the last great unknown in weight research: Why do people get fat? And, more specifically, why do some people get fat and others do not? This is a very different question from asking why people who have gotten fat find it so hard to lose weight. The answer to this latter question lies with the set point and with lifestyle habits that people form over a lifetime. But the original weight gain is a different matter, and the why of it is still a mystery waiting to be solved.

Here is what we know. People's bodies have a preferred weight, a set point, that they will defend against any push away from it, either up or down. The set point defense includes both changes in metabolism and changes in appetite. Despite its name, the set point is not truly set. It tends to drift upward as you get older, and in some cases it will jump more sharply, rising steadily over months or years, until it finally settles in at a new, higher weight. There is even some evidence that the set point can be adjusted downward, but, if so, it is only with hard, conscious, sustained effort.

If you are not consciously watching your weight, you will tend to remain at your set point. Many people stay ten or twenty pounds below their set point by dieting and exercise. Depending upon their commitment and tenacity, they may maintain this lower weight for months or years, but if they lose focus, their weight will start to climb. Some people can even maintain a weight fifty or a hundred pounds below their set point, usually through a combination of rigid calorie-counting and regular exercise, but these are exceptional sorts for whom weight is a constant obsession. In rare cases—football players, say, or sumo wrestlers—a person will maintain a weight above his set point by consciously overeating. Here, too, staying away from the set point demands constant attention, and the body's natural tendency is to push back to where it is more comfortable.

But what sets the set point? And when? Is it set at birth, or is it responsive to influences during childhood and even adult life? If doctors are to have any hope of keeping people from getting fat in the first place, instead of simply trying to help them lose weight later on, they need answers.

Unfortunately, there aren't any. No one really knows why some people get fat and others don't. The answer is a work in progress, and the best we can do is sketch out its current, very incomplete status.

Three forces shape how much you or I or anyone else weighs. The environment in which we live, our genes, and our behavior—the choices that we make throughout our lives. We do not know just how these forces fit together, but we do have these isolated fragments whose significance and place in the larger framework is not clear but which plainly have some role. So we shall proceed to view some of the fragments that seem today to be most important.

The starting place is the one detail that everyone agrees with: The root of our weight problems lies with the cushy environment that we in the Western world have created for ourselves. One could track the march of Westernization across the globe by observing the percentage of overweight. Indeed, the average BMI of a country's population is probably as good a measure of Westernization as any single number you could come up with. But what is it in particular that makes Western civilization so fattening? No one knows for sure, but we do have some clues.

The most popular candidate for explaining our widening waistlines is the amount of fat in our diets. Nutritionists say we should get somewhere between 10 and 20 percent of our calories from fat, about what traditional societies have done. The eighteenth-century Pima Indian diet, for instance, had about 15 percent of its total calories from fat. But today, people in Western countries generally get 30 to 40 percent of their calories from fat, and studies have shown that people offered a high-fat meal will consume more calories than those given a low-fat version of the same meal, even when the two meals seem identical.

High-fat foods encourage overeating in several ways. Fatty foods tend to taste better, so people eat more of them. You may leave some broccoli on your plate because you feel full, but you still manage to have room for that double fudge chocolate cake. Fatty foods have a higher energy density—that is, they pack more calories into an ounce—than other foods, so you can ingest more calories before you start to feel full. And some researchers have suggested that while the body regulates its carbohydrate intake, monitoring how many carbohydrate calories come in and sending out satiety signals when they reach a certain point, it does not regulate fat intake. If this is the case, then a person would have to eat more of a high-fat, low-carbohydrate meal to feel satiated than a person eating a low-fat, high-carbohydrate meal.

The effects of a high-fat diet have been demonstrated in a number of studies on animals. In one experiment, half of a group of squirrel monkeys were fed commercial monkey biscuits, which have 13 percent fat, and the other half were raised on high-fat foods, with from 21 to 31 percent fat content. At four years of age the monkeys were tested. Those raised on the biscuits had just 7 percent body fat, while the others had ballooned out to 30 percent body fat—more than four times as much.

Something similar may happen in humans. No one has taken a group of people and fed them high-fat diets, but several researchers have tried the reverse, putting subjects on low-fat diets and seeing what happens. In one such trial, reported in 1994, scientists from the University of Minnesota School of Public Health taught overweight women to cut the amount of fat in their diets to 20 grams a day, or about a fourth of what they had typically been eating, while allowing them to eat as much as they wanted of foods rich in complex carbohydrates and low in fat. Over six months, the women lost an average of nearly ten pounds, slightly more than another group of overweight women who had been put on low-calorie diets.

Strangely enough, and despite all the evidence about the short-term effects of fat in the diet, we have no direct proof in humans that a high-fat diet will by itself lead to overweight and obesity. Similarly, and equally strange, researchers have not been able to prove that, over the long term, less fat in the diet will lead to a weight loss. The University of Minnesota scientists found, for instance, that the weight lost by their subjects in the first six months gradually returned over the next year, so that by the end of eighteen months they were back where they started. It is not known whether the patients backslid and started eating high-fat foods or simply began eating more of the low-fat stuff, but other long-term studies in people have found the same thing: switching someone to a lower-fat diet does not guarantee weight loss.

And, indeed, the experience of the United States as a society indicates that weight gain and loss are not as simple as the amount of fat in the diet. Since the 1970s, the average percentage of fat in the American diet has been steadily declining, as people have become more health-conscious and food producers have pushed low-fat versions of everything from milk and bread to ice cream and candy bars. Yet the U.S. population has gotten much fatter during the same time. In the early 1970s, one out of every four adult Americans was overweight; by the early 1990s, that number was one out of every three. Or, by the new, stricter definition of overweight offered by the National Institutes of Health in 1998, the number of overweight adults grew from 46 percent of the population in the early 1970s to 55 percent during the early 1990s. Things were even worse in the higher weight categories, as the percentage of the population that was obese—at least 20 percent above a healthy weight—almost doubled during that twenty-year stretch, from 13 percent to 23 percent. It's hard to see how cutting the amount of fat in the American diet has helped.

Not everyone is willing to believe these numbers. The idea that we could sharply cut the amount of fat in our diets and get much fatter is so counterintuitive that many experts have questioned it, and the debate over what really happened during those twenty years can get quite detailed and arcane. For example, the percentage of fat in the American diet is not an easy number to calculate, and people disagree on just how much it has changed. One survey, the Nationwide Food Consumption Study performed by the U.S. Department of Agriculture, reported that the amount of fat in the American diet declined from 40 percent of calories in 1977–78 to 33 percent in 1994–95. But another study, the National Health and Nutrition Examination Surveys conducted by the National Center for Health Statistics, saw a drop less than half as large, from just under 37 percent in 1971–74 to 34 percent in 1988–91. Both of these surveys are based on food-recall questionnaires, and people—particularly obese people—are known to consistently report eating less food than they really do, so the numbers cannot be completely trusted. It's possible that with the growing realization that fat is bad for you, people have fudged even more on how much fatty food they eat, so that the apparent decline in fat is merely a collective self-deception on the part of American eaters.

In short, although there is good evidence that high-fat foods cause people to overeat at a single meal and that they lead to obesity in some lab animals (although not in others), it has been surprisingly difficult to prove a connection between our high-fat diet and the current plague of overweight and obesity. Most researchers suspect that fat must be playing some role, but they can't say exactly what. Perhaps only certain people are vulnerable to high-fat diets, or perhaps the decrease in fat consumption has come about because so many of the overweight have tried to improve their diets by cutting out the fat. They got fat initially by eating too much fat and then, worried about their weight, they went low-fat, but it was too late. Once the set point was pushed up, it would not come back down in response to a low-fat diet.

If fatty foods are not driving the fattening of America, a number of other potential culprits remain. It could be something as simple as the growth in portion sizes and the easy availability of tasty, inexpensive foods. At 7-Eleven you can get 44-ounce Super Big Gulps and 64-ounce Double Gulps of Coca-Cola—enough sugar in one large cup to last you for a week. At McDonald's you can get anything super-sized except the booths. In cities and, increasingly, in small towns it is possible to get food quickly and conveniently at any time of day and night. People driving around in their cars don't wait until they get home to eat; if they're hungry, they pull into a Taco Bell and grab a little something for the road. And almost all of the convenience foods are energy-dense—high-calorie, if not also high-fat.

It seems reasonable that this cornucopia pushes people to eat a little more than their bodies need, but if this is what is making people fatter, there should have been an increase in caloric intake over the past several decades, and the nutrition surveys don't show it. If anything, they find a slight decrease in calories in the average American diet. Again, however, these surveys depend on people reporting how much food they ate in the previous twenty-four hours, which is open to all sorts of errors. Furthermore, it doesn't take many extra calories to fatten someone up. If, as the Mayo researchers calculated, 40 percent of the calories you eat above your maintenance requirement are destined to end up as fat deposits, a surplus of only 100 calories a day would add four pounds within a year, forty within a decade. It is conceivable that the average American is eating 100 calories a day more than in 1970 and the nutrition surveys have missed it, but we have no way of knowing that. For now, at least, the connection between easily available, large-portion food and the obesity epidemic is nothing more than conjecture.

Given that we seem to be cutting back on the fat and calories in our diet but we keep getting fatter, a number of researchers have suggested that the culprit behind the obesity epidemic may be not our diets but our lack of physical activity. Historically, other societies have had plentiful food, but the couch-potato and desk-potato syndromes we have today are unique. Our cars, our televisions and computers, our leaf blowers, our riding lawn mowers, our self-propelled vacuum cleaners—all of these make it easier for us to get through the day without doing something that might leave us out of breath or cause us to break out in a sweat. And, unlike the situation with calories and fat in our food, there is no sign that things have gotten better over the past two or three decades. Year by year the average American exerts himself less and expends less energy in physical activity, with no sign of a turnaround.

This decline in physical activity could fatten people up in a number of ways. The most obvious is that a less active person burns fewer calories. The difference in energy expenditure between a person who exercises regularly and a person whose job and hobbies are sedentary can be hundreds of calories a day—in many cases, 1000 or more. Of course, people who are active must eat more than the sedentary types in order to have the energy for all that running around, but on the whole they still come out ahead.

One of the great misconceptions about exercise and weight is that physical exertion causes an increase in appetite that makes a person eat more, canceling out whatever weight loss might come from exercise. The exercise-appetite connection has been studied in great detail in rats. It is true that normal-weight rats that get a normal amount of exercise will respond to extra exercise by eating more. In this way they keep their weight stable even as they are burning more calories than before. But below a certain exercise threshold, this effect reverses itself. Rats that have not been exercising respond to a new exercise program by eating less and losing weight. The few studies done on humans generally find the same thing: inactive, overweight people who start an exercise program will eat less and lose weight. Reasoning from these studies, it seems likely that if people become less and less active, at some point their appetite will no longer drop enough to counter the decrease in energy expenditure, and they gain weight.

Physical activity also appears to affect weight by altering how much energy the body burns while at rest. People who exercise regularly have higher resting metabolic rates than those who don't. Various types of exercise, particularly weight lifting and other strengthening activities, build muscle mass, which in turn increases the body's basal metabolic rate. And there is some evidence that exercise decreases the appetite for fatty foods. In all of these ways, exercise helps a person lose weight.

Still, despite the experimental evidence, it has been difficult to prove the converse: that being overweight is the result of not getting enough exercise. What we do know is that the obese tend to be less active than the non-obese. The classic study of this connection was performed in the early 1960s by Jean Mayer, a professor of nutrition at Harvard and one of the early giants of weight research. Mayer and his colleagues took motion pictures of teenaged girls at two summer camps on Cape Cod. One of the camps, Camp Seascape for Girls, catered to overweight teens. The other, Camp Wono, had girls of mostly normal weight. When Mayer reviewed movies of the girls swimming, playing tennis, and playing volleyball and rated, second by second, how much energy each girl was expending, he found the non-obese girls to be far more active. During swimming periods, for instance, an average of only 9 percent of the obese group were swimming at any one time; the rest were standing and talking or walking casually in the water. By contrast, typically 55 percent of the non-obese group would be swimming.

Such studies are not conclusive, however. For one thing, they are inconsistent. Over the years a number of such studies have found a difference as Mayer did, but others have found obese subjects to be just as active as their non-obese counterparts. It seems to vary according to the type of activity and also on how fat the obese subjects are. Those who are only moderately obese may have activity levels similar to the non-obese. The biggest problem with these studies, however, is that they cannot distinguish between two equally likely possibilities: that people get fat because they are not active enough, or that fat people are less active because exercise is less fun for them, or less comfortable, or demands more effort.

The bottom line is that no one can point to a particular factor and say with confidence, "This is why people are getting fatter." Which, when you stop to think about it, should not be not surprising. The various factors are all interconnected, pushing on each other and being pushed on in turn. Activity levels reflect weight, and weight reflects activity levels. Appetite shapes body weight, and body weight influences appetite. Activity levels alter appetite. And on and on.

Perhaps the best we can do is to draw two safe, if rather tepid, conclusions about the precise ways that our Western society pushes people toward obesity. First, it is almost certainly a combination of factors, not any one thing by itself. The decline in physical activity is surely a player, as is the increase in fatty foods in our diet. The cultural influences that spur people to eat more—the oversized servings, the easy availability of food, the emphasis on convenience and eating whenever you want—probably also play a role, but it is very difficult to test that.

The second conclusion is that we will not find any one-size-fits-all explanation. Different people get fat for different reasons. Some may be particularly susceptible to a high-fat diet, others to the effects of a sedentary lifestyle, some to overfeeding as an infant, others to the wealth of food choices as an adult. And, of course, some people don't get fat at all, despite eating just as badly and exercising just as little as anyone else.

To explain these differences, one must look to the genes.

In the early 1990s, researchers at the Pennington Biomedical Research Center in Baton Rouge, Louisiana, set out to see how different strains of mice respond to a high-fat diet. They ordered ten each of eight strains of mice from the Jackson Laboratory—Black-6, DBA, and six others—as well as ten mice from a strain bred at the Roswell Park Memorial Institute in Buffalo, New York. Once the mice were about a month old, each strain was divided into two groups of five. One group in each strain was fed the standard Purina Rodent Chow, and the other a modified chow that was high enough in fat to practically congeal their little rodent arteries overnight. Served in pellets that looked much like their usual food, the high-fat diet contained 47 percent rodent chow, 44 percent sweetened condensed milk, 8 percent corn oil, and 1 percent corn starch. For seven weeks the mice were allowed to eat as much as they wanted of their respective diets, then they were killed, dissected, and their fat content analyzed.

Of the nine strains, six had grown quite chubby on the condensed milk diet. Among the Black-6 mice, for instance, the mice fed the modified chow had an average body fat content of nearly 22 percent, compared with less than 9 percent for those who had been eating the usual stuff. Surprisingly, though, three of the strains had resisted the effects of the high-fat diet. Indeed, in two of the strains, the rats fed the modified chow actually had lower average body fat than the others, although the differences were small enough that they could be chalked up to chance.

The lesson here is an important one, and often overlooked: Environmental factors such as high-fat diets may cause obesity, but only in the presence of genetic susceptibility. In the example of the nine mice strains, a majority of the animals were indeed susceptible to high-fat diets, but some of them, for reasons the researchers could only guess at, were able to subsist on corn oil and sweetened condensed milk with impunity.

The field of weight research is rife with such stories. While squirrel monkeys get fat when raised on a high-fat diet, cebus monkey do not. Among dogs kept as pets, Labradors and, to a lesser degree, cairn terriers and cocker spaniels are the breeds most likely to become fat, while German shepherds, greyhounds, and Yorkshire terriers are the least likely. A Labrador is four times as likely to be obese as a German shepherd. No one knows why dogs get fat, but the best guess is that it is for much the same reasons as their owners: high-fat diets, not enough exercise, or the easy availability of too much food.

Among humans, of course, something very similar happens. Some "breeds"— the Pimas and certain other American Indian tribes as well as the inhabitants of various Pacific islands—get much fatter on the Western lifestyle than do others. And in general, not just among populations but among individuals within a population and even among individuals within a family, genes play a large role in determining who succumbs to the environmental pressures to get fat.

In one classic study, a precursor to the fidgeting work at the Mayo Clinic, Canadian researchers recruited twelve pairs of identical twins and had them overeat by 1,000 calories a day for twelve weeks. At the end of that time, the subjects—all young males—had put on an average of eighteen pounds, but the gain varied widely from subject to subject. The least that any of the subjects gained was nine pounds, the most twenty-nine, and the rest were scattered between those two extremes. Within the pairs of twins, however, the weight gain was not nearly so random. Most subjects gained about the same amount of weight as their twin did, to within a few pounds. Clearly the genes had a lot to say about how much each person gained from the forced overfeeding.

Well into the 1980s, genetic studies of weight were mainly concerned with the general question of how important genes are in the development of overweight and obesity. Since the answer to that question has become clear—genes are very important, though not all-important—researchers have turned their attention to tracing out the particulars of how genes influence weight. Which genes are involved? Exactly what do they do? How do they interact with the environment? And what can we learn about the genetics of obesity that will point to ways to prevent it? Weight researchers have taken two tacks to find the answers.

The first of these is a straightforward search for the genes that affect weight, the expectation being that once these genes have been discovered, it will be possible to study their structures, map out what they do and how they do it, see how they interact with other genes, and determine how different versions of the genes lead to different physiological characteristics. The leptin gene is the big success story of this approach, of course. As we have seen, its discovery allowed researchers to understand why the *obese* mutation causes obesity in mice—and in a few humans—and has also opened the door to an exploration of the entire weight-regulating system. Unfortunately, it has not offered a direct explanation of why some people get fat and others don't, since almost everyone has the same version of the leptin gene.

Since the isolation of the leptin gene in late 1994, researchers have identified a number of other genes that do seem to affect a person's tendency to gain weight. None of these genes plays a major role, but each adds a little piece to the picture of how weight is controlled.

In August 1995, for instance, three different teams of scientists announced simultaneously that the gene for the beta-3-adrenergic receptor plays a role in the development of both obesity and diabetes. The beta-3-adrenergic receptor sits in fat tissue and, when signaled by adrenaline or a related chemical, turns on a fat-burning process inside the fat cells. All three teams reported subtle differences between subjects with a particular version of that gene and people who had the more common version. Those with the less common variant of the gene were likely to have lowered metabolic rates, had earlier onsets of diabetes, and—among a group of very obese subjects—had gained more weight over their adult lives than comparison subjects. It is not a particularly rare mutation—depending on the population it affects anywhere from one in every ten people to one in every four—and its consequences are weak enough that some studies do not even see an effect, but quite a few researchers have examined the gene now, and the consensus is that it is an—admittedly minor—obesity gene.

This sort of very subtle effect may well be typical of the obesity genes that will be discovered in the coming years. Genetic studies imply that a large number of genes have a role in shaping how much a person weighs, and most of them have only bit parts. That makes sense—the body's control of its fat levels must involve or touch on many different systems in the body, most of which are likely to affect weight only indirectly.

There is, however, tantalizing evidence that at least a few genes exist that wield a major influence on body weight. No one knows yet what they might be, although it's a good guess that one or two will have some connection with the leptin system. If researchers were to find such major genes, it could help doctors predict which people are most at risk of becoming obese and eventually lead to truly effective treatments. Otherwise, if there are no major obesity genes and only dozens of minor ones in which the interaction is more important than the independent actions of the genes, it will be difficult to find a simple treatment.

Even if major obesity genes exist, though, the genetic research implies that it will not be enough simply to isolate the genes and understand them individually, for much of the power these genes wield over us arises from how they interact with each other. The evidence comes from twin studies. If each gene that has an effect on weight were acting in isolation, then pairs of fraternal twins—who have, on average, half the same genes—should be half as similar as pairs of identical twins. Yet genetic studies find that identical twins are far more than twice as similar as fraternal twins. This implies that the precise combination of genes plays a role in determining weight over and beyond the contribution of the individual genes by themselves. The whole is greater than the sum of the parts.

Genetic researchers refer to the effects that depend only on individual genes as "additive" because it is possible to calculate the entire effect by adding the individual effects. The effects that depend on combinations of genes are called "non-additive." According to one careful study that looked at identical and fraternal twins raised together and apart, the non-additive genetic component is actually more important than the additive component. In men, additive genetic effects were found to explain only 17 percent of twins' weights, while non-additive genetic effects explained an incredible 57 percent; the environment accounted for the remaining 26 percent of their weights. Among women, additive genetic effects accounted for 32 percent of the differences in weight and non-additive genetic effects for 37 percent; the environment explained 31 percent. In each case, the single most important factor shaping a person's weight was the particular combination of genes a person had inherited and how those genes interacted with one another. Researchers are a long way from being able to explain, or even guess at, what these interaction effects are.

Instead of looking for specific genes that affect weight and trying to understand how they work, some researchers are working backward, starting not with the genes themselves but with their effects. That is, they are looking for inherited physiological characteristics that make people more or less likely to become overweight. Once these characteristics are found, then the search for obesity genes can be sharpened considerably by knowing what to look for.

A number of scientists, for example, have examined the connection between metabolic rates and how likely a person is to gain weight. It is an approach that goes back to the early 1900s, when doctors believed much of obesity could be attributed to abnormally slow metabolisms, but today researchers see it in somewhat different terms. A slow metabolism is probably not a determining factor in making a person fat but rather just one piece of a larger, more complex picture. Even if your basal metabolic rate is a hundred calories a day lower than your friend Fred's, you can—theoretically, at least—make up for it by eating 100 calories a day less than Fred does. If you cannot, there must be more at work than the sluggish metabolism.

That said, however, a number of reports have found a slow metabolism to be a risk factor for obesity. One study done in the late 1980s found that infants who expended less energy at three months—mostly by moving less than other infants—were more likely to be overweight by the time they were a year old. A second report found that five-year-old girls who expended less energy than their peers were heavier when they reached adolescence. One of the most detailed studies was performed on Pima Indians in 1987. Eric Ravussin and colleagues at the NIDDK measured total energy expenditure among a number of Pima subjects by having them spend twenty-four hours in a metabolic chamber, then they waited from two to four years to see how much weight their patients would gain. They found that a subject's total energy expenditure, adjusted for body composition, age, and sex, predicted quite well which of the subjects would gain weight. When Ravussin focused on two subsets of his patients—high-energy sorts, whose twenty-four-hour expenditures were at least 200 calories greater than expected, and low-energy types, who burned off at least 200 calories less than expected— he found that the low-energy subjects were four times as likely to gain at least eighteen pounds over the next two years as the high-energy group.

But the slow metabolism could explain only a part of the subjects' weight gains, Ravussin found. He calculated the deficit between how much energy his subjects would have burned off if they had normal metabolisms and how much energy they actually were burning, and then figured out how many pounds of extra fat that metabolic deficit explained. On average, he reported, only about a third of the weight gain could be attributed to their low metabolisms. Furthermore, a number of subjects with low metabolisms did not gain weight at all.

The most intriguing part of Ravussin's study was the suggestion that the weight gain might be a compensatory mechanism, intended to bring the subjects' bodies into a "normal" metabolic state. After the subjects with a low metabolism had gained weight, their bodies burned energy at the same rate as those of the other subjects. The parallel with the reduced-obese patients whom Leibel and Hirsch tested is striking: after losing weight, the Rockefeller patients had lower-than-normal metabolic rates which did not return to normal until they had gained weight back to their usual overweight state. The Pimas whom Ravussin examined had not lost weight like Leibel and Hirsch's subjects, but a similar mechanism may have been at work. Their bodies may have felt as if they had too little body fat and pushed—by keeping the metabolism low and perhaps by other means—to gain weight. If this is the case, then the low metabolism may not be so much a cause of the weight gain as a sign that the body is not where it wants to be.

Ravussin went on to measure twenty-four-hour energy expenditure in a group of ninety-four siblings from thirty-six Pima families. He found that his subjects had metabolisms much closer to those of their brothers and sisters than to those of Pimas outside their families. Other studies have found similar familial effects. Although no one knows exactly which genes influence metabolism, there is no doubt that the metabolic differences between people are, to a large extent, inherited.

In his ongoing studies of the Pimas, Ravussin has tracked down two other genetically based physiological differences that affect weight. Both of these traits influence how the body responds to a high-fat diet. The first of these traits is the "respiratory quotient," the ratio of carbohydrate oxidation to fat oxidation, or, in other words, a measure of how much of the energy a body burns in a day comes from carbohydrates versus how much from fats. People with high respiratory quotients burn proportionately more carbohydrates and conserve fats; those with low respiratory quotients burn more fats and fewer carbohydrates. Ravussin's group found that people with the highest respiratory quotients—that is, those whose bodies had the most resistance to burning off stored fat for energy—were two and a half times more likely to gain at least eleven pounds over the course of the study as were people with the lowest respiratory quotients.

The second, related trait that Ravussin observed was insulin resistance. Insulin prepares the body to metabolize carbohydrates, so people who are less sensitive to insulin—who are "insulin resistant"—will tend to burn more fat and less carbohydrates. Not surprisingly, among the Pima Indians that Ravussin tested, the insulin-resistant subjects gained less weight than those who were sensitive to insulin's effect and thus burned more carbohydrates.

Just as was the case with twenty-four-hour energy expenditure, Ravussin's group found that weight gain acted to "normalize" the respiratory quotient and the sensitivity to insulin. Once the subjects gained weight, their respiratory quotients dropped and their insulin resistance increased, and, at this point, their bodies began to resist gaining further weight. They were where they wanted to be.

Thus, depending on their genes, different people will respond in different ways to a particular environment, and the answer to why a person gets fat will inevitably entail this interaction between the genetic and environmental contributions. But there is a third piece of the answer, one that is usually ignored or downplayed these days. Since the 1970s, when the externality hypothesis imploded, little attention has been paid to the role of behavior. It is a factor that makes many uncomfortable because of the worry that it will offer support for those who would stigmatize the obese, but it is something that cannot be ignored if one is to paint a complete picture of weight.

The initial discovery of a connection between socioeconomic class and weight was a classic bit of scientific serendipity. In the early 1960s, Mickey Stunkard and two colleagues, Mary Moore and Leo Srole, set out to see, in the objective, data-driven way for which Stunkard was well known, whether there were correlations between obesity and various psychological measures—depression, anxiety, and so forth. For two decades, psychiatrists and psychologists had claimed that the obese suffered disproportionately from mental problems, and many thought that mental disturbances were a major cause of obesity, but there was little besides anecdotal data to back this up. So Stunkard hooked up with Srole, the originator of the Midtown Manhattan Study, a survey of 700 men and nearly 1000 women designed to examine the epidemiology of mental illness in a metropolitan area. The idea was to analyze the data in Srole's survey to see whether the obese indeed were more likely to be psychologically abnormal. And since earlier work had shown a relationship between the socioeconomic class of the subject's parents and the occurrence of mental illness, the researchers examined the relationship between parental socioeconomic class and obesity as well.

What they found surprised them. Whether a person had been raised in an upper or lower socioeconomic bracket turned out to have a much greater effect on weight than any of the psychological variables they had been considering. Classifying the subjects into eleven socioeconomic levels based on the occupation and the education of the respondent's father when the respondent was eight years old, they calculated the percentage of obese at each level. Among women the effect was particularly striking: 30 percent from the lowest socioeconomic classes were obese, compared with only 4 percent from the highest. For the men, the pattern was muted but still there: men from the lower classes were twice as likely to be fat as those from the higher classes.

Later, Stunkard and Moore, working with Phillip Goldblatt, expanded on the original report by looking at the relationship between obesity and the current socioeconomic status of the respondent instead of the socioeconomic status during childhood. The researchers found a similar pattern: 30 percent of the women in the low socioeconomic group were obese, compared with just 16 percent of the women in the middle group and a mere 5 percent of the women in the high socioeconomic group. For the men, obesity was twice as common among the low-class respondents as among those of high socioeconomic status.

The natural reaction upon hearing of a relationship between social class and obesity is to suspect discrimination against fat people. Fat men, for instance, might find it harder to make it to the tops of their fields, no matter how talented they were, because of a perception that they were not competent. Fat women might be frozen out of the higher socioeconomic classes because the more successful men preferred to marry thin women. This was still a time when relatively few women worked after marriage and when a married woman's status was largely dependent on the status of her husband. (Indeed, for the purposes of the survey, a married woman, whether working or not, was ranked on the occupation scale according to her husband's occupation.)

The survey provided some evidence that this might be happening. When Stunkard, Moore, and Goldblatt looked at social mobility and obesity, they found that women who moved upward in socioeconomic status were much less likely to be obese (12%) than those who moved down (22%). Those who stayed in the social class in which they were born were in between these two extremes (17% obese).

But this could not explain all, or even most, of the relationship between social class and obesity. After all, the relationship between obesity and the socioeconomic class in which one was raised was, if anything, stronger than the relationship between obesity and current socioeconomic status. And there was so much social mobility—44 percent of the women in the survey belonged to a different class than their parents—that each of the two relationships was significant in its own right.

No, something about a child's socioeconomic status was clearly making a big difference in how likely he or she—particularly she—was to become obese later in life. It seemed unlikely that the effect was purely genetic—thin, higher-class parents passing on thin genes to their offspring—or else there would not have been such a large discrepancy between the men and the women. The only reasonable conclusion, the researchers said, was that obesity must be, in part, a social phenomenon. Someone raised in a high-status household where obesity was frowned upon as a character flaw and, worse, a sign of low class, would have developed a strong aversion to being overweight and would work much harder to keep from getting fat. Furthermore, they suggested, the same sort of social pressures were probably at work throughout a person's life. A woman in a high socioeconomic class would know that all her peers looked down on those who were overweight; even if she herself had not been raised to feel this way, she would pick up the attitude from them. Because overweight men were not so uniformly rejected, the effects of socioeconomic class on their weight would be much less.

Since that original work, dozens of studies have examined the relationship between socioeconomic class and weight. In 1989, when Stunkard and Jeffery Sobal, a specialist in medical sociology, looked back on a quarter-century of these studies, they concluded that the situation is much like the one that Stunkard initially perceived.

Throughout the developed world, women in higher socioeconomic brackets are thinner than those in lower. Only one study has found an exception, and it looked at women who had migrated into Belgium from outside the country. For men, the situation is more complicated. Some studies found what Stunkard's original ones did—that upper-class men are less likely to be fat than lower-class men but that the difference is not nearly as strong as for women. Others found just the opposite, that men in the upper classes are more likely to be fat. The contradictory findings could have arisen for any number of reasons, Sobal and Stunkard said. The various studies used different measures of obesity and socioeconomic class, which could have affected the results; some cultures might place more importance on men being thin than others; some secondary factor such as smoking, which generally causes weight loss, might be confusing the results. Whatever the reasons, the class effect in men is never as pronounced as in women, no matter which direction it points. Among children in developed countries there seems to be little relationship between class and weight, and what little relationship there is seems to point in the opposite direction from adult women: children from the higher socioeconomic classes may weigh a little more. It is only as the girls are growing into women that the class difference in weight makes its appearance.

By contrast, in developing countries the situation is reversed—and much closer to what it has been throughout much of human civilization. The wealthy classes are fatter than the poorer classes, both women and men. The explanation seems obvious: only the wealthy classes can reap the same "benefits" that are ubiquitous in the Western world, such as plenty of tasty, high-fat food and little need to exert oneself physically. The poorer people are kept thinner by a limited diet and hard labor.

In analyzing the collection of studies, Stunkard and Sobal explained the weight-class connection among women in much the same way Stunkard had in the beginning. Certainly social mobility is playing some role. Even today, many women's places in the socioeconomic hierarchy are largely dependent on their husbands, and wealthier men still prefer thinner wives. Furthermore, we still have discrimination against the obese, making it less likely they will land high-paying, high-status jobs. Genetic inheritance must also explain part of it. Those thin women who marry into the upper classes pass their thin genes along to their children. But, just as clearly, behavior is behind much of the pattern. Otherwise it would be impossible to explain, for example, why the class-weight connection appears only in adults. Two of the most convincing studies followed large groups of British subjects from childhood to adulthood. No weight differences were found between boys of different classes and only insignificant differences between girls, but by the time they were adults the usual pattern had emerged, in this case for both sexes. In this study, social mobility played no role because the comparison was made strictly on the basis of the social class the subjects inhabited as children. And if genetics were the explanation, the weight differences should have been visible in childhood. So we are left with the inescapable conclusion that people's behavior—as shaped by the expectations of their social class—can exert a very noticeable degree of control over how much they are going to weigh.

There are two ways in which that might be done. One is through increased physical activity, and a number of studies have found that people in higher socioeconomic brackets do indeed spend more time jogging, biking, going to exercise classes, and the like, all of which make up, to at least some degree, for the fact that they no longer physically exert themselves in their jobs, their homes, or most of the rest of their lives. The second way to keep control of one's weight is to watch what one eats, either with a formal diet or simply by being careful to eat well and not take in too much fatty or high-calorie food. And, again, studies have found that, especially among women, those in the upper socioeconomic brackets are more likely to diet than those in the lower.

The message here is that the fattening effects of Western civilization can be resisted to a large degree with the right behavior or, more accurately, with the right social pressures. Living in a high-fat world does not inevitably lead to being fat.

Just this point was made in a study performed in The Netherlands in 1996–97. The researchers recruited a couple of hundred volunteers and gave them two tests designed to measure restraint in eating. Based on the test scores they selected twenty subjects who were restrained eaters—that is, they consciously ate less than their appetites requested in order to lose weight or to keep from gaining. Then they chose twenty subjects, carefully matched for sex, weight, and age, who were unrestrained eaters.

Since the idea of restrained and unrestrained eaters was first introduced in the 1970s, research has proved that restrained eaters do indeed form a class of people with a set of psychological characteristics that distinguishes them from others. Restrained eaters are generally overweight and are restraining their eating in an attempt to lose weight, or else they may be at their desired weight and restrict their eating in order to maintain that weight. Either way, they are likely to be below their set points, so that their metabolisms have slowed and their appetites increased. These are often the people who are perpetually on a diet, who seldom lose much weight, yet who swear they eat less than their skinny friends—and indeed they do. Because of their lowered metabolism, they need fewer calories to maintain their weight.

In the Dutch experiment, once the twenty restrained and twenty unrestrained eaters had been selected, for six months the researchers allowed their subjects to get much of their food for free from a laboratory "supermarket." Half the restrained eaters and half the unrestrained eaters went to a low-fat supermarket with reduced-fat versions of butter, cheese, meats, prepared dishes, cakes, cookies, and much more. The other half's supermarket had exactly the same items but in full-fat versions. In this way, half the subjects got a high-fat diet—higher than most were used to in their pre-experiment lives—and half got a diet much lower in fat than they had been eating.

Not surprisingly, the unrestrained eaters put on the high-fat diet began taking in more fat and more calories. By the end of the experiment, the average weight of the group had increased, although not by so much that it couldn't be dismissed as chance. The unrestrained eaters on the low-fat diet took in less fat as a percentage of their total intake, but they made up for it by eating more, and their total calorie intake—and their weights—stayed the same.

By contrast, the restrained eaters who shopped in the low-fat supermarket not only took in less fat as a percentage of their total diet but also consumed fewer calories, and they lost weight over the course of the experiment. Perhaps the most interesting group was the restrained eaters sent into the high-fat supermarket. Initially their fat intake shot up as did their total calorie intake, but after the first month they reestablished control and began to cut down on both. By the end of the experiment they were taking in no more calories than at the beginning, and they gained no weight over the six months.

In short, the subjects who consciously restricted their eating were able to counter the usual effects of a high-fat diet. In the beginning they did take in more calories than they were used to, probably because they ate the same amounts of food that they were accustomed to eating but now the food was higher in fat. Once they had a chance to adapt to the new high-fat diet, however, they squelched this overeating. If the results can be generalized to the world outside the laboratory—and this experiment was designed to be as close to real life as an experiment can get—the lesson would be that some people, at least, are not slaves to the environment and their genes.

Restrained eaters, conscious exercisers, and the persistent class differences in obesity speak to one of the most contentious debates in the area of weight research:

How great a role does behavior—consciously directed behavior, in particular—play in determining weight? The issue is controversial not just because the evidence is inconclusive but also because of what the answers might say about the obese. No one wants to go back to the bad old days of the 1930s and 1940s when fat people were routinely pilloried, even by many doctors, as sloths, gluttons, and worse. The argument that obesity is a disease and that its victims have no real control over their fate has helped remove some of the stigma of being fat, but is that argument too simplistic? Does it ignore evidence that something is at work besides genes and environment?

In discussing this subject, it is important to make a distinction between two different arenas in which behavior can play a role. The first comes in efforts to lose weight once one's set point is higher than desired. Here, as we have seen, the body resists efforts to drop much below the set point, and losing a large amount of weight can demand a strength of will that borders on obsession.

Of course, it's likely that the resistance to losing weight varies from person to person. Some, like the man in Turkey whose body does not produce leptin, may find it impossible, for all practical purposes, to lose weight much below what their body demands. Others may have far less resistance from their bodies and, for them, the greater obstacle to losing weight may well be behavioral. They have developed certain habits over a lifetime and, although they may be able to change them for a short time, they eventually fall back into old patterns.

This is one of the major areas of disagreement among obesity experts: how much of the inability to maintain a weight loss is due to biology, and how much to behavior. Rudy Leibel and Jules Hirsch are among those who argue for biology, pointing to their laboratory studies of the metabolic changes in people who gained or lost at least 10 percent of their body weight. Others think a bigger problem may be that people have tremendous difficulty making major lifestyle changes—not just the obese, but anyone.

Much of the debate here centers on studies of patients who have lost weight and kept it off for a year or more—the "reduced obese" or "formerly obese." Leibel got it started with his study of four reduced-obese women, which found the women to have depressed metabolisms similar to those of patients who had recently lost weight. Since then, a raft of similar studies have been done, with mixed results. In 1999, a group of Danish researchers performed a meta-analysis on a dozen such studies, analyzing their combined results, and concluded that the formerly obese do tend to have lower-than-expected metabolic rates, but it is a smaller effect than Leibel had originally found. Indeed, they said, it seems to be only a minority of the reduced obese—about one in seven—that have significantly lower metabolic rates than expected. Most formerly obese people have completely normal metabolisms.

It might seem that the Danish study supports those who argue for weight regain being a behavioral problem, since most of the reduced obese did not have a low metabolism that would indicate a body trying to return to a higher set point. The problem with this conclusion is that it assumes that the reduced obese in these studies are representative of everyone who tries to lose weight, but they are not—they are part of a highly selected subgroup that has lost weight and kept it off long enough to be included in these studies. Another, equally plausible, interpretation would be that the bodies of the obese respond in different ways to losing weight. Some fight the loss every step of the way, lowering the metabolism and increasing hunger; most of the people in this category fail to keep weight off, and such people will make up a disproportionate number of the subjects in studies at places like Rockefeller, where the most desperate obese go to try to lose weight. Other people probably meet less resistance. Their bodies' metabolisms may drop temporarily with the initial weight loss but then return to normal or near normal; these people are more likely to keep weight off and thus more likely to be included in studies of the formerly obese. If they regain their lost weight, it is more likely because they have returned to the same habits that made them fat in the first place than because they were pushed back upward toward an elevated set point.

In short, it seems likely that behavior and biology play their roles to differing degrees in different people, and that the debate over whether weight regain is due to biological or behavioral factors is an artificial one, asking "Black or white?" of a half-tone mosaic. At some point in the future it may be possible to perform a genetic test on an obese patient and discover how much of the resistance to weight loss is biological and how much behavioral, but it will not any time soon. For now, we simply cannot tell, which implies both that we should not castigate the obese for their lack of willpower, for many of them truly cannot help themselves, nor should we stop looking for ways to help them lose weight, since many others may well be able to become formerly obese with the right program.

The second arena in which behavior plays a role is the setting of the set point, and here we have a similar debate. Some researchers, such as Leibel and Hirsch, do not believe that behavior has much to do with where a person's set point ends up. It is, they argue, mainly beyond an individual's control, fixed by the interaction between a person's genes and the particular environment in which he or she grows up. An analogy is often made with height. Genes and environment set height completely, or at least so close to completely that the difference doesn't matter. As long as you get decent nutrition growing up, you will reach a height that your genes predetermine; if your nutrition is lacking, you will come up short. The same sort of thing is probably true of weight, the reasoning goes. Once we are living in a society that provides as much extra nutrition as our bodies can absorb, we will float up to a weight that is mostly dependent on our genes. It could be 120 pounds, it could be 520 pounds, but we don't have much say over it.

On the other hand, researchers like Stunkard believe that the data on socio-economic class and weight imply that something more is going on here. If women in upper socioeconomic classes are much thinner than women in the lower brackets, it is not likely because many of them are, by sheer force of will, staying well below their set points. Instead, it must be because these women somehow managed to keep their set points from becoming so high in the first place. And this could be true only if the set point is not determined solely by the interplay of genes and environment but responds to behavior as well.

There is some evidence that this is the case. When people gain weight, the pattern of weight gain is often a series of spurts. A person will maintain one weight for a while, quite effortlessly, then for some reason find that the reading on the scale has jumped by ten or twenty or thirty pounds in a matter of months. A teenaged boy is depressed about school and his social life, and eats to compensate. A girl breaks her leg and has to stay in bed, so she gets no exercise and eats out of boredom. A man goes on an extended business trip and takes three meals a day in nice restaurants. A woman gains fifty pounds during pregnancy and only twenty drops off in the weeks after birth. Much of the time, as dozens of over-feeding experiments over the past four decades have shown, this extra weight will disappear once things get back to normal. But sometimes the weight stays. In 1964, when Ethan Allen Sims performed his classic overfeeding experiment with inmate volunteers from Vermont State Prison, only two of the twenty-plus subjects found it easy to meet the goal of gaining 20 percent of their starting weight. Sims later discovered that these two had family histories of obesity and diabetes, so they probably had some genetic predisposition to gain weight. Once the over-feeding phase of the experiment was done and the convicts set about losing the weight they had gained, these two were the only subjects who had difficulty taking off the extra pounds.

No one knows exactly what happens at this point when someone has gained weight over his usual set point and does not easily lose it once life returns to normal. It seems reasonable that the previous set point should still be within reach, even if it takes a little discipline to get back there. But at some point, the set point may get fixed at this higher level. This would lead to a ratchet effect, where the set point would jump by ten or twenty pounds at a time, stabilize for a while, and then, when conditions were right, move upward again.

The converse question of whether it is possible to move the set point back down—and, if so, how—is equally up in the air. It's possible that the set point is more flexible in some than in others, so that some people, having settled in at a certain weight, will never again be comfortable at a lower weight, while others will find that the right combination of diet and exercise can reset the set point downward.

Jeffrey Friedman, the discoverer of the leptin gene, has suggested one scenario for how the set point could ratchet upward. Since leptin is the chemical signal by which the brain knows how much fat is in the body, losing weight below the set point causes the amount of leptin in the blood to drop below the desired level and triggers the hypothalamus to send out signals that increase appetite and slow the metabolism. Conversely, a weight gain above the set point pushes the leptin level past where it is supposed to be, leading the brain to decrease appetite and increase metabolism. But suppose, Friedman suggests, that in some people a sharp increase in the leptin levels causes the brain to make an adaptation: it becomes less sensitive to leptin. It now demands more leptin than before to trigger it to send out signals that slow appetite and increase metabolism.

Studies of fat mice have found exactly this sort of "leptin resistance." These mice do not respond as strongly as expected to leptin injections—their bodies have developed a tolerance for leptin and require much higher-than-normal levels for a response. It seems reasonable that obese humans have a similar impaired response to leptin, since most have higher-than-normal levels circulating in their bloodstream. We don't know, however, since no one has yet done extensive trials on the effects of leptin in people.

Whatever the precise mechanism is, it seems likely that, in some people at least, the set point probably does ratchet up. And, if this is the case, then behavior probably does play a role in regulating where the set point eventually ends up. Someone who was religious about watching his or her weight, who would cut back on the calories or increase the exercise at the first sign of an extra couple of pounds, might well avoid this ratcheting effect by never allowing the weight to creep up in the first place. A person who did not worry so much about weight, on the other hand, might gain twenty pounds and promise himself that he would diet sometime in the future, and later find it was too late—the weight had settled in. This could explain why higher-socioeconomic-class women stay so much thinner than those from the lower brackets—they are much more conscious of even minor weight gains and take immediate steps to correct them.

If behavior does play a role in obesity, alongside genetics and the environment, what does this say about how we should view the obese? Does it push us back to the days of condemning the fat among us for their flaws? Can we still view them as innocent victims? Such questions ultimately take us beyond science and into the realm of philosophy and ethics, but science can at least inform the philosophical and ethical debate.

In that vein, the first thing to keep in mind is that the scientific research on weight is statistical in nature—it says nothing about a particular individual, but speaks only of groups of people. Even if it is true, for instance, that some people could have avoided becoming fat by watching their weight more vigilantly and fighting back with diet and exercise each time it threatened to increase, it is equally true that some people—the leptin-deficient patients are the most extreme examples—had no choice about their obesity. They were born to be fat. So it is not necessary to argue that every fat person is a victim in order to argue that none of them should be condemned out of hand. No one knows, and present-day science offers no way to know, just what forces have pushed any particular person to become fat.

Furthermore, it is clear that, despite the role that behavior plays, there is no reason to think of the obese as gluttons and sloths. They, like most of the rest of us, have merely followed their bodies' directions for how much to eat. The worst that can be said is that they—some of them, anyway—were not as conscientious about fighting the weight from the very beginning as perhaps others would have been, and this is not so much a statement about them as about the sort of people around them. As far as we know, the best way to escape the push of genes and environment is to grow up in a culture that abhors obesity, and not everyone does.

Indeed, some might go so far as to argue that the studies of weight and social class actually tell us little about individual behavior but instead are one more aspect of the influence that environment wields over weight. After all, one's cultural environment—the beliefs and attitudes that one grows up with—is every bit as real and powerful as the physical environment. The problem with this line of argument is that one quickly wanders into an area in which freedom of action and personal responsibility have vanished and everything about a person from leptin levels to ability to adhere to a diet is explained as being set by the interaction of genes and environment. Such an absolute determinism is a philosophy of despair, leaving no hope that a person can rise above what genes and environment have decreed, and most people prefer to believe that they have some control over their actions. Assuming that they do, the studies of weight and social class inform us that our actions—and therefore our decisions about how to act—can indeed influence our weight.

It would be nice to be able to conclude that the studies of weight and social class offer us some hope for a way out of the obesity plague. After all, if we could bring the overall rate of obesity down near the rate we see among women in the highest socioeconomic bracket, that would be a major victory. There would be millions fewer obese and tens of millions fewer overweight adults in the United States alone, health care costs would drop dramatically, and people would live longer, healthier lives. It's hard to see how this could be done, however. The standard approach would be education: teach children about the dangers of being overweight, and tell them that they can make a difference in their weight if only they become fanatic about snuffing out any weight gain almost before it happens. To see how likely this is to succeed, one has only to look at the failure of anti-smoking campaigns aimed at kids. Theoretically, it should be much easier to convince young people not to form a habit—smoking—than to get them to train themselves into doing something quite unnatural—eating less than their bodies tell them to—but with all the Surgeon General's warnings and all the Don't Start campaigns, teenagers continue to put cigarettes in their mouths. So the chances of creating a thin-conscious culture that extends across our entire society seem slim.

One final, related observation is that the drive to remove the stigma from obesity may well, to the extent that it succeeds, have unanticipated and unwelcome consequences. The more undesirable obesity is seen, the harder people work to avoid it, and the fewer people become fat. This is the lesson of the studies on social class and weight. If it were possible somehow to wave a magic wand and remove the stigma of obesity overnight—if suddenly fat people were thought of as just as competent, intelligent, attractive, and fashionable as thin people—what would happen? Three things, at least. First, fat people would be happier and less frustrated. Second, the rates of anorexia, bulimia, and the other eating disorders that arise from an obsession with thinness and which plague mostly girls and women from upper socioeconomic brackets would go down. And, third, there would be a lot more fat people in the world. Is this a reasonable trade-off? The answer depends on a number of factors, including how many more people would become fat, the health effects of obesity, and one's attitudes toward personal responsibility. Reasonable people can differ on the answer. But it is important to realize, in discussions about removing the stigma, that it is not so simple an issue as it might seem. But, of course, nothing in this field ever is.

EIGHT

One Pill Makes You Larger, and One Pill Makes You Small

Redux was going to be the dream drug, the little pill that made it easy to lose weight. Then sometime in 1996, in a medical center in Fargo, North Dakota, it all began to unravel. But we're getting ahead of ourselves. The story actually begins long before that, with a drug called Pondimin.

Pondimin, better known by its chemical name, fenfluramine, had been in the diet doctor's black bag since the 1970s. Because it tends to make people drowsy, it was often paired with phentermine, a chemical that is both a weak appetite suppressant and a stimulant. The combination, known as fen-phen, was just one of many diet pill options, no more popular than any other, until the 1992 publication of a series of papers by pharmacologist Michael Weintraub of the University of Rochester. Weintraub found fen-phen to be effective in helping many patients lose 10 percent or more of their body weight and keep it off for two years or more, as long as the drugs were continued.

That report triggered a fen-phen fad. After reading accounts of the Weintraub study in the popular press, patients demanded that their doctors prescribe them fen-phen. Weight-loss boutiques sprang up whose main purpose was to hand out fen-phen prescriptions, sometimes without a doctor even seeing the patients who were getting the pills. Even such staid, normally antidrug, weight-loss programs as Nutri/System began handing out fen-phen to clients. The manufacturer of fenfluramine, Wyeth-Ayerst Laboratories, could not keep up with demand, and pharmacists across the country began running out.

In the middle of this binge, Redux appeared. Fenfluramine is actually a mixture of two drugs with the same chemical formula but in which the atoms arrange
themselves in mirror images. The left-handed version is called levofenfluramine,
the right-handed one dexfenfluramine. It is dexfenfluramine that acts as an
appetite suppressant, while levofenfluramine causes many of the side effects but
does little or nothing to help a person lose weight. When fenfluramine had first
been manufactured there was no way to produce just the right-handed version,
so pills had to include both dexfenfluramine and levofenfluramine, but in the
1970s the French pharmaceutical company Servier developed a method of turning out pure dexfenfluramine. By the mid-1990s, after working its way through
the Food and Drug Administration's multiyear testing process, dexfenfluramine—or Redux, as it would be called when marketed in the United States—
was up for final approval. As Wyeth-Ayerst saw it, Redux was a can't-miss deal, a
fen-phen with fewer side effects, and the company envisioned hundreds of millions of dollars in annual sales for years to come.

And, for a short while after the FDA's okay, Redux looked as if it would fulfill
those expectations. As the first prescription weight-loss drug approved by the FDA
in twenty years, Redux was immediately embraced by those looking for help in
their diets. *Time* recognized it with a cover story in September 1996, and Sheldon
Levine, a New Jersey diet doctor, touted it in his much-publicized book, *The
Redux Revolution: Everything You Need to Know About the Most Important
Weight-Loss Discovery of the Century.* According to one stock analyst, Redux's
first three months were probably "the fastest launch of any drug in the history of
the pharmaceutical industry." But even then there were signs that not all was perfect with Redux.

In 1995, as the FDA was considering whether to approve Redux for sale as an
appetite suppressant, one of the arguments against it was that, in large doses, it
causes brain damage in monkeys. The FDA judged that to be a relatively insignificant risk for people, however, and in April 1996 gave Redux the go-ahead. Four
months later, a report in *The New England Journal of Medicine* revealed that in
Europe—where prescribing Redux had been legal for years—people who had
taken it or the closely related Pondimin were at a much higher risk for primary
pulmonary hypertension, a disease of the heart and lungs that eventually kills
about half the people who contract it. Still, the risk was low enough that only
about twenty-eight people per million users were expected to get the disease, and
many researchers judged this a reasonable price for helping thousands of people
lose weight and thus avoid heart attacks or the other complications of obesity. So,
even after the risk of primary pulmonary hypertension was known, the drugs
remained on the market in both the United States and Europe. It was around this
time that Jack Crary, a heart specialist at the MeritCare Medical Center in Fargo,

began to notice an ominous pattern among obese patients who had been taking Pondimin. An extremely rare form of heart damage was showing up in these patients with alarming regularity.

The first whom Crary found was a forty-four-year-old woman, five-foot-three and 200 pounds, who had been taking fen-phen for a year when her doctor noticed that she had developed shortness of breath and a heart murmur. She was referred to Crary, who found that three of her heart's four valves had become thick and rigid, allowing blood to leak backward as the heart was pumping. Such leaks force the heart to work harder, and when severe enough—as they were in this case—they can lead to congestive heart failure. Crary sent the woman to a surgeon, who replaced two of the damaged valves and repaired the third. Examining one of the extracted valves under a microscope, Crary found that a plaque-like growth covered both of its sides.

This sort of valvular heart disease, Crary knew, appears sometimes in people who have a type of cancer called carcinoid and also in people who have taken the migraine medications ergotamine or methysergide for many years, but his patient had none of these risk factors. She was a mystery, one more patient whose malady had no apparent cause.

And a mystery she would likely have remained, had not others like her appeared soon after. One forty-eight-year-old woman, five-foot-two and 187 pounds, had taken fen-phen for nine months when her doctor noticed a heart murmur, breathlessness, and swollen ankles. When Crary examined her, he again found a thickened heart valve that needed replacement; the valve, inspected after the surgery, showed the same plaques as in the previous patient. A fifty-one-year-old woman, five foot tall and 293 pounds, on fen-phen for seven months, exhibited shortness of breath and a heart murmur. Three of her valves were thickened, although not so severely that they demanded surgical replacement. And on it went. By the end of 1996, Crary had found twelve patients with almost identical damage to their heart valves and none of the normal predisposing factors for valvular heart disease. Not all of them were obese—some were just twenty or thirty pounds above their optimum weight—but all of them, Crary noticed, had been taking fen-phen.

Despite its location in Fargo, population 75,000, the MeritCare Medical Center prides itself on its advanced facilities—it was the first hospital between Minneapolis and the West Coast to open a pediatric intensive care unit, for instance, and the first to be certified as a Level II trauma center—but no one there could tell Crary what might be going on with these patients. So in January 1997 he approached the Mayo Clinic, 300 miles to the south and east, in Rochester, Minnesota, to ask: Did anyone there know of a connection between diet medications, fen-phen in particular, and valvular heart disease?

As it happened, doctors at Mayo had already seen a patient similar to those that Crary had found: a forty-one-year-old woman, five-foot-five, 238 pounds, on fen-phen for more than two years, who had none of the risk factors for valve disease but nonetheless had a valve damaged so badly that it needed to be replaced. And a second fen-phen user with valve damage had appeared at Mayo in January, shortly before Crary came to call, so the doctors there were happy to work with him. Convinced that there must be a connection, Crary and a Mayo cardiologist, Heidi Connolly, continued to look for other fen-phen users with heart valve damage.

By April, Connolly had identified three more and Crary seven, for a total of twenty-four cases. Their symptoms varied, from a barely noticeable heart murmur to shortness of breath, heart palpitations, chest pain, and congestive heart failure. All of them had at least one leaky valve, some two or three. Of the two dozen, five needed surgery to replace or repair the valves.

Crary and Connolly submitted their report to *The New England Journal of Medicine* with a cautious interpretation: Fen-phen might be causing valvular heart disease in some patients, but they could not prove it. In particular, they did not know *how* the drugs might be causing the damage. Both fenfluramine and phentermine increase the amount of the neurotransmitter serotonin circulating in the brain, and it seemed likely that they also raise the amount of serotonin in the heart. Perhaps the extra serotonin was somehow damaging the valves, but that was no more than speculation. No one could be sure what was going on.

The news broke July 8. Normally the *New England Journal* would not have allowed Crary and Connolly to speak about their findings publicly until they were actually published in the journal—a standard practice for top journals in science and medicine—but the magazine's editors decided that keeping the story quiet for another six weeks would be irresponsible. Crary had seen patients with valve damage who had been taking fen-phen for as little as one or two months. The Mayo Clinic held a press conference with Connolly to announce the results. Ironically, although Crary had identified nineteen of the twenty-four patients in the study, it was Connolly—because she had assembled a team from Mayo to study the heart damage in depth—who was the lead author for the report and who became the spokesman for the research. Press accounts of the findings generally referred to them as the work of Connolly and ignored Crary's role altogether.

At this point only fen-phen had been implicated in the damage, not Redux. But Redux, as the right-handed version of fenfluramine, was immediately suspect too. Since it had been on the market less than a year during the time that Crary and Connolly were identifying their twenty-four heart valve victims, it seemed likely that there simply had not been enough time for a large number of dieters to be damaged by Redux.

And indeed, as the FDA accumulated more information over the next two months, that proved to be the case. By mid-September the agency had more than 100 reports of people who had been on appetite suppressants and developed heart valve damage. Most of them were on fen-phen, but some had been taking fenfluramine alone or Redux. The most damning evidence came from a group of doctors who had examined about 300 people who had been taking fen-phen or "dexfen-phen"—Redux in combination with phentermine—but who had no obvious signs of heart problems. When the doctors looked closely at the hearts of these seemingly healthy patients, they found that 30 percent—three out of every ten—had valve damage of one sort or another, generally in the early stages. Not good odds.

On September 15, 1997, sixteen and a half months after it had approved Redux for sale, the FDA announced that it had asked the manufacturers of both fenfluramine and Redux to remove their drugs from the market and that they had agreed. The FDA also recommended that anyone still using fenfluramine or Redux should quit. It made no move against phentermine because there was no evidence that phentermine by itself had caused any damage.

Since then, the case against fenfluramine and Redux has grown stronger. A trio of studies published in *The New England Journal of Medicine* almost exactly a year after the FDA's action found a clear connection between the drugs and valve damage. The most alarming of these reported the results of echocardiograms on nearly 500 subjects, both those who had been taking appetite-control drugs and a control group who had not. It found heart-valve problems in only 1.3 percent of the subjects who had never taken appetite suppressants, but in 12.7 percent of those who had used Redux, 24.5 percent of those who used Redux in combination with phentermine, and 26.3 percent of those who had taken fen-phen. In other words, someone who had taken fen-phen or dexfen-phen had one chance in four of damaged heart valves. Redux alone looked safer, but the researchers noted that this might have been because the Redux users had taken the drug for a shorter time than the other two groups. A second study looked at patients who had taken Redux for only two and a half months. They, too, had more heart valve problems than a control group who had not used the drug, but the difference was much smaller, again perhaps because they had taken the drug for so short a time. The third study examined how many users of appetite suppressants had been diagnosed by their doctors with valve problems. Among the more than 18,000 patient records they studied, they found only a handful of cases of valve disorders, but all of them appeared in users of appetite suppressants.

If the three studies are to be believed, fenfluramine and Redux cause valve damage in a large percentage of people who use them, but the damage usually takes more than a couple of months to develop, and it is rarely serious enough that it is detected by a doctor who is not looking for it. The risk seems to increase with length of drug use, but the evidence for that is still weak.

The moral, as one Mayo Clinic doctor observed, is, "It's not nice to fool Mother Nature." But, then, anyone who had been paying attention to more than sixty years of attempts to control weight with drugs could have told you the same thing.

The modern era of weight-loss drugs might be said to have begun in June 1892, when an American doctor treated an overweight patient with an underactive thyroid gland by injecting her with an extract from the thyroids of sheep. This was not the first time doctors had attempted to treat obesity with elixirs of one form or another, of course. We can trace that practice back to at least the second century, to Soranus of Ephesus, a Greek physician living and working in Rome. For weight loss, Soranus suggested combining a restricted diet with harsh laxatives, drugs to induce vomiting, and heat, massage, exercise, and bathing. No doubt many doctors before Ephesus were recommending elixirs of one sort or another, as did many that followed him, but the sheep thyroid extract took treatment to a new level. With it, doctors were directly manipulating the messengers that the body uses to control its functions and to communicate within itself. And that was quite different from helping a patient lose weight by causing him to throw up.

The thyroid gland is the conductor of the body's metabolism. A butterfly-shaped organ that stretches around the sides and front of the windpipe, it produces two closely related hormones, thyroxine and triiodothyronine, which quicken the body's metabolism. When signaled by the pituitary gland—via a hormone called, reasonably enough, thyroid-stimulating hormone—the thyroid releases these two chemicals into the bloodstream. Carried around the body in the blood, the thyroid hormones intensify the activity of every cell they touch, speeding up carbohydrate metabolism and boosting the synthesis and breakdown of proteins. When the levels of thyroid hormones drop, cellular activity slows back down.

In some people, an oversized thyroid or a tumor prompts the gland to secrete abnormally high levels of these hormones, pushing the body's metabolism into high gear. This cellular speed-up raises the body's temperature, increases physical activity, and causes nervousness and irritability. In other people, damage to the thyroid causes it to produce too little of the hormones. These people are sluggish, both physically and mentally, tire easily, are susceptible to cold, and tend to gain weight. In extreme cases, the skin thickens and becomes puffy with underlying fluid, the tongue becomes bloated, the heart enlarges, and, in women, menstruation ceases.

It was just such people that James J. Putnam, a Boston doctor, treated with sheep's thyroid beginning in 1892. His first patient was a forty-seven-year-old woman whom he had been seeing since 1885. Her skin was thick, dry, and stiff, her eyelids swollen. "The nutrition of the teeth and nails was defective," he wrote, "and the hair had fallen out except for a few bunches here and there. Formerly slender and with delicate coloring, she now looked overgrown and old." Furthermore, she was listless and apathetic. "Her friends would leave her with one boot on and the other in her hand, and return an hour later to find her in the same condition and attitude."

For years Putnam had been unable to help, but in 1892 he came across the work of the English physician George Redmayne Murray. Doctors had known since the 1880s that myxedema—the collection of symptoms that Putnam found in his patient—was caused by a lack of thyroid hormones, and Murray had hit upon the idea of dissolving the thyroid glands of sheep and injecting an extract of the glands into myxedematous patients. His trial worked, he wrote it up in the medical literature, and so Putnam set out to repeat the experiment in his own bald, apathetic patient. Over the next seven months, Putnam would later report, the woman gradually returned to normal health, her swelling diminishing, her energy increasing, her hair coming back, and her excess flesh melting away. "[S]he was rapidly growing thinner and slenderer, while her hands were becoming softer and more shapely. The clothes that she had worn were now hanging in folds, and in fact she became at this time really too thin." Putnam continued to treat her with thyroid, now in the form of the sheep's glands themselves, dried and powdered, and by the time of his report in August 1893 she was almost completely healthy. "She is still an anemic and delicate person, as she always was [before her thyroid problems], but as regards any distinct myxedema she is practically well."

The implications of his patient's weight loss were not lost on Putnam. It was natural to ask, he noted, whether the thyroid treatments might help obese people lose weight, even if their thyroids were functioning perfectly. He had heard from a doctor in Liverpool who had treated five cases of "ordinary corpulence" with thyroid: "One lost twenty-eight pounds in six weeks, three a moderate amount, and all lost more or less." Putnam himself was testing the treatment on two obese patients but at the time had nothing to report.

Soon after, thyroid became a standard treatment for myxedema, but it would not be until the 1920s and 1930s that thyroid became popular for treating obesity in otherwise healthy patients. Because research had implied that a small percentage of the obese had lower-than-normal metabolisms even though they had no obvious glandular disorders, it made sense that a little extra thyroid would boost their metabolic rate and help them lose weight. The theory became more questionable for the vast majority of the obese whose metabolisms were clearly normal, and many doctors argued against using thyroid pills for such patients. But there were few other options for people who couldn't or wouldn't lose weight through diet and exercise, and plenty of physicians were willing to prescribe the thyroid metabolism boosters even for those without low metabolisms. By this time, scientists had learned how to isolate thyroxine, the more important of the two thyroid hormones, from thyroid tissue, and had also discovered how to synthesize it, so thyroid could be taken as a chemically pure drug as well as in the form of powdered sheep thyroid glands. Through the 1960s, thyroid pills of both types would be a standard weight-loss prescription for the obese.

And the thyroid pills did work, at least as well as anything else. Doctors found that some obese patients would lose weight on just the thyroid medication, and others could lose weight by combining the thyroid with a low-calorie diet. There were side effects, of course—racing pulse, heart palpitations, tremors, sleeplessness, suppression of menstruation—but these affected only a minority of patients as long as the dose was not too high. Later, researchers would discover that as much as two thirds of the weight loss caused by the thyroid hormones came from muscle instead of fat, but that was not understood in the early years and, when it was understood, doctors found they could block much of the muscle loss by feeding the patient more protein.

The major problem with thyroid treatment was the same one that would bedevil every other weight-loss drug that followed in its wake: After an initial weight loss, usually rather small, the drug was not particularly helpful, and if its use was discontinued, the patient almost inevitably regained the weight.

This was not something that doctors in the 1930s worried much about, however. If a patient's excess weight was due to an identifiable glandular deficiency, then a doctor was willing to keep the patient on hormone medications for the rest of his or her life. And if there was no metabolic abnormality—if the obesity was due simply to overeating—then doctors saw their job simply as helping the patients lose the excess weight and bringing them back to a normal state. Once the weight was gone, keeping it off was the patient's problem, since doctors assumed that overeating was simply a behavioral issue. The thyroid drugs were intended as an initial boost to help get the patient started losing weight, but they were never intended for the long term.

If the 1930s saw the first commonly prescribed and relatively safe weight-loss drug in thyroxine, it also saw the first weight-loss drug to prove too dangerous to keep on the market. Dinitrophenol, discovered during the First World War in a munitions factory, increased the body's metabolic rate in a very direct and efficient way, by triggering cells to burn extra sugars and fat molecules. During normal metabolism, mitochondria, the cell's power plants, oxidize—or burn—sugar and fat molecules and use the resulting chemical energy to create molecules of adenosine triphosphate. ATP, as it is abbreviated, is the power source for most of the cell's operations. An ATP molecule is like a tiny rechargeable battery, discharging itself to provide energy to the cell and being recharged with the oxidation of the food molecules. Dinitrophenol works by "uncoupling" the recharging from the oxidation so that the mitochondria continue to burn the fat and sugar molecules, but little of the chemical energy is used to recharge the ATP. It is instead mostly dissipated as heat.

In 1933 three researchers from the Stanford University School of Medicine reported promising results for dinitrophenol in treating obesity. As measured in a group of 113 obese patients, the drug's effect on metabolism was unmistakable. Within a couple of hours of taking the drug, the patients' basal metabolic rates had increased by 20 to 30 percent and their body temperatures had risen slightly but measurably; they also reported feeling warmer, and their perspiration increased. More to the point, almost all of the patients lost weight—an average of one and a half pounds a week for six weeks. For a short while it seemed as if the answer to obesity had been found: with dinitrophenol the obese could sweat off their extra pounds by turning up the body's internal thermostat.

Then came the side effects. The Stanford researchers had reported relatively minor difficulties with the drug, but as more dieters tried it, more problems appeared. Skin rashes. Swelling and redness in the hands and feet. Headaches, weakness, nervousness, dizziness. Vomiting and diarrhea. A decreased sensitivity to sweet and salty foods. About 20 percent of the people taking the drug experienced at least one of them, and these were the milder side effects. Less fortunate users saw their skin peel off, their hair fall out, their livers fail, their eyes develop cataracts, or their white blood cells die off. This last side effect killed at least five people. And all of these reactions were recorded in patients taking "therapeutic" doses—the amount needed to see any effect on the metabolism. If one got careless and took much more than the recommended dosage, the body almost literally burned itself up. One unfortunate user's temperature reached 115 degrees before he died. By the end of the 1930s, such horror stories had driven dinitrophenol from the market.

Except for thyroid pills and dinitrophenol, the most popular weight-loss methods of the 1930s had not advanced much past those of Soranus of Ephesus. Drugstores sold a variety of "purgatives"—laxative herbs, pills, and such—that would send whatever food might be in the intestines careering through the body and out. Sold alongside the laxative products were diuretics—natural products, often high in salt, that would cause the body to expel much of its water and thereby lose several pounds over several days. Also popular were steam cabinets, reducing creams, and special soaps and bath powders.

Meanwhile, a steady stream of fad diets came and went, and although their developers had probably never heard of Soranus, most of them nonetheless abided by his advice to offer "in limited amounts, foods that do not give much nourishment." There was the Hollywood diet, which consisted mainly of grapefruit and Melba toast. The Hay diet, in which proteins and carbohydrates were never to be eaten at the same meal—it confused the stomach, supposedly—and whose users were encouraged to take daily purgative enemas. There was the bananas and milk diet. The raw tomato and hard-boiled egg diet. The lamb chop and pineapple diet. The baked potato and buttermilk diet. Each was guaranteed to work, but not for the reasons most people assumed: since few dieters could stomach more than 800 or 1000 calories a day of the prescribed foods, as long as they limited themselves to the raw tomato and boiled eggs or the bananas and milk, they would lose weight by simple calorie restriction. On the other hand, few could stay on such diets for long, which was probably for the best, since most of the diets failed to provide the minimum essential nutrients that the body needs to function properly. According to a 1937 article in *Hygeia*, the popular health magazine published by the American Medical Association, at least one of the diets—the citrus-fruit-and-toast plan—had "chalked up a number of deaths to its credit."

Throughout the 1930s the main purpose of weight-loss drugs was burning calories and, to a lesser degree, purging food from the system after it had been eaten. What was missing from the diet armamentarium was anything that curbed the appetite. In small part, this may have been a reflection of the prevailing consensus that an individual is—or at least should be—in control of what he eats, but mostly it was a practical matter: although drugs were known that made a person too sick to feel like eating, no one had found a drug that slowed eating but let a person feel good. Benzedrine would change that.

It was 1894 when two British physiologists, Edward Sharpey and George Oliver, showed that extracts from the adrenal gland raised blood pressure in experimental animals. This, combined with the work that has been done on the thyroid gland over the previous two years, heralded the birth of a new field: endocrinology, the study of hormones and the glands that produce them. Ironically enough, research on the gland that seemed to have the more obvious application to obesity—the thyroid—would ultimately lead to little more than what James Putnam was already able to offer his patient in 1893, while the adrenal gland, which had no obvious connection with weight, would point the way to an entire pharmacopoeia of weight-control drugs.

The adrenal glands sit half a body away from the thyroid, atop the upper end of each kidney. ("Adrenal" is Latin for "adjacent to the kidney.") Roughly triangular in shape, each gland is about an inch wide, two inches long, and less than a quarter of an inch thick. Although they appear to be single organs, each is composed of two nearly independent parts: the adrenal cortex on the outside, and the adrenal medulla within. The cortex is, by almost any measure, the more important part of the adrenal gland. It accounts for about 90 percent of the gland's volume. It produces and secretes several dozen steroid hormones, including such important ones as aldosterone, which regulates the body's salt and water balance, and cortisone and hydrocortisone, which are involved in the metabolism of fat, protein, and carbohydrate. It is an essential organ — remove it, and the person will die.

By contrast, the adrenal medulla would seem to be the junior partner. It is tucked away inside the cortex, just one-ninth the cortex's size. It produces only two hormones, whose jobs are mainly fine-tuning. Neither is essential to life. Yet it was the adrenal medulla that would set researchers on the path that would lead eventually to fenfluramine, phentermine, Redux, and at least a dozen other drugs that doctors have used in attempts to help patients lose weight.

The better-known of the two hormones produced by the adrenal medulla is epinephrine, or adrenaline, the flight-or-fight hormone that floods the body in times of excitement or stress. Adrenaline produces the flight-or-fight response by stimulating the sympathetic nervous system, the part of the involuntary nervous system that directs glands and various smooth muscles, such as those in the heart. A jolt of adrenaline pushes the heart to pump faster and harder, causes the blood vessels in muscles to dilate, providing greater blood flow to the muscles, and signals the liver to break down glycerol into glycogen, sending extra sugar into the bloodstream for quick energy. The second hormone produced by the adrenal medulla is norepinephrine, or noradrenaline, which is closely related to adrenaline and has very similar effects in the body.

It was adrenaline and, to a lesser degree, noradrenaline whose action Sharpey and Oliver observed when they fed bits of adrenal tissue to lab animals and saw blood pressure climb, and so it was these two hormones and not some of the more vital products of the adrenal cortex that were named for the adrenal gland. And it was adrenaline that became the first hormone to be isolated from the gland — in 1901, by Jokichi Takamine, a Japanese chemist working in the United States at the time.

The chemical structure of adrenaline is vaguely comet-like: a large head with a tail tagging along behind. The head is a benzene ring, a circle of six carbon atoms each with a hydrogen atom attached. The tail is a line of three carbon atoms with several hydrogen atoms and an ammonia molecule (one nitrogen and two hydrogen atoms) clinging to it at various points. Beginning in the early 1900s, chemists and biochemists studied a large number of adrenaline-like molecules.

They would create variations by changing the length of the tail, by hanging different atoms and molecules off the sides of the tail, and by attaching different atoms to the benzene ring. They would then test the new chemical on experimental animals, usually by observing the effect on blood pressure. As early as 1910 it was clear that a number of these adrenaline-like molecules had effects on the sympathetic nervous system very similar to adrenaline's.

In this way, a whole new line of research opened up: the development of drugs whose actions mimicked those of adrenaline and noradrenaline but which would affect the body in different—and, it was hoped, more medically useful—ways. One of the earliest drugs to come out of this research program was ephedrine, which was used as a decongestant in the United States beginning in the 1920s. (A related drug, pseudoephedrine, is still a common decongestant today.) Ironically, after ephedrine was synthesized in 1923, Western doctors discovered that they were not the first to put it to work clearing noses. It occurs naturally in the mahuang shrub, which had been the basis for asthma and hay fever remedies in China for some 5000 years. Ephedrine works by constricting the tiny blood vessels in the mucous lining of the nose, cutting off blood flow in the nasal lining, and reducing the inflammation that leads to the feeling of congestion.

Up until this point, researchers had thought of the adrenaline-like drugs mainly in terms of their effect on the sympathetic nervous system: increasing blood pressure, speeding up heart rate, dilating the pupils and the bronchial tubes, and so on. But doctors discovered that their patients who took ephedrine often experienced nervousness, tremors, or insomnia alongside the effects on the cardiovascular system. Ephedrine, it seemed, was a mental stimulant as well as a physical one.

Realizing this, physicians in the early 1930s put ephedrine to work in a different manner: reversing the effects of narcotic drugs and treating victims of narcolepsy. For reasons that are still not well understood today, narcolepsy causes a person to fall asleep at almost any time—while reading, eating, carrying on a conversation, even while walking—and then wake a few seconds or a few minutes later as if nothing had happened. Regular doses of ephedrine helped many of them stay awake.

In 1935, Myron Prinzmetal and Wilfred Bloomberg, two doctors at the Harvard medical school, reported that a new drug worked dramatically better than ephedrine at keeping narcoleptics awake. Benzedrine, also known as amphetamine, was another of the family of drugs with a chemical structure similar to adrenaline. In the mid-1930s it was mainly being used in spray form to treat congestion and inflamed nasal membranes. Earlier researchers had tried benzedrine spray in the treatment of narcolepsy and found it useless, but Prinzmetal and Bloomberg decided to give it orally. And when they did, they found it stopped the sleep attacks in every one of the nine patients they studied, including some for whom ephedrine had done no good at all.

From there, one thing quickly led to another. M. H. Nathanson, a doctor at the University of Minnesota's medical school, wondered whether benzedrine might also help people who complained of constant fatigue and exhaustion but did not actually fall asleep at inappropriate times. It seemed reasonable that narcolepsy was merely an exaggerated version of this fatigue syndrome, so Nathanson gave benzedrine to forty such patients. Most of them felt that their fatigue had lessened, but, Nathanson found, benzedrine's effects did not stop there. His patients experienced an increased energy and ability to do work, he reported, and often even a feeling of exhilaration. "Many patients volunteered that there had been a definite increase in mental activity and efficiency. Another striking reaction was a tendency to loquaciousness. This was very marked in many instances and was noted both by the patients and by those around them."

Soon after, researchers in the University of Minnesota psychology department gave benzedrine tablets to normal subjects in a test of "mental efficiency" and found that the drug prevented sleepiness and generally "pepped up" those who took them. It didn't take long for word to spread through the university's student body, and by early 1937 the local drugstores were being visited by students who wanted the drug in order to stay awake and alert while preparing for exams or writing papers. Within a couple of months, students at a number of colleges around the country were taking benzedrine, and by June the editors of the *Journal of the American Medical Association* were inveighing against this unplanned use of the drug, citing side effects such as insomnia, fainting, and collapse. "Benzedrine sulfate," they intoned, "thus becomes one more example of a drug which is useful in a limited field of therapeutics but which has been diverted to uncontrolled use by the public for related, but not similar, purposes."

The editorializing did no good. The use of benzedrine for the purposes of staving off sleep and increasing mental alertness would only increase in the coming years. Not just students but pilots, long-distance truckers, shift workers, and anyone else who needed to stay awake for long stretches was apt to try it.

In his test of benzedrine on patients with constant fatigue, Nathanson had noticed another effect, this one completely unexpected. Ten of his forty subjects reported that their appetite had decreased noticeably and that they had lost weight. Nathanson was not interested in weight loss and did not follow up on the findings, but others would. This was a side effect that could prove useful — and profitable.

Over the next several years, a series of studies tested the effectiveness of benzedrine in weight loss. In 1938, for instance, two psychiatrists from the Boston State Hospital reported the effects of benzedrine in seventeen obese patients, most of them with some sort of psychological problem as well. All but one lost weight, even though no attempt was made to keep the patients on a diet. The average weight loss ranged from one pound a week to more than four.

Clearly benzedrine worked, although some researchers did notice a tendency for its effects to lessen after a few weeks. But no one knew just how it worked. Mark Lesses and Abraham Myerson, the Boston State Hospital psychiatrists, theorized that it cured the "anhedonia" of the obese. Most fat people, they suggested, eat because they are bored, because other parts of their lives no longer give them pleasure. Benzedrine, by increasing mental energy and making life seem more interesting, cured this inability to take pleasure in their lives and removed the major reason they were eating too much. Lesses and Myerson also suspected that benzedrine was causing patients to burn a few more calories each day: they moved around and exercised more because they felt better and had more energy. Other researchers suggested that the weight loss might come from shedding excess water, or that the benzedrine decreased the appetite by relaxing the muscles of the stomach and intestine and thus decreasing the number and strength of hunger contractions.

It was 1947 before doctors realized that benzedrine works primarily by suppressing the appetite. The proof came in a series of experiments performed by three physiologists at the Northwestern University Medical School in which they fed benzedrine to both dogs and human volunteers. The researchers had let the human subjects eat as much as they wanted and measured their intake while they were kept on either benzedrine or a placebo. Almost without exception the subjects ate less and lost more weight on the drug. Next the subjects were put on a constant 3000 calories per day and given the benzedrine again. Some of them had a small initial weight loss, which the researchers attributed to their moving around more on the drug, but after the first few days their weight stayed steady. Benzedrine, the researchers concluded, must work almost exclusively by decreasing the appetite. To nail down their case, they reported that the benzedrine had worked the same way in dogs, cutting their appetite to the point where they would refuse food for days on end.

Finally, the researchers cut the nerves to the dogs' intestines so that the dogs could not perceive hunger contractions and repeated the experiment. The benzedrine, they found, worked just as well as before, which the researchers took as proof that the drug was doing its work not in the stomach and intestines but directly in the brain.

It was, or so it seemed at the time, a turning point in the battle against obesity. Here was a drug that could break the pattern of overeating in the obese in the most direct way possible, by damping their overactive appetites. Combined with drugs to speed up the metabolism, it should help the obese return to a healthy weight. That, at least, was the hope.

Slowly, almost imperceptibly, from the 1940s through the 1950s and on into the 1960s, the use of pills to help people lose weight grew more widespread and more common. It was mostly a hidden phenomenon, taking place as millions of individual transactions between doctor and patient, so it is difficult to track directly, but the indirect evidence is considerable. Certainly, interest in losing weight was growing. Articles in popular magazines on dieting were relatively rare in the 1940s, more common in the 1950s, and by the 1960s were becoming nearly as ubiquitous as they are today. And the number of drugs available for fighting fat was growing as well.

Phentermine, half of the fen-phen combination, was approved by the FDA for use as a diet drug in 1959. Fenfluramine, the other half, was under development and testing in the 1960s and was approved in 1973. A 1976 review of weight-control drugs listed a score of them in use: thyroid compounds; various hormones, including human chorionic gonadotropin and human growth hormone; drugs that slowed the absorption of food in the intestines; the heart stimulant digitalis; and a dozen appetite suppressants, from several amphetamines to phentermine and phenylpropanolamine, widely used as a decongestant but also packaged in diet pills. The combination of readily available diet drugs with a population increasingly fixated on being thin would result, in the late 1960s, in the worst episode in the checkered history of the weight-loss industry.

By the beginning of the 1960s the FDA had choked off most of the obvious abuses of diet-pill use. In contrast to the 1930s, when dinitrophenol and benzedrine were available at drug stores to anyone who asked, now the more powerful drugs could be bought only with a doctor's prescription. Some diet aids were still available over the counter—phenylpropanolamine, for instance, and benzocaine, a topical anesthetic that supposedly dulled the nerve endings in the mouth and cut the appetite—but they were generally safe. Of course, they were almost completely ineffective, too, but enterprising businessmen could, with a good advertising campaign and the right trade name (Ayds, Figure-Aid, Appedrine, and so on), make them sound like winners. The more dangerous and more effective drugs were to be reserved for those patients whom a doctor judged to be in medical need of losing weight. Unfortunately, different doctors had different ideas of what constituted medical need, and for some of them, anyone who walked in the front door with cash in hand fit the bill.

The diet pill scandal broke in September 1967, when Russell Henry, Oregon's chief medical investigator, accused diet pills of killing six Oregon women in the previous two years. Henry had become suspicious of the pills when the parents of a nineteen-year-old student at Oregon State University had questioned an autopsy report that blamed her death on "probably viral pneumonia." Upon looking into it, Henry found that the woman, Cheryl Oliver, had been trying to lose weight on a "rainbow pill" regimen—a package of half a dozen or so brightly colored pills taken in a prescribed sequence throughout the day. The collection generally included one of every type of pill that had been shown to—or been rumored to—help in weight loss: amphetamine, thyroid hormone, digitalis, thiazide or some other diuretic, and a laxative. A barbiturate such as phenobarbital was often thrown into the mix to cancel out any nervousness caused by the amphetamine. Henry blamed Oliver's death and those of at least five other women on an unanticipated interaction among the drugs: the thiazide and the laxative flushed potassium out of their systems, while the amphetamine, by cutting appetite and reducing food intake, prevented their bodies from replenishing the potassium as fast as necessary; the lowered potassium levels then made the heart muscle overly sensitive, so that a normally safe dose of digitalis sent the heart into spasms. Henry couldn't prove it, but his case was convincing enough that the *Journal of the American Medical Association* and two other medical journals published his warning about the pills.

Henry's charges triggered an intense scrutiny of the diet-pill business, including a Senate investigation led by Philip Hart, a Democratic senator from Michigan. One of the abuses that immediately became apparent was the practice of packaging two drugs into a single pill. One of the most common combinations was digitalis and thyroid hormone, which both stimulate the heart and whose interaction might have unpredictable results, and in early 1968 a U.S. district judge ordered the Lanpar Company, the largest diet pill manufacturer in the country, to stop selling such pills and destroy its stocks of them. At about the same time, prodded by Hart's hearings, the FDA seized some 45 million pills from various manufacturers, claiming that they were not "safe and effective" for losing weight. But the most disturbing details Hart uncovered dealt not with the drugs but with the doctors who were dispensing them.

The hearings found that most dieters were getting their pills not from a pharmacy via a doctor's prescription but directly from the offices of "fat doctors." According to testimony before Hart's committee, about 5000 doctors, half of them osteopaths, were specializing in obesity. Many were legitimate, but a portion of them ran thinly disguised pill outlets, to which almost anyone could come and, with a minimum of fuss or physical examination, walk out with a bag of diet drugs.

Susanna McBee, a reporter for *Life*, set out to see just how easy it was to obtain diet pills. At five-foot-five and 125 pounds, she was trim, and certainly well within any recommended weight categories for her height. Even after stuffing herself in preparation for her assignment, she weighed no more than 130 or 131 — still not a candidate for medical weight loss by any definition. Yet of the ten diet doctors she visited across the country, not one refused to supply her with pills, even though three of them told her she didn't need to lose weight. At the end she had received an average of 150 pills per doctor. Of course, she had picked the doctors ahead of time as being well known for running pill clinics, but the ease with which she accumulated amphetamines, barbiturates, thyroid tablets, diuretics, laxatives, digitalis, and even sex hormones was arresting. At some of the clinics McBee had only her height and weight checked; at others she filled out questionnaires or had more detailed measurements and tests, such as temperature, blood pressure, and hemoglobin. The result, as she noted in her article for *Life*, was always the same: the doctor decided she needed pills.

One obvious problem with this system, as Hart's hearings brought out, was that the doctors had a conflict of interest. As doctors, they should be looking out for the health of their patients, which should mean that they would never prescribe pills for someone like McBee. As businessmen, however, they had a strong incentive to sell pills to everyone who walked in the door: the pills were much more profitable than the office visit. One doctor, Hart's committee heard, paid $71 for 100,000 pills which he then sold to his patients for $12,000. It had reached the point where many of the diet clinics assumed that you would leave the office with a bag of pills, so that the cost of the visit, extracted up front, included the price of the pills. By 1967, the country's fat doctors were grossing half a billion dollars a year on annual sales of two billion diet pills. Some of them were seeing as many as 100 patients a day, bringing them a total income of around $2000 daily, or half a million dollars a year — more than $2 million a year in today's dollars.

The solution, Hart suggested, was to remove the conflict of interest. He proposed legislation to prevent doctors from owning pharmacies or drug-repackaging companies and to restrict their sales of drugs to patients to certain extraordinary circumstances, such as during emergencies or in rural areas where pharmacies are scarce. Today, doctors are generally not permitted to sell drugs directly except in special cases, as when there are no nearby pharmacies.

As the dangers of the rainbow-pill regimen were being uncovered and the abuses of the pill doctors being addressed, yet a third problem of diet drugs was emerging, and it was this that would tar the industry for a generation. Of all the drugs prescribed for losing weight, benzedrine was by far the most appealing. It had few of the physical side effects and risks of thyroid or digitalis, and it did not flush out potassium and other nutrients as did the diuretics and the laxatives. It was psychologically satisfying, for it worked by making it easy to eat less and giving the illusion of increased willpower. It also made a person feel, at least for a few hours, happier and more energetic—an effect that made it a favorite of the pill-popping drug culture that had grown up in the late 1960s. So as digitalis, thyroid, and other weight-loss drugs were removed from the weight-loss arsenal, benzedrine—now usually referred to as amphetamine—came to be the drug of choice for many doctors trying to help patients lose weight.

But as their use grew, amphetamines' dark side came into view. Although people taking it did lose weight for a few weeks, their bodies quickly developed a tolerance for it. The weight loss—and the emotional highs—stopped, which led people to up the dose, trying to regain the magic of those first few weeks. Again and again they would increase the dosage, and although amphetamine is not physically addictive, doctors found that this pattern of abuse could be as difficult to break as narcotic addiction. If the amphetamine use continued, the patient could expect insomnia, increased anxiety, and, in the long term, a psychosis much like paranoid schizophrenia. On the other hand, if the patient used amphetamine for a few weeks and stopped, the lost weight generally returned.

The FDA finally banned amphetamine in diet pills in 1979. By that time, thanks to many well-chronicled stories of amphetamine abuse, amphetamine-containing diet pills—and, by association, prescription diet drugs in general—had developed a reputation as sleazy and disreputable. It would be more than a decade before the industry recovered.

If the history of weight-loss drugs teaches us anything, it is that tricking the body into losing weight by pharmaceutical means inevitably carries a certain amount of risk. Time and time again, drugs that were thought to be safe and effective have been misused or had unexpected consequences. Dinitrophenol in the 1930s. Rainbow pills in the late 1960s. Amphetamines in the late 1960s and early 1970s. In Europe, during the late 1960s and early 1970s, an epidemic of pulmonary hypertension struck users of the adrenaline-like diet drug aminorex; by the late 1970s, nearly half of the seventy-two known victims had died. Later, fenfluramine users would be struck by the same disease, although with not nearly the same frequency as users of aminorex. And, of course, there was the valvular disease that followed fen-phen and Redux use in the 1990s. It seems almost a rule of thumb that the more effective a drug is in helping a person lose weight, the more likely it is to have some negative consequences for the body as well.

Prescribing a diet drug then becomes a matter of balancing risk and benefit. Because the obese are prone to such syndromes as diabetes, high blood pressure, and heart disease, there is generally a benefit to losing weight, but some patients benefit more than others. The most obese—those who weigh 400 and 500 pounds—are at such risk that some doctors will take the extreme measure of surgically reducing the size of the stomach or bypassing it altogether. On the other hand, those who are just five or ten pounds overweight carry so little extra risk that only the most benign measures—diet, exercise, over-the-counter drugs—make sense. People in between should be willing to risk some negative effects from a weight-loss strategy, but how much risk is a judgment call.

The FDA played just such a balancing game with Redux. When considering whether to approve the drug, the problems with valvular disease were unknown but other risks were not. Researchers knew, for instance, that Redux increased the chances that a patient would develop pulmonary hypertension. It was also known that Redux causes brain damage in laboratory animals, although at higher doses than likely to be taken by dieters.

The risks seemed substantial enough that the FDA's advisory committee debated vigorously and often contentiously whether to recommend approval. It first voted against advising the FDA to approve Redux, then later reconsidered and voted for approval by a one-vote margin. When the FDA, which was not bound by the advisory committee's vote, decided to go ahead, it explicitly acknowledged the risks of Redux and advised that its use be limited to those most in need of losing weight. In particular, the agency found that Redux was indicated for people with a BMI of 30 or more—someone, for instance, who was five-foot-six and weighed 185 pounds or more—or for people with a BMI of 27 or higher who had some other health problem, such as diabetes or high blood pressure, that was exacerbated by being overweight. Redux, the FDA warned, should not be used for cosmetic weight loss.

So far, so good, but once it had approved the drug for sale, the FDA had no further say on how it would be used. And the second lesson to be learned from the history of weight-loss pills is that no matter how hard the medical establishment preaches that drugs such as these are for medical weight loss only, inevitably they will be picked up by people for whom they were never intended.

The decision to prescribe or not to prescribe is up to individual doctors, many of whom have traditionally paid scant attention to the finer points of the FDA's approval process. Fenfluramine and phentermine, for example, were never approved for use together, but only singly, yet when the 1992 paper by Weintraub reported that the two in concert worked better than either alone, fen-phen quickly became the most commonly prescribed diet regimen in the country. Few doctors worried that the combination had never been rigorously tested.

More to the point, for much of the past decade there has been a small cadre of diet doctors willing to prescribe diet pills to almost anyone for any reason. Like their predecessors at the 1960s pill clinics, they take your money and give you drugs, no matter whether you're a hundred pounds overweight or ten; the only difference is that you now have to take the prescription down the street to a pharmacy instead of walking out of the doctor's office with a bag of pills. In recent years, a number of journalists have followed Susanna McBee's lead, visiting diet doctors and reporting how easy it is to get the pills, but it somehow no longer seems as shocking as it did in 1968. Perhaps because the doctors are no longer handing out the pills directly, they can more plausibly claim to be looking after the patients rather than themselves.

It was the 1992 fen-phen paper that gave these pill mills a fresh start. Throughout the 1980s they had languished, suffering both from the residual stigma of the diet pill fiascoes of the 1960s and 1970s and from the lack of any drug that could be touted as the new miracle cure. By the early 1990s, however, a generation had grown up that wasn't put off by the idea of diet drugs, and when fen-phen appeared they embraced it. The more traditional and reputable obesity specialists reserved it for their heaviest patients, but others were willing to give it to anyone who asked—and the patients who wanted fen-phen quickly learned who those doctors were. By 1996, when Redux came on the market, fen-phen was already big business. An article in *Time* reported that one chain, California Weight Loss Medical Associates, had nineteen centers in the Los Angeles area and "a catchy toll-free number (1-888-4FEN-FEN) that it advertises in the *Los Angeles Times*, the *Los Angeles Daily News* and on Howard Stern's syndicated radio show." Other clinics, the article said, offered discounts for bulk orders. The clinics would apply the same tactics to the selling of Redux, helping give it a spectacular start.

As a result of this pills-for-everyone attitude, the list of victims of fenfluramine- and Redux-induced heart valve problems included a number of people, mostly women, who had been just slightly overweight. One was Sabine Sisk-Bisson, Patient 4 in the report that Jack Crary and Heidi Connolly published in *The New England Journal of Medicine*. In the spring of 1995 she started fen-phen, hoping to lose the fifteen pounds she had gained after quitting smoking. At five-foot-two and 150 pounds, she was heavy, but her BMI of only 27.6 was well below the cutoff of 30 that the FDA would suggest the following year for Redux and which was a benchmark that more conservative doctors had applied to fen-phen. The drugs did help her drop from a size 10 to a size 6, but soon she noticed that she was having trouble breathing and often felt exhausted. When she complained to her doctor, he discovered that her heart was weakened and enlarged. By the spring of 1996, a year after she started on fen-phen, the problem had become bad enough that she needed surgery at the Mayo Clinic to repair one of her heart valves. Two and a half years later, Sisk-Bisson was still unable to walk up hills or talk on the phone for long, and she told a newspaper reporter that she expected to need more heart surgery in the future.

People like Sisk-Bisson were never factored into the equation when fenfluramine and Redux were approved by the FDA. Of course, no one knew then that the drugs could damage heart valves, but no one believed that the drugs were completely safe, either. That's why—in theory, at least—the drugs were to be reserved for the truly obese, people who weigh a good deal more than Sabine Sisk-Bisson.

In practice, though, it doesn't happen this way. A huge demand for weight-loss drugs exists, not just from those who are fifty, 100, 200 pounds overweight, but from those who are five or ten or twenty pounds heavier than they'd like to be. And once the FDA has given its imprimatur to a new drug, patients and their doctors tend to assume that it is safe for anyone to take, ignoring the delicate cost-benefit calculations that may be part of the FDA's decision.

The FDA knows that any weight-loss drug it approves will be prescribed for people who are not obese. With Redux in particular, the agency could look to Europe to see how it was being prescribed there before it had been approved for sale in the United States: the majority of people taking it in Europe were looking to lose only ten or twenty pounds. The agency also knew that fen-phen was being widely prescribed in the United States for people who were only slightly overweight. Nonetheless, it approved Redux, taking into account only its implications for the obese.

It is easy to sympathize with the FDA. The agency is under constant pressure, both from pharmaceutical companies who have invested hundreds of millions of dollars into developing the drugs under consideration and from doctors and patients' groups who push for faster approval of new drugs. And always the debate over a drug is framed in the context of its value for the purported target group. There is no place in the approval process for a representative of the people for whom the drug is not intended but who may be tempted to take it. Perhaps that is how it should be. One could argue that it is not the FDA's place to consider these people in its decisions; whether they take a drug not specifically intended for them is between them and their doctors, and if they want to take a one-in-20,000 risk of developing pulmonary hypertension just to lose ten or fifteen pounds, so be it.

But one could also argue that the FDA's job is to look out not just for the patients for whom a drug is intended but for all the patients who are going to be taking the drug. If so, then the benefits of the drugs for the truly obese should outweigh the risks not just to the obese but to all of the people likely to take it, fat and nonfat alike.

Either way, the calculation depends not just on the risks but also on the benefits, and the third lesson from the history of weight-loss drugs is that where benefits are concerned, there is often less there than meets the eye.

The spring and summer of 1996 saw a flurry of articles in newspapers and magazines on a coming generation of diet pills. Excited by the advent of Redux, which had become the first new antiobesity drug approved by the FDA in twenty-three years, journalists looked to the future and thought they saw a new era. The amphetamine-induced antipathy toward weight-loss medications was gone, and obesity, finally recognized as a disease instead of a failure of willpower, would soon be attacked with a variety of new drugs. It was a stirring vision, and it even had a certain foundation in reality.

It was true, for instance, that a number of new and different weight-control drugs were in the pipeline. The first was sibutramine, a drug that would be approved by the FDA in November 1997. Manufactured by Knoll Pharmaceutical Company and sold under the trade name Meridia, sibutramine works in a way reminiscent of Redux. Like Redux, it increases the amount of serotonin available in the brain by slowing its absorption back into the neurons that release it. Unlike Redux, however, it does not increase the amount of serotonin released from nerve cells, which may explain why it does not seem to cause valvular heart disease or pulmonary hypertension. And unlike Redux, it also increases the brain's levels of a second neurotransmitter, norepinephrine. In ways that are still not understood, increasing the levels of serotonin and norepinephrine seems to make people feel full sooner once they begin eating, and clinical trials find that people dieting and taking sibutramine lose more weight than those dieting alone.

Sibutramine does increase blood pressure in some patients, so that, as with Redux, the FDA recommended it be used only for people with a BMI of 30 or more. And, in the beginning at least, it seemed as though people were listening. With the highly publicized Redux withdrawal occurring just three months before sibutramine's approval, its sales in the first six months were much more modest than Redux's had been, and the moderately overweight seemed to be staying away. Whether they will continue to stay away is questionable, given that sibutramine is, at least as this is written, the most effective appetite suppressant available in the United States.

In April 1999 sibutramine was joined on the FDA-approved list by orlistat, a rather unusual drug made by Roche and trade-named Xenical. Orlistat is not an appetite suppressant like most other weight-loss drugs but rather a lipase inhibitor. Lipase enzymes work in the intestines to cut up fat molecules into smaller pieces that can be absorbed by the intestinal wall. Orlistat slows down this process and so decreases the amount of fat digested in the intestines by about one-third. The fat that is not digested is excreted, which can result in such unpleasant side effects as diarrhea, cramping, and oily spotting. People taking orlistat seem to learn rather quickly to keep the amount of fat in their diet down so as to avoid these consequences, and this monitoring of fat intake may have something to do with the weight loss that has been seen in a number of studies.

Two *obese* mice, one treated with leptin injections, the other untreated. Photo credit: John Sholtis, The Rockefeller University, New York City. Reprinted with permission of Rockefeller University.

By inhibiting fat absorption, orlistat decreases the amounts of certain fat-soluble vitamins—A, D, E, and K, as well as beta carotene—that are taken in by the body, but the FDA was willing to overlook that, since people could take vitamin supplements. The clinical trials also found a mysterious increase in breast cancer among women taking the drug. Roche argued that the orlistat could not have led to the cancers since, given how long it takes them to develop, they must have started before the women began the trial. After examining more data, the FDA accepted that position.

Beyond sibutramine and orlistat, a number of weight-loss drugs are under development or in the early phases of testing. Some, like Redux and sibutramine, are drugs that increase the amount of serotonin in the brain and increase the feeling of fullness with a meal. But the more intriguing are the drugs that act in ways quite different from the traditional diet pills.

Most obvious is leptin, in Phase I clinical trials by Amgen. Although Phase I is designed merely to determine whether a drug is safe, Amgen has reported that the subjects of these safety tests have lost weight. The weight loss has been relatively minor, however, and the leptin must be injected. Amgen and other companies are looking for drugs that can be taken orally that will bind to the same receptors in the brain that leptin does.

A collaboration between Hoffman-LaRoche and Millennium Pharmaceutical hopes to bypass leptin and manipulate the leptin receptor directly, perhaps by finding a way to make it more sensitive to leptin. Since the obese do not have too little leptin—they generally have higher levels of leptin than people who are thinner—the idea is that the receptors of the obese do not respond well to the leptin their bodies produce. This is all highly speculative, though, and no one knows whether drugs to modify the leptin receptor can be found or, if they are found, whether they will be effective.

Several drug companies are looking into hormones or neurotransmitters that are known to affect food intake in rats or mice, in the hope that they can manipulate eating in people with similar success. One is neuropeptide Y, the hormone that induces lab rats to eat ravenously even when they have just been fed. In 1996, researchers from Synaptic Pharmaceutical and Ciba-Geigy found the particular brain receptor on which neuropeptide Y acts in passing along its "eat" signal. The researchers were testing a drug they hoped would block the neuropeptide Y receptor and, they hoped, make people less hungry. Another drug target is melanocyte-stimulating hormone (MSH), which acts to slow down eating in lab rats. Since MSH works by binding to the melanocortin-4 receptor, a number of companies are working on drugs that will stimulate this receptor and, it is hoped, decrease appetite.

Some pharmaceutical firms are also looking into cholecystokinin (CCK), the satiety-response hormone that Rosalyn Yalow thought might be involved in the *ob* mutation. Scientists at Glaxo Wellcome have uncovered a number of chemicals that mimic the action of CCK and have shown that rats fed these chemicals eat less than normal.

Yet another group of drug candidates are molecules that can stimulate the so-called beta-3-adrenergic receptors and, it is hoped, increase the metabolism and burn off fat. A number of these molecules have been shown to work in rats and other lab animals, and they are in preliminary testing at a number of companies, including Pfizer and Merck. The main problem here is that in rats the drugs work mainly by causing the rat's body to burn brown fat, a type of tissue common in rats but rare in humans.

Finally, some researchers are trying to go one step beyond the beta-3 adrenergic receptor, into the cell itself. The receptor sits on the surface of a cell and, when triggered, sends a message into the cell instructing it to make a particular sort of protein called an uncoupling protein. These molecules have the same effect on the cell as dinitrophenol, the drug responsible for a number of deaths in the 1930s: they uncouple the burning of fat molecules from the storage of energy in molecules of ATP. If the cell cannot store the energy from the burning of the fat, that energy simply goes to raising the temperature of the surrounding tissue. For some time, researchers have known of an uncoupling protein that works in brown fat, but only in 1997 did they uncover a similar uncoupling protein that functions in white fat and muscle tissue. Millennium and Hoffman-LaRoche are collaborating to find a drug that will mimic the action of this new uncoupling protein. If they find one and it works as expected, the pill would raise a person's metabolic rate and cause the body to burn more calories each day—without, it is hoped, the dangerous risk of overheating that came with dinitrophenol.

All in all, the coming generation of drugs is an impressive one, even if it is mostly potential at this point. The tools of molecular biology have allowed researchers to identify a number of genes, proteins, and receptors that play a role in regulating body weight, and increasingly sophisticated methods of pharmaceutical research have let researchers zero in on drugs that mimic the actions of the proteins or affect the receptors in one way or another. It is no longer a hit or miss affair, trying out a few chemicals whose structure is similar to adrenaline and observing their effects on the blood pressure of laboratory animals. Instead, it has become an intelligent, directed process in which scientists know what sort of control they would like to exert over the body and set out to find the best way to do it.

And yet—

And yet in reading over the descriptions of these marvelous drugs and what they do, or what it is hoped they will do, one has the nagging feeling that something important has been overlooked, some detail that puts all this in a different light. And with a little thought, one finds the neglected item in the Clinical Research Center of the Rockefeller University Hospital. It is P. J. Nelson, preparing to leave Rudy Leibel's weight-loss experiment, having brought her weight from 300 pounds to 188 by the simple expedient of taking in only 800 calories a day for a year or so, not counting the months she spent maintaining her weight at one plateau or another. But despite her determination that she would keep the weight off, a determination that had her sticking her finger down her throat the first few weeks out of the hospital, P.J. had gained back fifty pounds within nine months and all the rest of it within another three years.

Here's the rub: Losing weight has never been the real problem. Almost anybody can lose weight. P.J. had lost sixty to seventy-five pounds several times simply by strict dieting or, once, because of an extended illness. The real problem has always been keeping the weight off.

When doctors or pharmaceutical companies discuss weight-control drugs, they normally present them as a way to take weight off. Sometimes they will describe them as a way to help people who have difficulty dieting get over the initial hump, with the implication that once the dieters have started losing weight on the drug, they can keep it up on their own using diet and exercise. Sometimes—and this has become much more common in the past few years— obesity specialists will assume the drugs will be continued at least as long as the patient is losing weight and probably for some time after that, to help the patient maintain and get used to the new, lower weight. But here the job of the drug, at least as traditionally envisioned, ends. The weight has come off, the drug is discontinued, and . . . what?

Now, according to everything we have learned about weight loss over the past sixty years, the patient begins a slow, or sometimes not so slow, return to his previous weight. The rare patient, one in ten or one in twenty, will maintain most or all of the weight loss, but the rest will see their drug-driven weight loss evaporate.

What has been gained? Well, at least that one patient out of ten or twenty has gone from obese to a much healthier weight. Ironically, though, this patient probably didn't need the drugs at all. The people who maintain a major weight loss— fifty, eighty, a hundred pounds or more—do it mainly by changing their lifestyles completely. They eat healthy foods and watch every calorie, they exercise religiously, and they never forget how easy it would be to gain it all back. In short, they are exactly the sort of people who have the character traits necessary to lose a lot of weight by the traditional means of diet and exercise. It seems likely, although I am not aware of any study that has tested this explicitly, that the people most likely to gain a long-term benefit from diet drugs are exactly those who need them least.

For more than sixty years, beginning with the thyroid extracts and benzedrine of the 1930s, weight-loss drugs have been seen as a way to fix a medical problem in much the same way as a doctor cures an infection or sets a broken bone to allow it to heal. Once the weight is lost, the body is returned to its normal healthy state. Mission accomplished. Of course, a patient seldom lost enough weight to be pronounced "cured," but a doctor could hope that the patient would at least be better after the treatment than before. Today, however, it is clear that a better metaphor for obesity would be high blood pressure or some other ongoing condition. The treatments, to the extent they work at all, do not cure the patient but rather ameliorate the side effects—the excess weight, the heightened risk of diabetes and cardiovascular diseases—that spring from the underlying syndrome, which is a body that wants to be fat. Like recovering alcoholics, who learn never to think of themselves as "former alcoholics," the recovering obese have not gotten rid of the physiological characteristics that pushed them to be obese in the first place; they have simply overcome them for the time being. Given that, the only approach to weight-loss drugs that makes sense is to accept that the drug therapy must be an ongoing process and to proceed from there.

The FDA and drug companies have been moving in just this direction, test-ing the safety and efficacy of drugs over periods of two years or more, rather than a few months, with the expectation that patients will stay on the drugs for at least several years, if not indefinitely. This demands a good deal more from the drugs than has previously been asked. They must be safe to take for years, not weeks or months, and they must continue to work. Weight loss on the drugs always stops, usually after three to six months, but the question is whether a patient can main-tain the weight loss by staying on the pills. With some drugs, the body compen-sates for them to such a degree that the patient regains the lost weight even while continuing to take the medication; with others, such as fen-phen, the weight stays off for two years or more. It was this staying power that made fen-phen so popu-lar. In the future, it seems likely that the FDA will approve only those drugs that have proved themselves over these longer periods.

But if the drugs are to become a permanent part of the lives of obese people, then the rationale for their use merits a renewed and increased scrutiny, for this change is not just quantitative—from, say, three months to two years—but is also qualitative. If drug use is to become a way of life for the obese, there should be good reasons.

And a growing number of doctors, albeit still a seeming minority, are deciding that the case for giving drugs to the obese is not a good one. In January 1998, for instance, the editors of *The New England Journal of Medicine* called for rethink-ing the usual New Year's resolution of losing weight. People should keep in mind, they wrote, "that the cure for obesity may be worse than the condition," and they suggested that the medical profession's determination to reduce the obese may not stem from a clear-eyed assessment of the risks and benefits of weight loss. Doctors and, increasingly, the general public have a tendency to "medicalize" behaviors and conditions that they disapprove of, to settle on a particular stan-dard of what is healthy and then to treat all deviations from that ideal as things that need to be corrected. Thus smokers should be urged to quit, the sedentary be put on exercise programs, the depressed be medicated or given counseling, and the obese be reduced.

In the case of obesity, this urge to medicalize is combined with the desire of many doctors to remove the stigma from overweight, which in turn leads them to embrace the idea of obesity as a disease. But, as the drug developers and phar-maceutical companies are well aware, it is just a short step from pronouncing obesity a disease to deciding that it should—it must—be treated with drugs. The traditional argument is actually the converse: Because it is so hard to lose weight without drugs, obesity should be considered a disease. But the two arguments reinforce each other nicely, if one doesn't mind a bit of circular logic: If obesity can be fixed only with drugs, it must be a disease; and if obesity is a disease, we need drugs to fix it.

The editors of the *New England Journal* urged a more dispassionate approach, comparing the costs and benefits of weight loss, and they argued that the medical benefits are not as great as most assume. Granted, there are health risks to being obese, but they are often exaggerated. The single most common health statistic about obesity is that it, depending on who is talking, "causes" or "contributes to" 300,000 deaths in the United States each year, making it the second leading preventable cause of death after smoking. The FDA itself put this number in its press releases announcing the approval of both Redux and sibutramine, although the agency did qualify this somewhat by adding "combined with other risk factors." The reality isn't nearly so dramatic. The 300,000 figure had its origin in a 1993 study by Michael McGinnis and William Foege which appeared in *JAMA*, the journal of the American Medical Association. What McGinnis and Foege actually calculated was that "dietary factors and activity patterns that are too sedentary" contributed to 300,000 American deaths each year, but not just via obesity. They noted that the health effects of these dietary factors and activity patterns also include high blood pressure, heart disease, and cancer and that it is difficult to sort out how many of those deaths should be chalked up to any one particular cause. In 1999, another study appeared with conclusions much like the earlier one, and with exactly the same shortcomings. Although this one was phrased more dramatically than that of McGinnis and Foege, stating that nearly 300,000 American deaths each year were "attributable to obesity," what the paper really found was that 300,000 obese Americans were dying earlier than expected each year from *something*. No one knows how many of these untimely deaths are caused by having too much fat.

It is also not clear, the editors noted, how much benefit there really is to losing weight. People with health problems such as heart disease, hypertension, and diabetes do seem to be helped by losing at least 10 to 15 percent of their body weight, but the moderately obese and those who are otherwise healthy may not gain much at all from losing weight. Furthermore, it seems that much of the benefit attributed to losing weight may actually come from a person's changing over to a healthier diet and a more active lifestyle. If so, the emphasis on losing weight is misplaced. In particular, it is hard to justify putting people on a long-term drug regimen to help them lose weight if the reason is to make them healthier. There is little evidence that weight loss by itself, without changes in diet composition or exercise habits, will have many health benefits.

Is there, then, a role for drugs in weight loss? Jules Hirsch, the Rockefeller researcher who pioneered the study of the fat cell and who collaborated with Rudy Leibel in his seminal study of the effects of weight loss and gain on metabolism, believes there is, but not for the current generation of drugs. None of today's drugs, he notes, treats the root cause of obesity, which is a body with a set point that is too high. Instead, the drugs attempt to keep the body artificially below that set point by affecting appetite, metabolism, or the absorption of food in the intestines. The body maintains its set point through a variety of interrelated systems, and when a drug affects one of these systems—appetite, say—the body will compensate in another area, for instance, by slowing down the metabolism. To get around this, the drug treatment must push exceptionally hard on one system or moderately hard on several systems, and either of these approaches makes it likely that the drugs will have unwanted side effects. Using drugs to modify the behavior of systems that are functioning perfectly is asking for trouble, Hirsch concludes.

The better approach, he says, is to learn how obesity develops, to understand how a person's genetic makeup interacts with the environment to determine the set point, and then to develop treatments and preventive strategies based on that understanding. Such treatments would be more effective and less likely to be harmful in unforeseen ways. This is no help for someone who wants to lose weight right now, but it could prevent a repeat of the Redux/fen-phen fiasco.

NINE

Just Who's in Charge Here?

Let us return briefly to 1967, a time of near-despair in the obesity field. For thirty years, doctors had been attempting to help patients lose weight, with little success. The traditional "eat less, exercise more" approach had failed. Psychoanalysis was fading, as its practitioners realized how few patients they were actually helping. And Oregon medical investigator Russell Henry had just charged the rainbow-pill regimen with killing six otherwise healthy women, a claim that would trigger an intense examination of the diet-pill industry and tarnish the reputation of weight-loss drugs for the next twenty years.

It was at this time that Richard Stuart, a psychologist at the University of Michigan's School of Social Work, announced a result that seemed almost too good to be true. Working with eight obese women over the course of a year, Stuart had helped all of them lose at least twenty-five pounds, and three had lost more than forty-five pounds. They had begun his program weighing from 170 to 225 pounds and ended it from 140 to 180. All had continued losing weight throughout the year—no rebounds, and not even a slowing of the weight loss. And it had been done without drugs and without psychoanalysis.

Stuart's tool was behavioral therapy, an approach that was still sparking controversy among psychologists. It had had its antecedents in the work of Ivan Pavlov, the Russian psychologist best known for showing that dogs could be conditioned to salivate at the sound of a bell, and B. F. Skinner, who had expanded upon Pavlov's work, using rewards and punishments to train lab animals to perform tasks that were sometimes astonishingly complex. One of his more famous tricks was teaching pigeons to play table tennis.

In the 1950s, a few psychologists had begun to apply the same sorts of techniques to people. If birds could learn to hit a ping-pong ball with a paddle, it seemed that humans should be able to overcome their phobias, control their destructive impulses, or, at the very least, stop smoking, but the behavioral approach demanded that psychologists treat their patients in a radically different way from what they were used to. Traditionally, psychologists had concerned themselves with what was going on inside a person's head: the likes and dislikes, the thoughts and fears, the hopes, the insecurities. But in teaching a dog to salivate at the sound of a bell or a pigeon to play ping-pong, none of these mentalisms mattered. All that one cared about was what could be directly observed: the actions of the subject and the relevant stimuli in the external environment.

In Pavlov's best-known work, by training a dog to associate the ringing of a bell with the presentation of food, he caused the dog to salivate upon hearing the bell whether or not food was present. This was all done in terms of stimulus (the presentation of food, the ringing of the bell) and response (salivation). There was no need to worry about what was going on inside the dog's head. Later, Skinner showed how an action such as lever pressing could be encouraged in rats by offering a reward—usually food—each time they performed the correct action. Conversely, an electric shock or other unpleasant stimuli could be used to train an animal to avoid certain behaviors. In all of his work, Skinner spoke only of what could be observed directly. He was very deliberate in removing any mention of "mentalisms"—that is, thoughts, emotions, or any other goings-on in the head that were not observable. In this way he thought to make psychology more scientific by putting it on a solid experimental and observational basis.

All this struck many psychologists as too demeaning to apply to humans. It didn't help that people still remembered how Skinner had modified his "Skinner box" for rats to create the "Air-Crib," a soundproof, air-conditioned box intended to provide a completely controlled environment in which to raise a child for the first two years of life. (A never-confirmed but persistent rumor had it that Skinner used the device on his own daughter.) All in all, behavior therapy seemed uncomfortably close to the sorts of things Skinner had advocated in his 1948 book, Walden Two, which offered a vision of a perfect, socially engineered world in which humans are shaped by techniques much like those he used on his rats.

Still, a cadre of psychologists—both Skinner disciples and those who were simply disenchanted with traditional psychoanalysis—were willing to ignore the Big Brother trappings and apply the insights gained from the animal experiments to humans. It was they who created the discipline that would be called behavior therapy. And, as it turned out, there was nothing to worry about. Patients were not, for the most part, treated like rats by their therapists, wired up to generators and given a shock each time they stepped out of line. Instead, they were taught to take the roles of both lab rat and rat handler, manipulating their own environments to modify their own behavior.

By 1967, behavior therapists had attacked anorexia, compulsive behavior, and smoking with some success, and Stuart applied almost exactly the same principles in his assault on obesity. The patients began by keeping a list of everything they ate and drank throughout the day, noting when, where, what food and how much, and what the circumstances were. Was it during a regular meal? Snacking as they read the newspaper? When they felt tense or depressed? By identifying what sorts of things triggered their eating, the patients could work with the doctor to avoid them. They also kept close track of their weights, recording them at four different times during the day. The weighings were intended to remind the patients constantly of what they were trying to do as well as to attach an immediate and unpleasant consequence to overeating: Eat too much, and the scale would notice.

Behaviorists believed that people ate too much in part because the effects of overeating were too indefinite and too removed from the act of eating itself, so one of the main goals of behavior therapy was to have patients associate eating directly with consequences that they wished to avoid. Stuart did this by a "sensitization" technique in which he had patients imagine themselves about to eat a favorite food and then immediately imagine some unpleasantness that could be tied to eating. One woman imagined taking her favorite cookie from the package, bringing it to her lips, and then switched to an image of her husband seducing another woman. She had told Stuart earlier that she feared her fatness might lead to such unfaithfulness, and he taught her to attach that fear to between-meal snacks.

Stuart also spent a great deal of time teaching his patients to modify their habits so that they would avoid many of the stimuli that triggered their overeating. If a patient regularly snacked at 10 a.m., for example, she was directed to schedule another activity—reading the newspaper, calling a friend—at that time.

Much of the rest of the program was designed to make eating a more complicated, less automatic experience, so that the stimuli that normally triggered overeating would have less power. Patients were told to get rid of all food in the house except in the kitchen and to make sure that everything in the kitchen needed preparation. Furthermore, they were to prepare only one portion at a time. While eating, they were to do nothing else—no reading, no watching T.V., no talking on the telephone—so that the eating was less likely to proceed unnoticed. These changes were designed not so much to get the patient to eat less as to make the eating more amenable to control by the patient by separating it from other behaviors. Finally, to slow the one-bite-leads-to-another phenomenon, patients were taught to take small bites, eat deliberately, and put their utensils down between bites.

There were a number of ironies in the success of Stuart's program. Perhaps the most obvious was that the Orwellian-seeming behaviorist approach, with its roots in the practice of turning rats into lever-pressing automatons, actually gave patients more control over their own lives. Instead of feeling as if food controlled them, they learned to control their relationship with food. Granted, it was not the direct match-up of willpower versus the desire to eat that doctors had focused on for so long, but that was just the point. Most obese patients had shown they could not win in such a head-to-head confrontation. Eventually their desire to eat would overcome whatever willpower they could muster. So Stuart showed them how to win a guerrilla war with their appetites, striking behind the lines at all the cues and circumstances that gave their urge to eat such force. And with each success, each time they avoided that 10 o'clock snack or ate a carrot instead of a candy bar because that's what they had in the house, they gained more confidence and a greater sense of self-control. It may not have been self-control in the way it had traditionally been conceived, with the human will conquering all, but it was self-control nonetheless.

A more subtle irony was that although behavior therapy had its roots in the Skinnerian behaviorist program and its practitioners tended to think of themselves as Skinnerians, the classic Skinnerian approach to psychology had no place for the sense of self-control that behavior therapists were creating in their patients. In his attempt to make psychology scientific, Skinner had banished any talk of mental states, for they were things that could not be measured or detected by outside observers. All was to be stimulus and response, two elements that were observable. And, indeed, some of the more radical of the Skinnerians denied the reality of mental states altogether: if they could not be measured or detected, they were not real. But while this may have worked reasonably well for describing what happened with rats, it fell miserably short in explaining what was going on with patients in behavioral therapy programs, for these patients were not only responding to environmental stimuli but were also manipulating those stimuli, and the decisions to perform those manipulations and just how to do it were impossible to account for in stimulus-response terms. The fact that patients were manipulating their own environments implied that more was going on in their minds than Skinner had allowed.

The role of food held yet another irony. In behavioral experiments on rats and other animals, food was almost always used as a reward, the thing that encouraged the animals to engage in some particular behavior, since animals instinctively want food and will perform almost any trick to get it. In behavioral therapy, very similar techniques—with different rewards—were used to make food less appealing.

But perhaps the biggest irony of all was the way in which Stuart's method of obesity treatment came to be accepted by the psychological mainstream. As we saw in Chapter 2, from 1968 to the early 1970s Stanley Schachter and his students piled up evidence that the obese were particularly susceptible to external eating cues. Because they could not read their bodies' internal hunger signals, they had to depend on such things as time of day, the appearance of food, and so on.

Stuart could not have scripted it better. Schachter's work did two things. First, it explained why behavioral therapy should work so well: the patients were learning to manipulate precisely those cues that were most important in determining when they ate. The technique would presumably not be as effective in helping the normal-weight to modify their eating habits, since they were not as sensitive to external stimuli. And, more important, Schachter's hypothesis implied that behavior therapy was exactly the right approach to helping the obese because it addressed the cause of their obesity directly. If the obese overate because they were responding to various cues in their environment, the best way to fight that was to change the cues. Behavior therapy taught patients to do that.

Throughout the early part of the 1970s, behavior therapy and the external hypothesis grew in importance in part because they were feeding off each other's success. In his 1972 book, *Slim Chance in a Fat World: Behavioral Control of Obesity*, Stuart spent much of one chapter detailing Schachter's work, using it to provide a rationale for why behavioral therapy could be expected to work. By the late 1970s, however, the external hypothesis had come tumbling down. The obese, it turned out, were not more sensitive to external cues after all and were no better candidates for behavior therapy than anyone else.

Nonetheless, behavior therapy for obesity was here to stay. Although much of its early acceptance had been due to the popularity of Schachter's externality hypothesis, by the time the evidence had turned against Schachter, Stuart's approach had proven itself well enough to hang around. Over time, its effectiveness has turned out to be much more limited than hoped—no one after Stuart ever had quite the same success he did—but it does work. And, in the obesity field, that is saying a lot. Today, behavior therapy, modified somewhat from Stuart's initial approach but still recognizable, is an integral part of many clinical and commercial weight-loss programs and is probably the single most successful approach to losing weight.

Today, weight-control strategies can be divided roughly into three categories that correspond to the three types of factors that play a role in determining weight:

FAT (218)

behavioral, physiological, and environmental. Behavioral approaches seek to change the behavior of the overweight person, to make him or her eat less and exercise more. They can be as simple as a kindly lecture from the family physician or as complicated as hypnotherapy or the twelve-step approach of Overeaters Anonymous. Physiological approaches work by altering the level of various chemicals in the body that play a role in the regulation of appetite or energy expenditure. The modification is usually done with drugs, although some try to accomplish it indirectly by a radical shift in diet. And environmental methods change, in big ways and small, the world in which the dieter lives.

Despite its name, behavior therapy is essentially an environmental approach to losing weight. Although the goal is to change the dieter's behavior, there is little attempt to affect behavior directly. Instead, the basic strategy, going back to Skinner, is to alter various things in the dieter's environment that in turn will affect the dieter's behavior. In this case, "environment" is defined very broadly to include anything that affects how much one eats, from the types of food in the cupboard and one's mealtime ritual to the eating habits of friends and food advertisements on television. Behavior therapy's credo is that it is difficult to change behavior directly by willpower, much easier to change it indirectly by modifying those things that influence behavior.

The effectiveness of behavior therapy seems to be rooted in its ability to attack both of the things that keep people fat. To the extent that losing weight is difficult because people develop habits of eating and cannot get away from them, behavior therapy offers a strategy for breaking those habits: identify the various triggers for eating and remove them from your environment. And to the extent that weight loss is resisted by the set point, behavior therapy's modification of the environment may help there, too. Although the evidence for this is fragmentary and tentative, it seems that the set point may not be completely fixed but instead may depend to some degree on one's environment.

In 1978, just as the external hypothesis was fading away, Jeffrey Peck at the University of Utah was reporting a series of experiments in which he manipulated the set point in rats. Peck had been intrigued by the fact, which a number of researchers had noticed, that rats maintain different body weights depending on the diets they are offered. A rat fed with quinine-adulterated chow, for example, will eat less of it and weigh less than a rat given regular chow. Earlier scientists had thought little of the experiments, assuming that the rats wanted to be at the higher weights but could not because the taste or the bulk of the food limited how much they could eat. Thus, the rats were being kept artificially below their set points by these manipulations of their food.

Peck thought it was something else. He believed that the set point was not completely fixed by the internal state of the animal but also depended on the animal's environment—that it was a much more dynamic thing than most people had assumed. And he set out to prove it.

Working with more than 100 rats, Peck fed some of them rat chow, some of them rat chow adulterated with varying concentrations of quinine, and some of them rat chow mixed with sugar and lard. Unsurprisingly, those who ate the sweet, greasy food became obese, while those raised on the bitter food were leaner than the rats fed normal chow, and the higher the quinine concentration, the thinner the rat. Peck's question was: Were these different weights evidence of different set points or evidence that some of the rats were staying artificially above or below their set points because of the palatability of their food? To distinguish between the two possibilities, Peck tested the rats in three ways.

One group of rats, including animals that were fat, lean, and of normal weight, was deprived of food for two days. After losing nearly 10 percent of their body weight during that time, all three types of rats ate hungrily when they were once again offered food, and by the fourth day after the fast, the rats were back at almost exactly where they had been before the fast, at which point they began again their slow weight gain. Although the groups of rats eating the greasy food, the normal food, and the bitter food had started at different weights, they all defended their weights in exactly the same way, by overeating enough after the fast to regain their lost weight in half a week.

With another group of rats Peck inserted tubes directly into their stomachs and force-fed them an eggnog mixture that contained anywhere from 50 percent to 85 percent of the daily calories they had been ingesting. If a rat did not curtail its eating sharply, it would gain weight much more rapidly than it had been doing. But all three types of rats compensated by eating less and kept their weights approximately where they had been.

With a third group, Peck moved the rats's cages into a refrigerator. When a rat is kept at a lower temperature in this way, it compensates by burning off brown fat to raise its internal temperature. If it does not eat more to compensate, the burning of the fat will cause the rat to lose weight. In this test Peck found that all three types of rats ate just enough extra calories to maintain their body weights.

The implication, Peck said, was that the rats on different diets were defending different body weights, but defending them with the same persistence. Those on quinine-adulterated diets weighed less than the others, but when the stomach tube gave them the chance to gain weight without eating any more of the unpalatable chow, they refused, cutting back on their chow instead. Conversely, they would eat more of the bad-tasting food to maintain their weights when kept in the refrigerator. In short, Peck had changed the set point of the rats by putting them on different diets. The set point was not some fixed thing but rather varied according to the food environment in which the rats lived.

If something similar is true for people, it could help explain the success of behavior modification therapy. By changing the types of food they keep around the house, their eating habits, and other parts of their food environment, people may not only be making it easier to maintain their discipline, but may also be shifting their set points down slightly.

Still, behavior therapy is only a partial solution to obesity. It helps some people lose some of their excess weight. A very few people may find that it helps them return to a normal weight, but others find it does little or nothing for them. Ultimately, behavior therapy suffers from the same obstacle that has frustrated every other weight-loss strategy: the curse of the sand rat. As long as we live in this world of plenty, powerful forces will push us to be fat, and those of us whose bodies are most sensitive to these forces will have difficulty resisting no matter what technique—drugs, behavior modification, willpower—we choose to rely on.

So here we are. Some 30 percent of the adult population in the United States is obese, and the number is growing rapidly. We know what is behind this obesity epidemic: it is a plague of plenty, a product of the luxurious environment we have created for ourselves. We understand why the overweight and obese have so much trouble losing weight and keeping it off. And we have started to trace out the molecular pathways involved in the body's weight-regulating system, so that we can identify many of the particular hormones and other chemicals that affect appetite and metabolism. But none of this knowledge has been of much use in stopping the plague. What can we do?

First, we must accept that relying on individuals to take control of their weight has not worked and is not likely to work. For more than sixty years doctors have lectured us on the importance of good nutrition; and for the past thirty we have been indoctrinated about the value of physical fitness; and over the last two decades low-calorie and low-fat foods have been as easy to find as white bread. Today the overweight get help and advice from Weight Watchers, Overeaters Anonymous, a variety of commercial weight-loss programs, and more diet books than any one person could read, all of them dedicated to helping individuals change their behavior. None of it has helped. Yes, some individuals do succeed in losing weight, but the society as a whole is steadily getting fatter. If individual willpower and good intentions have not worked over the past sixty years, there's no reason to think they will in the next sixty. Halting the obesity epidemic will demand something more.

Many obesity specialists believe that the best chance for the obese lies with pharmaceuticals. Although drugs have not performed particularly well in the past, the future could well be different. With detailed knowledge of the body's weight-regulating system that researchers are now assembling, drug designers may be able to develop drugs that zero in on specific parts of that system, controlling appetite and metabolism with great power but with few side effects. Some researchers have gone so far as to suggest that appetite could be turned on and off like a switch.

Looking further down the road, it is possible that genetic engineering could be used to help the obese. In June 1999, researchers at the University of Florida announced that they had treated fat mice and rats with gene therapy, giving them copies of genes that produced appetite-suppressing hormones. Working with *obese* mice, who have a mutated copy of the leptin gene, the researchers inserted working copies of the gene into the mice, who then began producing leptin and lost weight. The researchers also injected copies of the gene for ciliary neurotrophic factor (CNTF) into rats. CNTF is known to suppress appetite in lab animals, and, indeed, the rats with the CNTF genes inserted did eat less and lose weight after they received the genes. Although gene therapy is still in its infancy, its potential is profound, and it is quite possible that obese patients would prefer this treatment, which could last for months or years at a stretch, to taking drugs every day. Even more speculative, someday doctors might be able to genetically engineer human embryos, replacing genes that make it likely a person would become fat with other genes that would predispose that person to thinness. People like the Pimas, with their genetic disposition for obesity and diabetes, would be good candidates for such genetic engineering.

Even if such remedies do prove effective, however, they should not be thought of as anything other than temporary, stop-gap measures. They are fine in the short term. After all, if someone is 100 or 200 pounds overweight, it's difficult to argue that he or she should not be given drugs—or, eventually, gene therapy—to take as much of that weight off as possible. But this is not something we should be satisfied with as a long-term solution. Already 30 percent of the adult population is obese and that number could well be 40 or 50 percent in the next few decades if current trends continue. Do we want to live in a world where 30, 40, maybe 50 percent of the population is taking drugs to control their obesity—especially when that obesity is caused by an environment that we have created? I don't think so. In the long run, the only goal that makes sense is to find some way to change the environment so that it does not push people so strongly to be fat.

In theory at least, we certainly could stop the obesity epidemic by changing the environment. If it were possible, for instance, to live as our ancestors did a few centuries ago, we would almost certainly have the same low obesity rates they did.

In the mid-1980s, an Australian researcher named Kerin O'Dea performed just such an experiment on a group of Australian aborigines. Like the Pimas and other American Indians, Australian aborigines have developed high rates of diabetes in moving from their traditional diet and lifestyle to a Westernized one and have also become overweight, though not as fat as the Pimas. O'Dea convinced ten middle-aged, overweight Aborigines, five men and five women, to spend seven weeks living as their ancestors did. They resided as hunter-gatherers in the same remote part of Australia in which their tribe had traditionally lived, eating nothing except what they themselves caught or collected. At the end of that time, the aborigines had lost an average of eighteen pounds and their diabetes had improved markedly by a number of measures: levels of blood sugar were down, the amount of insulin secreted after a meal was up, and the rate at which glucose was cleared from the blood after a meal had increased. Had they returned to this life permanently, it seems possible that they would have left behind completely the fattening effects of Western civilization.

This, of course, is not a practical option for the general population. We are no more likely to return to the lifestyle of our ancestors than the United States is to revert to being a collection of English colonies. Fortunately, we don't have to. All we need do is identify the particular features of the Western lifestyle that are so fattening and deal with them. Is it the high fat content of our foods? The sugar? The taste? The easy availability? The large serving sizes? Our eating patterns? The way that advertising and parenting practices have turned the foods that are worst for us—sweets, pastries, ice cream—into psychological rewards? And what role does the decreased amount of physical activity play? Are short bursts of intense physical activity more useful than extended periods of low-level movement in keeping the fat off? Up to now there has been relatively little research aimed at teasing apart these various factors, but until we know specifically what needs to be changed, we can't rework our environment to be more human-friendly.

The reworking will take various forms. Every now and then someone—usually the author of a weight-loss book—suggests returning to various habits of the past, such as replacing some of today's foods with the sorts of dishes that were common several hundred years ago, but that is just not going to happen. A few dedicated individuals might pull it off, but not the society as a whole. Instead, our best chance is to start with the environment we have and engineer it in various ways that don't demand a great deal of commitment from individuals. This is the idea behind sugar and fat substitutes—someone can move into a lower-calorie, lower-fat world with a minimum of effort—but the fake fat in particular is still not a satisfactory replacement for the real thing. Better, more widely used substitutes might make a difference. Another tack, suggested by Adam Drewnowski, a researcher at the University of Michigan who studies eating preferences, would be to start with foods that are healthy—broccoli, carrots, and so on—and find ways to make them more appealing, perhaps by modifying their taste and texture.

The food industry has been quite assiduous in finding ways to make snacks and other unhealthy foods even more appealing than they normally would be; maybe it can turn its talents to a somewhat more virtuous goal. The most difficult environmental changes to make will likely be those that encourage greater physical activity. Quite consistently, people have shown a preference for machines that relieve them of as much exertion as possible, from automobiles to the remote channel changer. It will be hard to sell them on anything that makes them work a little harder, even if it promises to help them stay thinner in the long run.

Once researchers have figured out which changes in the environment will be the most effective, those changes will have to be carried out, and that will not be easy. If we lived in a totalitarian society where the nutrition czar could order us all to live on rice and fish and the exercise czar could confiscate our cars and force us to ride bicycles everywhere, those benevolent dictators might be able to change our environment from the top and force us to be healthy in spite of ourselves. But we don't. We won't even restrict the sale of cigarettes when they are killing tens of thousands of people a year, so top-down changes in our diet or exercise habits are out of the question. The best hope is for a bottom-up approach, starting with individuals and working from there.

There is some evidence that this is already happening, albeit in a small way. For the past forty years, obesity researchers have been generally pessimistic about an obese person's chances for losing weight and keeping it off. The statement one hears most often is that only about 5 percent of overweight people lose a significant amount of weight and keep it off. That statistic got its start in a 1959 paper by Mickey Stunkard in which he reviewed the results of a number of studies by other researchers and found that only 5 percent of grossly overweight subjects were able to lose forty pounds or more. Since then, the number has been repeated regularly, often by obesity researchers who wish to make the case that the obese should not be stigmatized or held responsible for their weight. But while it is true that many of the clinical studies have had depressingly low success rates, it is also true that these studies tend to attract the hard-core obese who have had difficulty losing weight in any other way, and so they are not necessarily representative of the experience of all overweight people. The 5 percent figure is mainly a myth, a convenient fiction repeated often enough that almost no one questions it anymore.

Recent studies indicate that many more people than suspected have been able to lose weight and keep it off all by themselves. They do it by the boring but effective method of changing their lifestyles—altering their eating patterns, eating different sorts of foods, increasing their physical activity. The National Weight Control Registry, a project run by Rena Wing at the University of Pittsburgh and James O. Hill at the University of Colorado, has assembled thousands of cases where people have lost at least thirty pounds and kept it off for at least a year. The people in the registry, found mostly through solicitations in newspapers and magazines, have averaged a sixty-seven-pound weight loss for five years.

According to interviews with these successful losers, they tend to use many of the same techniques that behavior therapy employs, even if they don't think of what they're doing as behavior therapy. They keep only certain types of food in the house, for instance, and invent eating rituals, such as putting only small portions on a plate, that focus attention on eating and slow it down. They find ways to treat themselves with food that is not high-calorie and high-fat. They get involved in exercise programs, often with a friend who keeps them going when they might otherwise quit.

In essence, much of what these people are doing is aimed at shielding themselves from the fat-promoting effects of the larger society. They cannot change that social environment, but they can alter their own "mini-environments," the small parts of the overall environment that are most salient to them. In other words, these people are changing the world around them in little ways that make it easier for them to maintain healthy habits. As long as they can maintain their mini-environments, like little bubble worlds that insulate them from the things that made them fat in the first place, these people can maintain their weight loss. But if the bubble collapses and the outside world impinges, they will likely gain it back.

To go beyound these individual successes, people will need help from the scientific community. Researchers must learn about which things in the environment are making us fat, how they interact, and what the relative importance of each is. Is it more important, for example, to limit children's fat intake or to get them away from the television or computer and have then play outside? Besides studying what makes us fat in the first place, scientists should determine which changes in the environment are most effective in helping a person lose weight. These changes may not be exactly the same as the changes needed to keep people from becoming fat.

Ultimately, if the obesity epidemic is to be stopped, it will be necessary to move beyond manipulating the mini-environments of individuals to making changes in the social environment that we all share. If we could create a society free of the worst of the forces pushing people to be fat, then everyone, even those most vulnerable to those forces, could live his or her life at a normal weight without drugs and without a constant struggle to fight those forces with diet programs, behavior therapy, or sheer willpower. It is an appealing vision, but it will take an attitude adjustment of the same magnitude as the environmental movement pulled off in the 1960s and 1970s, when it succeeded in convincing society that clean air and clean water were important enough to demand a complete rethinking of how we were behaving with respect to the physical environment.

Nothing will be as difficult or as important in the fight against the obesity epidemic as this changing of attitudes. Throughout the twentieth century, we have insisted on seeing obesity as a problem of the individual. This was a perfectly reasonable attitude in the 1930s, when relatively few people were fat and the best medical minds saw obesity as the result of gluttony and sloth. It is problematic today, however, with some 30 percent of the adult population obese and clear evidence from cross-cultural studies showing that the major factor pushing populations toward obesity is the Western lifestyle.

Unfortunately, obesity researchers themselves inadvertently help sustain this emphasis on the individual. When researchers look for genetic differences that distinguish the obese from the non-obese, for instance, it creates the perception that genes are responsible for obesity. Yet the distribution of genes in our society has not changed in the past twenty years, while the percentage of the population that is obese has doubled. Genes did not cause that doubling of the obesity rate. They simply determined which individuals were more susceptible to the forces pushing on everyone in society.

More generally, there are a number of institutional factors that keep the emphasis on the individual. Doctors are trained to treat individuals, not societies, and when a fat person walks through a doctor's door, the doctor's job is to figure out what will help that individual. The exceptions are public health specialists and epidemiologists, who look at obesity and other diseases from a broader perspective, but so far they have had little influence on the broader society's view of obesity. Pharmaceutical companies, which fund a large amount of research on obesity, are interested in finding drugs that will help individuals overcome their weight problems, not in finding ways to change the environment so that people won't need drugs. Even public health campaigns generally focus on what individuals can do to lose weight or to keep from getting fat in the first place. The net result of all this is that people naturally think of obesity as caused by factors within an individual—the wrong genes, the wrong upbringing, the wrong behavior— and so they assume that obesity should be treated on an individual level, with diets, drugs, hypnosis, or some other personalized approach.

Furthermore, we in Western countries and especially the United States have a long tradition of emphasizing personal responsibility and personal accountability. Humans are endowed with free will, and what they do with their lives is up to them. Granted, there has been a muting of this attitude in recent decades, with various movements pushing to hold individuals blameless for a number of things they would have been condemned for in the past—mental illness, delinquency, even criminal activity—but this forgiveness has not yet been extended to the obese. Because any rational human being has control over what goes into his or her mouth, it seems intuitively obvious that someone who is 100 pounds overweight bears some blame for that situation. Even the obese themselves tend to see the problem as being within them, either because of their own personal failings or because of a genetic tendency to get fat.

From a practical point of view, however, debates about free will and personal responsibility do not get us very far. The bottom line is that we have tried dealing with obesity as a matter of personal responsibility for a long time, and it has done no good. We keep getting fatter and fatter. If we wish to create a world in which people are neither fat nor constantly fighting a tendency to be fat, it simply won't work to continue thinking of obesity as a problem of individuals. We must learn to see obesity as a product of the environment and to see the obese as people who are more vulnerable to that environment than others. We need, in short, a new paradigm for thinking about the obesity epidemic.

Imagine for a moment that some unknown toxin was in the air over the United States, a toxin that created serious lung problems in some people, left others with shortness of breath, and did not affect others at all. Researchers might well spend their time figuring out the characteristics of those most affected in order to determine the nature of the toxin, and doctors would try their best to treat the afflicted. But would anyone describe this as a problem of the affected individuals and suggest that the best approach was to hand out oxygen masks to this group, or perhaps find some drug that would minimize the effects of the toxin? Of course not. Everyone would recognize that the only reasonable long-term goal was to identify the toxin and remove it from the air. And so it is with the obesity epidemic: We must identify the specific things in the environment that are making so many of us sick and get rid of them.

The trick will be to move toward this attitude without killing the sense of personal responsibility for one's weight. If people interpret the message that the environment is the culprit as meaning that they are powerless in the face of that environment, they may stop trying to control their weight, and the epidemic will get even worse. The message is not that individuals cannot make a difference in their own weight. They can, and they do. The message is that society as a whole has created the problem by constructing an environment that is unhealthy for many of us, and society as a whole must do something to fix it.

How well we fight this battle will likely have implications far beyond the obesity epidemic. For tens of thousands of years, humans have been modifying their environment to suit their own needs, from the taming of fire and the development of flint tools to all the wonders of modern technology. For much of that time the modifications were relatively minor, but with the invention of agriculture and the creation of large-scale, integrated societies, humans found themselves living in a world much different from the world they had evolved in. That disconnection has only grown more pronounced since then, and today's highly technological society has almost nothing in common with the hunting and gathering culture that characterized human society for most of human history. From this point of view, it is not surprising that we should be suffering from a mismatch between what our genes were evolved to expect—a world of limited food resources, with periodic shortages—and the luxurious environment we have created for ourselves. And from this point of view, we should expect other mismatches to appear as well.

With a little thought, it is not difficult to come up with examples of such mismatches. Our immune systems, for example, were never designed to deal with the sorts of diseases that can develop and spread in cities with millions of people living closely together. Our social instincts are intended for living in small groups; many of our social problems, from mental illness to crime, could conceivably be linked to the inability of many people to adapt to life in a large, impersonal society. And the psychologist Diane McGuinness argues in her book *When Children Don't Learn: Understanding the Biology and Psychology of Learning Disabilities* that attention-deficit disorder is nothing more than a mismatch between how some children, particularly boys, naturally behave and the environment in which these children find themselves. We are drugging a whole generation of schoolchildren, she says, simply because they are not equipped to thrive in the artificial environment of the home and classroom that we expect them to live in. From an evolutionary perspective their behavior is perfectly normal, but it is not normal for our world, and, instead of changing that world to fit them, we expect them to change to fit it—with drugs if necessary.

At some point we must stop and ask ourselves how much adaptation we expect from people. How much behavior modification therapy must they undergo, how many drugs must they take in order to fit in, to survive and to thrive in this environment of our own making? Could there be a better way? Can we learn to shape our environment so that it agrees—or at least does not disagree so badly—with us, its inhabitants?

How we answer these questions for the obesity epidemic will set the tone for how we deal with the many other environmental mismatches that we are sure to encounter. This is the first battle in what is going to be a long war with various effects of the environment we have created for ourselves. How well we do in this battle will go a long way toward determining whether we learn to create environments that fit us or whether we continue to force ourselves to fit our environments.

Notes

Introduction

Page

3 **Patient 24** Andreas Strobel, Tarik Issad, Luc Camoin, Metin Ozata, and A. Donny Strosberg, "A Leptin Missense Mutation Associated with Hypogonadism and Morbid Obesity," *Nature Genetics* 18 (March 1998), pp. 213–215.

Five-foot-six and 330 pounds The height and weight were not recorded in the paper describing Patient 24. They come from a personal e-mail communication from Metin Ozata, January 8, 1998.

body mass index Body mass index is defined as weight in kilograms divided by height in meters.

The researchers named the mutation *obese* Biologists use italics in writing the name of a mutation. This book follows that convention.

4 **the man desperately wishes to lose weight** Personal e-mail communication with Metin Ozata, July 31, 1998.

He has not been able to find a job Personal e-mail communication with Metin Ozata, August 4, 1998.

He has tried dieting Personal e-mail communication with Metin Ozata, August 7, 1998.

testing members of Patient 24's extended family Strobel et al., "A Leptin Missense Mutation."

Nine of them were unaffected. Of the unaffected family members, some had two normal genes and some had one normal gene and one mutant gene. Since the mutation is recessive, only those family members with two copies of the mutant gene were affected.

Ozata has discovered a distant cousin Personal e-mail communication from Metin Ozata, August 3, 1998.

In England, Carl T. Montague et al., "Congenital Leptin Deficiency Is Associated with Severe Early-Onset Obesity in Humans," *Nature* 387 (June 26, 1997), pp. 903–908.

5 **And, in Paris** Karine Clement et al., "A Mutation in the Human Leptin Receptor Gene Causes Obesity and Pituitary Disfunction," *Nature* 392 (March 26, 1998), pp. 398–401.

Page

6 **A key-word search of Amazon.com** Keyword search on Amazon.com performed on November 3, 1999.

in 1995 Americans were spending Institute of Medicine, *Weighing the Options: Criteria for Evaluating Weight-Management Programs*, National Academy Press, Washington, D.C., 1995, p. 2.

In October 1999, a group of doctors Ali H. Mokdad, Mary K. Serdula, William H. Dietz, Barbara Bowman, James S. Marks, and Jeffrey P. Koplan, "The Spread of the Obesity Epidemic in the United States, 1991–1998," *JAMA* 282 (October 27, 1999), pp. 1519–1522.

the situation is probably much worse Ibid., p. 1520.

overweight people generally underestimate Furthermore, all people tend to overestimate their height. Both these reporting biases will tend to cause a person to report a lower BMI than is actually the case.

A more trustworthy set of numbers Katherine M. Flegal, M.D. Carroll, R.J. Kuczmarski, and C.L. Johnson, "Overweight and Obesity in the United States: Prevalence and Trends, 1960–1994," *International Journal of Obesity* 22 (1998), pp. 39–47.

7 **We take it for granted** In 1990, 23 percent of men and 40 percent of women contacted by the National Health Interview Study were trying to lose weight by eating less, exercising more, or both. John Horm and Kay Anderson, "Who in America Is Trying to Lose Weight?," *Annals of Internal Medicine* 119 (1993), pp. 672–676.

annual health-care expenses for obesity Institute of Medicine, *Weighing the Options.*

obesity is a factor David B. Allison, Kevin R. Fontaine, JoAnn E. Manson, June Stevens, and Theodore B. VanItallie, "Annual Deaths Attributable to Obesity in the United States," *JAMA* 282 (October 27, 1999), pp. 1530–1538. It is not accurate to say, as some have, that obesity causes 300,000 deaths in the United States each year. That number, which is reported in this paper, was calculated by looking at the death rate among the obese and comparing it with the death rate for people with a body mass index between 23 and 25 (which is, statistically speaking, a very healthy condition). This comparison finds approximately 300,000 more deaths each year among the obese than would be expected among a non-obese population. This does not necessarily mean, however, that obesity was the cause of these deaths. It is possible, for instance, that the obese have a variety of unhealthy habits—eating fatty foods, not exercising enough—that increase their risk of disease and early death. If so, some or much of the increased mortality chalked up to "obesity" would actually be due to other factors. The studies cannot tease out these factors, so all the deaths are labeled as being caused by obesity. What is clear is that the obese, for whatever reasons, have a significantly lower life expectancy than people who are not overweight.

9 **a heartening success** I. Sadaf Farooqi et al., "Effects of Recombinant Leptin Therapy in a Child with Congenital Leptin Deficiency," *The New England Journal of Medicine* 341 (September 16, 1999), pp. 879–884.

leptin injections on a three-year-old girl Gina Kolata, "Hormone That Slimmed Fat Mice Disappoints as a Panacea in People," *The New York Times*, October 27, 1999, pp. A1, A21.

Ozata had not yet Personal e-mail communication with Metin Ozata, September 17, 1999.

the same pace it has for the past two decades Since the late 1970s, the percentage of obesity in the adult population has increased by about eight percentage points every ten years. This is actually an anomaly—there was only a minor increase in the percentage of obese in the population from the mid 1960s to the late 1970s—so there is little reason to believe that the increase will continue at this pace. On the other hand, it was quite surprising to find that the increase had been so sharp in the 1990s, so it is hard to know when it will slow down. And there is no reason at all to believe that the percentage of obese in the population will start to drop any time soon.

11 **Obesity specialists are still debating** See, for instance, James O. Hill and Holly R. Wyatt, "Relapse in Obesity Treatment: Biology or Behavior?" *American Journal of Clinical Nutrition* 69 (1999), pp. 1064–1065.

12 **Some doctors even expect** See, for example, Gina Kolata, "The Fat War: Hope Amid the Harm," *The New York Times*, October 31, 1999, section 4, pp. 1, 5. Kolata quotes Stephen Heymsfield, a leading obesity specialist at St. Luke's-Roosevelt Hospital in New York City, as saying, "This is my prediction. We are going to be able to turn off appetite completely—eventually. The therapeutics will be sophisticated enough to stop people from eating." Researchers whom I have spoken with have expressed similar opinions, although none quite so dramatically as Heymsfield.

avoid the complications she could otherwise expect There is actually some debate as to whether losing weight helps an obese person dodge the normal medical consequences of obesity. It is possible, for instance, that the obesity is a result of something else—unhealthy eating and exercise habits, say—that leads to higher risks of various diseases, so that losing the weight without changing these other risk factors would have little effect. See Chapter 9 for more details.

Page

ONE: Medicalizing Obesity

15 **a simple experiment** Walter Bradford Cannon and Arthur L. Washburn, "An Explanation of Hunger," *American Journal of Physiology* 29 (March 1, 1912), pp. 441–454. Some background to, and more details about, the experiment can be found in Horace W. Davenport, "Walter B. Cannon's Contribution to Gastroenterology," in Chandler McC. Brooks, Kiyomi Koizumi, and James O. Pinkston, eds., *The Life and Contributions of Walter Bradford Cannon 1871–1945*, State University of New York Downstate Medical Center, Brooklyn, 1975, pp. 3–25.

In years to come See various chapters in ibid., for descriptions of Cannon's work. For a more condensed narrative, see Jean Mayer, "Walter Bradford Cannon—A Biographical Sketch," *Journal of Nutrition* 87 (1965), pp. 3–8.

16 **Arthur Lawrence Washburn** I am indebted to Jack Eckert, reference librarian at Harvard's Francis A. Countway Library of Medicine, for digging up much of the material on Washburn. Details are from a personal communication from Eckert dated February 10, 1999.

An obituary *JAMA* 192 (May 3, 1965), p. 440.

The idea for this experiment Ibid.

Hunger was widely believed Cannon and Washburn, "An Explanation of Hunger," p. 442.

17 **he did not believe the body's nutrient levels** Ibid., pp. 443–444.

"In order to learn" Ibid., p. 449.

"a soft-rubber balloon" Ibid.

what Washburn was swallowing Davenport, "Walter B. Cannon's Contribution," p. 21.

"The condom has a place in physiology" Horace W. Davenport, "Past President's Lecture: Human Voices," *Physiologist* 5 (1961), pp. 265–269. Quote is from page 267.

"After this preliminary experience" Ibid.

18 **"a rather tedious period of waiting"** Ibid., p. 450.

it was later discovered Albert J. Stunkard and Sonja Fox, "The Relationship of Gastric Motility and Hunger: A Summary of the Evidence," *Psychosomatic Medicine* 33 (March-April 1971), pp. 123–134.

19 **a series of observations and experiments** For more details, see Reginald Horsman, *Frontier Doctor: William Beaumont, America's First Great Medical Scientist*, University of Missouri Press, Columbia, 1996.

Beaumont's book William Beaumont, *The Physiology of Digestion*, 2nd ed. Burlington, Massachusetts, 1847.

Page

he would not become hungry again Ibid., p. 51.

Beaumont speculated Ibid., p. 55.

Eighty years later Cannon and Washburn, "An Explanation of Hunger," pp. 446–447.

21 **four calories of energy** The "calorie" discussed here is the dietary calorie. As the scientifically minded are aware, the calorie is also a unit of energy from physics and chemistry, and in this context it refers to something different. A dietary "calorie" is the same thing as what the chemists call a kilocalorie, or kilogram calorie, or Calorie. Throughout this book I use the term calorie in the dietary sense. Those more comfortable with the physics and chemistry terms should substitute "kilocalorie" for "calorie."

Atwater continued his studies Atwater later worked with Francis Benedict. See, for example, Wilbur O. Atwater and Francis G. Benedict, *Experiments on the Metabolism of Matter and Energy in the Human Body, 1900–1902,* Bulletin No. 136 from USDA Office of Experiment Stations. U.S. Government Printing Office, Washington, D.C., 1903.

Two generations later another scientist Albert J. Stunkard and C. Koch, "The Interpretation of Gastric Motility: I. Apparent Bias in the Reports of Hunger by Obese Persons," *Archives of General Psychiatry* 11 (1964), pp. 74–82.

a decent amount of extra flesh was prudent Roberta Pollack Seid, *Never Too Thin: Why Women Are at War with Their Bodies,* Prentice-Hall, Englewood Cliffs, N.J., 1989, p. 73.

22 **Neurasthenia, or nervous exhaustion** Ibid.

"This is more easily accomplished" As quoted in Daniel McMillan, *Obesity,* Franklin Watts, New York, 1994, pp. 13–14.

it was not doctors but statisticians A good, short history of the role insurance companies played in changing attitudes toward overweight can be found in William Bennett and Joel Gurin, *The Dieter's Dilemma,* Basic Books, New York, 1982, pp. 123–138.

the death rate was 35 percent higher than expected O. H. Rogers, "Build as a Factor Influencing Longevity," in *Proceedings of the Association of Life Insurance Medical Directors of America from Organization to and Including the 16th Annual Meeting,* Knickerbocker Press, New York, 1901, pp. 280–288. As quoted in David P. Barr, "Health and Obesity," *The New England Journal of Medicine* 248 (June 4, 1953), p. 968.

23 **a German physician, Martin Hahn** "Plump Youth; Thin Old Age," *The Literary Digest,* September 8, 1928, p. 21.

a watershed paper detailing the specific maladies Louis I. Dublin,

Page

"Influence of Weight on Certain Causes of Death," *Human Biology* 2 (1930), pp. 159–184.

kidney disease Today there seems to be no direct connection between obesity and kidney disease, although there is a clear indirect connection, since kidney problems are one of the main complications of diabetes. Thus Dublin's identification of nephritis, or inflammation of the kidneys, as one of the main causes of excess deaths among the obese, is strange. He had a separate category for deaths from diabetes, so it seems that he was speaking of kidney disease unrelated to diabetes, and, from what we know now, there should have been no such surplus of kidney disease among the overweight. See Dublin, ibid., pp. 167, 170–171, 174. See also Bennett and Gurin, *Dieter's Dilemma*, p. 134.

a wave of research Barr, "Health and Obesity," p. 968.

it was pointed to as definitive proof Bennett and Gurin, *Dieter's Dilemma*, p. 134.

when Rogers first performed his analyses Bennett and Gurin, ibid., p. 126.

the subjects were mostly white males Ibid.

24 **a significant minority questions** The loudest voice questioning the health risks of obesity is undoubtedly Paul Ernsberger. His case is laid out most completely in Paul Ernsberger and Paul Haskew, "Rethinking Obesity: An Alternative View of Its Health Implications," *Journal of Obesity and Weight Regulation* 6 (Summer 1987), pp. 58–137. There are other dissenting voices as well, however, including the editors of the *The New England Journal of Medicine*: Jerome P. Kassirer and Marcia Angell, "Losing Weight—An Ill-Fated New Year's Resolution," *The New England Journal of Medicine* 338 (January 1, 1998), pp. 52–54. See also the letters in response to that editorial, particularly one from Glenn Gaesser, in Correspondence, *The New England Journal of Medicine* 338 (April 16, 1998), pp. 1156–1158.

careful statistical studies One of the best is a sixteen-year analysis of 115,000 women enrolled in the Nurses' Health Study: JoAnn E. Manson et al., "Body Weight and Mortality among Women," *The New England Journal of Medicine* 333 (September 14, 1995), pp. 677–685.

Do not attempt E. M. Geraghty, " . . . And So You're Reducing!" *Hygeia*, May 1937, pp. 422–425. Quote on p. 422.

25 **dieting had been popular** A good account of the history of dieting back to the early 1800s can be found in Hillel Schwartz, *Never Satisfied: A Cultural History of Diets, Fantasies and Fat*, Free Press, New York, 1986.

doctors and physiologists were accustomed Seid, *Never Too Thin*, pp. 95–96.

Page

"**Dieting may be difficult**" Jerome W. Ephraim, "The Truth About Reducing," *American Mercury*, November 1935, pp. 362–365. Quote on page 364.

Don't let your child get fat! Mildred Hatton Bryan, "Don't Let Your Child Get Fat!" *Hygeia*, September 1937, pp. 801–803. Quote on p. 801.

Most fat or plump persons John Grinde and Alice C. Jolivette, "Slimming Scientifically," *Hygeia*, December 1937, p. 1072.

26 **An attribute of man** Lemuel C. McGee, "The Fat of the Land," *Hygeia*, May 1939, pp. 411–413, 448. Quote on p. 448.

27 **a forty-seven-year-old woman whose thyroid gland** James J. Putnam, "Cases of Myxedema and Acromegalia Treated with Benefit by Sheep's Thyroids: Recent Observations Respecting the Pathology of the Cachexias Following Disease of the Thyroid; Clinical Relationships of Graves's Disease and Acromegalia," *American Journal of the Medical Sciences* 106 (1893), pp. 125–148.

the case of a fourteen-year-old boy Alfred Froehlich, "Ein Fall von Tumor der Hypophysis Cerebri Ohne Akromegalie, *Wiener Klinische Rundschau*. 15 (1901), pp. 883–906. As reported in Hilde Bruch, *The Importance of Overweight*, W. W. Norton, New York, 1957, pp. 20–23.

"**It is the general opinion**" Karl von Noorden, "Obesity," in Karl von Noorden, Isaac Walker Hall, and Adolf Magnus-Levy, eds., *Metabolism in Practical Medicine*, vol. 3, W. T. Keener, Chicago, 1907, pp. 693–715. Quote on page 695.

doctors tended to lean toward See, for instance, "Plump Youth, Thin Old Age."

research showed that very few See, for instance, Ephraim, "The Truth About Reducing," or Grinde and Jolivette, "Slimming Scientifically."

28 **one 1930 study designed to test** J. M. Strang, H. B. McClugage, and F. A. Evans, "Further Studies in the Dietary Correction of Obesity," *American Journal of the Medical Sciences* 179 (1930), pp. 687–694.

"**If it is not a glandular disturbance**" Bryan, "Don't Let Your Child Get Fat!" p. 801.

29 **a series of careful studies** L. H. Newburgh and Margaret Woodwell Johnston, "The Nature of Obesity," *Journal of Clinical Investigation* 8 (1930), pp. 197–213; L. H. Newburgh and Margaret Woodwell Johnston, "Endogenous Obesity—A Misconception," *Annals of Internal Medicine* 3 (1930), pp. 815–825; Strang, McClugage, and Evans, "Further Studies."

To discover what was going on Newburgh and Johnston, "Endogenous Obesity—A Misconception," p. 820.

"the treatment of obesity lost its glamour" Albert J. Stunkard and Mavis McLaren-Hume, "Results of Treatment for Obesity: A Review of the Literature and Report of a Series," AMA *Archives of Internal Medicine* 103 (1959), pp. 79–85. Quote on p. 84.

30 **"Most obese patients"** Albert J. Stunkard, "The Management of Obesity," *New York State Journal of Medicine* 58 (January 1, 1958), pp. 79–87.

a remarkably uniform record Ibid., p. 85.

Of all human frailties Stanley Schachter and Judith Rodin, *Obese Humans and Rats*, Lawrence Erlbaum Associates, Potomac, Md.: 1974, p. 1.

Everybody loves a fat man Robert B. Greenblatt, "The Fat and the Lean," *Hygeia*, January 1948, pp. 43, 58–59. Quote on p. 48.

31 **No longer were the obese jolly** For a more complete discussion of the attitudes toward the obese during this period, see Chapter 3, "The Cultural Frame," in Bruch, *Importance of Overweight*, pp. 35–59.

they could create rats that overate A. W. Hetherington and S. W. Ranson, "Hypothalamic Lesions and Adiposity in the Rat," *Anatomical Record* 78 (October 1940), pp. 149–172.

a hypothesis that was advanced for the first time See, for example, Jean Mayer, "The Glucostatic Theory of Regulation of Food Intake and the Problem of Obesity," *Bulletin of the New England Medical Center* 14 (1952), pp. 43–49; Jean Mayer, "Regulation of Energy Intake and the Body Weight: The Glucostatic Theory and the Lipostatic Hypothesis," *Annals of the New York Academy of Sciences* 63 (1955), pp. 15–43.

32 **"When food is taken in excess of"** George H. Reeve, "Psychological Factors in Obesity," *American Journal of Orthopsychiatry* 12 (1942), pp. 674–678. Quote on p. 674.

One of the earliest psychological explanations See, for instance, S. Charles Freed, "Psychic Factors in Development and Treatment of Obesity," *JAMA* 133 (February 8, 1947), pp. 369–373.

if a person had a predisposition "It is not considered that these factors are specific causes for overeating but simply that they influence the release of nervous energy into the channel of overeating in those persons who tend in that direction." Ibid., p. 371.

In 1947 Alfred Schick Alfred Schick, "Psychosomatic Aspects of Obesity," *Psychoanalytic Review* 34 (1947), pp. 173–183.

33 **In infancy,** Ibid., p. 175.

The analysis was designed Ibid., pp. 176–182.

35 **a catalog of some of the unconscious meanings** Harold I. Kaplan and Helen Singer Kaplan, "The Psychosomatic Concept of Obesity," *Journal*

Page

of Nervous and Mental Disease 125 (1957), pp. 181–201. List on pp. 195–196.

"Almost all conceivable psychological impulses" Ibid., p. 195.

"many symbolic meanings" In defense of the psychiatrists studying obesity, it should be noted that this sort of associational one-upmanship, where psychoanalysts seemed to be competing with one another to come up with the most tortured interpretation of a patient's problems, was not confined to overeating. Flip through the psychiatric and psychological journals of the time, and you find the same methods applied to almost any affliction. In a 1953 issue of the *Proceedings of the Nutrition Society*, for instance, immediately following an article on "Psychiatric Implications of Disturbances of Eating and Nutrition" is one on "Peptic Ulceration," in which the author discusses an earlier paper that advanced a psychoanalytic explanation of ulcers:

> Alexander, on the basis of six cases, presented the view that the characteristic feature in ulcer patients was a fundamental conflict originating in the infant's gratification at receiving milk from the mother's breast. More precisely, oral-receptive tenderness and the wish to be taken care of and loved are repressed and over compensated owing to a "narcissistic injury caused by the infantile claims and manifested on the surface in a sense of inferiority on the one hand and guilt and fear on the other."

(C.F.W. Illingworth, "Peptic Ulceration," *Proceedings of the Nutrition Society* 12 (1953) pp. 148–153. Quote on pp. 149–150.

Today doctors know that ulcers are caused by a bacterium, *Helicobacter pylori* (originally known as *Campylobacter pyloridis*), and not by stress as long thought, but even in the 1940s, the heyday of Freudian psychoanalysis, the idea of repressed oral-receptive tenderness as the root cause of ulcers was probably a bit of a stretch.

35 **obesity is best thought of** Kaplan and Kaplan, "Psychosomatic Concept," p. 197.

it received little attention See, for instance, Colleen S. W. Rand, "Treatment of Obese Patients in Psychoanalysis," *Psychiatric Clinics of North America* 1 (December 1978), pp. 661–672.

Even a number of psychoanalysts See, for example, Edmund Bergler, "Psychoanalytical Aspects of the Personality of the Obese Person," *International Record of Medicine* 171 (January 1958), pp. 5–8. Bergler wrote: "All these theories have worked to a limited and transitory degree, though for reasons unknown to their adherents: they produced 'successes because of unconscious fear.' Translated from 'psychoanalese' into English, the patient unconsciously projects a good deal of his own infantile ideas of omnipotence and omniscience onto the therapist, with the result that he is—frequently without justification—afraid that the x-ray eyes of the therapist will penetrate his deepest (hence, masochistic) inner motivations; to avoid this danger, he unconsciously gives up a symptom, to retain his neurosis." Bergler could not resist putting his own psychoanalytic spin on the phenomena, with the patients subconsciously fearing the loss of their neuroses, but the bottom line was that it was the act of therapy, not the content, that helped the patient deal with overeating.

36 **Study after study had shown** One of the earliest such studies, often referred to in later years, was the 1947 work by Freed, "Psychic Factors":

> Five hundred consecutive patients who requested treatment for their overweight were asked the question: "When you are nervous or worried do you eat more or less?" Three hundred and seventy answered that they either ate larger meals or ate more frequently, 95 of the remaining 130 answered that they did not believe that they ate more when nervous or worried but that they did eat more when they were idle, bored or tired. The remainder claimed that their appetites were always good, or that they just enjoyed food. (p. 370)

the Dr. Feelgoods See the description of pill doctors in Chapter 8.
"Most physicians regard obesity" Howard D. Kurland, "Obesity: An Unfashionable Problem," *Psychiatric Opinion* 7 (December 1970), pp. 20–24.

37 **the "medicalization of obesity"** Jeffery Sobal, "The Medicalization and Demedicalization of Obesity," in Donna Maurer and Jeffery Sobal, eds., *Eating Agendas: Food and Nutrition as Social Problems*, Aldine de Gruyter, Hawthorne, N.Y., 1995, pp. 67–90.

TWO: The Answer That Wasn't

41 **Bruch decided to specialize** Hilde Bruch, *The Importance of Overweight*, W. W. Norton, New York, 1957, pp. 5–10.
one of the most influential thinkers Peter Wyden, *The Overweight Society*, William Morrow, New York, 1965, pp. 263–264.
Bruch's idea Hilde Bruch, "Conceptual Confusion in Eating Disorders," *Journal of Nervous and Mental Disease* 133 (1961), pp. 46–54.

Page

"These people are unable" Ibid., p. 52.

42 **his 1955 paper describing it** Albert J. Stunkard, W. J. Grace, and H. G. Wolff, "The Night-Eating Syndrome," *American Journal of Medicine* 19 (1955), pp. 78–86.

the depression and emotional upset Albert J. Stunkard, "The 'Dieting Depression,'" *American Journal of Medicine* 23 (1957), pp. 77–86.

a detailed inquiry into binge-eating Albert J. Stunkard, "Eating Patterns and Obesity," *The Psychiatric Quarterly* 33 (1959), pp. 284–290.

Stunkard repeated the Cannon-Washburn experiment Albert Stunkard, "Obesity and the Denial of Hunger," *Psychosomatic Medicine* 21 (1959), pp. 281–289.

43 **they lost the ability to discriminate** Ibid., p. 287.

his long career Neil E. Grunberg, Richard E. Nisbett, Judith Rodin, and Jerome E. Singer, *A Distinctive Approach to Psychological Research: The Influence of Stanley Schachter*, Lawrence Erlbaum Associates, Hillsdale, N.J., 1987.

44 **a new way of thinking about human emotions** A good history of the path that Schachter took from his thinking on emotions in the 1950s to his work on obesity in the 1960s can be found in Stanley Schachter, "Cognitive Effects on Bodily Functioning: Studies of Obesity and Eating," in David C. Glass, ed., *Neurophysiology and Emotion*, Rockefeller University Press and Russell Sage Foundation, New York, 1967, pp. 117–144.

Schachter suggested that the subject Schachter, "Cognitive Effects," p. 120.

45 **a subject was put into the test room** Schachter, Ibid., p. 122.

Those subjects who had been given adrenaline Ibid., p. 123.

Later, Schachter used Ibid., p. 124.

46 **Richard Nisbett . . . a graduate student** Interview with Richard Nisbett, April 13, 1998.

"One day he told me" Ibid.

47 **Nisbett was put to work** Richard E. Nisbett, "Taste, Deprivation, and Weight Determinants of Eating Behavior," *Journal of Personality and Social Psychology* 10 (1968), pp. 107–116.

A variety of Schachterian twists The experiment was presented as a study on how hunger affects one's ability to concentrate. The subjects were asked to eat nothing for five or so hours before arriving. Once there, half were given sandwiches and soda and told to eat and drink as much as they wished, while the others were given nothing, in order to compare the amount of ice cream eaten between those who were hungry and those who were not. During this initial period, the subjects filled out a questionnaire on food preference and hunger level. Next came the ice cream and the taste evaluation test, with the ice cream presented as the food the effect of which on concentration was being studied. Finally the subjects were given their "concentration test."

overweight subjects were more influenced Stanley Schachter and Larry P. Gross, "Manipulated Time and Eating Behavior," *Journal of Personality and Social Psychology* 10 (1968), pp. 98–106.

the effects of fear on eating Stanley Schachter, Ronald Goldman, and Andrew Gordon, "Effects of Fear, Food Deprivation, and Obesity on Eating," *Journal of Personality and Social Psychology* 10 (1968), pp. 91–97.

48 **In high-fear conditions** Ibid., p. 93.

four back-to-back articles In addition to the three articles referenced above, there was a fourth article containing a hodge-podge of survey experiments and more memorable for its title than its contents: Ronald Goldman, Melvyn Jaffa, and Stanley Schachter, "Yom Kippur, Air France, Dormitory Food, and the Eating Behavior of Obese and Normal Persons," *Journal of Personality and Social Psychology* 10 (1968), pp. 117–123.

49 **a medical case described in 1840** The original report can be found in Mohr, *Wchnschr. f. d. ges. Heilk.*, 1840, pp. 565–571. I have relied on descriptions of the research in John R. Brobeck, J. Tepperman and C.N.H. Long, "Experimental Hypothalamic Hyperphagia in the Albino Rat," *Yale Journal of Biology and Medicine* 15 (July 1943), pp. 831–853, esp. p. 831, and John R. Brobeck, "Mechanism of the Development of Obesity in Animals with Hypothalamic Lesions," *Physiological Review* 26 (1946), pp. 541–559, esp. p. 541.

several other clues like this one Brobeck, Tepperman, and Long, "Experimental Hypothalamic Hyperphagia," 831.

the peculiar case of an obese fourteen-year-old boy Alfred Froehlich, "Ein Fall von Tumor der Hypophysis Cerebri Ohne Akromegalie," *Wein. Klin. Rundschau* 15 (1901), pp. 883–906. For a short description of the paper, see Bruch, *The Importance of Overweight*, pp. 20–22.

in later years he would complain Ibid., p. 23.

50 **Later, doctors found that** Ibid., p. 22. Also Brobeck, Tepperman, and Long, "Experimental Hypothalamic Hyperphagia," pp. 831–832.

the development of stereotaxic surgery George Clark, "The Use of the Horsley-Clarke Instrument on the Rat," *Science* 90 (1939), p. 92.

They proved that obesity is produced A. W. Hetherington and Stephen

Page

W. Ranson, "Hypothalamic Lesions and Adiposity in the Rat," *Anatomical Record* 78 (October 1940), pp. 149–172.

The hypothalamus controls Carol Turkington, *The Brain Encyclopedia*, Facts on File, New York, 1996, p. 125.

The next major study Brobeck, Tepperman, and Long, "Experimental Hypothalamic Hyperphagia," pp. 831–853.

51 **As the tale is usually told** See, for instance, Stanley Schachter and Judith Rodin, *Obese Humans and Rats*, LEA, Potomac, Md., 1974, p. 1.

The original account Brobeck, Tepperman and Long, "Experimental Hypothalamic Hyperphagia," pp. 834–835.

One of the most dramatic cases Alexander G. Reeves and Fred Plum, "Hyperphagia, Rage, and Dementia Accompanying a Ventromedial Hypothalamic Neoplasm," *Archives of Neurology* 20 (June 1969), pp. 616–624.

52 **"Although these [outbursts of violence]"** Ibid., p. 618.

voracious and frenzied Although the woman's violent behavior was not something seen in lesioned rats, who at most might become irritable, it was quite similar to what scientists had seen in cats with hypothalamic lesions. As one researcher reported in 1944, these cats were constantly in a rage, their backs arched, their hair standing on end, their eyes dilated, spitting, yowling, and lashing their tails. (M. D. Wheatley, "The Hypothalamus and Affective Behavior in Cats: A Study of the Effects of Experimental Lesions, with Anatomic Correlations," *Archives of Neurology and Psychiatry* 52 (October 1944), pp. 296–316.)

It was Schachter's student Nisbett Nisbett telephone interview, April 13, 1998.

In the quinine experiment Neal E. Miller, Clark J. Bailey, and James A. F. Stevenson, "Decreased 'Hunger' but Increased Food Intake Resulting From Hypothalamic Lesions," *Science* 112 (September 1, 1950), pp. 256–259.

53 **After his taste test** Richard E. Nisbett, "Determinants of Food Intake in Human Obesity," *Science* 159 (1968), pp. 1254–1255.

In a a series of experiments Miller, Bailey, and Stevenson, "Decreased 'Hunger.'"

he pointed out the similarities Nisbett, "Determinants of Food Intake," p. 1255.

54 **Schachter decided to test for parallels** Schachter and Rodin, *Obese Humans*, pp. 1–10.

shock-avoidance experiments Ibid., p. 21.

Page

"We assume," she wrote Ibid., p. 22.

The parallel with rats stood up Ibid., pp. 22–23.

55 "something awry with the hypothalamus" Ibid., p. 40.

the temptation offered by cashew nuts Lee Ross, "Effects of Manipulating Salience of Food upon Consumption by Obese and Normal Eaters," ibid., pp. 43–51.

56 almost every introductory psychology textbook Judith Rodin, "The Current State of the Internal-External Hypotheses: What Went Wrong?" *American Psychologist* 36 (1981), pp. 361–372, comment on p. 362.

"finicky, irascible, emotional," Schachter and Rodin, *Obese Humans*, p. 1.

No one took the externality hypothesis Flemming Quaade, "Untraditional Treatment of Obesity," in W. L. Burland, *Obesity Symposium*, Proceedings of a Servier Research Institute Symposium held in December 1973, Churchill Livingstone, Edinburgh, 1974, pp. 338–352.

57 When this section was tickled Jos M. R. Delgado and Bal K. Anand, "Increase in Food Intake Induced by Electrical Stimulation of the Lateral Hypothalamus," *American Journal of Physiology* 172 (January 1953), pp. 162–168. Although Anand and Delgado used cats instead of rats in this experiment—the larger animals made it easier to keep an electrode in the desired part of the brain—earlier research had already shown that cats respond to surgery on the hypothalamus in the same way as rats, so the new results could be combined with the old.

if the section was burned away Bal K. Anand and John R. Brobeck, "Hypothalamic Control of Food Intake in Rats and Cats," *Yale Journal of Biology and Medicine* 24 (November 1951), pp. 123–140.

It worked, he reported Quaade, "Untraditional Treatment," p. 342.

The medical world—or at least that part "It shows how ineffective the simpler forms of treatment are that anyone should think it reasonable to produce irreversible intracranial lesions in very obese patients" ("Infant and Adult Obesity," *The Lancet*, January 5, 1974, p. 17).

Quaade was unrepentant Flemming Quaade, "Stereotaxy for Obesity," *The Lancet*, February 16, 1974, p. 267.

when Stunkard revisited Albert J. Stunkard and Sonja Fox, "The Relationship of Gastric Motility and Hunger: A Summary of the Evidence," *Psychosomatic Medicine* 33 (March–April 1971), pp. 123–134.

58 a 1977 report by Rodin Judith Rodin, Joyce Slochower, and Barbara Fleming, "Effects of Degree of Obesity, Age of Onset, and Weight Loss on

Page

Responsiveness to Sensory and External Stimuli," *Journal of Comparative and Physiological Psychology* 91 (1977), pp. 586–597.

an analysis that challenged Richard E. Nisbett and Linda Temoshok, "Is There an External Cognitive Style?" *Journal of Personality and Social Psychology* 33 (1976), pp. 36–47.

Rodin spoke at an international conference Judith Rodin, "Has the Internal versus External Distinction Outlived Its Usefulness?" in George A. Bray, ed., *Recent Advances in Obesity Research II*, Newman, London, 1978, pp. 75–85.

Whether or not a person becomes obese Ibid., p. 77.

wrestling with what had gone wrong Judith Rodin, "The Current State of the Internal-External Hypotheses: What Went Wrong?" *American Psychologist* 36 (1981), pp. 361–372.

overweight people no more responsive Ibid., p. 363.

Because there is such a wide variation Ibid.

59 **In 1978, he was studying** Stanley Schachter, "Pharmacological and Psychological Determinants of Smoking," *Annals of Internal Medicine* 88 (January 1978), pp. 104–114.

the critical insight Richard E. Nisbett, "Hunger, Obesity and the Ventromedial Hypothalamus," *Psychological Review* 79 (1972), pp. 433–453.

work done in the 1960s Jerome L. Knittle and Jules Hirsch, "Effect of Early Nutrition on the Development of Rat Epididymal Fat Pads: Cellularity and Metabolism," *Journal of Clinical Investigation* 47 (1968), pp. 2091–2098; Jules Hirsch and Jerome L. Knittle, "Cellularity of Obese and Nonobese Human Adipose Tissue," *Federation Proceedings* 29 (1970), pp. 1516–1521. See Chapter 4 for details.

Later, Peter Herman C. Peter Herman and D. Mack, "Restrained and Unrestrained Eating," *Journal of Personality* 43 (1975), pp. 647–660; C. Peter Herman and Janet Polivy, "Anxiety, Restraint, and Eating Behavior," *Journal of Abnormal Psychology* 84 (1975), pp. 666–672. See also C. Peter Herman, "Restrained Eating," *The Psychiatric Clinics of North America* 1 (December 1978), pp. 593–607.

60 **In one typical study** Herman and Mack, "Restrained and Unrestrained Eating."

Drinking alcohol before Janet Polivy and C. Peter Herman, "Effects of Alcohol on Eating Behavior: Influences of Mood and Perceived Intoxication," *Journal of Abnormal Psychology* 85 (1976), pp. 601–606.

Many of the effects Herman, "Restrained Eating," pp. 602–603.

Page

THREE: There's No Place Like Homeostasis

61 **P. J. Nelson remembers** Telephone Interview with P. J. Nelson, August 21, 1998.

64 **Each fat droplet** Jules Hirsch, Susan K. Fried, Neile K. Edens, and Rudolph Leibel, "The Fat Cell," *The Medical Clinics of North America* 73 (January 1989), pp. 83–96. Numbers for the fat cells on p. 83.

one 450-pound man W. K. Stewart and L. W. Fleming, "Features of a Successful Therapeutic Fast of 382 Days Duration," *Postgraduate Medical Journal* 49 (1973), pp. 203–209.

"The biggest lipid compartment" Telephone interview with Jules Hirsch, November 3, 1998.

in 1960 he devised Jules Hirsch, John W. Farquhar, E. H. Ahrens, Jr., Malcolm L. Peterson, and Wilhelm Stoffel, "Studies of Adipose Tissue in Man: A Microtechnic for Sampling and Analysis," *American Journal of Clinical Nutrition* 8 (July–August 1960), pp. 499–511.

"[T]he buttock is usually" Ibid., p. 499.

65 **"In this manner"** Ibid.

"Over several years" Hirsch interview.

66 **in 1966 Hirsch developed** Jules Hirsch and E. Gallian, "Methods for the Determination of Adipose Cell Size in Man and Animals," *Journal of Lipid Research* 9 (1968), pp. 110–119. Although the article describing this method did not appear until 1968, Hirsch had already been using it for a couple of years.

their obesity was due Jules Hirsch, Jerome L. Knittle, and Lester B. Salans, "Cell Lipid Content and Cell Number in Obese and Non-Obese Human Adipose Tissue," *Journal of Clinical Investigation* 45 (1966), p. 1023.

67 **As researchers would later show** Joan M. Bulfer and C. Eugene Allen, "Fat Cells and Obesity," *BioScience* 29 (December 1979), pp. 736–741. See p. 740.

a simple but clever experiment with rats Jerome L. Knittle and Jules Hirsch, "Effect of Early Nutrition on the Development of Rat Epididymal Fat Pads: Cellularity and Metabolism," *Journal of Clinical Investigation* 47 (1968), pp. 2091–2098.

the rats from the small litters For convenience, Hirsch had measured the size of the epididymal pads, a well-defined deposit of fat near a male rat's testes. Later it would turn out that the epididymal pads were not completely representative of fat deposits throughout the rat's body, but much of what Hirsch learned from these pads was correct for the rest of the body's adipose tissue as well.

Page

From this evidence For decades it was an article of faith among most scientists that all brain cells were formed early in life, so that any that were lost were gone for good, and could not be replaced. Only recently have scientists discovered that new brain cells do indeed appear in the mature brain.

68 **Doctors now know** Jules Hirsch, Susan K. Fried, Neile K. Edens, and Rudolph Leibel, "The Fat Cell," *The Medical Clinics of North America* 73 (January 1989), pp. 83–96. See esp. p. 90.

one 1977 study M. Krotkiewski, L. Sjöström, P. Björntorp, C. Carlgren, and U. Smith, "Adipose Cellularity in Relation to Prognosis for Weight Reduction in Obesity," *International Journal of Obesity* 1 (1977), pp. 395–416.

Another study done Per Björntorp, G. Carlgren, B. Isaksson, M. Krotkiewski, B. Larsson, and L. Sjöström, "Effect of an Energy-Reduced Dietary Regime in Relation to Adipose Tissue Cellularity in Obese Women," *American Journal of Clinical Nutrition* 28 (1977), pp. 445–452.

a study tracking the size Jerome L. Knittle, K. Timmers, and F. Ginsverg-Fellner, "The Growth of Adipose Tissue in Children and Adolescents," *Journal of Clinical Investigation* 63 (1979), pp. 239–246.

adults rats could be induced Irving M. Faust, Patricia R. Johnson, Judith S. Stern, and Jules Hirsch, "Diet-Induced Adipocyte Number Increase in Adult Rats: A New Model of Obesity," *American Journal of Physiology* 235 (1978), pp. E279–E286.

69 **In 1988, Swedish doctors** I. Naslun, P. Hallgren, and L. Sjöström, "Fat-Cell Weight and Number Before and After Gastric Surgery for Morbid Obesity in Women," *International Journal of Obesity* 12 (1988), pp. 191–197.

In 1983, Hirsch W. H. Miller, I. M. Faust, A. C. Goldberger, and Jules Hirsch, "Effects of Severe Long-Term Food Deprivation and Refeeding on Adipose Tissue Cells in the Rat," *American Journal of Physiology* 245 (1983), pp. E74–E80.

Rudy Leibel Interview with Rudolph Leibel, Rockefeller University, New York City, August 7, 1997.

"Randall, let's get out of here." Ibid.

70 **a series of seminal experiments** Ethan A. H. Sims, Ralph F. Goldman, Charles M. Gluck, Edward S. Horton, Philip C. Kelleher, and David W. Rowe, "Experimental Obesity in Man," *Transactions of the Association of American Physicians* 81 (1968), pp. 153–170. See also Ethan A. H. Sims, E. Danforth, Jr., Edward S. Horton, George A. Bray, J. A. Glennon, and L. B. Salans, "Endocrine and Metabolic Effects of Experimental Obesity in Man," *Recent Progress in Hormone Research* 29 (1973), pp. 457–496.

Page

As Leibel listened Leibel interview.

71 **When Leibel walked** Ibid.

72 **"The abnormality is not"** Hirsch interview.

an almost obsessive preoccupation See, for instance: Myron L. Glucksman and Jules Hirsch, "The Response of Obese Patients to Weight Reduction: I. A Clinical Evaluation of Behavior," *Psychosomatic Medicine* 30 (1968), pp. 1–11; Myron L. Glucksman, Jules Hirsch, R. S. McCully, B. A. Barron, and Jerome L. Knittle, "The Response of Obese Patients to Weight Reduction: II. A Quantitative Evaluation of Behavior," *Psychosomatic Medicine* 30 (1968), pp. 359–373; and Myron L. Glucksman and Jules Hirsch, "The Response of Obese Patients to Weight Reduction: III. The Perception of Body Size," *Psychosomatic Medicine* 31 (1969), pp. 1–7.

Hirsch argued to an obesity conference The Second International Conference on Obesity, October 23–26, 1977, Washington, D.C. Hirsch's comments are included in the proceedings of that conference as Jules Hirsch, "Obesity: A Perspective," in George A. Bray, ed., *Recent Advances in Obesity Research, II*, Newman Publishing, London, 1978, pp. 1–5.

"When people lost fat" Hirsch interview.

Recently, Hirsch told the story Jules Hirsch, "Obesity: Definition of the Problem," in George A. Bray and Donna H. Ryan, eds., *Nutrition, Genetics, and Obesity*, Louisiana State University Press, Baton Rouge, 1999, pp. 1–13.

"I hospitalized him for weight reduction" Ibid.

73 **J.W. had reduced to 212** J.W. had been treated with the weight-loss drug dexfenfluramine, which was removed from the market after it was discovered that a large number of patients using it had developed heart valve disease of the sort that J.W. had.

the average American man or woman Michael Rosenbaum, Rudolph L. Leibel, and Jules Hirsch, "Obesity," in *The New England Journal of Medicine* 337 (August 7, 1997), pp. 396–407. Leibel's argument on p. 396.

The homeostatic balance "Why should the homeostatic mechanism which operates so efficiently in most people to enable them to maintain a desirable weight without their giving a second thought to what they eat, break down in the obese? The final answer, or answers, to these questions are unfortunately still lacking." From E. Philip Gelvin and Thomas H. McGavack, *Obesity: Its Cause, Classification, and Care*, Paul B. Hoeber, New York, 1957, p. 39.

74 **the body must contain a "lipostat"** Jean Mayer, "Regulation of Energy Intake and the Body Weight: The Glucostatic Theory and the Lipostatic

Page

Hypothesis," *Annals of the New York Academy of Sciences* 63 (1955), pp. 15–43.

the level of glycerol in the blood See, for instance, David Wirtshafter and John D. Davis, "Body Weight: Reduction by Long-Term Glycerol Treatment," *Science* 198 (December 23, 1977), pp. 1271–1274.

Leibel injected glycerol Joel Grinker, Alan J. Strohmayer, Jonathan Horowitz, Jules Hirsch, and Rudolph L. Leibel, "The Effect of the Metabolite Glycerol on Food Intake and Body Weight in Rats," *Brain Research Bulletin* 5 (1980), pp. 29–35.

it had no effect on their hunger Rudolph L. Leibel, Adam Drewnowski, and Jules Hirsch, "Effect of Glycerol on Weight Loss and Hunger in Obese Patients," *Metabolism* 29 (December 1980), pp. 1234–1236.

76 **the usual Rockefeller liquid formula** The formula was originally developed in the 1950s by Pete Ahrens to study how varying the types of fat in the diet would affect the composition of fats in the body.

The results were published Rudolph L. Leibel and Jules Hirsch, "Diminished Energy Requirements in Reduced-Obese Patients," *Metabolism* 33 (February 1984), pp. 164–170.

the important variable is a person's fat-free mass See, for example, Eric Ravussin, Stephen Lillioja, Thomas E. Anderson, Laurent Christin, and Clifton Bogardus, "Determinants of 24-Hour Energy Expenditure in Man," *Journal of Clinical Investigation* 78 (December 1986), pp. 1568–1578.

77 **Fat itself adds little** This does not mean, however, that a person's daily energy demands will not change when he gains weight. Every pound of fat demands a few ounces of fat-free mass — muscle, blood vessels, connective tissue — to support it, so a person who overeats and gains, say, forty pounds has really put on about thirty pounds of fat and ten pounds of nonfat tissue. (This number varies quite a lot. See Table 1 on p. 622 of Rudolph L. Leibel, Michael Rosenbaum, and Jules Hirsch, "Changes in Energy Expenditure Resulting from Altered Body Weight," *The New England Journal of Medicine* 332 (March 9, 1995), pp. 621–628.) The extra ten pounds of fat-free mass will add to the daily energy requirements; the thirty pounds of fat will not.

In a follow-up study Leibel and Hirsch, "Diminished Energy Requirements," p. 167.

78 **"We would do it right"** Leibel interview.

exactly the same formula In the earlier studies, the patients had received various formulations, which probably did not affect the outcome, but which did complicate things slightly.

Page

79 **Kelli Johnson** Telephone interview with Kelli Johnson, October 22, 1998.

80 **Naturally there were a few slip-ups** Telephone interview with Rudolph Leibel, October 23, 1998.

"You have to be able to keep yourself entertained" Nelson interview.

a simple, unchanging recipe The carbohydrate was polycose, a polymer of glucose. The protein was casein hydrolysate, one of the proteins in milk, which provides all essential amino acids.

81 **The formula was supplemented** Each patient's salt was carefully controlled. With too much salt, the body will retain water in order to maintain the correct salinity in the body's cells and fluids; with too little salt, the body will flush some of its water.

Scientists who study metabolism Eric Ravussin and Boyd A. Swinburn, "Effect of Calorie Restriction and Weight Loss on Energy Expenditure," in Thomas A. Wadden and Theodore B. Van Itallie, eds., *Treatment of the Seriously Obese Patient*, Guilford Press, New York, 1992, pp. 163–189.

82 **To measure the resting metabolic rate** Leibel also flew P.J. and other patients to Phoenix to use a metabolic chamber set up by the National Institute for Diabetes and Digestive and Kidney Diseases to study the Pima Indians (see Chapter 6) for up to twenty-four hours at a stretch. The room is equipped with radar detectors that sense how much the subject moves around and with temperature gauges so accurate that the researchers can calculate how much heat a subject's body produces during a stay. Other devices in the chamber monitor the levels of various gases in the air, providing a measure of the subject's oxygen consumption, carbon dioxide production, and nitrogen excretion. From all these data it is possible to get an accurate measure of a person's metabolic rate throughout an entire day.

"That was not always so easy" Nelson interview.

Leibel analyzed the results and published them Leibel, Rosenbaum, and Hirsch, "Changes in Energy Expenditure."

about a fourth of their weight gain The percentage of lean tissue in the weight gain was actually 20 percent in the non-obese and more than 40 percent in the obese. In other words, when the obese gained weight, a good deal less of it, in percentage terms, was actually fat tissue. On the other hand, during weight loss, lean tissue accounted for about 20 percent of the weight loss in the obese and nearly 40 percent in the non-obese. See Table 1 in ibid., p. 622.

83 **when Leibel observed his patients' movements** The observations were carried out in the metabolic chamber in Phoenix.

From Leibel's perspective Leibel interview, August 7, 1997.

Page

84 **The reason, he suspects** Leibel, Rosenbaum, and Hirsch, "Changes in Energy Expenditure," p. 624.

It is certainly true for rats See, for instance, Jeffrey W. Peck, "Rats Defend Different Body Weights Depending on Palatability and Accessibility of Their Food," *Journal of Comparative and Physiological Psychology* 92 (1978), pp. 555–570.

"He got six people" Interview with Bruce Schneider, Washington, D.C., July 24, 1998.

It was late 1994 Johnson interview.

85 **Leibel recommended her to reporters** He recommended her for this book as well.

"It was nice for my mom" Johnson interview.

86 **"They are always back to normal"** Leibel interview, October 23, 1998.

"It's an enormous discipline" P.J. Nelson interview, August 21, 1998.

88 **P.J. Nelson has come to see** Ibid.

FOUR: The Legacy of the Great Fire

89 **the '47 Fire** The most comprehensive source on the Great Fire of 1947 is Joyce Butler, *Wildfire Loose: The Week Maine Burned*, Durrell Publications, Kennebunkport, Maine, 1978. See also a series of articles entitled "The '47 Fire" that appeared in the *Portland Press Herald and Maine Sunday Telegram* in October 1997; I found them on the Internet at http://spider.biddeford.com/ph/fire/.

The damages Clarke Canfield, "1947 and Maine Was Ablaze," from "The '47 Fire."

90 **B. F. Goodrich** Butler, *Wildfire Loose*, p. 53

as did members of Mark Shanahan, "Ravaged Resort," in "The '47 Fire."

Edsel Ford Jean Holstein, *The First Fifty Years at the Jackson Laboratory*, The Jackson Laboratory, Bar Harbor, 1979, p. 4.

A. T. Stotesbury Butler, *Wildfire Loose*, p. 53.

Summer was a gay time Holstein, *First Fifty Years*, p. 3.

Gone were houses "Disaster: A Lovely Time of Year," *Time*, November 3, 1947, p. 26.

many of the summer homes Butler, *Wildfire Loose*, p. 232.

91 **The Jackson Lab had opened** Holstein, *First Fifty Years*, pp. 1–15. Holstein's book is the official history of the Jackson Laboratory, the institution that Little founded.

Page

92 **Most of the 90,000-plus mice** Ibid., pp. 13, 26, 35–36; Butler, *Wildfire Loose*, p. 66.

   the mouse keepers used kerosene Holstein, *First Fifty Years*, pp. 39–40.

93 **When Jackson Laboratory** Butler, *Wildfire Loose*, pp. 66, 183.

   "Rebuild? Of course we'll rebuild" LaRue Spiker, "Like a Giant Blowtorch," *The Ellsworth American*, October 19, 1972. As quoted in Butler, *Wildfire Loose*, p. 183.

   sent mice from their own labs Butler, ibid., p. 211.

   it was able to reestablish Patricia Lauber, *Of Man and Mouse: How House Mice Became Laboratory Mice*, Viking Press, New York, 1971, p. 14.

94 **the Jackson Laboratory had rebuilt** Holstein, *First Fifty Years*, pp. 43–46.

   Kaliss took up residence Ibid., p. 40.

   he brought a breeding pair The details of Kaliss's accidental creation of a new strain of mice can be found in J. K. Naggert, J.-L. Mu, W. Frankel, D. W. Bailey, and B. Paigen, "Genomic Analysis of the C57BL/Ks Mouse Strain," *Mammalian Genome* 6 (1995), pp. 131–133.

   It could be traced back to a line Holstein, *First Fifty Years*, p. 75.

   The first hint that something Naggert et al., "Genomic Analysis," p. 131.

95 **In 1995, a team** Ibid.

   The first truly obese mice Ann M. Ingalls, Margaret M. Dickie, and George D. Snell, "Obese, a New Mutation in the House Mouse," *Journal of Heredity* 41 (1950), pp. 317–318.

   The picture published Ibid., p. 317.

   The two women who discovered In crediting Margaret Dickie and Priscilla Lane as the discoverers of the *obese* mouse, I am relying on the account in Holstein, *First Fifty Years*, p. 154. Since this is an official history of the Jackson Laboratory, which should have been checked carefully by lab officials before it was released, I assume this is correct. Douglas Coleman points out, however, that the paper announcing the discovery of the mouse and describing its traits has as its authors Ann Ingalls, Margaret Dickie, and George Snell. Thus the official record indicates those three as the discoverers of the *obese* mouse, and Coleman recommended that I give them credit for that in this book. I chose to name Dickie and Lane here because I am more interested in who actually came across the mouse first than in who initially studied the mouse once it had been found, and the record implies to me that Dickie and Lane were the actual finders.

96 **often not bothering to produce** Maintaining a pure inbred line was much more difficult for *obese* than for other strains because mice with two copies of the *obese* mutation tended to be sterile, or at least have very low fertility.

Page

This forced the mouse breeders to take extraordinary measures, such as transplanting the ovaries from *obese* mice into normal mice in order for the eggs of the *obese* mice to mature and be fertilized. Ibid., pp. 155–156.

As a result Ibid., p. 156.

another fat mutant Katharine P. Hummel, Margaret M. Dickie, and Douglas L. Coleman, "Diabetes, a New Mutation in the Mouse," *Science* 153 (September 2, 1966), pp. 1127–1128.

"The mouse was picked up" Interview with Douglas Coleman, Jackson Laboratory, Maine, October 27, 1997.

97 **In the days before inexpensive** Holstein, *First Fifty Years*, pp. 1–2.

98 **they knew the basic details** Hummel, Dickie, and Coleman, "Diabetes."

99 **"Skippy Lane brought in another mouse"** Coleman interview.

100 **What he found** Katherine P. Hummel, Douglas L. Coleman, and Priscilla W. Lane, "The Influence of Genetic Background on Expression of Mutations at the Diabetes Locus in the Mouse. I. C57BL/KsJ and C57BL/6J Strains," *Biochemical Genetics* 7 (1972), pp. 1–13.

the *db-2J* mutation behaved like Later Coleman would perform the same test on the original *db* mutation, comparing the *db* mutation in Black-6 mice with Black Kaliss mice and, as would be expected, got the same result. Black Kaliss mice with *db* got fat, developed diabetes, and died. Black-6 mice with *db* got fat but never developed diabetes.

In Black-6 mice, by contrast Ironically, *ob* had originally appeared in a line of mice in which it did lead to diabetes, and it was only when the mutation was transferred to a line of Black-6 mice that the diabetes disappeared. Coleman remembers that Jean Mayer, a well-known nutrition researcher who was later president of Tufts University, worked with the earliest strains of the *obese* mouse. Mayer called it the obese-hyperglycemic mouse, giving its high levels of blood sugar equal billing with its obesity. As the *ob* gene was bred into the Black-6 line, Mayer complained that he no longer got the diabetic mice that he was interested in studying, but it did no good. The Jackson Lab breeders put *ob* onto Black-6 and the diabetes disappeared, a phenomenon that no one was interested in pursuing at the time.

101 **Beverly Paigen, the Jackson Lab geneticist** Telephone interview with Beverly Paigen, January 20, 1998.

102 **"Research is a hard business"** Coleman interview.

103 **"I never complained about my career"** Ibid.

104 **"I was just in the right place"** Ibid.

It was an exciting time Ibid.

106 **the correct answer was** Douglas L. Coleman and Katharine P. Hummel,

Page

"Effects of Parabiosis of Normal with Genetically Diabetic Mice," *American Journal of Physiology* 217 (November 1969), pp. 1298–1304.

"The first few that died" Coleman interview.

the blood sugar of the individual mice The blood sugar levels of the two mice in a joined pair can be quite different even though their circulatory systems are joined because the mice exchange only about 1 percent of their blood each minute, and glucose in the blood is produced and metabolized on such short time scales that each mouse in the pair can maintain a separate equilibrium.

a paper published nearly ten years earlier G. R. Hervey, "The Effects of Lesions in the Hypothalamus in Parabiotic Rats," *Journal of Physiology* 145 (1959), pp. 336–352.

107 **a "satiety factor"** Coleman and Hummel, "Effects of Parabiosis," p. 1303.

In 1971, Coleman had figured out The paper did not appear until 1972, but the work was finished in 1971. Hummel, Coleman, and Lane, "Influence of Genetic Background."

in 1973 he had shown that Douglas L. Coleman and Katharine P. Hummel, "The Influence of Genetic Background on the Expression of the Obese (*Ob*) Gene in the Mouse," *Diabetologia* 9 (1973), pp. 287–293.

108 **one of the two most important** Douglas L. Coleman, "Effects of Parabiosis of Obese with Diabetes and Normal Mice," *Diabetologia* 9 (1973), pp. 294–298.

the discovery of leptin Yiying Zhang, Ricardo Proenca, Margherita Maffei, Marisa Barone, Lori Leopold, and Jeffrey M. Friedman, "Positional Cloning of the Mouse *Obese* Gene and Its Human Homologue," *Nature* 372 (December 1, 1994), pp. 425–432. See Chapter 6 for details.

109 **interpretation of Coleman's experiments** See, for instance, Jeffrey M. Friedman and Jeffrey L. Halaas, "Leptin and the Regulation of Body Weight in Mammals," *Nature* 395 (October 22, 1998), pp. 763–770.

the body had a "lipostat" G. C. Kennedy, "The Role of Depot Fat in the Hypothalamic Control of Food Intake in the Rat," *Proceedings of the Royal Society* B140 (1953), p. 578–592; Jean Mayer, "Regulation of Energy Intake and the Body Weight: The Glucostatic Theory and the Lipostatic Hypothesis," *Annals of the New York Academy of Sciences* 63 (1955), pp. 15–43.

110 **One, for instance** Jean Mayer, "The Glucostatic Theory of Regulation of Food Intake and the Problem of Obesity," *Bulletin of the New England Medical Center* 14 (1952), pp. 43–49; Mayer, "Regulation of Energy Intake.

Another suggested that John R. Brobeck, "Food Intake as a Mechanism of Temperature Regulation," *Yale Journal of Biology and Medicine* 20 (1948), pp. 545–552; John R. Brobeck, "Neural Control of Hunger, Appetite and Satiety," *Yale Journal of Biology and Medicine* 29 (1957), pp. 565–574.

Coleman set off on a series Douglas L. Coleman, "Thermogenesis in Diabetes-Obesity Syndromes in Mutant Mice," *Diabetologia* 22 (1982), pp. 205–211.

Eventually, he says Telephone interview with Douglas Coleman, September 10, 1997.

in a completely wrong direction Coleman interview, October 27, 1997.

FIVE: That Eureka Moment

111 **MacLagan discovered** N. F. MacLagan, "The Role of Appetite in the Control of Body Weight," *Journal of Physiology* 90 (1937), pp. 385–394.

previous work that had found T. Kosaka and R.K.S. Lim, "Demonstration of the Humoral Agent in Fat Inhibition of Gastric Secretion," *Proceedings of the Society for Experimental Biology and Medicine* 27 (1930), pp. 890–891.

112 **Zvi Glick and Jean Mayer** Z. Glick and J. Mayer, "Preliminary Observations on the Effect of Intestinal Mucosa Extract on Food Intake of Rats," *Federation Proceedings* 27 (1968), p. 485; Andrew V. Schalling, Tommie W. Redding, Harold W. Lucien, and Joe Meyer, "Enterogastrone Inhibits Eating by Fasted Mice," *Science* 157 (July 14, 1967), pp. 210–211.

the ingredient of interest James Gibbs, Robert C. Young, and Gerard P. Smith, "Cholecystokinin Decreases Food Intake in Rats," *Journal of Comparative and Physiological Psychology* 84 (1973), pp. 488–495.

CCK's main job See, for example, Viktor Mutt, "Cholecystokinin: Isolation, Structure, and Functions," in George B. Jerzy Glass, ed., *Gastrointestinal Hormones* (New York: Raven Press, 1980), pp. 169–221.

the effects of CCK on appetite Gibbs, Young, and Smith, "Cholecystokinin Decreases Food Intake."

one of the classic papers James Gibbs, Robert C. Young, and Gerard P. Smith, "Cholecystokinin Elicits Satiety in Rats with Open Gastric Fistulas," *Nature* 245 (October 12, 1973), pp. 323–325.

113 **the act of eating itself** Gibbs, Young, and Smith were not the first to observe that eating by itself is not enough to cause satiety. In 1949, Janowitz and Grossman, confirming an observation that Ivan Pavlov had made years earlier, showed that dogs in whom the esophagus had been removed so that

Page

no food reached the stomach or intestines, kept eating long after intact dogs were satiated. H. D. Janowitz and M. I. Grossman, *American Journal of Physiology* 159 (1949), pp. 143–148.

The food had to make its way Later, in a series of experiments designed to test the effect of food in the intestines directly, Smith and Gibbs would insert a catheter through the fistula, into the stomach, and from there into the small intestine. With this they were able to inject liquid food directly into the intestines even as the food the rats were ingesting was draining out through the fistula. Now the rats behaved as normal when fed after a fast: They stopped eating a few minutes after the food had begun flowing into their intestines, they licked their fur for a while, and fell asleep. It was the passage of food into the intestines that provoked the satiety response. Gerard P. Smith and James Gibbs, "Cholecystokinin and Satiety: Theoretic and Therapeutic Implications," in Donald Novin, Wanda Wyrwicka, and George A. Bray, eds., *Hunger: Basic Mechanisms and Clinical Implications,* Raven Press, New York, 1976, pp. 349–355.

Once the CCK hit Gibbs, Young, and Smith, "Cholecystokinin Elicits Satiety."

114 **a 1976 experiment** G. J. Dockray, "Immunochemical Evidence of Cholecystokinin-Like Peptides in Brain," *Nature* 264 (December 9, 1976), pp. 568–570.

their article describing the results Eugene Straus and Rosalyn S. Yalow, "Cholecystokinin in the Brains of Obese and Nonobese Mice," *Science* 203 (January 5, 1979), pp. 68–69.

the study "unequivocally" showed Ibid., p. 69.

115 **It was Bruce Schneider** Interview with Bruce Schneider, Washington, D.C., July 24, 1998.

"She announced that she had discovered" Ibid.

116 **He wrote up his own results** Bruce S. Schneider, Joseph W. Monahan, and Jules Hirsch, "Brain Cholecystokinin and Nutritional Status in Rats and Mice," *Journal of Clinical Investigation* 64 (November 1979), pp. 1348–1356.

Schneider himself went back Schneider interview.

Schneider's group localized the CCK gene Jeffrey M. Friedman, Bruce S. Schneider, D. E Barton, and U. Francke, "Level of Expression and Chromosome Mapping of the Mouse Cholecystokinin Gene: Implications for Murine Models of Genetic Obesity," *Genomics* 5 (1989), pp. 463–469.

researchers are still not sure See, for example, A. S. Levine and C. J. Billington, "Peptides in Regulation of Energy Metabolism and Body

Page

Weight," in Claude Bouchard and George A. Bray, eds., *Regulation of Body Weight: Biological and Behavioral Mechanisms*, John Wiley and Sons, New York, 1997, pp. 179–191. Details on CCK on pp. 185–186.

Jeffrey Friedman Details about Friedman and his search for the *ob* gene are taken mainly from a series of interviews with Friedman both in person at Rockefeller University and on the telephone conducted between March 27, 1997, and July 31, 1998.

117 **Friedman remembers loafing** Telephone interview with Jeffrey Friedman, July 31, 1998.

"The world of science was opening up" Interview with Jeffrey Friedman at Rockefeller, September 27, 1997.

"There is no ceiling" Friedman interview, July 31, 1998.

118 **Friedman decided to go back to school** It was David Baltimore, a Nobel Laureate at MIT and one of the country's leading molecular biologists, who advised Friedman to stay at Rockefeller and enter its Ph.D. program. Baltimore had graduated from the Rockefeller Ph.D. program himself, and later returned to Rockefeller as its president.

"among the handful of leading molecular biologists" Friedman interview, July 31, 1998.

he had been intrigued Ibid.

He showed that it was the same gene The paper was not published until 1985. Jeffrey Friedman, Bruce S. Schneider, and Donald Powell, "Differential Expression of the Mouse Cholecystokinin Gene During Brain and Gut Development," *Proceedings of the National Academy of Science* 82 (September 1985), pp. 5593–5597.

119 **"If it's not CCK, what is it?"** Telephone interview with Jeffrey Friedman, August 23, 1997.

"I'm going to go and clone the gene" Schneider interview.

each of them contains The exception is the Y chromosome, which contains relatively few genes. Its major purpose is to hold the instructions for the extra few developmental steps that are required for creating a male.

120 **the three billion letters** The mouse genome has twenty pairs of chromosomes, three fewer pairs than the human genome, but approximately the same number of genes.

Steps on the ladder are the base pairs The paired structure explains DNA's ability not only to carry the genetic code but to be passed on from generation to generation. The sequence of the base pairs carries the genetic information, and knowing one member of a base pair implies what the other must be: A with T, C with G. Because of this redundancy, the recipe

Page

encoded in the DNA is usually abbreviated simply by following the bases along one side of the ladder: . . .AATGCCGATA. . . .The bases on the other side are implied, but seldom written. It is this redundancy that allows a molecule of DNA to be copied easily, either inside a cell or inside a test tube. A strand of DNA reproduces by splitting down the middle, which creates two single strands, each a half-ladder consisting of a phosphate backbone and a sequence of bases attached to it. From each of these half-ladders a full ladder identical to the original is reconstructed by tacking onto each base its complementary base, A onto T, T onto A, C onto G, and G onto C, and then adding a second phosphate backbone on the other side. Now each of the half-ladders is a full ladder identical to the first, and there are two copies of the DNA molecule where once there had been one. The process can be repeated indefinitely, creating an exponentially growing number of strands of identical DNA.

a needle looks different Credit for this particular analogy goes to David A. Micklos and Greg A. Freyer, *DNA Science: A First Course in Recombinant DNA Technology*, Carolina Biological Supply Company, Burlington, N.C., 1990, p. 62. "The problem is even worse than searching for the proverbial needle in a haystack, where at least the needle looks different from the surrounding hay."

121 **Morgan found that this was not quite right** Ibid., pp. 16–17.

122 **Friedman recalls** Friedman interview, September 29, 1997.

123 **Suppose, for example** The technical term here is restriction fragment length polymorphism, or RFLP, pronounced "riflip."

124 **He and Friedman agreed to collaborate** Today, Friedman and Leibel disagree on exactly what went on during their first meeting, in particular on whose idea it was to clone the *obese* gene. Friedman says that he was already planning to clone the gene before he met Leibel, and, from interviews with other researchers, I know that this is the case. On the other hand, Leibel insists that the idea for cloning the gene grew out of his program to find out why the obese have so much trouble losing weight and that, having conceived of the idea of looking for the gene, he approached Friedman and asked if he would like to collaborate. While it is certainly true that an attempt to clone the *obese* and *diabetes* genes would seem to be a natural follow-up to Leibel's earlier work, such as testing glycerol to see if it might be the body's fat signal, I have not been able to confirm independently that Leibel was planning to clone the genes before meeting Friedman. For his part, Friedman insists that Leibel did not really understand cloning before meeting with him and that Leibel had not been planning to clone the genes.

It has been impossible for me to determine with certainty the truth about this meeting that took place between the two of them fourteen years ago, and for the purposes of this book the specifics are not particularly important. But I offer these extra details because apportioning credit for the discovery of the *obese* gene is not something to be taken lightly, and Leibel insists that his part in the discovery has been unfairly overlooked.

I have chosen to tell the story of the cloning of the *obese* gene from Friedman's point of view because, after discussing the issue with a number of people familiar with the work, it seems to me that Friedman was the one irreplaceable person on the project. Leibel made many contributions, and it's quite probable that the discovery would have taken longer without his help, but it is clear that the discovery would not have been made at all without Friedman's vision, determination, and understanding of molecular biology and cutting-edge cloning techniques.

By the fall of 1986 Friedman interview, September 27, 1997.

125 **"CCK was a safer bet"** Ibid.

126 **"It took a long time to make it work"** Friedman interview, September 27, 1997.

"When the project started" Interview with Jeffrey Friedman at Rockefeller, July 21, 1998.

he was an investigator Friedman was an employee—an assistant investigator—of the Howard Hughes Medical Institute (HHMI) with a position as assistant professor at Rockefeller. In other words, although he had an affiliation with Rockefeller, his salary was paid by HHMI. He is now an investigator with HHMI and professor at Rockefeller.

"Over the years" E-mail communication with Jeffrey Friedman, July 16, 1998.

127 **The two complemented each other** Telephone interview with Nathan Bahary, January 28, 2000.

tensions grew The tensions seem to have had their roots in the first meeting between the two and the different perceptions that each had of it. Friedman, who sees himself as the one who understood what it took to clone a gene and sees Leibel as someone who could help in that search but who would not have been able to take it on by himself, considered himself the main figure in the collaboration and saw Leibel's contribution as secondary. Leibel, who had been working in the obesity field longer than Friedman and who was better known among the researchers in that field, saw the effort to clone the *obese* gene as part of the longstanding effort in the Hirsch laboratory to understand obesity and considered Friedman as

Page

someone who had been recruited into that effort. With each of the two men considering himself to be the primary figure in the collaboration, it was perhaps inevitable that they would have a falling out. To this day, the two find little to agree on when talking about whose project it was.

early in 1994 researchers had described D. M. Church et al., "Isolation of Genes from Complex Sources of Mammalian Genomic DNA Using Exon Amplification," *Nature Genetics* 6 (1994), pp. 98–105.

128 **"When I saw something"** Friedman interview, September 27, 1997.

"All this time" Ibid.

129 **"I knew when I saw this"** Telephone interview with Jeffrey Friedman, July 31, 1998.

"We sat outside" Ibid.

130 **In December, he published** Yiying Zhang, Ricardo Proenca, Margherita Maffei, Marisa Barone, Lori Leopold, and Jeffrey M. Friedman, "Positional Cloning of the Mouse *Obese* Gene and Its Human Homologue," *Nature* 372 (December 1, 1994), pp. 425–432.

Friedman, in collaboration with Jeffrey L. Halaas, Ketan S. Gajiwala, Margherita Maffei, Steven L. Cohen, Brian T. Chait, Daniel Rabinowitz, Roger L. Lallone, Stephen K. Burley, and Jeffrey M. Friedman, "Weight-Reducing Effects of the Plasma Protein Encoded by the *obese* Gene," *Science* 269 (July 28, 1995), pp. 543–546.

Amgen announced it was buying rights Richard Stone, "Rockefeller Strikes Fat Deal with Amgen," *Science* 268 (May 5, 1995), p. 631.

131 **researchers in hundreds of labs** For a review of the leptin research, see Jeffrey M. Friedman and Jeffrey L. Halaas, "Leptin and the Regulation of Body Weight in Mammals," *Nature* 395 (October 22, 1998), pp. 763–770.

leptin-treated mice grew more slowly Farid F. Chehab, Khalid Mounzih, Ronghua Lu, and Mary E. Lim, "Early Onset of Reproductive Function in Normal Female Mice Treated with Leptin," *Science* 275 (January 3, 1997), pp. 88–90.

Leptin returned the immune systems to normal Graham M. Lord, Giuseppe Matarese, Jane K. Howard, Richard J. Baker, Stephen R. Bloom, and Robert J. Lechler, "Leptin Modulates the T-Cell Immune Response and Reverses Starvation-Induced Immunosuppression," *Nature* 394 (August 27, 1998), pp. 897–901.

Leptin, they found, causes the corneas R. Rocio Sierra-Honigmann et al., "Biological Action of Leptin as an Angiogenic Factor," *Science* 281 (September 11, 1998), pp. 1683–1686.

132 **the level of leptin in the blood** Margherita Maffei et al., "Leptin Levels in

Human and Rodent: Measurement of Plasma Leptin and *ob* RNA in Obese and Weight-Reduced Subjects," *Nature Medicine* 1 (November 1995), pp. 1155–1161; Robert V. Considine et al., "Serum Immuno-reactive-Leptin Concentrations in Normal-Weight and Obese Humans," *The New England Journal of Medicine* 334 (February 1, 1996), pp. 292–295.

levels in the blood vary widely See Figure 1 in Considine et al., "Serum Immunoreactive-Leptin Concentrations."

when the obese lose weight For example, see Table 1 in Maffei et al., "Leptin Levels."

133 **leptin does indeed seem to help** Andrew Pollack, "Weight-Loss Drug Shows Some Success in Humans," *The New York Times*, June 15, 1998, p. D7.

leptin is most potent Friedman and Halaas, "Leptin and the Regulation of Body Weight," p. 769.

what we now know See, for example, Ibid., pp. 765–766.

134 **the leptin level is more subtle** Ibid.

135 **the brain seems to have two different** Jeffrey Friedman, "The Alphabet of Weight Control," *Nature* 385 (January 9, 1997), pp. 119–120.

genetically engineered mice Jay C. Erickson, Kathy E. Clegg, and Richard D. Palmiter, "Sensitivity to Leptin and Susceptibility to Seizures of Mice Lacking Neuropeptide Y," *Nature* 381 (May 30, 1996), pp. 415–418.

mice that had neither NPY nor leptin Jay C. Erickson, Gunther Hollopeter, and Richard D. Palmiter, "Attenuation of the Obesity Syndrome of *ob/ob* Mice by the Loss of Neuropeptide Y," *Science* 274 (December 6, 1996), pp. 1704–1707.

The melanocortin-4 receptor Wei Fan, Bruce A. Boston, Robert A. Kesterson, Victor J. Hruby, and Roger D. Cone, "Role of Melanocortin-ergic Neurons in Feeding and the *Agouti* Obesity Syndrome," *Nature* 385 (January 9, 1997), pp. 165–168; Dennis Huszar et al., "Targeted Disruption of the Melanocortin-4 Receptor Results in Obesity in Mice," *Cell* 88 (January 10, 1997), pp. 131–141.

when the receptor is blocked This discovery, made in late 1996, explained a fifty-year-old mystery: Why the yellow agouti mouse is fat. These mice, which were raised at Jackson Lab years before the *obese* mouse was discovered, are distinguished by their bright yellow fur and their weight—not as fat as *obese*, but twice as fat as normal mice. For decades, no one could guess why the same mutation should both turn the mice yellow and make them fat. The answer is that the *agouti* gene causes a mouse to make large

Page

amounts of a protein that has effects on two different systems. The agouti protein blocks the action of melanocyte-stimulating hormone on melanocortin-1 receptors in the skin, shutting down normal pigment production and causing the yellow color. (See Friedman, "The Alphabet of Weight Control," p. 120.) It also blocks the melanocortin-4 receptor in the hypothalamus, leading to overeating and obesity.

when mice are genetically engineered Huszar et al., "Targeted Disruption."

136 **two neuropeptides—small proteins** T. Sakurai et al., "Orexins and Orexin Receptors: A Family of Hypothalamic Neuropeptides and G Protein-Coupled Receptors That Regulate Feeding Behavior," *Cell* 92 (February 20, 1998), pp. 573–585.

Corticotropin-releasing hormone Mariarosa Spina et al., "Appetite-Suppressing Effects of Urocortin, a CRF-Related Neuropeptide," *Science* 273 (September 13, 1996), pp. 1561–1564.

an increased production of CRH Michael W. Schwartz, R. J. Seeley, L. Arthur Campfield, P. Burn, D. G. Baskin, "Identification of Targets of Leptin Action in Rat Hypothalmus," *Journal of Clinical Investigation* 98 (1996), pp. 1101–1106.

Other chemicals involved For a recent overview, see Stephen C. Woods, Randy J. Seeley, Daniel Porte, Jr., and Michael W. Schwartz, "Signals That Regulate Food Intake and Energy Homeostasis," *Science* 280 (May 29, 1998), pp. 1378–1383.

when NPY is applied C. J. Billington, J. E. Briggs, M. Grace, A. S. Levine, "Effects of Intracerebroventricular Injection of Neuropeptide Y on Energy Metabolism," *American Journal of Physiology* 260 (1991), pp. R321–R327.

SIX: The Parable of the Pimas

137 **dwelt the Pimas** The classic—and still the best—reference on the Pimas is Frank Russell, *The Pima Indians*, University of Arizona Press, Tucson, 1975. Russell was a young Harvard anthropologist who spent the first few years of the twentieth century among the Pimas. Before he died at thirty-five, he finished the work on the Pimas, which originally appeared as part of the *Twenty-Sixth Annual Report of the Bureau of American Ethnology, 1904–1905*. Seventy years later the work was reissued by the University of Arizona Press. It is still available through the press's Books on Request program.

"Bread is to eat" See, for instance, *The Pima Indians: Pathfinders for*

Page

Health, NIH Publication No. 95–3821, National Institutes of Health, Bethesda, Md., 1995, p. 1.

138 **the Pimas offered supplies** Russell, *Pima Indians*, p. 31.

"Every three or four days" Ibid., pp. 200–201.

an important part of a boy's education Anna Moore Shaw, *A Pima Past*, University of Arizona Press, Tucson, 1974, pp. 35–46.

"In those days" George Webb, *A Pima Remembers*, University of Arizona Press, Tucson, 1959, p. 25.

a thousand or more warriors Ibid., pp. 201–202.

One of the great battles Accounts can be found in several places, including: Russell, *Pima Indians*, pp. 46–47; Shaw, *A Pima Past*, pp. 11–12; Webb, *A Pima Remembers*, pp. 22–25.

139 **"the ground was strewed"** Russell, *Pima Indians*, p. 47, n. a. Russell is quoting from John C. Cremony, *Life Among the Apaches*, A. Roman and Company, San Francisco, 1868, p. 148; rpt., Arizona Silhouettes, Tucson, 1951; Rio Grande Press, Glorieta, N.M. 1969.

"Since the year 1849" Ibid., p. 31, n. d.

"could not have inhabited" *Eleventh Annual Report of the Board of Indian Commissioners for the Year 1879*, Washington, D.C., 1880, p. 54. As quoted in Malcolm L. Comeaux, "Creating Indian Lands: The Boundary of the Salt River Indian Community," *Journal of Historical Geography* 17 (1991), pp. 241–256. Quote on p. 244.

140 **The average Pima man** The data on the Pimas are usually given in terms of body mass index. Anyone with a BMI over 27 is considered overweight; over 30 is obese. For Pimas in their thirties, men average a BMI of about 34 and women about 36. See, for example, R. Arlen Price, Marie Aline Charles, David J. Pettitt, and William C. Knowler, "Obesity in Pima Indians: Large Increases Among Post-World War II Birth Cohorts," *American Journal of Physical Anthropology* 92 (1993), pp. 473–479.

Because most people are unfamiliar with BMI, I have transformed the average BMI figures into heights and weights. I used a number for average height from another publication (S. Lillioja and Clifton Bogardus, "Obesity and Insulin Resistance: Lessons Learned from the Pima Indians," *Diabetes/Metabolism Reviews* 4:5 (1988), pp. 517–540) and calculated what the weight would be to give the appropriate BMI.

weigh as much as 500 pounds Malcolm Gladwell, "The Pima Paradox," *The New Yorker*, February 2, 1998, pp. 44–57.

141 **Half of all adults** Ibid., p. 45.

diabetes strikes the Pimas Among those Pimas who contract diabetes, the

Page

average age of onset is thirty-six, as compared with sixty among diabetes in the general population. *The Pima Indians: Pathfinders for Health*, p. 26.

It was 1694 Russell, *Pima Indians*, p. 27.

Whenever a Pima man Shaw, *A Pima Past*, p. 113.

the Pimas gradually acquiesced Russell, *Pima Indians*, p. 153.

Pima parents sent their children Ibid., p. 34.

142 **At first the Pimas** Comeaux, "Creating Indian Lands," p. 242.

drought shrunk the Gila Russell, *Pima Indians*, p. 66.

These demands on the Gila's water Comeaux, "Creating Indian Lands," p. 242.

143 **"One summer afternoon"** Russell, *Pima Indians*, p. 39.

"Two Apaches were discovered" Ibid., p. 45.

"Those stricken with it usually died" Ibid., p. 42.

Later, epidemics caused by contact Ibid., pp. 48, 52, 53, 55, 58, 59, 64.

The Pimas had always brewed Ibid., pp. 198–199.

"Tizwin was made at Gila Crossing" Ibid., p. 61.

144 **made them partly dependent** Vicky L. Boyce and Boyd A. Swinburn, "The Traditional Pima Indian Diet," *Diabetes Care* 16 (January 1993), pp. 369–371.

They relied less and less Russell, *Pima Indians*, pp. 80–83.

Pimas were "noticeably heavier" Ibid., p. 66.

A poor and mostly forgotten people Price et al., "Obesity in Pima Indians," p. 475.

the U.S. Department of Agriculture expanded Cynthia J. Smith, Sally F. Schakel, and Robert G. Nelson, "Selected Traditional and Contemporary Foods Currently Used by the Pima Indians," *Journal of the American Dietetic Association* 91 (March 1991), pp. 338–341.

Gradually traditional dishes Ibid., p. 340.

the traditional Pima diet Vicky L. Boyce and Boyd A. Swinburn, "The Traditional Pima Diet: Composition and Adaptation for Use in a Dietary Intervention Study," *Diabetes Care* 16 (January 1993), pp. 369–371.

By the 1950s the proportions had changed F. G. Hesse, "A Dietary Study of the Pima Indian," *American Journal of Clinical Nutrition* 7 (1959), pp. 532–537. As quoted in Boyce and Swinburn, "The Traditional Pima Diet," p. 369.

In 1971 it was J. M. Reid et al., "Nutrient Intake of Pima Indian Women: Relationships to Diabetes Mellitus and Gallbladder Disease," *American Journal of Clinical Nutrition* 24 (1971), pp. 1281–89. As quoted in Boyce and Swinburn, "The Traditional Pima Diet," p. 369.

Page

145 **It was not until late in the nineteenth century** Ibid., p. 84.

   Pimas practiced running Shaw, *A Pima Past*, p. 86.

146 **it was still relatively rare** William C. Knowler, David J. Pettitt, Peter H. Bennett, and Robert C. Williams, "Diabetes Mellitus in the Pima Indians: Genetic and Evolutionary Considerations," *American Journal of Physical Anthropology* 62 (1983), pp. 107–114.

   Russell's extensive report Russell, *Pima Indians*, p. 268.

   In 1940, an epidemiologist E. P. Joslin, "The Universe of Diabetes: A Survey of Diabetes Morbidity in Arizona," *JAMA* 115 (1940), pp. 2033–2038.

   The researchers who study the Pimas See, for example, Price et al., "Obesity in Pima Indians," pp. 475–477.

   Many of the Indians Ibid., p. 477.

   the federal government leased a site "Evacuees Operate Factory Vegetable Farm at Rivers," *This Is Your America*, Literary Classics, New York, 1943. This article was originally published in *The Phoenix Republic*, possibly in late 1942. I found a copy on the web site of the Museum of the City of San Francisco: www.sfmuseum.org/ war/relocate.html.

147 **The sand rat** Details about the sand rat can be found in various places. Most of the information here comes from a special double issue of the *Journal of Basic and Clinical Physiology and Pharmacology* 4, nos. 1–2 (1993).

   This arrangement allows Berry Pinshow, "The Fat Sand Rat: A Quintessential Desert Rodent," *Journal of Basic Clinical Physiological Pharmacology* 4 (1993), pp. 5–12.

   The advantage of this choice A. Allen Degen, "Energy Requirements of the Fat Sand Rat When Consuming the Saltbush: A Review," *Journal of Basic Clinical Physiological Pharmacology* 4 (1993), pp. 13–28.

   an appalling transformation K. Schmidt-Nielsen, H. B. Haines, and D. B. Hackel, "Diabetes Mellitus in the Sand Rat, Induced by Standard Laboratory Diets," *Science* 143 (1964), pp. 689–690.

148 **Its basal metabolic rate is low** Degen, "Energy Requirements," p. 13.

   it is superefficient in storing R. Kalman, J. H. Adler, G. Lazarovici, H. Bar-On, and E. Ziv, "The Efficiency of Sand Rat Metabolism Is Responsible for Development of Obesity and Diabetes," *Journal of Basic Clinical Physiological Pharmacology* 4 (1993), pp. 57–68, esp. pp. 67–68.

   Many chow-fed sand rats Ibid.

149 **genetic tests on the Pimas** At least one study has found a gene in Pimas that seems to affect metabolic rate and the onset of diabetes. A particular mutation in the gene for the beta-3 adrenergic receptor is more common

among Pimas than in the rest of the U.S. population and is associated with both metabolism and diabetes, but the effect of the gene, if it exists, is rather small: People with two copies of the gene develop noninsulin-dependent diabetes at an average age of thirty-six, compared with an average age of forty for those with one copy and forty-one for those with no copies of the mutant gene. Subjects with the gene also tend to have a lower resting metabolic rate. See Jeremy Walston et al., "Time of Onset of Non-Insulin-Dependent Diabetes Mellitus and Genetic Variation in the Beta-3-Adrenergic-Receptor Gene," *The New England Journal of Medicine* 333 (August 10, 1995), pp. 343–347.

When genetics researchers compare The most thorough review of the genetic contribution to weight is Claude Bouchard, ed., *The Genetics of Obesity*, CRC Press, Boca Raton, Fla.:, 1994.

Adopted siblings Thorkild I. A. Sorensen and Albert J. Stunkard, "Overview of the Adoption Studies," in, ibid., pp. 49–61. Also see Albert J. Stunkard, Thorkild I. A. Sorensen, Craig Hanis, Thomas Teasdale, Ranajit Chakraborty, William J. Schull, and Fini Schulsinger, "An Adoption Study of Human Obesity," *The New England Journal of Medicine* 314 (1986), pp. 193–198.

one's family environment In particular, the "shared environment"—that part of the environment which is the same for the siblings—has almost no effect on BMI or other measures of weight. There may be unshared environmental effects in a household, things that vary from sibling to sibling, which play a role in weight, but it is difficult to say what those might be.

identical twins who were separated at birth Joanne M. Meyer and Albert J. Stunkard, "Twin Studies of Human Obesity," in Bouchard, ed., *Genetics of Obesity*, pp. 63–78. Also see Albert J. Stunkard et al., "The Body-Mass Index of Twins Who Have Been Reared Apart," *The New England Journal of Medicine* 322 (May 24, 1990), pp. 1483–1487.

a heritability of about 70 percent Ibid., p. 72.

By comparison, the heritability for IQ See, for example, Richard J. Herrnstein and Charles Murray, *The Bell Curve*, Free Press, New York, 1994.

150 **much lower heritabilities** See, for instance, Claude Bouchard and Louis Pérusse, "Genetics of Obesity: Family Studies," in Bouchard, ed., *Genetics of Obesity*, pp. 79–92.

Perhaps the best known study Stunkard et al., "Body-Mass Index of Twins."

the !Kung San The "!" in !Kung San represents a clicking noise at the front

Page

of the word that has no equivalent in the English language and cannot be reproduced with letters.

151 **the ancestors of today's Pimas** Eric Ravussin, Mauro E. Valencia, Julian Esparza, Peter H. Bennett, and Leslie O. Schulz, "Effects of a Traditional Lifestyle on Obesity in Pima Indians," *Diabetes Care* 17 (September 1994), pp. 1067–1074.

When the NIDDK team Ibid., p. 1068.

152 **A few of the Mexican Pimas were obese** The highest BMI for any woman among the Mexican Pimas was 31.5, while the average BMI for an age-matched group of Arizona Pimas was 35.5, so the fattest woman from Maycoba would appear relatively thin among her U.S. cousins. On the other hand, at least one man among the Mexican Pimas had a BMI of 35.7, which was higher than the average BMI of 30.8 for a randomly selected, age-matched sample of male Arizona Pimas. Still, he would not stand out as particularly heavy among a crowd of the Pimas from Gila River.

"These people have a very tough life" Telephone interview with Leslie Schulz, August 15, 1997.

Among the few tribes today Peter J. Brown, "The Biocultural Evolution of Obesity," in Per Björntorp and Bernard Brodoff, eds., *Comprehensive Textbook on Obesity*, Lippincott, New York, 1992, pp. 320–329.

153 **according to the anthropologist Peter J. Brown** Ibid.

SEVEN: Setting the Set Point

157 **the latest in a long line** James A. Levine, Norman L. Eberhardt, and Michael D. Jensen, "Role of Nonexercise Activity Thermogenesis in Resistance to Fat Gain in Humans," *Science* 283 (January 8, 1999), pp. 212–214.

a technique called doubly labeled water The doubly labeled water technique involves giving the subjects water in which both the oxygen and the hydrogen atoms are radioactive isotopes. By knowing how much water is drunk and by measuring the amount of radioactive oxygen and radioactive hydrogen that is excreted from the body, it is possible to calculate very accurately how much carbon dioxide the body has produced over a day or so, which in turn implies the total energy expenditure during that time. A similar calculation can be made by keeping the subject in a closed room and keeping track of the production of carbon dioxide, but the doubly labeled water technique can be used with people who are allowed to go about their normal daily activities.

Page

159 **other researchers, such as Leibel and Hirsch** Rudolph L. Leibel, Michael Rosenbaum, and Jules Hirsch, "Changes in Energy Expenditure Resulting from Altered Body Weight," *The New England Journal of Medicine* 332 (March 9, 1995), pp. 621–628.

The subject who gained only thirteen ounces See Figure 1 in Levine, Eberhardt, and Jensen, "Role of Nonexercise Activity," p. 213.

160 **The eighteenth-century Pima Indian diet** Vicky L. Boyce and Boyd A. Swinburn, "The Traditional Pima Diet: Composition and Adaptation for Use in a Dietary Intervention Study," *Diabetes Care* 16 (January 1993), pp. 369–371.

people offered a high-fat meal See, for instance, James O. Hill and John C. Peters, "Environmental Contributions to the Obesity Epidemic," *Science* 280 (May 29, 1998), pp. 1371–1374, and also the references cited in n. 11 of that article.

High-fat foods encourage overeating Walter C. Willett, "Is Dietary Fat a Major Determinant of Body Fat?" *American Journal of Clinical Nutrition* 67 (March 1998), pp. 556S–562S.

161 **And some researchers have suggested** J. P. Flatt, "Energetics of Intermediate Metabolism," in J. S. Garrow and D. Halliday, eds., *Substrate and Energy Metabolism in Man*, John Libbey, London, 1985, pp. 58–69.

The effects of a high-fat diet David B. West and Barbara York, "Dietary Fat, Genetic Predisposition, and Obesity: Lessons Learned from Animal Models," *American Journal of Clinical Nutrition* 67 (March 1998), pp. 505S–512S.

group of squirrel monkeys L. M. Ausman, K. M. Rasmussen, and D. L. Gallinam, "Spontaneous Obesity in Maturing Squirrel Monkeys Fed Semipurified Diets," *American Journal of Physiology* 241 (1981), pp. R316–R321.

In one such trial Meena Shah, Paul McGovern, Simone French, and Judith Baxter, "Comparison of a Low-Fat, Ad Libitum Complex-Carbohydrate Diet with a Low-Energy Diet in Moderately Obese Women," *American Journal of Clinical Nutrition* 59 (May 1994), pp. 980–984.

they were back where they started Robert W. Jeffery, Wendy L. Hellerstedt, Simone A. French, and Judith E. Baxter, "A Randomized Trial of Counseling for Fat Restriction Versus Calorie Restriction in the Treatment of Obesity," *International Journal of Obesity* 19 (1995), pp. 132–137.

other long-term studies See, for instance, Willett, "Is Dietary Fat a Major Determinant?" pp. 559S–560S, and the references therein.

Page

the average percentage of fat in the American diet See, for example, Susan M. Krebs-Smith, "Progress in Improving Diet to Reduce Cancer Risk," *Cancer* 83 (October 1, 1998), pp. 1426–1432.

162 **In the early 1970s** Robert J. Kuczmarski, Katherine M. Flegal, Stephen M. Campbell, and Clifford L. Johnson, "Increasing Prevalence of Overweight Among U.S. Adults," *JAMA* 272 (July 20, 1994), pp. 205–211. Esp. see chart on p. 208.

Or, by the new, stricter definition Katherine M. Flegal, M. D. Carroll, Robert J. Kuczmarski, and C. L. Johnson, "Overweight and Obesity in the United States: Prevalence and Trends, 1960–1994," *International Journal of Obesity* 22 (1998), pp. 39–47.

a drop less than half as large Figure 1 in Krebs-Smith, "Progress in Improving Diet."

a collective self-deception The only other measure of how much fat we eat comes from food supply data collected by the agriculture department. These figures represent the amount of food sold yearly to American retail distributors, expressed in terms of pounds of food per person. From that form they are transformed by various nutrition calculations into estimates of, for example, the number of calories consumed yearly by the average person or the number of grams of protein. The tallies are rough estimates only, since they do not account for how much food is thrown out or how many nutrients are lost in cooking. These food survey data show a small increase in the amount of fat the American food industry has consumed over the past few decades, but this does not necessarily mean that people have been eating more fat. During the same period, Americans were using more fats and oils for frying, and, since much of that is thrown away, it is quite possible that the actual consumption of fat dropped. See ibid., p. 1428. See also J. J. Putnam and J. E. Allhouse, *Food Consumption, Prices, and Expenditures, 1970–92*, 1993 Statistical Bulletin No. 867, Food and Consumer Economics Division, Economic Research Service, U.S. Department of Agriculture, Washington, D.C., 1993.

163 **It could be something as simple as** Hill and Peters, "Environmental Contributors," p. 1371.

a slight decrease in calories See, for example, Eileen T. Kennedy, Shanthy A. Bowman, and Renee Powell, "Dietary-Fat Intake in the US Population," *Journal of the American College of Nutrition* 18 (1999), pp. 207–212. As noted on page 208, U.S. Department of Agriculture surveys showed a decrease in calorie intake from 1965 to 1991. Surveys taken in 1994 and 1995 showed a sharp increase from 1991, but the surveys had changed their

Page

method of asking questions in an effort to improve the accuracy of the data, and that change probably explains the jump. People generally underreport their calorie intake, and any change in the survey aimed at improving the accuracy could be expected to cause an increase in the reported calorie intake. In short, it is not valid to compare the numbers for 1994 and 1995 with the earlier ones, so the only secure conclusion is that the years between 1965 and 1991 showed a small decrease in the amount of calories that the average American adult takes in each day.

164 **The exercise-appetite connection** Ibid., pp. 257–258.

The few studies done on humans Ibid.

Physical activity also appears Ibid., p. 258.

People who exercise regularly Angelo Tremblay, Elisabeth Fontaine, Eric T. Poehlman, Denyse Mitchell, Lynda Perron, and Claude Bouchard, "The Effect of Exercise Training on Resting Metabolic Rate in Lean and Moderately Obese Individuals," *International Journal of Obesity* 10 (1986), pp. 511–517.

exercise decreases the appetite for fatty foods Carlos M. Grilo, Kelly D. Brownell, and Albert J. Stunkard, "The Metabolic and Psychological Importance of Exercise in Weight Control," in Albert J. Stunkard and Thomas A. Wadden, eds., *Obesity: Theory and Therapy*, 2nd ed., Raven Press, New York, 1996, pp. 253–273.

The classic study of this connection Beverly Bullen, Robert B. Reed, and Jean Mayer, "Physical Activity of Obese and Nonobese Adolescent Girls Appraised by Motion Picture Sampling," *American Journal of Clinical Nutrition* 14 (April 1964), pp. 211–223.

165 **others have found obese subjects to be just as active** See Grilo, Brownell, and Kelly, "Metabolic and Psychological Importance of Exercise," pp. 258–259. See esp. the discussion on pp. 253–254 and the references mentioned there.

how different strains of mice respond David West, Carol N. Boozer, Deborah L. Moody and Richard L. Atkinson, "Dietary Obesity in Nine Inbred Mouse Strains," *American Journal of Physiology* 262 (1992), pp. R1025–R1032.

166 **While squirrel monkeys get fat** Ausman, Rasmussen, and Gallinam, "Spontaneous Obesity."

Among dogs kept as pets A. T. Edney and P. M. Smith, "Study of Obesity in Dogs Visiting Veterinary Practices in the United Kingdom," *Veterinary Record* 118 (1986), pp. 391–396. See esp. Table 7 on p. 393.

Page

genes play a large role A good summary of modern genetic studies of obesity is Joanne M. Meyer and Albert J. Stunkard, "Genetics and Human Obesity," in Stunkard and Wadden, eds., *Obesity*, pp. 137–149.

In one classic study Claude Bouchard, Angelo Tremblay, Jean-Pierre Després, André Nadeau, Paul J. Lupien, Germain Thériault, Jean Dussault, Sital Moorjani, Sylvie Pinault, and Guy Fournier, "The Response to Long-Term Overfeeding in Identical Twins," *The New England Journal of Medicine* 322 (May 24, 1990), pp. 1477–1482.

Most subjects gained about the same amount Ibid. See Figure 1 on p. 1179.

167 a number of other genes See, for instance, Anthony G. Comuzzie and David B. Allison, "The Search for Human Obesity Genes," *Science* 280 (May 29, 1998), pp. 1374–1377.

the gene for the beta-3 adrenergic receptor The three papers appeared in the August 10, 1995, issue of *The New England Journal of Medicine*: Jeremy Walston et al., "Time of Onset of Non-Insulin-Dependent Diabetes Mellitus and Genetic Variation in the ß3-Adrenergic-Receptor Gene," pp. 343–347; Elisabeth Widen et al., "Assocation of a Polymorphism in the ß3-Adrenergic-Receptor Gene with Features of the Insulin Resistance Syndrome in Finns," pp. 348–351; and Karine Clément et al., "Genetic Variation in the ß3-Adrenergic Receptor and an Increased Capacity to Gain Weight in Patients with Morbid Obesity," pp. 352–354. See also the accompanying editorial, Peter Arner, "The ß3-Adrenergic Receptor—A Cause and Cure of Obesity?" *The New England Journal of Medicine* 333 (August 10, 1995), pp. 382–383.

It is not a particularly rare mutation A. Donny Strosberg, "Association of ß3-Adrenoreceptor Polymorphism with Obesity and Diabetes: Current Status," *TiPS* 18 (December 1997), pp. 449–454.

168 tantalizing evidence that at least Comuzzie and Allison, "The Search for Human Obesity Genes."

one careful study that looked Albert J. Stunkard, Jennifer R. Harris, Nancy L. Pedersen, and Gerald E. McClearn, "The Body-Mass Index of Twins Who Have Been Reared Apart," *The New England Journal of Medicine* 322 (May 24, 1990), pp. 1483–1487.

169 a slow metabolism to be a risk factor Eric Ravussin and Boyd A. Swinburn, "Pathophysiology of Obesity," *The Lancet* 340 (August 15, 1992), pp. 404–408, esp. p. 406.

infants who expended less energy S. B. Roberts, J. Savage, W. A. Coward,

Page

B. Chew, and A. Lucas, "Energy Expenditure and Intake in Infants Born to Lean and Overweight Mothers," *The New England Journal of Medicine* 318 (February 25, 1988), pp. 461–466.

One of the most detailed studies Eric Ravussin et al., "Reduced Rate of Energy Expenditure as a Risk Factor for Body-Weight Gain," *The New England Journal of Medicine* 318 (February 25, 1988), pp. 467–472.

the slow metabolism could explain Ibid., p. 471.

170 **Ravussin went on to measure** Ibid., p. 469.

"respiratory quotient" Francesco Zurlo et al., "Low Ratio of Fat to Carbohydrate Oxidation as a Predictor of Weight Gain: Study of 24-h RQ," *American Journal of Physiology* 259 (1990), pp. E650–E657.

insulin resistance Boyd A. Swinburn et al., "Insulin Resistance Associated with Lower Rates of Weight Gain in Pima Indians," *Journal of Clinical Investigation* 88 (1991), pp. 168–173.

weight gain acted to "normalize" Ravussin and Swinburn, "Pathophysiology of Obesity," p. 406.

171 **The initial discovery of a connection** Mary E. Moore, Albert J. Stunkard, and Leo Srole, "Obesity, Social Class, and Mental Illness," *JAMA* 181 (September 15, 1962), pp. 962–966.

if there were correlations In particular, they compared obesity rates with scores on eight psychological scales: immaturity, suspicious, rigidity, frustration-depression, withdrawal, tension-anxiety, neurasthenia, and childhood anxiety. Ibid., p. 965.

the Midtown Manhattan Study Leo Srole et al., *Mental Health in the Metropolis: Midtown Manhattan Study*, McGraw-Hill, New York, 1962.

Later, Stunkard and Moore Phillip B. Goldblatt, Mary E. Moore, and Albert J. Stunkard, "Social Factors in Obesity," in Norman Kiell, ed., *The Psychology of Obesity*, Charles C. Thomas, Springfield, Ill., 1973, pp. 57–66, esp. p. 58.

the socioeconomic status of the respondent This was assessed simply and directly on the basis of four pieces of information from the original survey: the respondent's occupation, education, weekly income, and monthly rent. Each response was rated on a scale of 1 to 6, and the four numbers were added together to create a socioeconomic rating for each person. Thus a respondent who ranked lowest in each category—unskilled labor, no education, an income of less than $49 a week, and monthly rent less than $30— received a cumulative score of 4. Someone who ranked highest in each category—elite white-collar, graduate school education, a weekly income of more than $300, and a rent of more than $200—was given a score of 24. The

Page

respondents were then grouped into three socioeconomic classes: low, from 4 to 10 points; medium, from 11 to 16 points; and high, from 17 to 24 points. **The researchers found a similar pattern** Ibid., p. 61.

172 **evidence that this might be happening** Ibid., p. 60.

obesity must be, in part, a social phenomenon Ibid., p. 63.

173 **In 1989, when Stunkard** For an extensive review of these studies, see Jeffery Sobal and Albert J. Stunkard, "Socioeconomic Status and Obesity: A Review of the Literature," *Psychological Bulletin* 105 (1989), pp. 260–275.

Only one study has found Ibid., p. 261.

The contradictory findings Ibid., p. 262.

Stunkard and Sobal explained Ibid., pp. 268–269.

174 **Two of the most convincing studies** F. E. Braddon, B. Rodgers, M. E. Wadsworth, and J. Davies, "Onset of Obesity in a 36-Year Birth Cohort Study," *British Medical Journal* 293 (August 2, 1986), pp. 299–303; and C. Power and C. Moynihan, "Social Class Changes and Weight-for-Height Between Childhood and Early Adulthood," *International Journal of Obesity* 12 (1988), pp. 445–453. As quoted in Sobal and Stunkard, "Socioeconomic Status and Obesity," p. 261.

a study performed in The Netherlands Margriet S. Westerterp-Plantenga et al., "Energy Intake and Body Weight Effects of Six Months Reduced or Full Fat Diets, as a Function of Dietary Restraint," *International Journal of Obesity* 22 (January 1998), pp. 14–22.

subjects who were restrained eaters For a review of restrained eating, see Karl M. Pirke and Reinhold G. Laessle, "Restrained Eating," in Stunkard and Wadden, eds., *Obesity*, pp. 151–162.

Since the idea of restrained C. Peter Herman and D. Mack, "Restrained and Unrestrained Eating," *Journal of Personality* 43 (1975), pp. 647–660; C. Peter Herman and Janet Polivy, "Anxiety, Restraint, and Eating Behavior," *Journal of Abnormal Psychology* 84 (1975), pp. 666–672. See also C. Peter Herman, "Restrained Eating," *Psychiatric Clinics of North America* 1 (December 1978), pp. 593–607.

restrained eaters do indeed Karl M. Pirke and Reinhold G. Laessle, "Restrained Eating," in Stunkard and Wadden, eds., *Obesity*, pp. 151–162.

175 **By the end of the experiment** Westerterp-Plantenga et al., "Energy Intake and Body Weight," pp. 17–19.

176 **one of the major areas of disagreement** James O. Hill and Holly R. Wyatt, "Relapse in Obesity Treatment: Biology or Behavior?," *American Journal of Clinical Nutrition* 69 (1999), pp. 1064–1065.

Page

laboratory studies of the metabolic changes Rudolph L. Leibel, Michael Rosenbaum, and Jules Hirsch, "Changes in Energy Expenditure Resulting from Altered Body Weight," *The New England Journal of Medicine* 332 (March 9, 1995), pp. 621–628.

tremendous difficulty making major lifestyle changes Thomas A. Wadden, "What Characterizes Successful Weight Maintainers?" in David B. Allison and F. Xavier Pi-Sunyer, eds., *Obesity Treatment*, Plenum Press, New York, 1995, pp. 103–111.

Leibel got it started Rudolph L. Leibel and Jules Hirsch, "Diminished Energy Requirements in Reduced-Obese Patients," *Metabolism* 33 (February 1984), pp. 164–170.

a meta-analysis on a dozen such studies Arne Astrup, Peter C. Gotzsche, Karen van de Werken, Claudia Ranneries, Soren Toubro, Anne Raben, and Benjamin Buemann, "Meta-Analysis of Resting Metabolic Rate in Formerly Obese Subjects," *American Journal of Clinical Nutrition* 69 (1999), pp. 1117–1122.

178 **In 1964, when Ethan Allen Sims** Ethan A. H. Sims et al., "Experimental Obesity in Man," *Transactions of the Association of American Physicians* 81 (1968), pp. 153–170.

179 **how the set point could ratchet upward** Jeffrey M. Friedman and Jeffrey L. Halaas, "Leptin and the Regulation of Body Weight in Mammals," *Nature* 395 (October 22, 1998), pp. 763–770.

most have higher-than-normal levels Robert V. Considine et al., "Serum Immunoreactive-Leptin Concentrations in Normal-Weight and Obese Humans," *The New England Journal of Medicine* 334 (February 1, 1996), pp. 292–295.

EIGHT: One Pill Makes You Larger

183 **pharmacologist Michael Weintraub** Michael Weintraub, "Long-Term Weight Control Study" (in six parts plus conclusion), *Clinical Pharmacological Therapy* 51 (May 1992), pp. 581–646.

Weight-loss boutiques sprang up See, for instance, Robert Langreth, "Critics Claim Diet Clinics Misuse Obesity Drugs," *Wall Street Journal*, March 31, 1997, pp. B1, B7.

Even such staid Laura Fraser, "The New Diet Drugs," *Health*, July/August 1996, pp. 52, 57.

Wyeth-Ayerst Laboratories Ibid., p. 52.

Page

184 **a cover story in September 1996** Michael D. Lemonick, "The New Miracle Drug?" *Time*, September 23, 1996, pp. 60–67.

"the fastest launch of any drug" David Crossen, an analyst for Montgomery Securities in San Francisco, as quoted in ibid., p. 62.

the arguments against it For a review of the effects of fenfluramine and dexfenfluramine (Redux) on the brain, see Una D. McCann, Lewis S. Seiden, Lewis J. Rubin, and George A. Ricaurte, "Brain Serotonin Neurotoxicity and Primary Pulmonary Hypertension from Fenfluramine and Dexfenfluramine: A Systematic Review of the Evidence," *JAMA* 278 (August 27, 1997), pp. 666–672.

a report in the *New England Journal* Lucien Abenhaim, Yola Moride, François Brenot, et al., "Appetite-Suppressant Drugs and the Risk of Primary Pulmonary Hypertension," *The New England Journal of Medicine* 335 (August 29, 1996), pp. 609–616. This was not the first time that primary pulmonary hypertension was linked with the use of fenfluramine and dexfenfluramine (Redux), but this report found that the risks for getting the disease were significantly higher than previously thought.

researchers judged this a reasonable price See, for example, JoAnn E. Manson and Gerald A. Faich, "Pharmacotherapy for Obesity—Do the Benefits Outweigh the Risks?" *The New England Journal of Medicine* 335 (August 29, 1996), pp. 659–660.

185 **an ominous pattern among obese patients** Details of the discovery of valvular heart disease in users of fen-phen can be found in Heidi M. Connolly, Jack L. Crary, Michael D. McGoon, Donald D. Hensrud, Brooks S. Edwards, William D. Edwards, and Hartzell V. Schaff, "Valvular Heart Disease Associated with Fenfluramine-Phentermine," *The New England Journal of Medicine* 337 (August 28, 1997), pp. 581–588.

all of them, Crary noticed Ibid., p. 584.

187 **A trio of studies** Mehmood A. Khan et al., "The Prevalence of Cardiac Valvular Insufficiency Assessed by Transthoracic Echocardiography in Obese Patients Treated with Appetite-Suppressant Drugs," *The New England Journal of Medicine* 339 (September 10, 1998), pp. 713–718; Hershel Jick et al., "A Population-Based Study of Appetite-Suppressant Drugs and the Risk of Cardiac-Valve Regurgitation," *The New England Journal of Medicine* 339 (September 10, 1998), pp. 719–724; Neil J. Weissman et al., "An Assessment of Heart-Valve Abnormalities in Obese Patients Taking Dexfenfluramine, Sustained-Release Dexfenfluramine, or Placebo," *The New England Journal of Medicine* 339 (September 10,

Page

1998), pp. 725–732. See also the accompanying editorial: Richard B. Devereux, "Appetite Suppressants and Valvular Heart Disease," *The New England Journal of Medicine* 339 (September 10, 1998), pp. 765–767.

It found heart-valve problems Khan et al., "Prevalence of Cardiac Valvular Insufficiency," p. 713.

They, too, had more heart valve problems Jick et al., "A Population-Based Study," p. 719.

they found only a handful of cases Weissman et al., "An Assessment of Heart-Valve Abnormalities," p. 725.

188 **"It's not nice to fool Mother Nature"** From Brooks S. Edwards, medical editor of the Mayo Clinic's publication *Mayo Health Oasis*. Edwards was commenting on Heidi Connolly's initial report in an editorial released the same day as her and Crary's work was made public. It can be found on Mayo's web site: www.mayohealth.org/mayo/ednote/htm/ed970708.htm.

an American doctor treated an overweight patient James J. Putnam, "Cases of Myxedema and Acromegalia Treated with Benefit by Sheep's Thyroids: Recent Observations Respecting the Pathology of the Cachexias Following Disease of the Thyroid; Clinical Relationships of Graves's Disease and Acromegalia," *American Journal of the Medical Sciences* 106 (1893), pp. 125–148.

For weight loss, Soranus suggested K. Guggenheim, "Soranus of Ephesus on Obesity," *International Journal of Obesity* 1 (1977), pp. 245–246.

189 **"The nutrition of the teeth and nails"** Putnam, "Cases of Myxedema and Acromegalia," p. 125.

"Her friends would leave her" Ibid., p. 126.

"[S]he was rapidly growing thinner" Ibid., p. 127.

"She is still an anemic and delicate person" Ibid., p. 128.

It was natural to ask Ibid., p. 130.

"One lost twenty-eight pounds" Ibid.

it made sense Hugo R. Rony, *Obesity and Leanness*, Lea and Febiger, Philadelphia, 1940, p. 257.

190 **many doctors argued against** Ibid., pp. 257–258.

By this time, scientists It was in 1919 that the American biochemist Edward Calvin Kendall described a way to isolate thyroxine, making it possible to produce relatively pure thyroid extracts and freeing patients from having to swallow bits of dried sheep tissue. In 1927 the British scientist Charles Harington discovered how to manufacture thyroxine synthetically.

some obese patients would lose weight Ibid., p. 257. See also the detailed discussion of the use of thyroid hormones in weight loss in George A. Bray,

Page

The Obese Patient, W. B. Saunders, Philadelphia, 1976, pp. 381–390.

side effects, of course Rony, *Obesity and Leanness*, pp. 257–258.

as much as two-thirds of the weight loss Bray, *The Obese Patient*, p. 388.

in a munitions factory John Grinde and Alice C. Jolivette, "Slimming Scientifically," *Hygeia*, December 1937, pp. 1072–1074, 1148.

increased the body's metabolic rate Bray, *The Obese Patient*, pp. 390–391. The understanding of dinitrophenol as uncoupling the burning of fat and sugar molecules from the production of ATP came sometime after the 1930s. Rony, in his 1940 description of the drug (*Obesity and Leanness*, pp. 264–265), concluded only that it worked through the "oxidation of fat."

191 **promising results for dinitrophenol** M. L. Tainter, A. N. Stockton, and W. C. Cutting, "Use of Dinitrophenol in Obesity and Related Conditions: A Progress Report," *JAMA* 101 (November 4, 1933), pp. 1472–1475.

Then came the side effects Rony, *Obesity and Leanness*, p. 264.

One unfortunate user's temperature Grinde and Jolivette, "Slimming Scientifically," p. 1074.

Drug stores sold a variety of "purgatives" Ibid., pp. 363–364.

Also popular were Ibid., p. 1074.

192 **a steady stream of fad diets** Jane Foster, "Dieting Daughters," *Hygeia*, February 1937, pp. 141–143.

"in limited amounts, foods" Guggenheim, "Soranus of Ephesus," p. 245.

"a number of deaths to its credit" Foster, "Dieting Daughters," p. 143.

What was missing from the diet Rony, *Obesity and Leanness*, p. 254.

endocrinology, the study of hormones The word "hormone" itself would not be coined until 1905.

193 **an ammonia molecule** More precisely, an ammonia molecule is a nitrogen atom with three attached hydrogen atoms. The ammonia molecule gives up one of its hydrogen atoms in order to bond with the carbon atoms in adrenaline's tail.

194 **As early as 1910** G. Barger and H. H. Dale, "Chemical Structure and Sympathomimetic Action of Amines," *Journal of Physiology* 41 (1910), pp. 19–26.

patients who took ephedrine M. H. Nathanson, "The Central Action of Beta-Aminopropylbenzene (Benzedrine): Clinical Observations," *JAMA* 108 (February 13, 1937), pp. 528–531. Details about ephedrine on pp. 528–529.

physicians in the early 1930s Ibid., p. 529.

a new drug worked dramatically better Myron Prinzmetal and Wilfred

Page

Bloomberg, "The Use of Benzedrine for the Treatment of Narcolepsy,"
JAMA 105 (December 21, 1935), pp. 2051–2054.

195 **Nathanson gave benzedrine** Nathanson, "Central Action of Beta-
Aminopropyl-benzene," p. 529.

"Many patients volunteered" Ibid.

"pepped up" those "Benzedrine Sulfate 'Pep Pills,'" *JAMA* 108 (June 5,
1937), pp. 1973–1974.

"Benzedrine sulfate" Ibid., p. 1973.

their appetite had decreased noticeably Nathanson, "Central Action of
Beta–Aminopropylbenzene," p. 529.

effects of benzedrine in seventeen obese patients Mark F. Lesses and
Abraham Myerson, "Human Autonomic Pharmacology: XVI. Benzedrine
Sulfate as an Aid in the Treatment of Obesity," *The New England Journal
of Medicine* 218 (January 20, 1938), pp. 119–124.

196 **it cured the "anhedonia" of the obese** Ibid., p. 120.

benzedrine was causing patients Ibid., p. 124.

weight loss might come from shedding Gerhard Rosenthal and Harry A.
Salomon, "Benzedrine Sulfate in Obesity," *Endocrinology* 26 (May 1940).

benzedrine decreased the appetite Cary Eggleston and Soma Weiss, "The
Rationale of Amphetamine (Benzedrine) Sulphate Theraphy," *American
Journal of the Medical Sciences* 199 (May 1940), pp. 729–737. Speculation
about the hunger contractions on pp. 733–734.

experiments performed by three physiologists Stanley C. Harris, A. C. Ivy,
and Laureen M. Searle, "The Mechanism of Amphetamine-Induced
Weight Loss," *JAMA* 134 (1947), 1468–1475.

they were kept on either benzedrine Some of the patients were actually
given an amphetamine closely related to benzedrine, but its action was the
same.

The benzedrine, they found, Ibid., p. 1472.

197 **A 1976 review of weight-control drugs** Bray, *The Obese Patient*, Chap. 9.

Russell Henry, Oregon's chief "End of the Rainbow," *Newsweek*, October
2, 1967, p. 56.

198 **Henry had become suspicious of the pills** "New Enemy Within: Drug
Inter-action," *Business Week*, October 14, 1967, pp. 114, 116.

a U.S. district judge Susanna McBee, "A Legal Blow at the Diet Pill
Business," *Life*, September 27, 1968, p. 86A.

the FDA seized some 45 million pills Ibid.

most dieters were getting their pills Ibid.

Page

about 5,000 doctors "Facts About Those 'Diet Pills,'" *U.S. News & World Report*, February 19, 1968, p. 63.

Susanna McBee, a reporter Susanna McBee, "A Slender *Life* Reporter Visits 10 'Fat Doctors,'" *Life* 64 (January 26, 1968), pp. 24–27.

199 **One doctor, Hart's committee heard** McBee, "A Legal Blow."

the country's fat doctors were grossing Ibid.

Some of them were seeing "Facts About Those 'Diet Pills.'"

He proposed legislation McBee, "A Legal Blow."

200 **amphetamines' dark side came into view** See, for instance, Eliot Marshall, "FDA Bans Speed in Diet Pills," *Science* 205 (August 3, 1979), pp. 474–475.

The FDA finally banned amphetamine Ibid.

an epidemic of pulmonary hypertension H. P. Gurtner, "Aminorex and Pulmonary Hypertension: A Review," *Cor Vasa* 27 (1985), pp. 160–171.

201 **Researchers knew, for instance** A study released several months after Redux's approval found that as many as fifty out of every million people who used the drug for more than three months could be expected to develop pulmonary hypertension, and, of those, half would die of the disease within five to ten years (Lucien Abenhaim, Yola Moride, François Brenot, et al., "Appetite-Suppressant Drugs and the Risk of Primary Pulmonary Hypertension," *The New England Journal of Medicine* 335 (August 29, 1996), pp. 609–616). The risk had not been known with this precision during the debate over Redux's approval, but doctors did know that Redux led, in rare instances, to often-fatal cases of pulmonary hypertension.

It was also known that Redux Ibid.

advised that its use be limited See, for instance, the FDA press release, "FDA Approves Dexfenfluramine to Treat Obesity," April 29, 1996. Available on the FDA web site, www.fda.gov.

202 **how easy it is to get the pills** See, for instance, Jeannie Ralston, "Pill Mill," *Allure*, July 1997, pp. 78–80. See also Robert Langreth, "Critics Claim Diet Clinics Misuse Obesity Drugs," *Wall Street Journal*, March 31, 1997, pp. B1, B7.

California Weight Loss Medical Associates Lemonick, "New Miracle Drug?" p. 66.

Sabine Sisk-Bisson Details on Sabine Sisk-Bisson come from Brooke A. Masters, "Va. Woman Settles with Diet-Drug Firm," *Washington Post*, December 8, 1998, p. D3.

Page

203 **the majority of people taking it in Europe** Lemonick, "New Miracle Drug?" p. 66.

a flurry of articles Ronald Rosenberg, "'Take-a-Pill,' Lose Some Weight: Firms Near Release of Fat-Fighting Products," *Boston Globe*, April 14, 1996; Anastasia Toufexis, "Diet Pills Are Coming Back," *Time*, May 13, 1996, p. 78; Melinda Beck, "A Pill to Help Dieters," *Newsweek*, May 13, 1996, pp. 76, 79; Laura Fraser, "The New Diet Drugs," *Health*, July/August 1996, pp. 52, 57. Interestingly, business publications were ahead of the curve on this trend, describing the new generation of diet drugs several months before the other magazines: David Stipp, "New Weapons in the War on Fat," *Fortune*, December 11, 1995, pp. 164–174; Naomi Freundlich, "Is There a Cure for Obesity?" *Business Week*, February 5, 1996, pp. 64, 66.

204 **its sales in the first six months** Dana Canedy, "Predecessors' Woes Make Diet Drug a Tough Sell," *The New York Times*, April 11, 1998, pp. D1, D4.

In April 1999 sibutramine Sheryl Gay Stolberg, "F.D.A. Approves New Type of Anti-Obesity Drug," *The New York Times*, April 27, 1999, p. A1, A19.

205 **a mysterious increase in breast cancer** Gina Kolata, "Obesity Drug Can Lead to Modest Weight Loss, Study Finds," *The New York Times*, January 20, 1999, p. A14

206 **researchers from Synaptic Pharmaceutical** Christophe Gerald et al., "A Receptor Subtype Involved in Neuropeptide-Y-Induced Food Intake," *Nature* 382 (1996), pp. 168–171.

The researchers were testing a drug Kathryn S. Brown, "A Full Plate: Researchers Attempt to Digest the Biochemistry of Obesity," *The Scientist*, September 16, 1996, pp. 12, 15.

Since MSH works by binding Dennis Huszar et al., "Targeted Disruption of the Melanocortin-4 Receptor Results in Obesity in Mice," *Cell* 88 (January 10, 1997), pp. 131–141.

Scientists at Glaxo Wellcome Brad R. Henke et al., "3-(1H-Indazol-3-ylmethyl)-1,5-benzodiazepines: CCK-A Agonists That Demonstrate Oral Activity as Satiety Agents," *Journal of Medicinal Chemistry* 39 (1996), pp. 2655–2658.

A number of these molecules have been shown Michael H. Fisher, "A Selective Human ß3 Adrenergic Receptor Agonist Increases Metabolic Rate in Rhesus Monkeys," *Journal of Clinical Investigation* 101 (June 1998), pp. 2387–2393.

207 **a similar uncoupling protein** Ruth E. Gimeno et al., "Cloning and Characterization of an Uncoupling Protein Homolog," *Diabetes* 46 (May

Page

1997), pp. 900–906; Christophe Fleury et al., "Uncoupling Protein-2: A Novel Gene Linked to Obesity and Hyperinsulinemia," *Nature Genetics* 15 (March 1997), pp. 269–272.

209 **rethinking the usual New Year's resolution** Jerome P. Kassirer and Marcia Angell, "Losing Weight—An Ill-Fated New Year's Resolution," *The New England Journal of Medicine* 338 (January 1, 1998), pp. 52–54.

210 **its press releases announcing the approval** The FDA press release announcing the approval of Redux can be found at http://www.fda.gov/bbs/topics/ANSWERS/ ANS00728.html, and of sibutramine at http://www.fda.gov/bbs/topics/ANSWERS/ ANS00835.html.

The 300,000 figure J. Michael McGinnis and William H. Foege, "Actual Causes of Death in the United States," *JAMA* 270 (November 10, 1993), pp. 2207–2212.

it is difficult to sort out Ibid., p. 2207. See also a letter to the editor from McGinnis and Foege, *JAMA* 338 (April 16, 1998), p. 1157. The letter was in response to the *New England Journal* editorial, which had misrepresented McGinnis and Foege's findings in much the same way that others had, claiming their paper said that "every year 300,000 deaths in the United States are caused by obesity."

In 1999, another study appeared David B. Allison, Kevin R. Fontaine, JoAnn E. Manson, June Stevens, and Theodore B. VanItallie, "Annual Deaths Attributable to Obesity in the United States," *JAMA* 282 (October 27, 1999), pp. 1530–1538.

much of the benefit attributed to losing weight See, for instance, the letter to the editor by Glenn A. Gaesser, *The New England Journal of Medicine* 338 (April 16, 1998), p. 1157, and the references appended to it.

Jules Hirsch, the Rockefeller researcher Jules Hirsch, "The Treatment of Obesity with Drugs," *American Journal of Clinical Nutrition* 67 (January 1998), pp. 2–4.

NINE: Just Who's in Charge Here?

213 **a result that seemed almost too good** Richard B. Stuart, "Behavioral Control of Overeating," *Behavioural Research and Therapy* 5 (1967), pp. 357–365.

Working with eight obese women Ten women had begun his program, but one dropped out after becoming pregnant and the other, "a probable psychotic, wanted another type of therapy and was dropped from this project following the second session." Ibid., p. 363.

Page

215 **behavior therapists had attacked anorexia** A. J. Bachrach, W. J. Erwin,
     and J. P. Mohr, "The Control of Anorexia by Operant Conditioning
     Techniques," in L.P. Ullman and L. Krasner, eds., *Case Studies in Behavior
     Modification*, Holt, Rinehart and Winston, New York, 1965.
     compulsive behavior J. R. Cautela, "Treatment of Compulsive Behavior
     by Covert Sensitization," *Psychological Record* 16 (1966), pp. 33–41.
     and smoking S. Pyke, N. M. Agnew, and J. Kopperud, "Modification of an
     Overlearned Response Through a Relearning Program: A Pilot Study on
     Smoking," *Behavioural Research and Therapy* 4 (1966), pp. 197–203.

215 **Stuart applied almost exactly the same principles** Stuart, "Behavioral
     Control of Overeating," pp. 358–359.
     in his assault on obesity One earlier attempt to treat obesity—an effort five
     years earlier by three psychologists at the Indiana University Medical
     Center—had been disappointing: Half of the ten patients had lost less than
     ten pounds, and none had lost more than twenty. Charles B. Ferster, John
     I. Nurnberger, and Eugene E. Levitt, "The Control of Eating," *Journal of
     Mathetics* 1 (1962), pp. 87–109.

     Details of the outcome of the 1962 study come from Sydnor B. Penick,
     Ross Filion, Sonja Fox, and Albert J. Stunkard, "Behavior Modification in
     the Treatment of Obesity," *Psychosomatic Medicine* 33 (January–February
     1971), pp. 49–55; see p. 49 in particular. Strangely, the original paper
     describing the behavioral approach to treating obesity gave no details on
     how well the approach worked, although it did offer a rather obscure com-
     ment implying that the study had had little success: "The preliminary
     results of this pilot program are not included as a record of even mediocre
     success, but rather as a description of the medium within which the spe-
     cific techniques of control were imparted. A much longer follow-up period
     and a larger number of cases are necessary to develop a successful program
     as well as test it" (p. 108).
     Behaviorists believed that people See, for instance, Ferster, Nurnberger,
     and Levitt, "Control of Eating," p. 87.
     Much of the rest of the program Stuart, "Behavioral Control of
     Overeating," pp. 360–361.

217 **a rationale for why behavioral therapy** Richard B. Stuart and Barbara
     Davis, *Slim Chance in a Fat World: Behavioral Control of Obesity*, Research
     Press, Champaign, Ill., 1972, chap. 2, pp. 44–57.
     Today, behavior therapy See, for example, Thomas A. Wadden, "The
     Treatment of Obesity: An Overview," in Albert J. Stunkard and Thomas A.

Wadden, eds., *Obesity: Theory and Therapy* (2nd ed.), Raven Press, New York, 1996, pp. 197–217. Behavior therapy on pp. 200–206.

218 **a series of experiments in which he manipulated** See Jeffrey W. Peck, "Situational Determinants of the Body Weights Defended by Normal Rats and Rats with Hypothalamic Lesions," in Donald Novin, Wanda Wyrwicka, and George A. Bray, eds., *Hunger: Basic Mechanisms and Clinical Implications*, Raven Press, New York, 1976, pp. 297–311.

He believed that the set point Actually, Peck pointed out that it was not even necessary to talk about a set point. He offered a theoretical model that could explain why an animal will defend a certain body weight depending on various factors, including the environment, and the model itself did not include anything that could be called a set point. Ibid., pp. 304–310.

219 **Working with more than 100 rats** Jeffrey W. Peck, "Rats Defend Different Body Weights Depending on Palatability and Accessibility of Their Food," *Journal of Comparative and Physiological Psychology* 92 (June 1978), pp. 555–570.

different set points Actually, "set point" is a relative term here. Because all the rats kept growing throughout the course of the experiment, as rats do, Peck had to compare weight curves that were moving upward, not staying flat.

After losing nearly 10 percent Ibid., p. 563.

all three types of rats compensated Ibid., pp. 561–562.

all three types of rats ate just enough Ibid., p. 562.

rats on different diets were defending In one important part of the study, after testing how rats fed the greasy or bitter diets defended their body weights, Peck put those rats back onto a normal diet of unadulterated rat chow. Now the rats' weights reverted to weights typical of rats who had been eating the usual chow all along, and these rats—who had had set points higher or lower than normal—defended their new body weight with the same vigor that they had shown before. Peck had shown he could move the set point around by changing the rats' environment—in particular, by changing the type of food they were given.

220 **Some 30 percent of the adult population** This is a guess based on two studies. One, the National Health and Nutrition Examination Survey, found that 22.5 percent of the U.S. adult population was obese around 1990. See Katherine M. Flegal, M. D. Carroll, R. J. Kuczmarski, and C. L. Johnson, "Overweight and Obesity in the United States: Prevalence and Trends, 1960–1994," *International Journal of Obesity* 22 (1998), pp. 39–24.

Page

The second study, based on phone interviews conducted from 1991 to 1998, found that the percentage of the population that is obese increased by half during that period. See Ali H. Mokdad, Mary K. Serdula, William H. Dietz, Barbara Bowman, James S. Marks, and Jeffrey P. Koplan, "The Spread of the Obesity Epidemic in the United States, 1991–1998," *JAMA* 282 (October 27, 1999), pp. 1519–1522. The second study, because it relied on phone interviews, estimated a significantly smaller percentage of the population to be obese than had the earlier study, but it can be used nevertheless to examine the trend during those years.

221 **researchers at the University of Florida** "UF Researchers Explore Gene Therapy to Treat Obesity," University of Florida press release, June 10, 1999. The researchers also presented their findings at the annual meeting of the American Society of Gene Therapy in Washington, D.C., June 10, 1999.

an experiment on a group of Australian aborigines Kerin O'Dea, "Marked Improvement in Carbohydrate and Lipid Metabolism in Diabetic Australian Aborigines After Temporary Reversion to Traditional Lifestyle," *Diabetes* 33 (June 1984), pp. 596–603.

223 **a 1959 paper by Mickey Stunkard** Albert J. Stunkard and Mavis McLaren-Hume, "Results of Treatment for Obesity: A Review of the Literature and Report of a Series," AMA *Archives of Internal Medicine* 103 (1959), pp. 79–85.

many more people than suspected Jane Fritsch, "95% Regain Lost Weight. Or Do They?" *The New York Times*, May 25, 1999, p. F7.

224 **The people in the registry** Ibid.

Index